Vancouver

"All you've got to do is decide to go and the hardest part is over.

So go!"

TONY WHEELER, COFOUNDER – LONELY PLANET

THIS EDITION WRITTEN AND RESEARCHED BY

John Lee

Contents

CHRISTOPHER HERWIG / GETTY IMAGES ©

GRANT FAINT / GETTY IMAGES ©

(left) Fine dining in Gastown (p84)

(above) Beluga whale at Vancouver Aquarium (p53)

(right) Chinese New Year celebrations (p20)

LUCIDIO STUDIO, INC. / GETTY IMAGES ©

North Shore
p177

Downtown & West End
p48

Gastown & Chinatown
p80

Commercial Drive
p117

Yaletown & Granville Island
p98

Kitsilano & University of British Columbia (UBC)
p161

Main Street
p131

Fairview & South Granville
p146

Welcome to Vancouver

Cool neighborhoods, drink-and-dine hot spots and spectacular vistas: all good reasons why visitors fall for this lovely lotusland metropolis.

Neighborhood Villages

Don't make the mistake of thinking that downtown is exclusively what Vancouver is about. Walk or hop on public transportation and within minutes you'll be hanging with the locals in one of the city's distinctive 'hoods. Whether you're discovering the coffee shops of Commercial Dr, the hipster haunts of Main St, the indie bars and restaurants of Gastown or the heritage-house beachfronts of Kitsilano, you'll find this city perfect for easy-access urban exploration. Just be sure to chat to the locals wherever you go: they may seem shy or aloof at first, but Vancouverites love talking up their town.

Epicurean Adventures

Don't tell Montreal or Toronto but Vancouver is the culinary capital of Canada. Loosen your belt and dive right into North America's best Asian dining scene, from chatty Chinese restaurants to authentic *izakayas* (Japanese neighborhood pubs), and taste a rich smorgasbord of freshly caught seafood, including seasonal spot prawns and juicy wild salmon. The farm-to-table movement here has revitalized the notion of West Coast cuisine – anyone for succulent Fraser Valley duck and a side dish of foraged morels? And we haven't even started on the craft-beer scene that has led the nation in recent years.

Outdoor Wonderland

Those snow-dusted mountains that peek between downtown's glass towers? They're less than 30 minutes away by car. Vancouverites really can ski in the morning and hit the beach in the afternoon – although it's more relaxing to chill out and take your time. The city's North Shore nature doorstep offers snow sports, mountain biking and leisurely rainforest viewing, while the city itself is studded with sandy beaches, forest trails, kayaking routes, seawall bike lanes and Canada's urban green-space jewel, the mighty and beloved Stanley Park.

Grassroots Arts

A lack of Guggenheim-sized galleries means you'll have to go looking for the city's cultural side, but that's its main appeal. Vancouver's thriving artistic edge is local, grassroots and neighborhood-sized: think of it like a locavore movement for culture lovers. Mingle with the regulars at waterfront Shakespeare shows, electric dance performances, sparkling theatrical events, toe-tapping live music and a huge range of public art – as well as an open-house art crawl that enlivens East Vancouver every November.

DAVID NUNUK / GETTY IMAGES ©

Why I Love Vancouver

By John Lee, Author

Hummingbirds on my balcony, beaches in Stanley Park, and the annual dusting of snow on surrounding mountains. Although I moved here from the UK in the 1990s, I still gape at Vancouver's natural beauty. For me, it's the backdrop that sets this metropolis apart. But I'm a big-city boy at heart and I've also been delighted to see Vancouver grow up since I arrived. From amazing (and great-value) dining to a thriving local art scene, Vancouver continues to move forward – and I don't just mean the brilliant craft-beer movement (although, personally, that really helps).

For more about our author, see p288.

Top: Vancouver skyline

Vancouver's Top 10

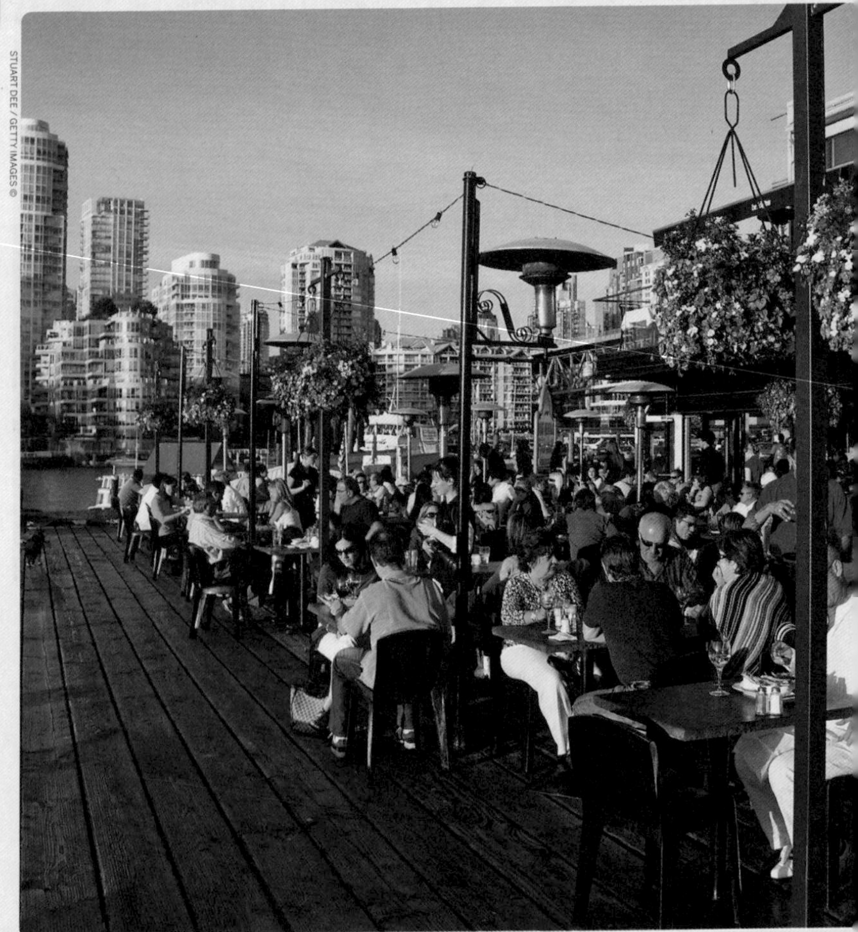

STUART DEE / GETTY IMAGES ©

Granville Island Public Market *(p100)*

1 Granville Island is crammed with busy backstreet studios and artsy little nooks, but the brimming Public Market lures everyone who comes here to the waterfront like a siren song. From pyramids of glistening fresh fruit to drool-triggering deli counters that inspire a picnicking approach to life, it's a taste-tripping stroll for browsers as well as those doing their regular shopping. Add a seat at the shoreline plaza, complete with cheery buskers and beady-eyed seagulls, and you've found what may be a perfect afternoon out. BELOW: OUTDOOR DINING ON GRANVILLE ISLAND

Yaletown & Granville Island

Gastown *(p80)*

2 The historic brick-paved neighborhood where 19th-century Vancouver began has seen a new wave of bars, restaurants and boutique shops opening in recent years. But rather than building afresh, these independent businesses have revitalized some of the city's oldest heritage buildings. The former skid row 'old town' area is now a picturesque and popular balance of old and new: just ask the jaunty bronze statue of 'Gassy' Jack Leighton in Maple Tree Sq, guarding the site where he built his first pub way back in 1867.

Gastown & Chinatown

DANITA DELIMONT / GETTY IMAGES ©

4

Asian Dining *(p27)*

3 Torn between visiting Canada or Asia? Come to Vancouver and try the richest, most authentic Asian dining scene outside of the continent itself. From bustling dim-sum joints and cozy *izakayas* (Japanese pubs), to *pho* (Vietnamese soup) houses and superfresh sushi joints, Vancouver is a culinary adventure. For the especially epicurious, dive into the Hong Kong–style summer night markets: there's one in Chinatown and two in Richmond, which also has more Asian restaurants than you'll ever be able to visit.

Eating

Grouse Mountain *(p179)*

4 Vancouver's favorite winter playground is only a short drive from downtown. But Grouse isn't just for goggle-eyed powder nuts. In summer, you'll have great views over the city – shimmering in the water far below – plus the perfect excuse for a flower-studded alpine hike. (Take the steep Grouse Grind to reach the summit if you fancy working up a sweat, or hop on the scenic gondola ride instead.) Either way, check out the grizzly bear enclosure: it's a great way to see sharp-toothed wildlife up close.

North Shore

Walking the Seawall *(p52)*

5 Few cities have democratized their waterfront better than Vancouver: you can stroll along a tree-fringed, wave-lapped walkway all the way from Canada Place to Kitsilano and the University of British Columbia. The highlight is the 8.8km stretch around Stanley Park. Like an immersive visual spa treatment, you'll encounter rippling ocean backed by looming mountains on one side and the gentle swish of dense forest and smiling cyclists on the other. The calming effect is an instant reminder of how good life can be. ABOVE: STANLEY PARK SEAWALL AT SUNSET

Downtown & West End

Vancouver Aquarium *(p53)*

6 There are few attractions that balance fun and education quite as well as this beloved family-friendly Stanley Park landmark. But while most parents bring their kids here to keep them occupied for a few hours, they end up having just as much fun themselves. Don't miss the mesmerizing displays of alien-like jellyfish and the smile-inducing feeding demonstrations with perky dolphins and jocular otters (the comedians of the aquatic animal world). If you're fully enthralled, get close to the action with a brilliant behind-the-scenes trainer tour. BELOW: BELUGA WHALE AT VANCOUVER AQUARIUM

Downtown & West End

Craft Beer *(p30)*

7 British Columbia has arguably become Canada's microbrewery capital in recent years, with dozens of beer makers popping up across the province like cheery drunks at an open bar. Luckily, Vancouver has jumped on board, with bars and restaurants across the city falling over themselves to stock the coolest local brews. Look out for hop-tastic Indian Pale Ales from the likes of Driftwood and Central City, and hunt down a tasting or three at a new wave of microbrewieries and nanobreweries opening in off-the-beaten-path locations around the city.

Drinking & Nightlife

6

Chinatown (p80)

8 Not all historic Chinatowns are created equal. The largest in Canada (and the third biggest in North America), Vancouver's Chinatown still has the bustling feel of a vibrant Chinese community, from its busy apothecary shops to its steam-shrouded barbecue-meat stores. The neighborhood is also chock-full of things to see: ornamental gardens, a towering Chinatown gate, a summertime night market and historic sites on corners and down side streets. It's an urban explorer's perfect afternoon out; ensure your camera is fully charged.

Gastown & Chinatown

Vancouver Art Gallery *(p55)*

9 The city's leading showcase for art has been exhibiting local photoconceptualist photographers, the nature-themed paintings of Emily Carr and an ever-changing roster of popular visiting exhibitions for many years, becoming western Canada's most important art space in the process. And while talks are afoot to move from its downtown heritage building space to a swanky new joint just a few blocks away, some things will endure, including the regular FUSE evening events when the gallery turns into a clubby late-night hangout for culture lovers.

Downtown & West End

Capilano Suspension Bridge *(p179)*

10 Arrive early to avoid the summer crowds and you'll have a great time inching over this swaying rope bridge, which stretches across a roiling, tree-lined river canyon. Even the bravest find their legs turn to jelly here, but it's all in good fun. At least that's what you should tell yourself, as you'll have to cross back at some point. There's plenty else to see in the temperate rainforest park, including a series of canopy bridges, a glass-floored cliffside walkway and nature trails through the towering trees.

North Shore

What's New

Gastown

Vancouver's oldest neighborhood is revitalizing, with hip bars and boutiques sprouting like Movember mustaches. Openings include Rainier Provisions. (p84)

Microbreweries

Canada's craft-beer city is getting hotter with a surfeit of microbrewery openings. Newbies include Powell Street Craft Brewery. (p125)

Gallery District

Galleries across Vancouver are migrating to a raft of former industrial spaces near Main St. Among them is Winsor Gallery. (p133)

Food Trucks

From 17 vendors in 2011 to more than 114 two years later, Vancouver's eclectic streetside food-truck dining scene is rapidly exploding, from Korean fusion to pulled-pork sandwiches. (p61)

Forbidden Vancouver Tours

Evoking Vancouver's historic underbelly, these entertaining guided walks are the best way to explore the city. (p248)

Chinatown Night Market

Reinvented with a funky hipster edge, the Chinatown Night Market remains the home of great alfresco grub – now with added ping-pong. (p84)

Storm Crow Tavern

Elf-eared locals flock to Storm Crow Tavern, Vancouver's only nerd pub for board games, craft beer and *Game of Thrones* screenings. (p122)

Vegetarian Restaurants

A miniwave of cool veggie eateries is sweeping Vancouver, making locals as giddy as heirloom tomatoes in a spin drier. Openings include Acorn. (p136)

Science World

One of Vancouver's best family-friendly attractions, the revamped Science World has a cool new outdoor area teeming with hands-on games and experiments. (p133)

Rosewood Hotel Georgia

A huge renovation has returned the handsome heritage Rosewood Hotel Georgia (p213) to former glory, complete with Hawksworth, Vancouver's top swanky restaurant. (p63)

Flying Pig

Yaletown's best new restaurant, Flying Pig has also opened an eatery in Gastown. Seasonal West Coast dining in a superfriendly setting. (p103)

For more recommendations and reviews, see **lonelyplanet.com/vancouver**

Need to Know

For more information, see Survival Guide (p243)

Currency
Canadian Dollar ($)

Language
English

Visas
Not required for visitors from the US, the Commonwealth and most of Western Europe for stays up to 180 days. Required by those from more than 130 other countries.

Money
ATMs are widely available around the city. Credit cards are accepted and widely used at all accommodations and almost all shops and restaurants.

Cell Phones
Local SIM cards may be used with some international phones. Roaming can be very expensive: check with your service provider.

Time
Pacific Time (GMT/UTC minus eight hours)

Tourist Information
Tourism Vancouver Visitor Centre (Map p266, 200 Burrard St; 8:30am-6pm; M Waterfront Station) provides maps, hotel booking and half-price theater tickets. At time of writing, the building was under renovation, so services were being conducted

Daily Costs

Budget: Less than $100
- Dorm bed: $30
- Food-court meal: $8; pizza slice: $1.75
- Beer special: $5
- All-day transit pass $9.75

Midrange: $100–$200
- Double room in a standard hotel: $120
- Dinner for two in neighborhood restaurant: $50 (excluding drinks)
- Craft beer for two: $15
- Museum entry: $15

Top End: More than $200
- Four-star hotel room: from $200
- Fine-dining meal for two: $100
- Cocktails for two: $20
- Taxi trips around the city: $5 and up

Advance Planning

Three months before Book summer season hotel stays and sought-after tickets for popular shows and festivals. Buy your Vancouver Canucks tickets.

One month before Book car rental and reserve a table at a fancy restaurant. Book theater tickets via Tickets Tonight (www.ticketstonight.ca).

One week before Check the *Georgia Straight*'s online listings (www.straight.com) to see what events are coming up.

Useful Websites

- **Inside Vancouver** (www.insidevancouver.ca) What to do in and around the city.
- **Miss 604** (www.miss604.com) Vancouver's favorite blogger.
- **Scout Magazine** (www.scoutmagazine.ca) Hip food and culture zine.
- **Tourism Vancouver** (www.tourismvancouver.com) Official tourism site.
- **Lonely Planet** (www.lonelyplanet.com/vancouver) Info for Vancouver travelers.

WHEN TO GO

December to March for skiing. Summer crowds roll in from June to September. Spring and fall for great weather and good-value hotel rates.

Vancouver, BC

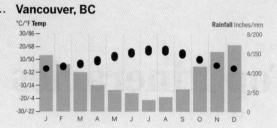

°C/°F **Temp**
30/86
20/68
10/50
0-32
-10/14
-20/-4
-30/-22

Rainfall Inches/mm
8/200
6/150
4/100
2/50
0

J F M A M J J A S O N D

Arriving in Vancouver

Vancouver International Airport Situated 13km south of the city in Richmond. Canada Line trains to downtown take around 25 minutes and cost $7.75 to $10.50, depending on the time of day. Alternatively, taxis cost up to $40.

Pacific Central Station Most trains and long-distance buses arrive from across Canada and the US at this station on the southern edge of Chinatown. Across the street is the SkyTrain Main St Station. From there it's just five minutes to downtown ($2.50).

BC Ferries Services from Vancouver Island and the Gulf Islands arrive at Tsawwassen, one hour south of Vancouver, or Horseshoe Bay, 30 minutes from downtown in West Vancouver. Both are accessible by regular transit bus services.

For much more on **arrival** see p244

Getting Around

SkyTrain Iconic train system winding through major downtown neighborhoods as well as out to the suburbs. There are only three lines, so walking and linking to local buses is often required.

Bus There's an extensive and generally reliable network in the downtown area and into major outlying areas such as Main St, Kitsilano and University of British Columbia (UBC).

Walk Downtown's city center area is eminently walkable with an easily navigated grid-like street system.

Bicycle There's an increasing network of dedicated bike lanes in the downtown core, plus access to much of the seawall.

Miniferries Two competing services ply the waters around False Creek. It's the best way to arrive or depart Granville Island.

For much more on **getting around** see p245

Sleeping

Downtown Vancouver is lined with boutique properties and chain hotels, several of them among Canada's swankiest sleepovers. If a character B&B is more your style, the West End and Kitsilano are home to several quality home-away-from-home spots, while budget options range from city-center hostels to student accommodation at UBC. Predictably, rates reach their peak here in summer, and advance booking is essential, but late spring or early fall can deliver serious deals and weather that's almost as good as August (sometimes).

Useful Websites

➡ **Tourism Vancouver** (www.tourismvancouver.com) Wide range of accommodation listings and package deals.

➡ **Hello BC** (www.hellobc.com) Official Destination British Columbia (BC) accommodation search engine.

➡ **Bed and Breakfast Online** (www.bbcanada.com) Listings site for B&Bs in the city and beyond.

For much more on **sleeping** see p209

Top Itineraries

Day One

Gastown (p80)

Start your wander around old town Gastown in **Maple Tree Sq**. Commune with the jaunty **'Gassy' Jack Deighton statue** and reflect on the fact that Vancouver might not be here today if it wasn't for the pub he built. Since it's a little too early for a drink, peruse the cool shops along Water St, including **Orling & Wu** and **John Fluevog Shoes**.

Lunch Rainier Provisions (p84) is perfect for great-value, hipster dining.

Chinatown (p80)

Your lunch spot is on the way to Chinatown, another top historic 'hood. Spend some time winding around the kaleidoscopically hued streets here. Don't miss the **Chinatown Millennium Gate** on Pender and the aromatic grocery and apothecary stores on Keefer St. Then go on the hunt for the **Jimi Hendrix Shrine**, before ending your afternoon at the delightful **Dr Sun Yat-Sen Classical Chinese Garden**.

Dinner Head east on Hastings for a carnivorous feast at Wildebeest (p88).

Downtown (p48)

Continue on foot to downtown and nip upstairs to the **Railway Club**, a great locals' hangout with craft beer and eclectic live music.

Day Two

Main Street (p131)

Have a lazy late start then get moving with coffee (plus a side order of hipsters) at **Gene Cafe**. Then head downhill on Main to explore the city's new gallery district, **the Flats**, colonizing a host of old industrial units. Next, hop on and off the number 3 bus southwards as you explore Main.

Lunch Join locals for a grilled cheese sandwich at Rumpus Room (p136).

Main Street (p131)

Bus to the 18th Ave intersection and hop off at the **Main Street Poodle** statue for some on-foot wandering. Check out Vancouver's best indie stores, from vinyl-loving **Neptoon Records** to the delightfully quirky **Regional Assemby of Text** stationery store. Back on the bus, head north to the intersection with Broadway and transfer to the 99B-Line express; you'll be at Commercial Dr in 10 minutes.

Dinner Head to Cannibal Café (p120) for perhaps the city's best burger.

Commercial Drive (p117)

Spend the evening bar (or coffeehouse) hopping around the area. Whatever you do, don't miss **Storm Crow Tavern**, Vancouver's only nerd pub.

Day Three

Stanley Park (p52)

Get here before the crowds to stroll the **seawall**, photograph the **totem poles** and nip into the **Vancouver Aquarium** to commune with the aquatic critters. Consider exploring the park by bike if you have time. You'll find some beady-eyed blue herons hanging out at **Lost Lagoon** – duck into the **Nature House** to find out more about them.

Lunch Exit the park for noodles nearby at Motomachi Shokudo (p64).

West End (p48)

Fully explore the tree-lined West End neighborhood, including Davie and Denman Sts. Save time for **English Bay Beach** and **Roedde House Museum**. There are also plenty of coffeehouses and shopping spots to lure your attention.

Dinner Consider some smashing Spanish tapas at Espana (p64).

West End (p48)

Davie St is the center of Vancouver's gay nightlife scene, and the area has plenty of cool options for folks of all persuasion to hang with the locals. Consider a sunset-viewing cocktail at **Sylvia's Lounge** in the neighborhood's ivy-covered heritage hotel. Or dive into **Lolita's** and drink yourself merry on cocktails.

Day Four

University of British Columbia (p161)

Start your day at the biggest university in British Columbia, exploring a surprising wealth of attractions. The **Museum of Anthropology** and **Beaty Biodiversity Museum** are must-sees, while the green-thumbed should also check out the **UBC Botanical Garden** and the **Nitobe Memorial Garden**. Stick around and explore the waterfront campus: it's dotted with intriguing public artworks.

Lunch Head for lunch at Kitsilano's Sophie's Cosmic Café (p170).

Kitsilano (p161)

It's all about shopping on West 4th Ave this afternoon. You'll find plenty of cool independent stores and boutiques here. Don't miss **Zulu Records** and travel-themed store **Wanderlust**, and pop into **49th Parallel Coffee** when you need a pit stop.

Dinner Tuck into a farm-to-table feast at Fable (p168).

Granville Island (p98)

Continue on to Granville Island for drinks at **Granville Island Brewing Taproom** before catching something theatrical at **Granville Island Stage** or a raucous improv show at **Vancouver Theatresports League** (just remember: if you sit in the front, they'll likely pick on you).

If You Like...

First Nations Art

Museum of Anthropology Vancouver's best museum presents an amazing array of Pacific Northwest artifacts. (p163)

Bill Reid Gallery of Northwest Coast Art Downtown showcase of Haida artists and those they inspired. (p57)

Hill's Native Art Gastown gallery with authentic art and crafts for sale. (p97)

Coastal Peoples Fine Arts Gallery Yaletown gallery selling aboriginal art, from jewelry to masks. (p113)

Salmon n' Bannock Vancouver's only authentic aboriginal restaurant is also lined with First Nations art. (p150)

Gardens

Vandusen Botanical Garden Manicured garden attraction with several themes and free guided tours. (p148)

Dr Sun Yat-Sen Classical Chinese Garden Tile-topped walls enclosing a symbolic Ming-style garden. (p83)

Vancouver Compost Demonstration Garden Ever-friendly hidden Kitsilano urban garden focused on sustainability. (p166)

Bloedel Conservatory Perfect rainy-day escape: a dome-covered tropical garden with exotic birds. (p148)

Queen Elizabeth Park Surrounding the Bloedel Conservatory, with curated gardens and great hilltop views. (p148)

MICHAEL WHEATLEY / GETTY IMAGES ©

Bloedel Conservatory, Queen Elizabeth Park (p148)

UBC Botanical Garden The university's greatest green space, with themed gardens and an annual Apple Festival. (p166)

Nitobe Memorial Garden Meticulous traditional Japanese garden with intricate symbolism. (p167)

Stanley Park Among the nature trails and seafront views, look out for rose and rhododendron gardens. (p52)

History

Gastown & Chinatown Vancouver's national historic neighborhoods recall Vancouver's earliest days with buildings from just after the 1886 Great Fire. (p80)

Forbidden Vancouver Tours into the city's sometimes sordid and dark past, from prohibition and beyond. (p248)

Roedde House Museum West End heritage mansion lined with period artifacts and antiques. (p59)

Old Hastings Mill Store Museum Vancouver's oldest building now houses eclectic artifacts from the city's past. (p166)

Museum of Vancouver The city's main history protector; check out Vancouver's recent past, including its neon signs. (p165)

Vancouver Police Museum The city's noirish past is traced in colorful detail. Consider the Sins of the City walking tour. (p82)

Views

Third Beach Stanley Park's best sunset spot, with mesmerizing panoramic waterfront vistas. (p54)

Vancouver Lookout The city's observation attraction, with 360-degree views over Vancouver and its surrounds. (p58)

Galley Patio & Grill Popular Kitsilano neighborhood hangout with great views of the city across the water. (p171)

Queen Elizabeth Park Camera-ready vistas of Vancouver backed by looming mountains. (p148)

Sylvia's Lounge Take in sunset views, with drink in hand, over the golden ripples of English Bay. (p68)

Tap & Barrel Olympic Village waterfront patio with handsome False Creek and cityscape views. (p135)

For more top Vancouver spots, see the following:

- Eating (p27)
- Drinking & Nightlife (p30)
- Entertainment (p35)
- Shopping (p37)
- Sports & Activities (p40)

Neighborhood Festivals

Eastside Culture Crawl Hundreds of East Vancouver studios and galleries invite folks in to see their work. (p93)

Car Free Day Streets across the city close to cars for a day of family-friendly partying. (p126)

UBC Apple Festival UBC's celebration of all things apple, from tastings to pies. (p174)

Pride Week The West End becomes party central with a week of events and a gigantic street parade. (p33)

Month by Month

TOP EVENTS

Vancouver International Film Festival, September

Vancouver International Jazz Festival, June

Eastside Culture Crawl, November

Pride Week, August

Car Free Vancouver, June

January

Vancouver's quietest month is usually cold, gray and dank weather-wise, with occasional sparkling blue skies to keep the locals from getting too miserable. Aside from the January 1 hangover cure, most happenings are indoors.

Polar Bear Swim

This chilly New Year's Day affair has been taking place annually in English Bay since 1920. At around 2:30pm more than a thousand people charge into the ocean…and most usually leap out shivering a few seconds later.

Dine Out Vancouver

From the second week of January, restaurants across the city offer 17 days of great-value, three-course tasting menus for $18, $28 or $38. Book ahead at www.dineoutvancouver.com – top spots always sell out.

PuSh International Performing Arts Festival

A three-week season of innovative theater, music, opera and dance from around the world, or around the corner. Adventurous performance-art fans will love this unusual showcase (www.pushfestival.ca), staged at venues across the city from the third week of January.

February

There are still good off-peak hotel deals to be had (except around Valentine's Day) and the weather may be warming a little – but don't count on it.

Chinese New Year

This multiday celebration (www.vancouver-chinatown.com) in and around Chinatown can take place in January or February, but it always includes plenty of color, dancing and great food. Highlights are the Dragon Parade and firecrackers.

Winterruption

Granville Island chases away the winter blues with a warming weekend-long roster of live music, theater and family-friendly events at Winterruption (www.winterruption.com). Dress warmly – many happenings are outdoors.

Vancouver International Wine Festival

The city's fave excuse for a drink – and one of North America's oldest wine fests – this week-long end-of-February wine festival (www.vanwinefest.ca) includes tastings, seminars and galas. Book ahead: many events sell out.

March

Spring is starting to bud around the city, which also means the rain is starting to kick in. Bring a waterproof jacket, complain about the

(Top) Fireworks display at the Celebration of Light festival (p23), English Bay
(Bottom) Dragon boat, False Creek

BARRY DUNCAN / GETTY IMAGES ©

BARRETT & MACKAY / GETTY IMAGES ©

relentless deluges and you'll fit right in.

Vancouver International Dance Festival

Local, national and international hoofers come together for this calf-stretching spree of performances (www.vidf.ca) showcasing the city's credentials as a major dance capital.

Celticfest Vancouver

Downtown's annual St Patrick's Day parade and multiday Irish cultural fiesta (www.celticfestvancouver.com) attracts those who like their beer green-hued. Expect some shamrock-tinged shenanigans and a chance to mix with local and visiting Irish folk.

April

Dry spells become longer as the month progresses. Expect to see the city's blossom trees in full and fragrant glory.

Vancouver Fashion Week

If you feel like hitting the catwalk, or at least watching others on it, check out the first of two annual fashion weeks – the second is in September. Fashion Week (www.vanfashionweek.com) shows, galas and educational events highlight the work of regional and international designers.

Sun Run

One of North America's largest street races, Sun Run lures 50,000 runners, speed walkers and wheezing wannabes for a spirited jaunt around the city in the fourth week of April.

May

The rain is intermittently forgotten as the promise of summer arrives. Several farmers markets start up for the season.

Vancouver International Children's Festival

Bristling with kid-friendly storytelling, performances and activities in a charming tented Vanier Park site, the eight-day Children's Festival (www.childrensfestival.ca) in late May is highly popular. Expect to be lured by face painters and balloon twisters while your ice-cream-smeared kids run riot.

Vancouver Craft Beer Week

Reflecting a surge in regional microbrewing, this popular late-May booze fest (www.vancouvercraftbeerweek.com) runs from pairing dinners to tasting events. Expect to rub shoulders with brewmeisters from Driftwood Brewing to Central City plus some from the US.

June

Let the summer good times roll as Vancouverites get used to wearing shorts and T-shirts for weeks on end (even when there's an unseasonal deluge). Neighborhood street parties kick off and it's time to crank up the barbecue.

(Top) The Olympic flame re-lit as part of Canada Day festivities
(Bottom) Chinese New Year celebrations (p20)

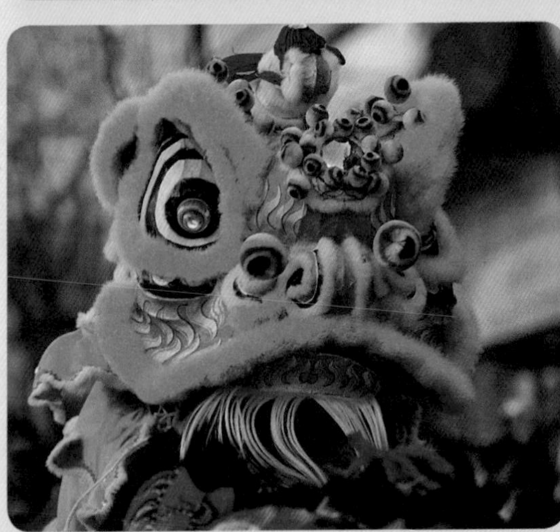

Bard on the Beach

Shakespeare performed the way it should be: in tents with the North Shore mountains peaking peacefully behind the stage. The four-play roster from Bard on the Beach (p173) runs from June to mid-September. Book ahead.

Car Free Vancouver

An increasingly popular day-long event, Car Free Vancouver (www.carfreevancouver.org) is held around mid-June, when the main streets of several neighborhoods – from Kitsilano to Main St – close to traffic and surrender to music, vendors, performers and food.

Dragon Boat Festival

An epic weekend splashathon during the third week of June, the colorful Dragon Boat Festival (www.dragonboatbc.ca) churns the normally placid waters of False Creek. Around 100,000 landlubbers turn up to cheer on close to 200 teams and partake of a minifestival of music, theater and food.

Greek Day

The local Hellenic community comes together for this rip-roaring late-June showcase of Greek culture (www.greekday.com). The one-day Kitsilano event (on W Broadway, between MacDonald and Blenheim Sts) features live music, street entertainers and lots of belt-challenging grub.

Vancouver International Jazz Festival

Vancouver's Jazz Fest (www.coastaljazz.ca) is a huge nine-day music party from late-June that combines superstar performances (Oscar Peterson and Diana Krall are past masters) with smile-triggering free outdoor shows in Gastown, Yaletown and on Granville Island.

July

The city is in full-on beach-bumming mode, with the very idea of rain a distant memory (except when there's an occasional cracking thunderstorm). Dress light and head outside from the first of the month onwards.

Canada Day

Canada Place is the main Vancouver location for Canada Day celebrations (www.canadaday.canadaplace.ca) marking the country's July 1 birthday. From 10am onwards expect music, food and (eventually) fireworks, plus an early evening street parade and impromptu renditions of 'O Canada.'

Vancouver Folk Music Festival

Kitsilano's Jericho Beach is the venue for the sunny, weekend-long Folk Music Festival (www.thefestival.bc.ca), featuring alfresco shows from folk to world music and beyond. Don your sunblock and join the 30,000-odd hippies and hipsters at one of Vancouver's most enduring music events.

Celebration of Light

One of North America's largest fireworks competitions, the Celebration of Light (www.hondacelebrationoflight.com) takes place in English Bay over three nights in late July and early August. Competing countries (which change every year) put on their most spectacular displays.

August

It's the peak of summer, which means locals are in full sun-kissed patio mode and a tasty menu of local-grown fruit – from blueberries to peaches – hits the city.

Pride Week

A multiday kaleidoscope of gay-, lesbian- and bisexual-friendly shows, parties and concerts culminating in western Canada's largest pride parade (p33). Typically the first Sunday of August, this saucy West End mardi gras draws up to 500,000 people with its disco-beat floats and gyrating, scantily clad locals.

Pacific National Exhibition

From the third week of August onwards, this ever-popular country fair (p127) has evolved into a three-week community party of live music, family-friendly performances (check out the Superdogs) and artery-clogging food stands: miss the minidonuts at your peril. Don't forget the fairground, with its kick-ass wooden roller coaster.

September

Summer is waning but there are usually still plenty of golden sunny days as the leaves start turning. The end of the month especially is many Vancouverites' favorite time of year.

Vancouver International Fringe Festival

One of the city's biggest arts events, the Fringe (p112) features a lively 11-day roster of wacky theatrics from the second week of September, drawing thousands to large, small and unconventional Granville Island venues. Expect short plays and comedy revues, with tickets typically around the $10 mark.

Vancouver International Film Festival

This giant, highly popular film festival (www.viff.org) celebrates smaller, art-house movies and international hidden gems. Its 17-day roster from late September covers hundreds of screenings of local, national and international films, and features gala events and industry schmoozes. Book ahead.

October

It's time to start heading back inside as the rains roll back into town and locals dig out their rainproof jackets for the rest of the year. Some sunny days remain though, illuminating the remainder of the fall foliage.

Vancouver International Writers Fest

A six-day, late-October literary event, the Writers Fest (www.writersfest.bc.ca) offers Granville Island readings, workshops and forums with dozens of local and international scribblers. Past guests have included Salman Rushdie and Margaret Atwood.

Parade of the Lost Souls

A spectral Day of the Dead celebration with a torch-lit procession of spookily dressed performers moving through the streets of East Vancouver. Parade of the Lost Souls (www.publicdreams.org) is Vancouver's main Halloween event.

November

Time to wrap up if you want to partake of the events around the city this month. Scarves and umbrellas are often a good idea in November.

Eastside Culture Crawl

Dozens of local artists in Vancouver's Eastside open their studios to visitors at this excellent three-day showcase (p93) in late November. Expect to come across a wild and wacky array of works, from found art installations to wood-block portraits of iconic Canadians.

Bright Nights in Stanley Park

Indicating that Christmas is on its way, this month-long event sees a swathe of the park covered in fairy lights, Yuletide displays and elfish dioramas. There's also a Christmas-themed train ride. Bright Nights (www.vancouver.ca/parks/events/brightnights) is Vancouver's most popular seasonal attraction, so book ahead.

December

Time to embrace the winter by either going into hibernation or adding a few extra layers of clothing. Events-wise, it's all about Christmas for the rest of the year.

Santa Claus Parade

Rivaling the Pride Parade for spectator numbers, this Christmas procession (www.rogerssantaclausparade.com) in the first week of December is a family favorite. Expect youth orchestras, carol-singing floats and, right at the end, the great man himself. And, yes, he's the real one.

With Kids

Family-friendly Vancouver is stuffed with activities for kids, including interactive science attractions, animal encounters and plenty of outdoor activities to tire them out before bed. Several festivals are especially kid-tastic, and local transportation options are highlights for many youngsters.

STEVE JOHNSON / GETTY IMAGES ©

ellyfish at Vancouver Aquarium (p53)

Animal Encounters

Kids often get a kick out of spotting Vancouver's indigenous critters, from hummingbirds that fly around the city to raccoons in Stanley Park. But for more organized encounters, take a summertime visit to Grouse Mountain (p179), where the resort's two resident grizzly bears have their own enclosure. While on the North Shore, combine it with a trip to Maplewood Farm (p179), where younger kids especially enjoy hanging out with the goats and chickens. If you have a half day to spare, make for the Vancouver Aquarium (p53), where the otters, iridescent jellyfish, and dolphin and beluga shows are popular; it's one of Vancouver's best kid-friendly attractions. And don't miss the bright parrots and wandering exotic birdlife at the jungly Bloedel Conservatory (p148).

Science & Nature

Science World (p133) is packed with hands-on activities and has mastered the art of teaching kids through an abundance of fun. Its new outdoor area is the city's favorite summertime hangout for children, especially under-10s. If you're traveling with a teen, Science World also stages regular after-hours social events for those aged 12 and up. And if your sprogs are of the astronomical persuasion, take them to the HR MacMillan Space Centre (p165) for push-button games and activities. But if learning about the region's natural backdrop is on your agenda, tackle the Capilano Suspension Bridge (p179). After inching over the canyon on the (deliberately) wobbly wooden bridge, take some short trails through the forest and learn about the towering trees and local critters that stud this coastal rainforest area. Take the kids even deeper at Stanley Park's Lost Lagoon Nature House (p53), where they can quiz the friendly volunteers about the park's flora and fauna: regular birdwatching tours are also available here.

NEED TO KNOW

- **Accommodation** Children can usually stay with parents at hotels for no extra charge. Some hostels have family rooms. Hotels can recommend trusted babysitting services.
- **Equipment** Strollers, booster seats and toys can be rented from Wee Travel (www.weetravel.ca).
- **Resources** Pick up the free *Kids' Guide Vancouver* around town and visit www.kidsvancouver.com for local tips, resources and family-focused events.

Outdoor Action

If your children have plenty of energy (or you just need to tire them out before bed), Stanley Park's Second Beach Pool (p76) is one of the city's best summertime hangouts. This side of the park also has a popular playground, as does the Lumberman's Arch area, where you'll also find a fun-tastic outdoor water park. An even bigger water park (p103) can be found on Granville Island, not far from the ever-popular Kids Market (p103). If your children prefer to make sandcastles, Kitsilano Beach (p165) is very popular with families and is highly recommended.

History Huggers

Richmond's excellent Gulf of Georgia Cannery (p200) is an evocative way to see how people used to work, while downtown's BC Sports Hall of Fame & Museum (p102) traces the region's sporting past via kid-friendly displays and activities. You can read up – or just catch an author reading – at the huge Kidsbooks (p175) store in Kitsilano, or book them in for some kid-focused swordplay lessons at Academie Duello (p75) and its ever-popular Knight Camp.

Festival Fun

The Vancouver International Children's Festival (p22) is packed with entertainers and face-painting shenanigans, while the Pacific National Exhibition (p127) is crammed with shows, activities and fairground rides for kids of all ages. You can also hang out with local families at Winterruption (p20), Car Free Vancouver (p23) and the Canada Day (p23) celebrations around Canada Place. For winter visitors, the Santa Claus Parade (p24) and Bright Nights in Stanley Park (p24) are the city's best Yuletide family events.

Transportation Hot Spots

Kids of a certain age really enjoy getting around Vancouver. Taking the seat at the front of a SkyTrain is all about pretending to be the driver, while the front window seats on a SeaBus jaunt to North Vancouver are almost as coveted. Hopping a bathtub-sized ferry around False Creek is also fun, while Stanley Park's miniature railway (p54) is a must.

NIGEL O'NEIL / GETTY IMAGES ©

Eating

Vancouver has an amazing array of dine-out options: authentic izakayas (Japanese neighborhood pubs), clamorous Chinese restaurants, food trucks and farm-to-table dining are all in the mix. You don't have to be a local to indulge: just follow your tastebuds and dinner will become the most talked-about highlight of your Vancouver visit.

Asian Rumble

There's no argument: Vancouver has Canada's best Asian dining scene outside Asia. Faced with a full and highly authentic menu of sushi, noodle and *izakaya* joints alongside taste-tripping Korean and Vietnamese *pho* (soup) and barbecue houses, you'll be salivating over your options. That's before we even get to the Chinese food: Vancouver has Canada's largest Chinatown plus dozens of options around the city for fans of everything from dim sum to chicken feet. Come hungry: you won't be disappointed.

Seafood

One reason Vancouver has great sushi and Chinese dining is the larder of top-table seafood available right off the boat. Given the length of British Columbia (BC) coastline, it's no surprise most restaurants (whether Asian, Mexican, West Coast or French) find plenty of menu space for local goodies such as salmon, halibut, spot prawns and freshly shucked

NEED TO KNOW

Price Ranges

The following price indicators are used in eating reviews:

$	up to $12 per main dish
$$	from $12 to $25 per main dish
$$$	over $25 per main dish

Opening Hours

➡ Restaurants generally open from 11:30am to 2pm for lunch and/or 5pm to 10pm (or later) for dinner.

➡ Breakfast is typically from 7am to 10am; later on weekends when many also serve brunch.

Reservations

➡ Reviews include phone numbers for restaurants typically requiring reservations. Many restos seat without bookings, especially for early dinners (from 5pm to 6pm).

Taxes & Tipping

➡ GST (Goods & Services Tax) of 5% is added to restaurant bills for food.

➡ Alcohol attracts GST plus 10% PST (Provincial Sales Tax).

➡ Some restaurants have corkage fees for BYO booze; typically $20 to $40.

➡ Tipping is standard; typically it's 15% of the bill. Some restos add a tip automatically for large groups: check your bill carefully.

oysters. If you're a seafood fan, you'll be in your element; even fish and chips is typically excellent. Start your aquatic odyssey at Granville Island, where the Public Market has seafood vendors and Fisherman's Wharf is just along the seawall.

Farm to Table

After decades of favoring imported ingredients over local, Vancouver now fully embraces regional food and farm producers. Restaurants can't wait to tell you about the Fraser Valley duck and foraged morels they've just discovered. Seasonal is key, and you'll see lots of local specials on menus; ask your server for insights. Adding to the feast, some restaurants showcase local cheese producers, and most have also taken their BC love affair to the drinks list: Okanagan wines have been a staple here for years but BC craft beer is the latest darling of thirsty Vancouver locavores.

International Dining

You'd be forgiven for thinking Vancouver's ethnic cuisine scene begins and ends with Asia, but locals know it's just the beginning. A city built on immigration, Vancouver's menu is a UN of dining options, from excellent French, Spanish and Italian eateries to highly popular Mexican joints. Follow the locals: they'll often lead you to unassuming family-run restaurants. Vancouver's dining is generally reasonably priced, so this is a great city to try something new.

Street-Food Extravaganza

A late starter to the North American street-food movement in 2011, Vancouver arguably now has the tastiest scene in Canada. The downtown core has the highest concentration of trucks. You'll find everything from Korean sliders and salmon tacos, to Thai green curry and barbecued brisket sandwiches. A visit that doesn't include at least one street-food meal isn't really a visit at all. If you're here in summer, consider the Chinatown Night Market (p84), which always has plenty of alfresco dining options plus the annual, highly popular Street Food Fest (www.foodcartfest.com).

Eating by Neighborhood

➡ **Downtown & West End** (p59) Food trucks and a full range of restaurants; many international midrange options in West End.

➡ **Gastown & Chinatown** (p84) Innovative independent eateries in Gastown; authentic Asian dining in Chinatown.

➡ **Yaletown & Granville Island** (p103) High-end restos in Yaletown; some good Granville Island seafood spots.

➡ **Commercial Drive** (p119) Brilliant neighborhood dining, with excellent patios.

➡ **Main Street** (p135) Quirky indie restaurants and neighborhood hangouts.

➡ **Fairview & South Granville** (p149) Fine dining and friendly neighborhood haunts.

➡ **Kitsilano & University of British Columbia (UBC)** (p168) Fine dining at midrange prices in Kits.

Lonely Planet's Top Choices

Forage (p64) Showcase of farm-to-table West Coast dining.

Flying Pig (p103) Perfect West Coast dining in a welcoming room.

Vij's (p153) Modern Indian cuisine at its finest.

Hawksworth (p63) Vancouver's leading fine-dining spot.

Bao Bei (p89) Vibe-tastic contemporary Chinese bistro.

La Taqueria Pinche Taco Shop (p149) Bright, cheery Mexican hangout.

Best by Budget

$

Rainier Provisions (p84) Great-value gourmet comfort food.

Budgie's Burritos (p135) Bulging vegetarian Mexican nosh.

$$

Rangoli (p152) Indian fusion without the Vij's lineup.

Cannibal Café (p120) Vancouver's best burger bar.

$$$

Hawksworth (p63) West Coast swanky dining.

Chambar (p63) Candlelit Belgian-influenced West Coast dining.

Best Breakfast

Medina (p62) Amazing for waffles.

Finch's (p59) Great-value fresh-cooked brekkies.

Templeton (p62) Diner joint with heaping breakfasts.

Paul's Omelettery (p152) Breakfast-specializing neighborhood haunt.

Sophie's Cosmic Café (p170) Kitsilano legend with belt-busting trad breakfasts.

Best Patios

Tap & Barrel (p135) Olympic Village waterfront hangout.

Galley Patio & Grill (p171) Kitsilano's sunset-hugging local fave.

Havana (p122) Vibing Commercial Dr haunt.

Gallery Café (p61) Perfect for a coffee and busy Robson St views.

Best Asian Dining

Bao Bei (p89) Supercool modern Chinese dining.

Guu with Garlic (p64) Authentic Japanese *izakaya*.

Sun Sui Wah Seafood Restaurant (p136) Top-notch traditional Chinese cuisine.

Sushi Mart (p63) West End's freshest sushi spot.

Phnom Penh (p89) Taste-tripping Cambodian and Vietnamese dining.

Best Vegetarian

Acorn (p136) Cool modern veggie diner with a hipster vibe.

Gorilla Food (p61) Downtown's raw and vegan specialist.

Heirloom Vegetarian (p152) Slick spot for a special dinner.

Budgie's Burritos (p135) Great-value Mexican-themed joint.

Naam (p170) Local vegetarian legend, open 24 hours.

Best Foodie Blogs

Follow Me Foodie (www.followmefoodie.com)

Eating in Vancouver (www.eatinginvancouver.ca)

Sherman's Food Adventures (www.shermansfoodadventures.com)

Chow Times (www.chowtimes.com)

LAWRENCE WORCESTER / GETTY IMAGES ©

Granville Island Brewing (p103)

Drinking & Nightlife

Vancouverites spend a lot of time drinking. And while British Columbia (BC) has tasty wines perfect for an aperitif and has undergone a recent cocktail renaissance, it's the regional craft-beer scene that keeps many quaffers merry. For a night out where a drink is the ideal side dish, join savvy locals supping in the bars of Gastown, Main St or Commercial Dr.

Craft Beer

Finally a real rival to the massive Pacific Northwest craft-brewing scene south of the border, BC is in the midst of a golden age of beer making. Luckily for Vancouver visitors, bars around the city are falling over themselves to showcase intriguing regional brews. Ask your server what's local on the draft list, and be sure to look out for favorite Vancouver-area beer makers including Central City Brewing (ESB recommended) and Storm Brewing (Black Plague Stout). The bars of Gastown, Main St and Commercial Dr are especially in tune with the BC beer scene. For more information on the city's beery happenings, visit www.camravancouver.ca.

Wine & Liquor

It's not just beer that has raised the bar recently in Vancouver. The city's drinking scene has improved immeasurably from the days when a badly made Manhattan was the height of sophistication. Grape-based quaffing kicked off the revolution, and several cool wine bars have popped up in recent years to satisfy thirsty oenophiles. Wine fans will now find plenty to crow about at bars around town. Cocktails are also set to impress, with a selection of taste-tastic little drinking joints, from traditional to quirky, joining the nightlife fray. Craft distilleries are the latest wave; look out for newly opened spots on your visit.

Clubbing

While downtown's Granville Strip draws the barely clad booties of mainstream clubbers, there are other, less limelight-hogging areas catering to just about every peccadillo. Cover charges run from $5 to $20 ('the ladies' often get in free before 11pm) and dress codes are frequently smart-casual – ripped jeans and sportswear will not endear you to the bouncers who are just looking for people to send home. Bring ID: most clubs accept over-19s but some want you to be over 25. You can put yourself on the VIP list (no waiting, no cover) at the websites of individual clubs or via www.clubvibes.com and www.clubzone.com.

Alternative Night Out

Pick up a copy of the free *Georgia Straight* weekly, the city's best listings newspaper, for additional night-out ideas. If you're stuck, consider the first Monday of the month at the Railway Club (p66) for the Hard Rock Miners group singalong; the monthly Green Drinks social mixer at Steamworks brewpub (p92); or just scratch your pinball itch with Pub 340's roomful of machines (p94).

Drinking & Nightlife by Neighborhood

- **Downtown & West End** (p66) Granville Strip is lined with party-hard clubs and bars while the West End's Davie St is gay nightlife central.
- **Gastown & Chinatown** (p89) Craft-beer taverns as well as indie bars and clubs.
- **Yaletown & Granville Island** (p108) Yaletown has some slick bars and a huge brewpub while Granville Island is fine for pre-theater drinks.
- **Commercial Drive** (p122) Neighborhood pubs and old-school coffee bars abound.
- **Main Street** (p137) Where in-the-know hipsters drink at some of the city's best indie bars.

NEED TO KNOW

Opening Hours

Pubs and bars serving lunch usually open before midday, with swankier, lounge-style operations waiting it out until 5pm. Most bars close sometime between 11pm and 2am, although some – mostly on the Granville Strip – stay open to 4am. Nightclubs usually open their doors at 9pm (although they don't really get going until 11pm) and most stay open until 3am or 4am. Many close from Monday to Wednesday.

How Much?

- Expect to pay $5 or $7 for a large glass of beer, but always ask if there are daily specials.
- A glass of wine will set you back anything over $6, while cocktails also often start at $6.
- Your bill will include an added 10% Provincial Sales Tax (PST), an extra that's enough to drive anyone to drink.
- Expect to pay $5 to $20 for entry to many clubs, with weekends being the most expensive time.

Tipping

Table servers expect around $1 per drink, or 15% when you're buying a round. Even if you order and pick up your beverage at the bar, consider dropping your change in the prominently placed tips glass.

Lonely Planet's Top Choices

Alibi Room (p89) Superb BC craft-beer selection wrapped in a friendly tavern vibe.

Railway Club (p66) Old-school pub feel with craft beer and nightly live music.

Storm Crow Tavern (p122) Sci-fi and fantasy nerd pub with board games galore.

Brickhouse (p93) Den-like locals' secret with eclectic decor.

Shameful Tiki Room (p138) Evocative, cave-like cocktail haunt.

Best Beer Bars

Alibi Room (p89) Vancouver's fave craft-beer tavern, with around 50 mostly BC drafts.

Railway Club (p66) Trad pub room with live music and beers served in dimpled pint glasses

Portland Craft (p138) Main St bar with dozens of craft brews, mostly from the US.

St Augustine's (p122) Sports-bar vibe with dozens of rare-for-Vancouver craft drafts.

Best Cocktail Joints

Shameful Tiki Room (p138) Windowless tiki-themed bar with strong concoctions.

Diamond (p91) Alluring upstairs room with perfect, classic cocktails.

Keefer (p93) Chinatown's fave lounge with great drinks and a cool-ass vibe.

George Lounge (p108) Yaletown's smoothest cocktail haunt.

Best Wine Lists

Salt Tasting Room (p91) Brick-lined wine, cheese and charcuterie bar with a chatty communal table.

Vancouver Urban Winery (p93) Barrel-lined tasting bar, popular on weekends.

Blue Water Café (p106) Swish seafood restaurant with one of the city's best wine lists.

Uva Wine Bar (p66) Slick, modern room with a great boutique wine list.

Best Guest Beer Casks

Whip (p137) Every Sunday from 4pm.

St Augustine's (p122) Every Monday from 6pm.

Railway Club (p66) Every Tuesday from 5pm.

Yaletown Brewing Company (p108) Every Thursday from 4pm.

Best Microbreweries for Tasting

Powell Street Craft Brewery (p125) Tiny art-lined nano-brewery.

33 Acres Brewing Company (p138) Hipster fave with lounge-like tasting room.

Parallel 49 Brewing Company (p125) Large tasting room with good array of taps.

Yaletown Brewing Company (p108) Brewpub with regular beers and seasonals.

Granville Island Brewing Taproom (p110) Lively taproom with popular brewery tours.

Best Bars for Live Music

Railway Club (p66) Local fave with eclectic nightly live acts.

Guilt & Co (p91) Subterranean bar with regular shows.

Backstage Lounge (p112) Granville Island bar hosting local bands.

Pat's Pub (p94) Old-school bar with live jazz shows.

Gay & Lesbian

Vancouver's gay and lesbian scene is part of the city's culture rather than a subsection of it. The legalization of same-sex marriage here makes it a popular spot for those who want to tie the knot in scenic style. But if you just want to kick back and have a good time, this is also Canada's top gay-tastic party city.

West End

The West End's Davie St is the center of Vancouver's gay scene. Sometimes called the Gay Village, this is Canada's largest 'gaybor-hood' and is marked by rainbow flags, hand-holding locals and pink-painted bus shelters. There's a full menu of scene-specific pubs and bars, and it's a warm and welcoming district for everyone, gay or straight. Find the perfect spot sitting at a street-side cafe pretending to read *Xtra!* while actually checking out the passing talent; you can expect to make friends pretty quickly here. Vancouver's Commercial Dr is a traditional center of the lesbian scene. Keep in mind, though, that Vancouver is highly gay-friendly, so you can expect events and happenings all around the city.

Nightlife

You're unlikely to run out of places to hang with the locals in Vancouver's lively gay scene. Davie St, in particular, is home to a full bar-crawl of diverse gay-driven watering holes, from pubby haunts to slick lounge bars. You'll also find places to shake your thang on the dance floor here. But it's not all about the West End: look out for gay-friendly nights at clubs and bars around the city. Peruse some options at www.gayvancouver.net/nightlife.

Pride Week

Showing how far the scene has progressed since the days when Vancouver's gay community was forced to stay in the closet, **Pride Week** (www.vancouverpride.ca) is now Canada's biggest annual gay celebration. Staged around the first week of August, the centerpiece is the parade – a huge street fiesta of disco-pumping floats, drum-beating marching bands and gyrating, barely clad locals dancing through the streets as if they've been waiting all year for the opportunity. The parade is only the most visual evidence of Pride Week; this is also the time to dive into galas, drag contests, all-night parties and a popular queer film fest. Book your area hotel far in advance, since this is a highly popular event for visitors. During the same week, East Vancouver's annual Dyke March concludes with a festival and beer garden in Grandview Park on Commercial Dr.

Gay & Lesbian by Neighborhood

- **Downtown & West End** West End's Davie St is Vancouver's gay scene central.
- **Gastown & Chinatown** The Cobalt stages regular gay-tastic events.
- **Commercial Drive** Traditional center of Vancouver's lesbian community.

NEED TO KNOW

➡ Pick up a free copy of *Xtra!* (www.xtra.ca) newspaper from sidewalk boxes on Davie St and beyond.

➡ Check the online directory of the Gay & Lesbian Business Association of BC (www.loudbusiness.com) for all manner of local businesses, from dentists to spas and hotels.

➡ For local events and the inside track on the community, check www.gayvancouver.net and www.gayvan.com.

➡ Head to www.superdyke.com for insights on the local lesbian scene.

➡ For support and resources of all kinds, Qmunity (www.qmunity.ca) provides discussion groups, a health clinic and advice for lesbians, gays, bisexuals and the transgendered.

➡ Contact Vancouver Pride Society (www.vancouverpride.ca) for the latest info on the Pride festival.

Lonely Planet's Top Choices

Pride Week (p33) Canada's best pride celebration, with a rocking street parade.

Cobalt (p95) Great events for gay and straight locals in a grunge-cool dive bar.

Fountainhead Pub (p67) Laid-back, beer-friendly gay community pub.

1181 (p68) Smooth lounge bar; great spot to see and be seen.

Little Sister's Book & Art Emporium (p74) Long-time 'gayborhood' legend, stocking books and beyond.

Best Gay Night Out

Cobalt (p95) Grunge-cool bar with great events.

Celebrities (p67) Pumping gay nightclub.

Pride Week (p33) Galas, parties and dancing galore.

Best Gay Bars

Fountainhead Pub (p67) Popular community pub with a lively patio.

Pumpjack Pub (p68) Sometimes raucous spot, great for making new friends.

1181 (p68) Smooth lounge bar with slick clientele.

Best for Watching the Pride Parade

Delany's Coffee House (p68) Denman St coffee shop with street-side tables.

Fountainhead Pub (p67) From the patio, wolf-whistling the passing locals.

Pumpjack Pub (p68) Watch the show through the window.

Vancouver Pride Society Float Catch it all from the back of a float.

Best Place to Recover After a Big Night Out

Little Sister's Book & Art Emporium (p74) Calm down and catch up on your reading.

Delany's Coffee House (p68) Grab a strong caffeine hit.

Raincity Grill (p65) Dive into brunch, then stroll the beach at English Bay.

Stanley Park Seawall (p52) Blow away the cobwebs with a jog, bike or hangover-busting walk.

Entertainment

You won't run out of options if you're looking for a good time here. Vancouver is packed with activities ranging from high to low brow, perfect for those who like catching a play one night, watching a football match the next, and rocking out at a gig in a grungy bar another. Whatever you do first, ask the locals for tips and they'll likely point out some grassroots happenings you never knew existed.

Live Music

Superstar acts typically hit the stages at sports stadiums and downtown theaters (and with the big venue comes a big ticket price), while smaller indie bands crowd broom-closet-sized spaces at a rag-tag of local-fave venues around town. Zulu Records (p174) and Red Cat Records (p143) are experts on the local scene and sell tickets to many grassroots shows. And the scene here is not all about brooding indie bands: Vancouver has a wide array of musical tastes and, with some digging, you'll find jazz, folk, classical and opera performances around the city, often with annual festivals to match.

Film

While some independent movie theaters have closed in recent years, there are still plenty of places to catch blockbusters as well as a couple of downtown art-house cinemas for those who like subtitles rather than car chases: visit www.cinemaclock.com to see what's on while you're here. Visiting cinephiles will be thrilled at the huge range of movie festivals. Consider the highly popular Vancouver International Film Festival (p24) in late September, as well as smaller film fests such as **DOXA** (www.doxafestival.ca) and the **Vancouver Asian Film Festival** (www.vaff.org). And when all you want is some popcorn fun, hit the summer alfresco screenings in Stanley Park, staged by **Fresh Air Cinema** (www.freshaircinema.ca).

Theater

Vancouver has a long history of treading the boards. The Arts Club Theatre Company is the city's leading troupe (particularly at its Granville Island stronghold), and there are many stages dotted around the city. Look out for challenging, fringe-like shows and visiting companies at the Cultch (p126) and Firehall Arts Centre (p95). Depending on the time of year you're visiting in, catch theater events such as January's PuSh International Performing Arts Festival (p20), September's Vancouver International Fringe Festival (p112) and the summer-long Bard on the Beach (p173), where Shakespeare plays are performed in tents against a mountain backdrop.

Entertainment by Neighborhood

- ➡ **Downtown & West End** (p69) Home to top entertainment venues, from theaters to cinemas, and local sports teams.
- ➡ **Gastown & Chinatown** (p94) Location of several under-the-radar venues.
- ➡ **Yaletown & Granville Island** (p112) Granville Island is a hotbed of theaters and festivals.
- ➡ **Commercial Drive** (p126) Location of several locally loved performance spaces.
- ➡ **Main Street** (p139) Home of some cool indie venues.

NEED TO KNOW

Opening Hours

- The theater season typically runs from October to May; shows usually start at 8pm.
- Live-music venues often start their shows after 9pm.

Price Ranges

- Music shows can be free at pubs (although a cover of up to $10 is also typical), while tickets at dedicated live venues can run from $20 to $60.
- Theater tickets typically start at $30; see www.ticketstonight.ca for half-price deals on the day.
- Cinema tickets often start at $12, with matinees and Tuesday shows sometimes cheaper.

Listings

- Pick up Thursday's freebie *Georgia Straight* (www.straight.com) for what's on in the week ahead.
- Look for *Discorder* magazine (www.discorder.ca) for local live-music insights.
- Head online to Live Van (www.livevan.com) for up-to-the-minute local gig listings.
- Browse a copy of *Preview* (www.preview-art.com) for gallery shows and events.

Lonely Planet's Top Choices

Commodore (p69) Vancouver's fave band venue.

Biltmore Cabaret (p139) Great low-ceilinged spot to catch indie acts.

Cultch (Vancouver East Cultural Centre) (p126) Brilliant theater space in a converted heritage building.

Bard on the Beach (p173) Shakespeare plays in waterfront tents.

Pacific Cinémathèque (p69) Art-house cinema.

Best Live-Music Venues

Commodore (p69) Springy-floored local legend.

Biltmore Cabaret (p139) Vancouver's favorite hipster venue.

Rickshaw Theatre (p94) Specializing in thrash and punk.

Cellar Jazz Club (p173) Kitsilano haunt for serious jazz musos.

Media Club (p72) Local and visiting indie acts.

Best Theaters

Granville Island Stage (p112) Granville Island's best stage.

Cultch (Vancouver East Cultural Centre) (p126) Heritage building converted into an excellent theater.

Stanley Theatre (p155) Heritage theater, specializing in musicals.

Firehall Arts Centre (p95) Cool fringe venue with an eclectic roster.

Pacific Theatre (p155) Small, intriguing theater, popular with locals.

Best Fests

Vancouver International Film Festival (p24) Giant showcase for global movies.

Vancouver International Fringe Festival (p112) Wacky shenanigans on Granville Island.

Vancouver International Jazz Festival (p23) Massive array of shows, including many freebies.

Bard on the Beach (p173) Summer Shakespeare shows in a tented waterfront venue.

Vancouver International Dance Festival (p21) Showcases modern dance performances.

Best Spectator Sports

Vancouver Canucks (p69) City's fave NHL hockey passion.

BC Lions (p112) Canadian Football League team, playing at BC Place.

Vancouver Whitecaps (p112) The city's MLS soccer team.

Vancouver Canadians (p156) Minor league fun at nostalgic old-school stadium.

AL HARVEY / GETTY IMAGES ©

Shopping on Commercial Drive (p128)

Shopping

Vancouver's retail scene has developed dramatically in recent years. Hit Robson St's mainstream boutiques then discover the hip independent shops and pop-up stores of Gastown, Main St and Commercial Dr. Granville Island is stuffed with artsy stores while South Granville and Kitsilano's 4th Ave are lined with higher-end indie boutiques.

Local Fashion

Vancouver has all the usual chain-store suspects, but it also has a bulging shopping bag of independent shops that focus on curated collections of fashions from around the world and locally designed togs for that perfect Vancouver look. Get off the beaten path to Main St and Commercial Dr for quirky vintage and artsy fashions. Or peruse the main drags and side streets of Gastown, South Granville and Kitsilano's 4th Ave for one-of-a-kind boutique gems. Keep your eyes peeled for pop-up shops and check the pages of *Vancouver* magazine and the *Georgia Straight* for retail happenings such as Gastown's 'shop hops' – seasonal evenings of late-opening shops with a party-like vibe. Before you arrive, peruse www.vitamindaily.com/vancouver for more retail therapy tips.

Arts & Crafts

The city's arts scene dovetails invitingly with its retail sector. There are dozens of intriguing private galleries, showcasing everything

NEED TO KNOW

Opening Hours

Typical downtown retail hours are from 10am to 5pm or 6pm Monday to Saturday, and from noon to 5pm Sunday. Independent stores in neighborhoods such as Main St and Commercial Dr typically don't open until 11am (noon on Sundays). Some stores and malls may stay open later on Fridays and Saturdays, especially during the Christmas season.

Consumer Taxes

The price on most items in shops does not include tax, which is added when you take it to the cash register to pay. The recently reinstated Provincial Sales Tax (PST) adds 7% to the cost of most items. The rate is 10% for alcohol, while there are some items – such as basic groceries – where no tax is charged at all.

from contemporary Canadian art to authentic First Nations carvings and jewelry. Check out the Flats emerging gallery district just off Main St and peruse the older gallery row on South Granville. There are also opportunities to buy art from indie galleries on Main St and from the many artisan studios on Granville Island. In addition, there are dozens of arts and crafts fairs here throughout the year and they're a great way to meet local producers and creative Vancouverites. Check local listings publications or www.gotcraft.com for upcoming events.

Souvenirs

For decades, visitors to Vancouver have been returning home with suitcases full of maple-sugar cookies and vacuum-packed smoked salmon in wooden boxes. You can still pick up these items, typically in the large souvenir stores lining the north side of Gastown's Water St. But it doesn't have to be this way. Consider consigning your Gastown-clock fridge magnet to the garbage and aiming for authentic First Nations art or silver jewelry; a book on Vancouver's eye-popping history (*Vancouver Noir* by Diane Purvey and John Belshaw, for example); some locally made pottery from Granville Island; or a Vancouver-designed T-shirt from the fashion stores on Main St.

Museum Goodies

The city's museums and galleries offer some unexpected buying opportunities. You don't have to see an exhibition to visit these shops, and keep in mind that you're helping to fund the institutions you're buying from. Perhaps the best of all the city's museum stores, the Museum of Anthropology (p163) shop has a fantastic array of First Nations and international indigenous artworks, ranging from elegant silver jewelry to fascinating masks. Back downtown, the Vancouver Art Gallery (p55) gift shop is like a lifestyle store for artsy types, with clever contemporary knickknacks and large art books to leave on your coffee table and impress guests.

Shopping by Neighborhood

- **Downtown & West End** (p72) Mainstream fashion boutiques on Robson St and in Pacific Centre mall.
- **Gastown & Chinatown** (p95) Independent fashion and homewares shops.
- **Yaletown & Granville Island** (p113) Swish boutiques in Yaletown; artisan studios on the island.
- **Commercial Drive** (p128) Eclectic fashions, vintage stores and hippy-esque shops.
- **Main Street** (p140) Local indie fashions, especially south of 18th Ave.
- **Fairview & South Granville** (p156) Independent stores on Cambie St; private galleries and swish boutiques on South Granville.
- **Kitsilano & University of British Columbia (UBC)** (p174) Hit Kitsilano's West 4th Ave for boutiques and homewares.

Lonely Planet's Top Choices

Regional Assembly of Text (p142) Creative stationery store with a little gallery nook.

Mountain Equipment Co-op (p142) Outdoor-gear and clothing megastore.

Erin Templeton (p95) Bags and accessories made from recycled leather.

Smoking Lily (p142) Quirky fashions for artistically minded locals.

Neptoon Records (p142) Old-school vinyl-hugging record shop.

Best Indie Designer Wear

Smoking Lily (p142) Cool togs for the pale and interesting set.

Lynn Steven Boutique (p96) Select local and international designer gear.

Barefoot Contessa (p128) Classic vintage-influenced womenswear.

John Fluevog Shoes (p95) Funky footwear, designed in Vancouver.

Best Bookshops

KidsBooks (p175) Giant child-focused bookstore.

MacLeod's Books (p72) Teetering stacks of used tomes.

Solder & Sons (p96) Tiny book nook with coffee.

Barbara-Jo's Books To Cooks (p175) Recipe books and cuisine-related volumes.

Best Record Shops

Neptoon Records (p142) Classic vinyl-focused store without hipster pretensions.

Red Cat Records (p143) Cool-ass array of vinyl and CDs.

Zulu Records (p174) Giant vinyl selection in a *High Fidelity*–like setting.

Audiopile (p128) Well-priced new and used recordings, especially in the bargain rack.

Best Homewares

Vancouver Special (p143) Double store of mod-designed knickknacks.

Orling & Wu (p96) Treasure trove of must-have goodies.

Peking Lounge (p97) Chinese-themed interiors store with arts and antiques.

Restoration Hardware (p159) Upmarket designer interior flourishes and furnishings.

Best Vintage Clothing

Deluxe Junk (p96) From prom dresses to costume jewelry.

Mintage (p129) Perfectly curated array of classic old-school togs.

Front & Company (p143) Hipster favorite with ironically cool used clothing.

Mis'cel'la'ny Finds (p129) Treasure hunt at this rambling used and vintage store.

Sports & Activities

Vancouver's variety of accessible outdoorsy activities is a huge draw: you can ski in the morning and hit the beach in the afternoon; hike or bike through a rainforest; windsurf along the coastline; or kayak to your heart's content – and indeed it will be content with grand mountain views as your backdrop.

Running

Vancouverites love to jog. For heart-pounding runs (or even just a walk at arm-swinging speed), the 8.8km Stanley Park Seawall (p52) is the city's number-one circuit. It's mostly flat, apart from a couple of uphill sections where you might want to hang onto a passing bike. The University of British Columbia (UBC) is another popular running destination, with tree-lined trails marked through Pacific Spirit Regional Park.

Cycling & Mountain Biking

Vancouver is a cycle-friendly city with a network of designated urban routes. For bike maps and resources, see www.vancouver.ca/cycling. There's a very active mountain-biking community in North Vancouver, where Mt Seymour (p185) offers some excellent forested runs. First-timers should consider the 10km Seymour Valley Trailway, which has only a few uphills and offers great wilderness views – as well as the occasional deer.

Skiing & Snowboarding

You'll find excellent alpine skiing and snowboarding areas, as well as cross-country skiing trails, less than 30 minutes from downtown – it's where you'll find most locals when the powder arrives. The season typically runs from late November to early April, and the main ski areas are Grouse Mountain (p185), Cypress Mountain (p185) and Mt Seymour.

Watersports

It's hard to beat the joy of a sunset kayak around the coastline here; it's a signature outdoor activity that many Vancouverites enjoy. But hitting the water isn't only about paddling: there are also plenty of opportunities to surf, kiteboard and stand-up paddleboard, especially along the shoreline of Kitsilano. Why not join the locals at the Jericho Sailing Centre (p176) to find out what's available.

Sports & Activities by Neighborhood

- **Downtown & West End** (p75) Home to Vancouver's top green space and Stanley Park Seawall.
- **Kitsilano & University of British Columbia (UBC)** (p176) Kits is the center of local watersports.
- **North Shore** (p185) Skiing and mountain-biking central.

Lonely Planet's Top Choices

Stanley Park Seawall (p52) Breathtakingly scenic walking, jogging and cycling trail.

Grouse Grind (p180) Steep rite-of-passage hiking trail.

Cypress Mountain (p185) Local-favorite ski and snowboard area.

Ecomarine Paddlesport Centres (p116) Perfect sunset paddling activity on False Creek.

Mt Seymour (p185) Ideal mountain-biking terrain.

Best Places to Ski

Grouse Mountain (p185) Popular and busy, especially for night skiing.

Cypress Mountain (p185) Former Olympic venue; great for snowboarding.

Mt Seymour (p185) Laid-back and quieter; popular with families.

Best Places to Get In or On the Water

Jericho Sailing Centre (p176) From sailing to surfing, this is Vancouver's watersports magnet.

Ecomarine Paddlesport Centres (p116) Everything from rentals to guided local paddles.

Deep Cove Canoe & Kayak Centre (p186) Tranquil kayaking in a mountain-shadowed setting.

Second Beach Pool (p76) Busy oceanfront pool that's popular with families.

Kitsilano Pool (p176) Giant saltwater swimming pool.

Best for Biking

Spokes Bicycle Rentals (p76) Kit out the whole family with various rental bikes.

Endless Biking (p186) Guided mountain-bike tours and rentals.

Reckless Bike Stores (p116) Longstanding organization with rental cruisers and mountain bikes.

False Creek Seawall Trail (p111) Follow the seawall trail on two wheels.

Pacific Spirit Regional Park (p167) Kilometers of trails in a 763-hectare park.

NEED TO KNOW

- Connect with Vancouver's urban bike scene at www.bikehub.ca.
- For information on area mountain biking, visit the North Shore Mountain Biking Association's website (www.nsmb.com).
- For a wide range of local hiking trails (plus maps), see www.vancouvertrails.com.
- Vancouver's full array of parks and recreation facilities are detailed at www.vancouver.ca/parks.
- For gear and equipment rentals (plus info on local outdoorsy events), see www.mec.ca.

IAN COOK / GETTY IMAGES ©

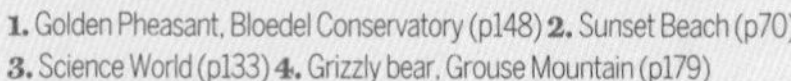

1. Golden Pheasant, Bloedel Conservatory (p148) **2.** Sunset Beach (p70) **3.** Science World (p133) **4.** Grizzly bear, Grouse Mountain (p179)

BY: KEN STRAITON / GETTY IMAGES ©

Vancouver Outdoors

Vancouver's sparkling natural setting is a key reason many visitors fall in love with this city. Plunge in at beaches, mountain promontories and perfect trails, both urban and on the city's tree-lined fringes.

Beaches

You're never far from great beaches in Vancouver, such as the busy, sandy swathes of Kits Beach and English Bay Beach or more tranquil gems such as Stanley Park's Third Beach and rustic Spanish Banks. Consider a picnic and plan for a sunset vista.

Grouse Mountain

It's hard not to take a deep breath when you step onto the smile-triggering summit of Grouse. Alpine trails, a grizzly bear refuge and some of the most spectacular natural views of the city shimmering in the water far below will have you itching to click that camera.

Queen Elizabeth Park

Stunning Stanley Park is hard to measure up to, but don't overlook these manicured gardens, jaw-dropping panoramic views of the city framed by mountains, and a tropical botanical garden teeming with beady-eyed, neon-hued birds.

False Creek Seawall

Vancouver's glittering waterfront has a spectacular seawall trail linking more than 20km of coastline, from downtown through Stanley Park and out to UBC. Don't miss the False Creek stretch; it's crammed with public art and water-to-city views.

Parks & Gardens of UBC

Pacific Spirit Regional Park rivals Stanley Park for stature and tree-hugging glory but it's UBC's manicured green spaces that attract the crowds. From a symbolic traditional Japanese garden to the verdant themed areas of the huge Botanical Garden, green-thumbed visitors have a ball here.

Explore Vancouver

VANCOUVER'S TOP SIGHTS

Neighborhoods at a Glance

❶ Downtown & West End p48

The heart of Vancouver occupies a jutting, ocean-fringed peninsula that's easily divided into three: the grid-pattern streets of shops, restaurants and businesses radiating from the city center's Granville and West Georgia Sts; the 1950s towers and dense residential side streets of the West End (also home to Vancouver's gay district); and Stanley Park, Canada's urban green-space gem.

❷ Gastown & Chinatown p80

The neighborhood where Vancouver began, Gastown is Vancouver's cobbled old-town district. Rapidly transforming in recent years, its heritage buildings are now home to some of the city's best independent shops, bars and restaurants. Almost as old, Chinatown is one of Canada's largest and most vibrant of its kind.

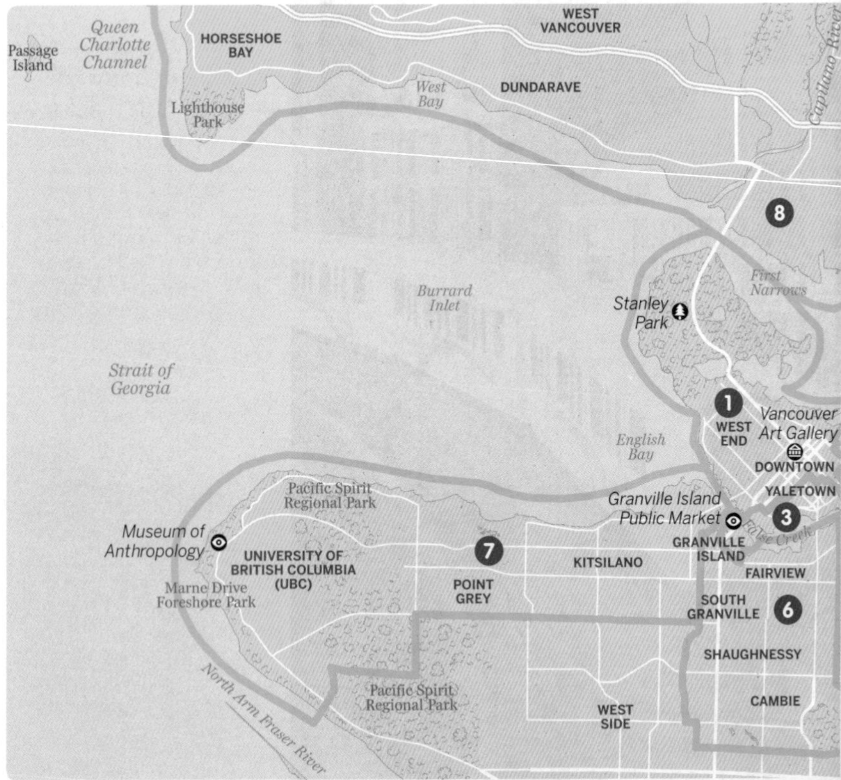

families. This is also a great dining strip and the home of Vancouver's best patios.

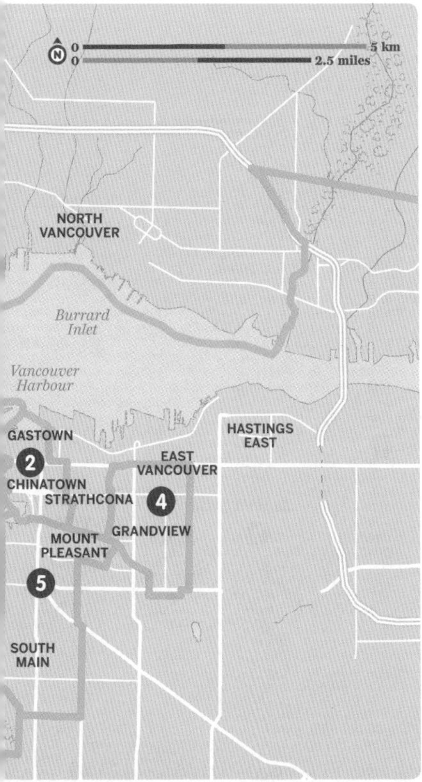

3 Yaletown & Granville Island p98

These shoreline neighborhoods exemplify Vancouver's development in recent decades. A former rail-yard and warehouse district on the edge of downtown, Yaletown is lined with chic restaurants and boutiques. Across the water, Granville Island was a grungy industrial area before being transformed in the 1970s into a haven of theaters, art studios and the best public market in British Columbia.

4 Commercial Drive p117

Settled by European immigrants in the 1950s and by counter-culture types in the 1960s, this is one of the city's most entrancing neighborhoods for a stroll. Eschewing chain stores, the main drag is studded with quirky shops, welcoming indie bars and coffee shops run by generations of Italian

5 Main Street p131

The skinny-jeaned heart of the hipster scene, Main has transformed into the city's coolest 'hood in recent years, boasting Vancouver's newest gallery district and its best independent cafes, shops, bars and restaurants. It's a great area to meet locals away from city-center crowds. Expect lots of changes: this area is developing rapidly.

6 Fairview & South Granville p146

Linked by Broadway, this area combines rows of clapboard residential avenues radiating from Fairview's Cambie St with, a few blocks west, the store- and gallery-lined South Granville, one of Vancouver's best walkable shopping strips. Green-thumbed visitors will also be drawn to its popular park and garden attractions.

7 Kitsilano & University of British Columbia (UBC) p161

Occupying the forested peninsula across the water to the south of downtown, Vancouver's West Side includes two major highlights: Kitsilano, with its wooden heritage homes, expansive beaches and browsable 4th Ave shopping strip; and, on the tip of the peninsula, UBC, a verdant campus with enough museums, galleries and attractions for a great half-day visit.

8 North Shore p177

Across the water and north of downtown, the mountain-shadowed North Shore is centered on the communities of West Vancouver and North Vancouver. Here you'll find the region's closest ski resorts as well as some of its best outdoor attractions and activities.

Downtown & West End

DOWNTOWN | WEST END

Neighborhood Top Five

❶ Strolling the entire **Stanley Park seawall** (p52) for smile-triggering views over the shimmering, mountain-framed shoreline – plus beaches, camera stops and bird-watching along the way.

❷ Hanging with the arty locals at **Vancouver Art Gallery** (p55) during an evening FUSE event.

❸ Supping a pint or three and watching a local band on the tiny **Railway Club** (p66) stage.

❹ Diving into the West Coast's lip-smacking regional bounty with a locally sourced feast at **Forage** (p64).

❺ Watching a pyrotechnic sunset from a log perch at Stanley Park's **Third Beach** (p53).

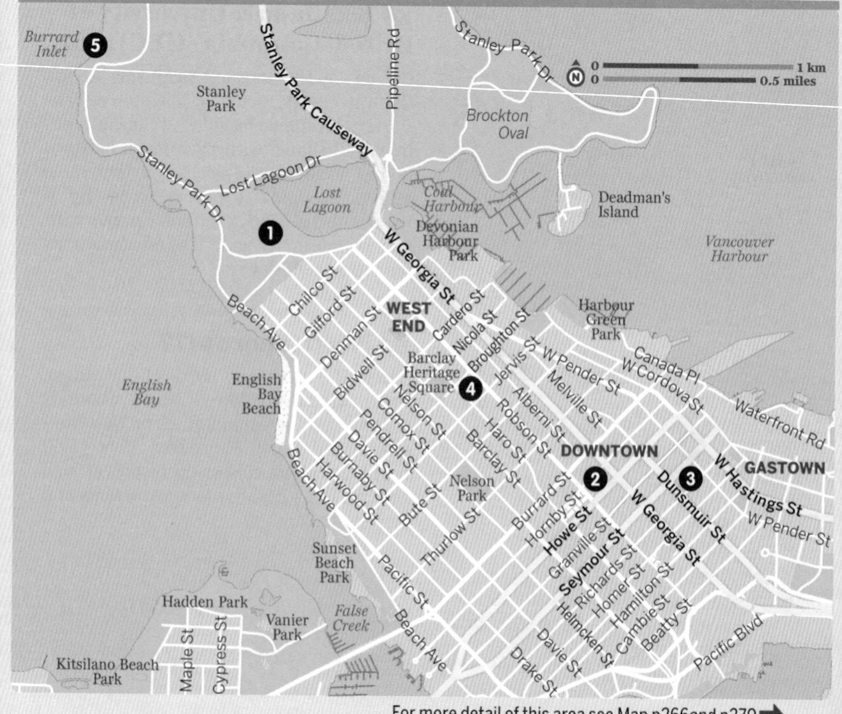

For more detail of this area see Map p266and p270

Explore Downtown & West End

Radiating from the central intersection of Granville and Georgia Sts, Vancouver's downtown core is easily walkable. Consider starting your exploration on the waterfront at Canada Place and then heading slightly uphill, with the mountain at your back, along Burrard or Granville Sts. You'll pass plenty of stores and cafes before reaching Robson St, the city's main shopping promenade. Wander along here (ducking into shops en route) before arriving at the intersection of Robson and Denman. Explore the West End and its menu of midrange restaurants, side-street wooden heritage homes and the friendly 'gayborhood' vibe. Davie St is the West End's main strip, and both Denman and Davie Sts lead to English Bay Beach, one of Vancouver's most popular summer hangouts. From either end of Denman St you can stroll into Stanley Park. Hitting the seawall here is the perfect way to commune with nature. See the totem poles and take in the Vancouver Aquarium, one of the city's best family-friendly attractions.

Local Life

➡ **Markets** Arrive early at the summertime West End Farmers Market (p74) to have your pick of the fresh, locally grown fruit before it sells out.

➡ **Restaurants** Robson St is always lined with tourists, but locals are much more likely to be dining out at the well-priced neighborhood eateries on Denman and Davie Sts in the West End.

➡ **Jogging** The Stanley Park seawall (p52) is a vista-hugging jogger's paradise. Avoid the summer crowds by hitting the trail early morning.

Getting There & Away

➡ **Walk** The downtown core is very walkable and the grid system of streets makes navigating easy. As a guide, strolling from Vancouver City Centre SkyTrain station to Stanley Park takes about 25 minutes.

➡ **Train** SkyTrain's Expo and Millennium Lines share the tracks through downtown, and the Canada Line also runs through the area. All three lines come together (via a short walk) at Waterfront Station.

➡ **Bus** The number 5 trundles along Robson St, the number 6 along Davie, the number 10 along Granville and the number 19 runs into Stanley Park. Numerous other services crisscross the city and beyond.

➡ **Car** There are parkades (parking lots) and parking meters throughout downtown. The West End has metered parking and Stanley Park has pay-and-display parking lots.

Lonely Planet's Top Tip

The Granville Strip nightlife stretch between Robson St and Granville Bridge is fine for a look (the twinkly neon is quite cool) but the generally humdrum bars and clubs here are aimed at partiers rolling into the city from the suburbs for vomit-inducing nights out. Especially on weekends, the area is a legless booze-fest abandoned by discerning locals. Instead, head to Gastown or the indie bars of Main St and Commercial Dr.

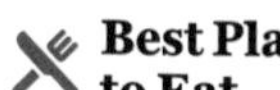

Best Places to Eat

- ➡ Forage (p64)
- ➡ Hawksworth (p63)
- ➡ Guu with Garlic (p64)
- ➡ Chambar (p63)
- ➡ Finch's (p59)

For reviews, see p59 ➡

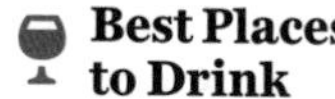

Best Places to Drink

- ➡ Railway Club (p66)
- ➡ Mario's Coffee Express (p67)
- ➡ Uva Wine Bar (p66)
- ➡ Vancouver Fanclub (p71)
- ➡ Sylvia's Lounge (p68)

For reviews, see p66 ➡

Best Places to Shop

- ➡ MacLeod's Books (p72)
- ➡ Mink Chocolates (p73)
- ➡ Holt Renfrew (p72)
- ➡ Golden Age Collectables (p72)
- ➡ West End Farmers Market (p74)

For reviews, see p72 ➡

A HALF-DAY TOUR

It's easy to be overwhelmed by Stanley Park, one of North America's largest urban green spaces. But there are ways to explore this spectacular waterfront swathe – from its top sites to hidden gems – without popping any blisters.

From the Georgia St entrance, trace the seawall around the shoreline to Brockton Point's **totem poles** 1. An early arrival means getting some snaps of these brightly painted carvings without fighting crowds.

From here, continue along the seawall. You'll pass a squat, striped lighthouse before reaching the Lumberman's Arch area. Duck under the road bridge and plunge into the park's tree-lined heart. Just ahead is **Vancouver Aquarium** 2, the park's most popular attraction.

Next up, follow the path to the **Miniature Railway** 3. If you have kids in tow, take them for a trundle on this replica of the locomotive that pulled the first transcontinental passenger train into Vancouver.

From here, follow Pipeline Rd to the Tudoresque pavilion a few minutes away. In front is the **Malkin Bowl** 4, a hidden outdoor theater. Poke around the nearby manicured gardens, then continue southwards to Lost Lagoon. Follow the shoreline clockwise to **Lost Lagoon Nature House** 5, where you can learn about the park's flora and fauna.

Continue to the lagoon's western tip, then head to the ocean front ahead. Now on the park's rugged western side, follow the seawall northbound to **Third Beach** 6. Find a log perch and prepare for Vancouver's best sunset.

TOP TIPS

- When cycling the seawall, keep in mind that wheeled traffic is one-way only.
- The park is home to raccoons. Take pictures, but don't feed them.
- There are restaurants in the park if you're peckish.
- The meadow near Lumberman's Arch is a top picnic spot.

Third Beach
Second Beach gets the crowds but Third Beach is where the savvy locals head. This is the perfect spot to drink in a sunset panorama over the lapping Pacific Ocean shoreline.

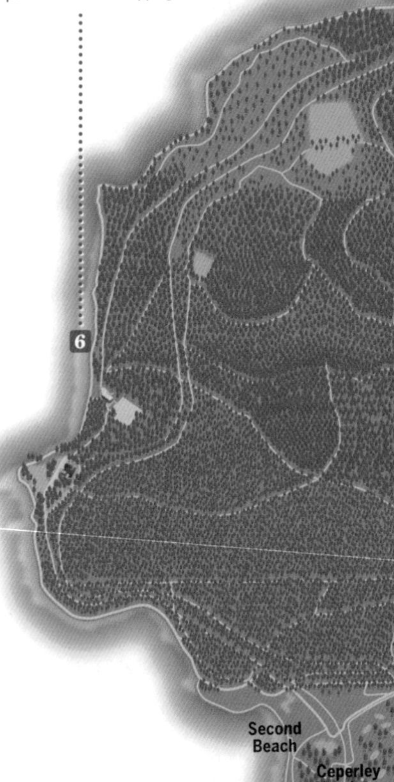

Lost Lagoon Nature House
The freshwater Lost Lagoon was created when the Stanley Park Causeway was built. Its shoreline Nature House illuminates the park's plant and animal life and runs guided walks.

PROSPECT POINT

DAVE FLEETHAM/GETTY IMAGES ©

Miniature Railway

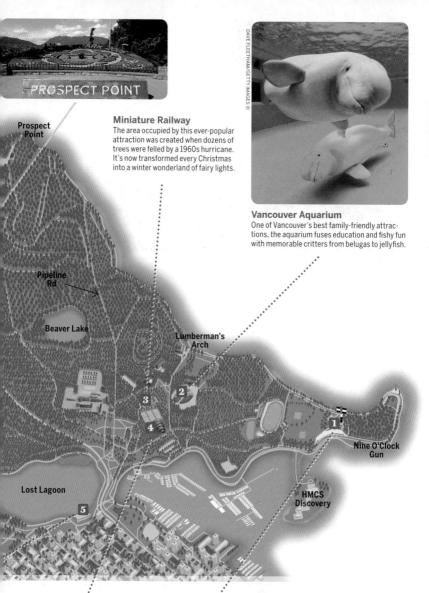

The area occupied by this ever-popular attraction was created when dozens of trees were felled by a 1960s hurricane. It's now transformed every Christmas into a winter wonderland of fairy lights.

Vancouver Aquarium

One of Vancouver's best family-friendly attractions, the aquarium fuses education and fishy fun with memorable critters from belugas to jellyfish.

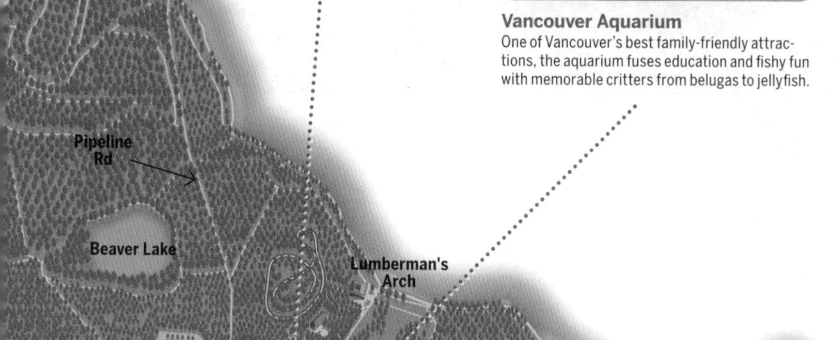

Prospect Point
Pipeline Rd
Beaver Lake
Lumberman's Arch
2
3
4
1
Nine O'Clock Gun
Lost Lagoon
5
HMCS Discovery

Malkin Bowl

Built by Vancouver mayor WH Malkin, this alfresco theater replaced an original bandstand. At the back of the seating area, you'll find a memorial statue to US president WG Harding.

Totem Poles

First Nations residents were still living here when Stanley Park was designated in 1888, but these poles were installed much later. The current poles are replicas of 1920s originals, carved in the 1980s.

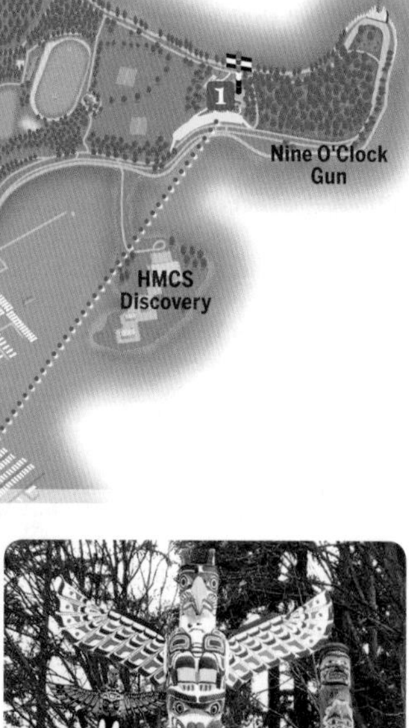

KORINA MILLER ©

MICHAEL WHEATLEY / GETTYIMAGES ©

TOP SIGHT
STANLEY PARK

One of North America's largest urban green spaces (even bigger than New York's Central Park), Stanley Park is revered for its dramatic forest-and-mountain oceanfront views. But there's more to this 400-hectare woodland than just its looks. The park is studded with nature-hugging trails, family-friendly attractions, sunset-loving beaches and a range of places to eat, from picnic spots to top-notch restaurants. There's also the occasional unexpected, off-the-beaten-path sight worth uncovering (and we're not just talking about the raccoons that call the area home).

DON'T MISS...

- Seawall
- Vancouver Aquarium
- Third Beach
- Lost Lagoon
- Miniature Railway

PRACTICALITIES

- Map p270
- www.vancouver.ca/parks
- [family-friendly icon]
- [bus icon]19

Stanley Park Seawall

Built in stages between 1917 and 1980, the park's 8.8km **seawall trail** is Vancouver's favorite outdoor hangout. Encircling the entire park, it offers spectacular waterfront vistas on one side and dense forest on the other. You can walk the whole thing in roughly three hours or rent a bike to cover the route far faster. Keep in mind: cyclists and rollerbladers must travel counterclockwise on the seawall, so there's no going back once you start. Also consider following the 24km of trails that crisscross the park's interior, including Siwash Rock Trail, Rawlings Trail and the popular Beaver Lake Trail (some routes are for foot-traffic only).

The seawall also delivers you to some of the park's top highlights. You'll pass alongside the stately **HMCS Discovery** naval station and a twee **cricket pavilion** that looks like an interloper from Victorian England. About 1.5km from the W Georgia St entrance, you'll come to the ever-popular **totem poles**. Remnants of an abandoned 1930s plan to create a First Nations 'theme village,' the bright-painted poles were joined by the addition of three exquisitely carved Coast Salish welcome arches in 2008. Once you've taken your photos, continue on to the nearby **Nine O'Clock Gun** (it fires at 9pm every night) and **Lumberman's Arch**, which is a good spot to see Alaska cruise ships sliding past. From here, you can cut into the park to the Vancouver Aquarium or continue around the seawall; it gets wilder and more scenic from here as you pass under the Lions Gate Bridge and face down the Pacific Ocean.

Natural Attractions

You don't have to be a child to enjoy Stanley Park's signature attraction. The **Vancouver Aquarium** (☎604-659-3474; www.vanaqua.org; 845 Avison Way; adult/child $27/17 Jul & Aug, reduced Sep-Jun; ⏰9:30am-6pm Jul & Aug, 10am-5pm Sep-Jun; 🚌19) combines exotic marine species with re-created local seascapes. Home to 9000 water-loving critters – including sharks, wolf eels, beluga whales and a somewhat shy octopus – it also has a small, walk-through rainforest of birds, turtles and a statue-still sloth. Also check out the mesmerizing iridescent jellyfish, and peruse the schedule for feeding times: there's almost always one hungry animal or another waiting for its dinner. If you're traveling with someone who really loves marine animals, consider an Animal Encounter tour (from $60). They'll get close to their chosen mammal and learn all about being a trainer: the sea otter encounter is recommended if you want to learn why they eat while lying on their backs, using their stomachs as dinner plates (always the best way to dine). The aquarium's latest draw is its 4D Experience: a 3D movie theater with added wind, mist and aromas. It generally shows nature-themed flicks and a seasonal movie at Christmas.

The aquarium isn't Stanley Park's only hot spot for flora and fauna fans. A few steps from the park's W Georgia St entrance lies **Lost Lagoon**, which was originally part of Coal Harbour. After a causeway was built in 1916, the new body of water was renamed, transforming itself into a freshwater lake a few years later. Today it's a nature sanctuary – keep your eyes peeled for blue herons – and its perimeter pathway is a favored stroll for nature nuts. The **Lost Lagoon Nature House** (Map p270; ☎604-257-8544; www.stanleyparkecology.ca; admission free, park walks adult/child $10/5; ⏰10am-7pm Tue-Sun May-Sep) here has exhibits on the park's wildlife, history and ecology – ask about the fascinating guided walks.

Beaches & Views

If it's sandy beaches you're after, the park has several options. **Second Beach** is a family-friendly area on the park's western side, with a grassy playground, an ice-cream-serving concession and a huge outdoor swimming pool. It's also close to **Ceperley Meadows**, where free outdoor movie screenings

STANLEY PARK TIPS

It typically takes around three hours to walk the 8.8km Stanley Park seawall. Alternatively, bike and in-line skate rentals are available at several stores on nearby Denman St. In summer the seawall is often packed with visitors, so arrive early morning or in the early evening. There are also often summertime queues to get into the Vancouver Aquarium, so try to make that one of your first stops when you arrive at the park. Dining-wise, although there are several restaurants here, this is the perfect destination for picnicking: consider the grassy swath near Lumberman's Arch.

The only person to be legally buried in Stanley Park is Pauline Johnson. A champion of First Nations culture, her book on Coast Salish legends was a huge bestseller. When she died in 1913, thousands of locals lined the streets to mark her passing. Her memorial is a few steps from the seawall's Siwash Rock landmark.

take place in summer. But for a little more tranquility, try **Third Beach**. A sandy expanse with plenty of logs to sit against, this is a favored summer-evening destination for Vancouverites. The sky often comes alive with pyrotechnic color here as chilled-out locals munch through their picnics.

There's a plethora of additional vistas in the park, but perhaps the most popular is at **Prospect Point**. One of Vancouver's best lookouts, this lofty spot is located at the park's northern tip. In summer you'll be jostling for elbow room with tour parties; heading down the steep stairs to the viewing platform usually shakes them off. Also look out for scavenging raccoons here (don't pet them). The area's Prospect Point Café (p65) offers refreshments – aim for a deck table.

Statue Spotting

Stanley Park is studded with statues, all of which come to life at night (okay, just kidding). On your leisurely amble around the tree-lined idyll, look out for the following and award yourself 10 points for each one you find. If you locate them all, partake of a gourmet dinner at the Fish House (p66). If you're on the seawall, it shouldn't be hard to spot *Girl in a Wetsuit*, a 1972 bronze by Elek Imredy that sits in the water. But how about the Robbie Burns statue unveiled by British Prime Minister Ramsay MacDonald in 1928 or the dramatic bronze of Canadian sprint legend Harry Jerome, who held six world records and won a bronze at the 1964 Summer Olympics? Here's a clue for the next one: it's near Malkin Bowl (p71). Marking the first official visit to Canada by a US president, this elegant statue is actually a memorial: after visiting in 1923, Warren Harding died a week later in San Francisco.

For Kids

It doesn't take much to plan an entire day with children here. In addition to the aquarium and Lost Lagoon Nature House, there are a couple of additional must-dos for under-10s. Look out for the **waterpark** overlooking the waterfront near Lumberman's Arch. There's also a playground here. Dry the kids off with a trundle on the **Miniature Railway** (adult/child from $5; ⌚hours vary, year-round; 🚌19); just a short stroll from the aquarium, this popular replica of the first passenger train that rolled into Vancouver in 1887 is a firm family favorite. The ride assumes several incarnations during the year: in summer, the ride through the trees has a First Nations theme; at Halloween it's dressed up for ghost fans; and from late November it becomes a Christmas-decorated theme ride that's the city's most popular family-friendly Yuletide activity.

If it's still light when you're leaving the park, visit the man behind the fun day you've just had. Take the ramp running parallel with the seawall near the W Georgia St entrance and you'll find an almost-hidden statue of Lord Stanley with his arms outstretched nestled in the trees. On his plinth are the words he used at the park's 1889 dedication ceremony: 'To the use and enjoyment of people of all colors, creeds and customs for all time.' It's a sentiment that resonates loudly here today.

TOP SIGHT
VANCOUVER ART GALLERY

Located in a heritage courthouse building, but aiming for a fancy new venue near the main library in the coming years, the VAG is the region's most important art gallery. Transforming itself in recent years, it's now a vital part of the city's cultural scene. Contemporary exhibitions – often showcasing Vancouver's wealth of renowned photoconceptualists – are combined with blockbuster traveling shows from leading galleries in North America and around the world.

DON'T MISS...

- Emily Carr paintings
- FUSE
- Gallery Café
- Offsite

PRACTICALITIES

- Map p266
- 604-662 4700
- www.vanartgallery.bc.ca
- 750 Hornby St
- adult/child $20/6
- 10am-5pm Wed-Mon, to 9pm Tue
- 5

VAG 101

Before you arrive, check online for details on the latest exhibition: the biggest shows of the year here are typically in summer, and it's often a good idea to arrive early or late in the day to avoid the crush, especially at the beginning or end of an exhibition's run. But the VAG isn't just about blockbusters. If you have time, explore this landmark gallery's other offerings. Start on the top floor, where British Columbia's most famous painter is showcased. Emily Carr (1871–1945) is celebrated for her swirling, nature-inspired paintings of regional landscapes and First Nations culture. Watercolors were her main approach, and the gallery has a large collection of her works, which it presents in different configurations during one or two exhibitions every year.

The city's more recent contribution to art is conceptual and postconceptual photography – usually referred to jointly as photoconceptualism. As you work your way around the gallery, you'll likely spot more than a few examples of works by the Vancouver School, a group of local photo artists from the 1980s onwards who have achieved national and international recognition. These include Roy Arden, Rodney Graham, Stan Douglas and – the most famous of the bunch – Jeff Wall. The best way to learn about these artists and others

VAG TIPS

While admission prices to the VAG are slightly reduced in winter, the gallery isn't the cheapest attraction in town. But if you're traveling on a tight budget (and you don't mind crowds), consider visiting on a Tuesday between 5pm and 9pm. This weekly by-donation night (most people pay $5 to $10) can save you enough for a latte at the Gallery Café. And since it's often very busy, you'll likely also make a few new local friends. Arrive early in summer; there's often a queue for entry.

With its columns and Trafalgar Square–style lions, the handsome 1907 gallery building was originally the Provincial Law Court. It was designed by Francis Rattenbury, who was responsible for many of the colonial-era buildings that still exist in the towns and cities of British Columbia (BC). His most famous constructions are in Victoria, the provincial capital, where the twin landmarks of the Parliament Buildings and the Empress Hotel still loom over the Inner Harbour.

on display at the gallery is to take a free guided tour: these are usually held throughout the day on Thursdays and Sundays.

Join the Locals

The gallery isn't just a place to geek out at cool art. In fact, locals treat it as an important part of their social calendar. Every few months, the gallery stages its regular **FUSE socials**, which transform the domed heritage venue into a highly popular night event with DJs, bars, live performances and quirky gallery tours. Vancouverites dress up and treat the event as one of the highlights of the city's art scene; expect a clubby vibe to pervade proceedings. Take the chance to hang out with local chin-scratching creative-types letting their hair down. You'll likely see some of the same crowd at the gallery's regular roster of lectures and art talks. There's also a Family FUSE event where arty kids can have some fun, usually with plenty of interactive shenanigans.

The Gallery Café (p61) is also one of downtown's most popular hangouts. Boasting the largest patio in the area, this cafe is the perfect spot to drink in the downtown vibe, even if you're not visiting an exhibition. On your way out, pop into the gallery shop: it's crammed with cool gadgets and artsy trinkets (and has a great collection of art books and cards).

Offsite

While the VAG is keen to move to a large space in order to display more of its vast collection, it has also opened a satellite space that even many locals don't know about. Located next to the towering Shangri-La Hotel near the intersection of W Georgia and Bute Sts, **Offsite** (Map p270; www.vanartgallery.bc.ca; 11 W Georgia St; M Burrard) is the gallery's highly eclectic outdoor exhibition space. With shows that change twice-yearly, the space typically has passers-by scratching their heads at installations that have ranged from undulating earthquake debris to exact scale replicas of traditional West Coast fishing shacks. Whether you like what's on display or not, it's hard to ignore: and that may be enough of an achievement.

SIGHTS

Downtown

VANCOUVER ART GALLERY — ART GALLERY

See p55.

CANADA PLACE — LANDMARK

Map p266 (www.canadaplace.ca; 999 Canada Place Way; Ⓜ Waterfront) FREE Vancouver's version of the Sydney Opera House, judging by the number of postcards it appears on, this iconic landmark is shaped like sails jutting into the sky over the harbor. Both a cruise-ship terminal and convention center (next door's grass-roofed West Building convention center expansion opened in 2010), it's also a pier, providing camera-worthy views of the North Shore mountains and some busy floatplane action.

Inside and outside the building, there are reminders of Canada's past, from temporary interactive exhibitions to a display in winter of vintage department store Christmas windows. At the time of research, a new movie screen attraction called Fly Over Canada was also gearing up to open inside the building. Check the website (www.flyovercanada.com) to see if they're up and running for your visit.

JACK POOLE PLAZA — PLAZA

Map p266 (North end of Thurlow St; Ⓜ Waterfront) FREE The heart of Vancouver's 2010 Olympic Games hosting duties, this handsome waterfront public space is the permanent home of the tripod-like Olympic Cauldron. The flame is lit for special occasions (you can pay $5000 to have it switched on). The plaza offers great views of the mountain-backed Burrard Inlet, and you can follow the shoreline walking trail around the Convention Center West Building for public artworks and historic plaques.

If you fancy a further taste of the 2010 Games, nip along the subterranean pedestrian tunnel between the two convention buildings. You'll find a small display of medals, Olympic torches and even a podium from the event, where you can pretend you won the skeleton event gold.

BILL REID GALLERY OF NORTHWEST COAST ART — GALLERY

Map p266 (www.billreidgallery.ca; 639 Hornby St; adult/child $10/5; ⏲11am-5pm Wed-Sun; Ⓜ Burrard) Showcasing carvings, paintings and jewelry from Canada's most revered Haida artist, this tranquil gallery is lined with fascinating and exquisite works – plus handy touch-screens to tell you all about them. The space centres on the Great Hall, where there's often a carver at work. Be sure to also hit the mezzanine level: you'll come face to face with an 8.5m-long bronze of intertwined magical creatures, complete with impressively long tongues.

The gallery offers a comprehensive intro to the creative vision of Reid and his Haida co-creators, and also hosts occasional artist talks – especially when there's a new exhibition – that bring the works to life.

CHRIST CHURCH CATHEDRAL — CATHEDRAL

Map p266 (www.cathedral.vancouver.bc.ca; 690 Burrard St; ⏲10am-4pm; Ⓜ Burrard) Completed in 1895 and designated as a cathedral in 1929, the city's most attractive Gothic-style church is nestled incongruously among looming glass towers. It's home to a wide range of cultural events, including regular choir and chamber music recitals, and the occasional Shakespeare reading. Self-guided tours of the 32 stained-glass windows are available: ask at the front desk for the highlights.

If you're short of time, head straight to the basement for a colorful, curlicue-patterned stained-glass window created by William Morris & Company. Also check out the church's dramatic hammerbeam ceiling as well as its newest window, the stunning *Tree of Life* by Susan A Point, located near the main entrance.

LOCAL KNOWLEDGE

HIDDEN ARTWORK

Enter the lobby of the Royal Bank building at the corner of W Georgia and Burrard Sts, and head up in the escalator that's directly in front of you. At the top you'll find one of the largest First Nations artworks in western Canada. Measuring 30m long and 2.5m high, the nine carved and painted red cedar panels of the spectacular 'Ksan Mural dramatically cover an entire wall of the building. It took five carvers three months to create in 1972, and it tells the story of Weget (or Man-Raven) and his often mischievous exploits. Well worth a look, the artwork seems a world away from the bustling streets outside.

VANCOUVER LOOKOUT VIEWPOINT

Map p266 (www.vancouverlookout.com; 555 W Hastings St; adult/child $15.75/7.75; 8:30am-10:30pm May-Sep, 9am-9pm Oct-Apr; Waterfront) Expect your lurching stomach to make a bid for freedom as the glass elevator whisks you 169m to the apex of this needle-like viewing tower. Once up top, there's not much to do but check out the awesome 360-degree vistas of city, sea and mountains unfurling around you. For context, peruse the historic photo panels that show just how much the landscape has changed over the years.

Tickets are pricey but are valid all day – return for a soaring sunset view of the city to get your money's worth.

ROGERS ARENA STADIUM

Map p266 (www.rogersarena.ca; 800 Griffiths Way; tours adult/child $12/6; tours 10:30am, noon & 1:30pm Wed, Fri, Sat; Stadium-Chinatown) This large, multipurpose stadium hosts the National Hockey League's Vancouver Canucks. On game nights, when the 20,000-capacity venue heaves with fervent fans, you'll enjoy the atmosphere even if the rules are a mystery. Rogers Arena was the main hockey venue during the 2010 Winter Olympics. It's home to a large Canucks team shop, and is also a favored arena for money-spinning stadium rock acts.

Behind-the-scenes tours (75 minutes) take you into the hospitality suites and the nosebleed press box up in the rafters, and are popular with visiting sports fans.

MARINE BUILDING HISTORIC BUILDING

Map p266 (355 Burrard St; 9am-5pm Mon-Fri; Burrard) FREE Vancouver's most romantic old-school tower block, and also its best art deco building, the elegant 22-story Marine Building is a tribute to the city's maritime past. Check out the elaborate exterior of seahorses, lobsters and streamlined ships, then nip into the lobby where it's like a walk-through artwork. Stained-glass panels and a polished floor inlaid with signs of the zodiac await.

You should also peruse the inlaid wood interiors of the brass-doored elevators. The Marine Building was the tallest building in the British Empire when completed in 1930. It now houses offices.

VANCOUVER PUBLIC LIBRARY LIBRARY

Map p266 (www.vpl.ca; 350 W Georgia St; 10am-9pm Mon-Thu, to 6pm Fri & Sat, noon-5pm Sun; ; Stadium-Chinatown) This dramatic, Colosseum-like building must be a temple to the great god of libraries. If not, it's certainly one of the world's most magnificent book-lending facilities. Designed by Moshe Safdie and opened in 1995, it contains 1.2 million books and other items spread out over seven levels, all of them seemingly populated by language students silently learning English from textbooks (and messaging each other).

There's free wi-fi available on-site, plus computer terminals if you don't have your laptop. The library hosts a lively roster of book readings and literary events. If you're traveling with kids, the downstairs children's section is an ideal hangout. Plans are also afoot to open the library's roof with a garden and cafe for visitors – ask at the front desk (quietly).

PENDULUM GALLERY GALLERY

Map p266 (www.pendulumgallery.bc.ca; 885 W Georgia St; 9am-6pm Mon-Wed, to 9pm Thu & Fri, to 5pm Sat; Burrard) FREE A creative use for a cavernous bank building atrium, this gallery offers an ever-changing roster of temporary exhibitions. It's mostly contemporary art, and can range from striking paintings to challenging photographs and quirky arts and crafts. The space also houses one permanent exhibit: a gargantuan 27m-long buffed aluminum pendulum that will be swinging over your head throughout your visit.

Designed by Alan Storey, the pendulum weighs 1600kg and moves about 6m (the swing is assisted by a hydraulic mechanical system at the top). There's also a coffee shop here if you need to rest your trek-weary feet.

CONTEMPORARY ART GALLERY GALLERY

Map p266 (www.contemporaryartgallery.ca; 555 Nelson St; noon-6pm Tue-Sun; 10) FREE Originally the Greater Vancouver Artists' Gallery, this small, off-the-beaten-path art space transformed itself into an independent gallery in 1996, and moved to a crisp, purpose-built facility a few years later. The gallery focuses on a wide range of modern art, and photography is particularly well represented here. Exhibitions are ever-changing, and include local and international artists. Check the gallery's website for events and openings.

Regular, free curator and artist talks are also held here.

West End

STANLEY PARK PARK

See p52.

ENGLISH BAY BEACH BEACH

Map p270 (cnr of Denman St & Beach Ave; 5) Wandering south on Denman St, you'll spot a clutch of palm trees ahead announcing one of Canada's best urban beaches. Then you'll see Vancouver's most popular public artwork: a series of oversized laughing figures that makes everyone smile. There's a party atmosphere here in summer as locals catch rays and busker shows…or just ogle the volleyballers prancing around on the sand.

Be sure to snap a few photos of the beach's towering *inukshuk* (Inuit sculpture), south of the main area, or just continue along the seawall into neighboring Stanley Park. The beach is a popular (but crowded) spot to catch the annual Celebration of Light fireworks festival, and it's also where the city's annual Polar Bear Swim takes place on 1 January.

ROEDDE HOUSE MUSEUM MUSEUM

Map p270 (www.roeddehouse.org; 1415 Barclay St; admission $5; 1-4pm Tue-Fri & Sun; 5) For a glimpse of what the West End looked like before the apartment blocks arrived, drop by this handsome 1893 Queen Anne–style mansion, now a lovingly preserved museum. Designed by infamous British Columbia (BC) architect Francis Rattenbury, the house is packed with antiques and the garden is planted in period style. Sunday entry includes tour, tea and cookies for just $8.

The abode is the showpiece of Barclay Heritage Sq, a one-block site containing nine historic West End houses dating from 1890 to 1908. If you don a top hat, monocle and waxed mustache, you'll fit right in. Pick up a free map covering the square's history highlights from Roedde House.

COAL HARBOUR SEAWALL WATERFRONT

Map p270 (Canada Place to Stanley Park; M Waterfront) An idyllic waterfront stroll from Canada Place to Stanley Park, this is a perfect way to spend a sunny afternoon. Along the 2km or so, you'll take in the West Building convention center's art and history-paneled seawalk, the cooling grassy nook of Harbour Green Park and the *Light Shed* artwork – a replica of one of the marine sheds that once lined this area.

Look out for the cozy houseboats in the marina near the Westin Bayshore hotel, where Howard Hughes holed up for three months in 1972. Continue a few more minutes and you'll be on the fringes of Stanley Park.

ROBSON STREET STREET

Map p266 (www.robsonstreet.ca; Robson St; 5) Locals, tourists and recent immigrants – count the number of accents you catch as you stroll here – throng the eateries and shops of Robson St, Vancouver's de facto urban promenade. While most shops are of the ubiquitous chain-store variety, the strip is worth a wander for the urban vibe, especially on summer evenings when buskers and street cartoonists set up shop.

It's also worth heading to the Stanley Park end of the strip, where you'll find a modern 'mini-Asia' of authentic *izakayas* (Japanese neighborhood pubs) and noodle bars populated by homesick Japanese and Korean language students. Turn the corner onto Denman to discover a United Nations of cheap-and-cheerful dining.

EATING

Downtown

You can't throw a Tim Hortons donut in the city center without hitting a restaurant. While there are plenty of midrange options and a smattering of celebrity-fave high-end locations radiating from Robson St, there are also rewarding ethnic eateries and quirky backstreet joints hidden slightly off the beaten path. Try either end of Robson for Japanese and Korean diners or the Granville Strip for brunch-serving bars.

FINCH'S CAFE $

Map p266 (www.finchteahouse.com; 353 W Pender St; mains $5-10; 9-5pm Mon-Fri, 11am-4pm Sat; 4) For a coveted seat at one of the dinged old tables, arrive off-peak at this sunny corner cafe that has a 'granny-chic' look combining creaky wooden floors and junk-shop bric-a-brac. You'll be joining in-the-know hipsters and creative types who've been calling this their local for years. They come for the well-priced breakfasts (egg and soldiers $2.95) plus freshly prepared gourmet baguette sandwiches and house-made soups.

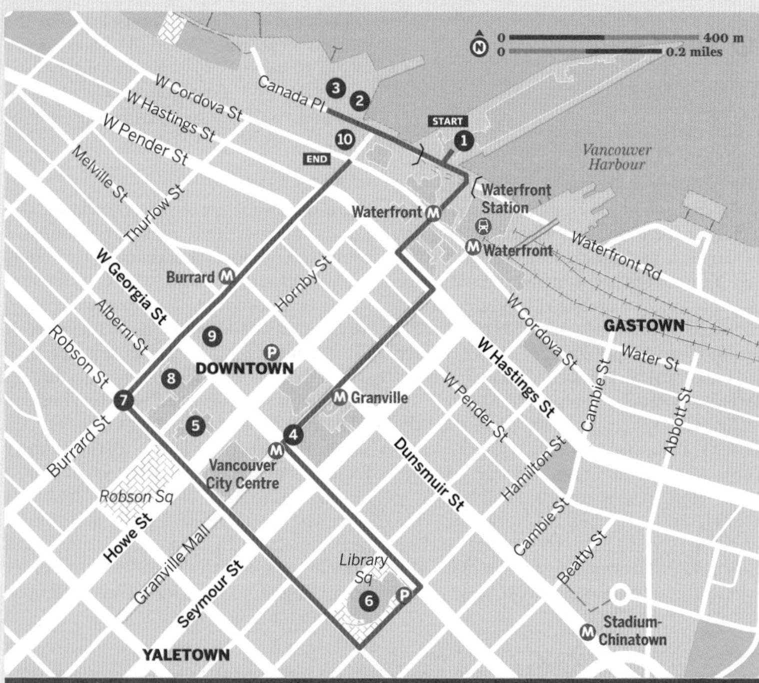

Neighborhood Walk
Downtown Grand Tour

START CANADA PLACE
END BELLA GELATERIA
LENGTH 3KM; ONE HOUR

Start at Vancouver's landmark **1 Canada Place** (p57), giving your camera finger free rein. Allow yourself time to walk along the outer promenade to watch floatplanes diving onto the water. There's often a giant cruise ship or two parked alongside. Next, stroll to the adjacent **2 Convention Center West Building**. Peruse the outdoor artworks and the **3 Olympic Cauldron**.

Head southwest along Howe St, turn left onto W Hastings St and then right onto bustling Granville St. Follow this uphill thoroughfare; it's one of the city's most important commercial streets. You'll pass coffee shops, clothing stores and the Pacific Centre, downtown's biggest mall.

Get your bearings at the busy intersection of **4 Granville & W Georgia Sts**, in the heart of the downtown core. Check out the shops around here or nip across one block to the **5 Vancouver Art Gallery** (p55) for a culture fix.

From here, stroll southeast a couple of blocks to the magnificent, Colosseum-like **6 Vancouver Public Library** (p58). The glass-enclosed atrium is a perfect place to grab a coffee, or you can pop inside and check your email for free.

Head northwest from here along Robson St, the city's mainstream shopping promenade, where you can wander to your credit card's content through boutiques, bookstores and shoe shops. There are many restaurants here, too, if it's time to eat.

Take a breather at the clamorous intersection of **7 Robson & Burrard Sts**, then turn right and head along Burrard toward the mountain vista glinting ahead of you. Duck into the **8 Fairmont Hotel Vancouver** (p214) to view the luxury lobby, then continue downhill to **9 Christ Church Cathedral**. You'll soon be back at Canada Place...but have a treat at **10 Bella Gelateria** (p64) first.

FOOD TRUCK FRENZY

Keen to emulate the legendary street-food scenes of Portland and Austin, Vancouver jumped on the kitchen-equipped bandwagon in 2011, launching a pilot scheme with 17 food carts. Things took off quickly and by mid-2013 there were 114 trucks dotted around the city, serving everything from halibut tacos to Korean sliders, pulled-pork sandwiches to French stews. While there are a number of experimental fusion trucks, several have quickly risen to the top: look out for local favorites TacoFino, Re-Up BBQ, Roaming Dragon, Feastro, Fresh Local Wild, Yolk's Breakfast, Pig on the Street and Vij's Railway Express. And don't miss JapaDog, which arguably kicked off the scene with nori-and-miso-flavored hotdogs.

There are usually a few vendors around the Art Gallery complex; downtown arteries such as Howe, Burrard, Georgia and Seymour are also good bets.

For up-to-the-minute listings, opening hours and locations for street-food carts, go to www.streetfoodapp.com/vancouver. And keep your eyes peeled for special appearances by the carts at events around the city. If you want some extra help, Vancouver Foodie Tours (p75) offers a tasty Street Eats Tour.

This quirky little hangout is a great spot for an afternoon cake and coffee, but be prepared to wait for a perch to call your own.

LA TAQUERIA MEXICAN $

Map p266 (www.lataqueria.ca; 322 W Hastings St; 4-taco combo $9.50; ⏲11am-6pm Mon-Sat; 🖉; 🚇14) Arrive off-peak at this tiny hole-in-the-wall to snag a seat at the turquoise-colored counter. Listening to the grassroots Mexican soundtrack and the kitchen staff chatting in Spanish is the perfect accompaniment to a few superbly prepared soft tacos: go for the four-part combo and choose from fillings such as grilled fish, pork cheeks and house-marinated beef, made with top-notch, locally sourced ingredients.

Vegetarians also have some tasty choices such as the veggie combo (cheaper than the meat combo) and quesadillas. Save room for a glass of cinnamon-flavored *horchata* (a milkshake-style traditional beverage).

JAPADOG JAPANESE $

Map p266 (www.japadog.com; 530 Robson St; mains $5-8; ⏲11am-10pm Mon-Thu, to 11pm Fri & Sat, to 9pm Sun; 🚇10) You'll have spotted the lunchtime line-ups at the Japadog hotdog stands around town, but a storefront was also opened in 2010 by the celebrated, ever-*genki* Japanese expats. The menu is almost the same here – think turkey smokies with miso sauce and bratwursts with onion, daikon and soy – but there are also naughty seasoned fries (try the wasabi version).

The tiny tables are usually taken, but the take-out window does a roaring trade. And this is the only location where you can get the perfect dessert: ice-cream in a deep-fried hotdog bun.

GALLERY CAFÉ CAFE $

Map p266 (www.thegallerycafe.ca; 750 Hornby St; mains $5-12; ⏲9am-6pm Mon & Wed-Fri, to 9pm Tue, 10am-6pm Sat & Sun; 🚇5) The mezzanine level of the Vancouver Art Gallery is home to a chatty indoor dining area complemented by what is possibly downtown's best and biggest patio. The food is generally of the salad and sandwiches variety, but it's well worth stopping in for a drink, especially if you take your coffee (or bottled beer) out to the parasol-forested outdoor area to watch the Robson St clamor.

This is one of the city's favorite meeting places so it's often packed: arrive late in the afternoon for your pick of tables. And if you're sitting outside, keep your eyes on your grub: the local birds are especially bold here.

GORILLA FOOD VEGAN $

Map p266 (www.gorillafood.com; 436 Richards St; mains $8-14; ⏲11am-6pm; 🖉; 🚇14) It's like stepping into a shaded forest nook at this well-hidden subterranean eatery. Gorilla Food is lined with woodsy flourishes and the kind of fresh-faced, healthy-living vegans who will make you want to adopt a new lifestyle. Organic, raw, vegan and gluten-free is the approach, which means treats such as curry-sauce veggie burgers and multilayered lasagna packed with seeds and 'walnut cheez.'

Save space for an icy almond shake dessert, and some carrot cake slathered with cashew cream.

MEDINA BREAKFAST **$$**

Map p266 (www.medinacafe.com; 556 Beatty St; mains $12-19; ⌚8am-4pm Mon-Fri; Ⓜ Stadium-Chinatown) At this lively breakfast-brunch-lunch cafe with bistro pretensions, finding a table can be an issue. But it's worth the wait if you're a Belgian waffle fan: the light and fluffy treats are the city's best and come with unexpected gourmet topping options such as chocolate lavender and fig-orange marmalade. Alternatively, go the savory route: excellent frittatas and cassoulets are also available.

There's a continental feel to the entire menu. Consider coming back for lunch and diving into the lovely spicy lamb and beef meatballs.

TWISTED FORK BISTRO FRENCH **$$**

Map p266 (www.twistedforkbistro.ca; 1147 Granville St; mains $20-22; ⌚5:30-11pm daily & 10am-2pm Fri-Sun; 🚌10) The best place to park your appetite among the Granville Strip's greasy pub-grub options, this narrow, art-lined bistro feels like it should be somewhere else. But even clubbers need to eat well sometimes. The menu of rustic French classics includes mussels, lamb shank and an excellent beef bourguignon, but there are also smaller tasting plates if you want to share.

The drinks menu here is never an afterthought, which means some excellent BC wines and good local craft beers to dive into. Also a popular weekend brunch spot.

TEMPLETON DINER **$$**

Map p266 (www.thetempleton.ca; 1087 Granville St; mains $10-14; ⌚9am-11pm Mon-Wed, to 1am Thu-Sun; 👪; 🚌10) A chrome-and-vinyl '50s-look diner with a twist, Templeton chefs up plus-sized organic burgers, addictive fries, vegetarian quesadillas and perhaps the best hangover cure in town – the 'Big Ass Breakfast.' Sadly, the mini jukeboxes on the tables don't work, but you can console yourself with a waistline-busting chocolate ice-cream float. Avoid weekend peak times or you'll be queuing for ages.

The java here comes from Oso Negro, a legendary Nelson, BC coffee roaster.

COMMUNE CAFE WEST COAST **$$**

Map p266 (www.communecafe.ca; 1002 Seymour St; mains $15-19; ⌚8am-10pm Mon-Wed, to 10pm Thu & Fri, 9am-11pm Sat & Sun; 🚌10) Like a modern-day cafeteria, this comfortable, no-nonsense spot offers good-value dining and a great little patio. Every week there's a special dish (usually around the $10 mark), while the main menu revolves around locally sourced gourmet comfort dishes such as duck confit and braised beef. It's also a good spot for weekend brunch, and be sure to ask about the daily drinks special.

If you're in the neighborhood in the afternoon, Commune has specials of the drink and snack variety between 3pm and 5pm: perfect for a balmy patio pit stop.

BIN 941 TAPAS **$$**

Map p266 (www.bin941.com; 941 Davie St; plates $10-19; ⌚5pm-midnight Sun-Thu, to 2am Fri & Sat; 🚌6) A hopping, intimate spot that's packed almost every night, cave-like Bin 941 kicked off Vancouver's small-plates fever a few years back, and they haven't lost their touch. The inventive menu, based on local and seasonal ingredients, often includes international-influenced dishes such as short ribs, seared scallops and steamed fresh mussels (go for the coconut-milk broth).

It's one of the best spots in town for late-night nibbles and a few glasses of wine with chatty friends – which will quickly include the people squeezed next to you at the small adjoining table. Reservations not accepted.

ZERO ONE SUSHI JAPANESE **$$**

Map p266 (559 W Pender St; mains $5-16; ⌚11am-8pm Mon-Thu, to 9pm Fri; Ⓜ Granville) Fueling city-center office workers for years (which is why it's closed on weekends), this unassuming hole-in-the-wall staple serves some of the freshest, no-nonsense sushi in the downtown core. Prices are very reasonable (*nigiri* rolls cost from $1 to $3, for example) and there's usually a special or two to entice you to try something other than your regular California rolls.

There's minimal seating, so consider taking your package to the waterfront and locating an alfresco perch with a view around Canada Pl, a 10-minute walk away.

LA BODEGA SPANISH **$$**

Map p266 (www.labodegavancouver.com; 1277 Howe St; tapas $3-13; ⌚4:30pm-midnight Mon-Fri, 5pm-midnight Sat, to 11pm Sun; 🚌10) It's all about the tasting plates at this rustic, checked-tablecloth tapas bar, arguably Vancouver's most authentic Spanish restaurant. Pull up a chair, order a jug of sangria and decide on a few shareable treats from the extensive menu – if you're feeling spicy, the chorizo sausage hits the spot and the Spanish meatballs are justifiably popular.

There's often a great atmosphere here – helped by the friendly servers – so don't be surprised if you find yourself staying for more than a few hours...and an extra jug of sangria.

★HAWKSWORTH WEST COAST **$$$**

Map p266 (☎604-673-7000; www.hawksworthrestaurant.com; 801 W Georgia St; mains $29-39; ⏰6:30am-11pm Mon-Fri, 7am-11pm Sat & Sun; Ⓜ Vancouver City Centre) Vancouver's current 'it' restaurant is the chic, fine-dining anchor of the top-end Rosewood Hotel Georgia. But unlike most hotel restaurants, this one has a starry-eyed local following. Created by and named after one of the city's top local chefs, the menu fuses contemporary West Coast approaches with clever international influences, hence dishes such as soy-roasted sturgeon. The seasonal tasting menu is also heartily recommended. This is the city's best restaurant for a special night out; reservations are recommended.

CHAMBAR EUROPEAN **$$$**

Map p266 (☎604-879-7119; www.chambar.com; 562 Beatty St; mains $23-33; ⏰5pm-midnight; Ⓜ Stadium-Chinatown) This candlelit, brick-lined cave is a great place for a romantic night out. The sophisticated Belgian-esque menu includes perfectly delectable *moules et frites* (mussels and fries) and a braised lamb shank with figs that's a local dining legend. An impressive wine and cocktail list (try a blue fig martini) is also coupled with a great Belgian beer menu dripping with tripels and lambics.

Also consider dropping by just to hang out in the restaurant's front-room bar: grab a perch and work your merry way down the drinks list.

LE CROCODILE FRENCH **$$$**

Map p266 (☎604-669-4298; www.lecrocodilerestaurant.com; 909 Burrard St; mains $26-42; ⏰11:30am-2:30pm Mon-Fri, 5:30-10pm Mon-Thu, 5:30-10:30pm Fri & Sat; 🚌2) Tucked along a side street (enter from Smithe) in an unassuming building that resembles a cast-off from a shopping mall, this excellent Parisian-style dining room is right up there with the city's top-end best. Instead of focusing on experimental shenanigans that only please the chefs, it's perfected a menu of classic French dishes, each prepared with consummate cooking skill and served by perfect, snob-free wait staff.

Try the sumptuous, slow-braised lamb shank, washed down with a smashing bottle from the mother country, or treat yourself to the five-course chef's tasting menu ($75).

West End

If you can walk along the West End's restaurant-packed streets without stopping to eat, you either have a newly installed stomach staple or the willpower of a particularly virtuous saint. But it's not just the sheer number of restaurants sardined along Robson, Denman and Davie Sts that is impressive; the vast variety and value of the eateries make this Vancouver's best mid-range dining 'hood. If you're a fan of Japanese and Korean food, you'll find plenty of authentic options radiating from the Georgia and Denman Sts intersection.

SUSHI MART JAPANESE **$**

Map p270 (www.sushimart.com; 1686 Robson St; sushi combos $7-18; ⏰11:30am-3pm & 5-9pm Mon-Sat; 🚌5) You'll be rubbing shoulders with chatty young Asians at the large communal dining table here, one of the best spots in town for a superfresh sushi feast in a casual setting. Check the ever-changing blackboard showing what's available and then tuck into expertly prepared and well-priced shareable platters of all your fave *nigiri*, *maki* and sashimi treats. Udon dishes are also available.

Wash it all down with a large bottle of Sapporo or a hot sake or two. Check the menu for sustainable fishing options, marked with a special decal.

DAILY GRIND CAFE CAFE **$**

Map p270 (1500 W Georgia St; mains $5-8; ⏰7am-4pm Mon-Fri; 🚌19) If all you really want is a freshly prepared sandwich, accompanied by a hearty bowl of soup or a crisp green salad, then this unpretentious local secret is recommended. Service is excellent, and the generously filled sarnies – bulging wraps or thick-cut door-stoppers – are great value: check the blackboard when you walk in for the day's specials.

A good spot for a cake-and-coffee pit stop. Also consider collecting lunch here for a picnic in Stanley Park, a 10-minute walk away.

WE ALL SCREAM FOR ICE CREAM

You'd be forgiven for feeling skeptical about just how good North American gelato can be. After all, this isn't Italy. But that's before you've found the time to step into downtown's little **Bella Gelateria** (Map p266; www.bellagelateria.com; 1001 W Cordova St; ⏱10am-10pm Mon-Thu, to 11pm Fri, 11am-11pm Sat, to 10pm Sun; Ⓜ Waterfront) and met James Coleridge. He learned his skills at a gelato university in Italy (yes, they *do* exist) and, in 2012, he won a gold medal at the Florence Gelato Festival, the world's biggest such event. He was the first non-Italian to win.

But since the proof of the pudding is in the eating, you need to judge for yourself. Dive into the dozens of ever-changing gelato and *sorbetto* flavors. On our last visit he was experimenting with beer varieties, and you'll likely find eye-rollingly amazing treats such as Amerana cherry, Thai coconut and salted caramel. And if you get Coleridge talking, you'll be swept up in his enthusiasm for discovering new and classic concoctions. If you're lucky, the frankly astonishing Persian-rosewater-infused *faloudah sorbetto* will be available: it's like no other dessert you've ever tried.

★FORAGE — WEST COAST $$

Map p270 (☎604-661-1400; www.foragevancouver.com; 1300 Robson St; plates $11-20; ⏱6:30-10am Mon-Fri, 7am-2pm Sat & Sun, 5pm-midnight daily; 🚌5) A champion of the local farm-to-table scene, this sustainability-loving restaurant is the perfect way to sample the flavors of the region. Brunch has become a firm local favorite (turkey sausage hash recommended), and for dinner the idea is to sample an array of tasting plates. The menu is innovative and highly seasonal, but look out for pork tongue ravioli and roast bison bone marrow.

Reservations recommended. If you're dining alone, the U-shaped central bar is ideal – and it's a good spot to launch into some BC beers and wine.

★GUU WITH GARLIC — JAPANESE $$

Map p270 (www.guu-izakaya.com; 1689 Robson St; plates $4-9; ⏱11:30am-2:30pm Tue-Sun, 5:30pm-midnight Mon-Thu & Sun, 5:30pm-12:30am Fri & Sat; 🚌5) Arguably the best of Vancouver's many authentic *izakayas*, this welcoming, wood-lined joint is a cultural immersion. Hotpots and noodle bowls are available, but it's best to experiment with some Japanese bar tapas, such as black cod with miso mayo, deep-fried egg and pumpkin balls or finger-lickin' *tori-karaage* fried chicken. Garlic is liberally used in most dishes. It's best to arrive before opening time for a seat.

Drinks-wise, go for the house-brewed Guuu'd Ale: a sparkling and surprisingly good pale ale made by a local craft brewer. Finish the night with a shot of *shochu,* a traditional distilled spirit, and you'll be looking for the nearest karaoke bar as soon as you hit the street.

ESPANA — TAPAS $$

Map p270 (www.espanarestaurant.ca; 1118 Denman St; tapas plates $5-12; ⏱5pm-1am Sun-Thu, to 2am Fri & Sat; 🚌5) Reservations are not taken but it's worth the line-up to get into Vancouver's best new Spanish tapas joint. The tables are crammed close and the atmosphere is warm and welcoming, triggering a hubbub of chat that's mostly centered on the great grub. The crispy squid and the cod and potato croquettes are delish, while the crispy chickpeas dish is a revelation.

There's a small but authentic sherry list to consider plus a good array of Spanish wines – why not go the Cava route and toast your lovely meal?

MOTOMACHI SHOKUDO — JAPANESE $$

Map p270 (740 Denman St; mains $9-14; ⏱noon-11pm Thu-Tue; 🚌5) A West End favorite, this incredibly tiny ramen house – it has fewer than 20 seats – combines lightning-fast service with perfect comfort dishes. First-timers should try the New Generation miso ramen, which comes brimming with bean sprouts, sweet corn, shredded cabbage and barbecued pork. An added plus is that most ingredients are organic.

Note that only cash or debit cards are accepted here. And if the queue's long, try its nearby sister noodlery, **Kintaro Ramen**, just a few doors south.

SURA KOREAN ROYAL CUISINE — ASIAN $$

Map p270 (www.surakoreancuisine.com; 1518 Robson St; mains $10-20; ⏱11am-11pm; 🚌5) From the 1400-block of Robson St on and around onto Denman and Davie Sts, you'll find a finger-licking smorgasbord of casual but authentic Korean and Japanese eateries. A cut above its ESL-student-luring siblings, slick Sura offers awesome Korean comfort dishes in a cozy, bistro-like setting. Try the spicy beef soup, kimchi pancakes and excellent *bibimbap*: beef, veggies and a still-cooking egg in a hot stone bowl.

The set-course lunches ($15 or $20) are a great deal if you want to try as many flavors as possible; each comes with lots of little plates to dip into.

COAST
SEAFOOD **$$**

Map p270 (☎604-685-5010; www.coastrestaurant.ca; 1054 Alberni St; mains $18-42; ⏲11:30am-1am Mon-Thu, to 2am Fri, 4pm-2am Sat, to 1am Sun; 🚌5) A buzzing seafood joint where Vancouver movers and shakers like to be seen scoffing a wide array of aquatic treats. Knowing reinventions of the classics include prawn or salmon flatbread pizzas, but it's the mighty seafood platter of salmon, cod, scallops and tiger prawns that sates true fish nuts. Lunchtime fish and chips to go costs $14, and there's also an excellent raw bar with oysters aplenty.

The menu is huge here, so feel free to ask your server for some navigational pointers.

LOLITA'S
MEXICAN **$$**

Map p270 (www.lolitasrestaurant.com; 1326 Davie St; mains $18-25; ⏲4:30pm-1am; 🚌6) This lively cantina is popular with in-the-know West Enders for good reason. It's a great place to find yourself late at night, when the warm party vibe makes you feel like you're hanging with friends at a beach bar. Turn your taste buds on with a few rounds of gold tequila, and be sure to sample some spicy, fusionesque nosh, including the wonderful halibut tacos.

It's superbusy here most weekends, so if you want to hear yourself think, consider dropping by on a weeknight.

RAINCITY GRILL
WEST COAST **$$$**

Map p270 (☎604-685-7337; www.raincitygrill.com; 1193 Denman St; mains $18-29; ⏲11:30am-3pm Mon-Fri, to 3pm Sat & Sun, 5-10pm daily; 🚌6) This venerable English Bay eatery was sourcing unique BC ingredients long before the fashion for Fanny Bay oysters took hold. A great showcase for West Coast cuisine, the weekend brunch is a neighborhood legend (Dungeness crab omelet recommended). But the early-bird (before 6pm) tasting dinner is a bargain: for $30 you'll have three superb courses – add $20 for wine pairing.

Once you're done, take a romantic evening stroll along the beach at English Bay. The next day, consider dropping by the restaurant's take-out window: it's a great place to pick-up quality fish and chips ($12) for an impromptu beach picnic.

LE GAVROCHE
FRENCH **$$$**

Map p270 (☎604-685-3924; www.legavroche.ca; 1616 Alberni St; mains $20-38; ⏲11:30am-2:30pm Mon-Fri, 5-10:30pm daily; 🚌5) Given a new lease of life – and a bright new interior – by fresh owners, this heritage-home charmer fuses local ingredients with contemporary French approaches, and is one of downtown's most romantic dining spots. Peruse the range of dishes from salmon tartare to *sous vide* venison then go straight for the $85 degustation menu: a taste-tripping cornucopia that's like a showcase of the entire kitchen. The offering changes weekly, based on seasonality.

Wine lovers should also rejoice: there's a fantastic selection – including many rare-for-Vancouver Burgundies and Bordeaux – that might just have you crying into your glass with gratitude.

Stanley Park

The park has several welcoming beaches and some tree-fringed grassy expanses ideal for alfresco noshing, but if you haven't brought a picnic with you, Vancouver's verdant green heart also has its own dining options covering a range of budgets. Wherever you eat, try for a window seat so you can enjoy a side dish of forest or panoramic sea-to-sky views.

PROSPECT POINT CAFÉ
FAST FOOD **$**

(www.prospectpoint.ca; Stanley Park Dr; mains $10-16; ⏲11am-8pm, reduced off-season; 🚌19) A typical family-style tourist eatery with an attractive forest-shadowed patio deck, this is the place most Stanley Park visitors end up eating – usually because their tour bus has dropped them outside to partake of the adjoining gift shop. The takeout includes the usual suspects (think burgers and hot dogs), while the seated patio cafe adds fish and chips and salmon platters to the mix.

VANCOUVER'S MOST BEAUTIFUL BRIDGE

The Lions Gate Bridge gets all the kudos and much of the postcard space, but that's arguably due to being bookended by Stanley Park and the looming mountains. For many, the huge green bridge itself is not nearly as picturesque as the **Burrard Bridge** that spans False Creek. Built to link downtown to Kitsilano and crammed with art deco flourishes – torch-like lamps at either end and a jutting ship's-prow motif signifying the region's seafaring heritage – the yellow-painted lovely was opened in 1932. But the inauguration wasn't just a simple ribbon-cutting affair. Instead, a Royal Canadian Airforce seaplane was flown under the bridge deck to kick things off in a rather nail-biting fashion. Perhaps there'll be an attempt to recreate the festive spectacle for the centenary in a few years time. Or perhaps not.

The view is the main reason for coming here, so consider just ordering a couple of beers and drinking it in.

TEAHOUSE RESTAURANT WEST COAST **$$**
(☎800-280-9893, 604-669-3281; www.vancouverdine.com; Stanley Park Dr, Ferguson Point; mains $15-36; ⏰11:30am-10pm Mon-Fri, 10:30am-10pm Sat-Sun; 🚌19) Recently returning to the name it started with in the 1930s, this lovely spot serves contemporary West Coast classics such as pan-seared BC halibut and Fraser Valley duck, along with smashing sunset patio views over Burrard Inlet. It's a good place for weekend brunch – crab eggs Benedict recommended. The park's Third Beach is a few steps away and is ideal for an evening stroll post dinner.

The wine list has some good BC bottles; here's your chance to dive into a tipple or two from popular regional wineries such as Quails' Gate and Burrowing Owl.

FISH HOUSE IN STANLEY PARK SEAFOOD **$$$**
(☎877-681-7275, 604-681-7275; www.fishhousestanleypark.com; 8901 Stanley Park Dr; mains $22-42; ⏰11:30am-10pm Mon-Fri, 11am-10pm Sat & Sun; 🚌19) The park's fanciest dine-out, this double-patioed joint serves some of the city's best seafood. The menu changes based on seasonality but typical favorites include salmon Wellington and smoked cod linguine, while fresh oysters are ever-popular with visiting shuckers. Weekend brunch is a highlight – try the smoked salmon Benedict. Fish House's commitment to serving sustainable seafood extends also to locally sourced beef, duck and chicken.

If you've room for more, come back for a rich treat-focused afternoon tea (served from 2pm to 4pm). Then run around the park four times to work it off.

DRINKING & NIGHTLIFE

The Granville Strip between Robson and Granville Bridge is lined with popular bars, where partying is the main attraction. A short walk away, you'll find more discerning options in the bustling West End, which has plenty of pubs and bars, including several gay-friendly haunts along Davie St.

Downtown

★**RAILWAY CLUB** PUB
Map p266 (www.therailwayclub.com; 579 Dunsmuir St; ⏰4pm-2am Mon-Thu, noon-3am Fri, 3pm-3am Sat, 5pm-midnight Sun; Ⓜ Granville) A local-legend, pub-style music venue, the upstairs 'Rail' is accessed via an unobtrusive wooden door next to a 7-Eleven. Don't be put off: this is one of the city's friendliest bars. You'll fit right in as soon as you roll up to the bar – unusually for Vancouver, there's no table service. The Rail has live music nightly.

Expect regional microbrews from the likes of Tree Brewing and Central City (go for its ESB) and hit the hole-in-the-wall kitchen for late-night nosh, including burgers and quesadillas. Arrive early enough and you might snag the corner window table overlooking the streets. Don't forget your hot nuts – from the vending machine by the bar.

UVA WINE BAR WINE BAR
Map p266 (www.uvawinebar.ca; 900 Seymour St; ⏰noon-1:45am Mon-Sat, noon-12:45am, Sun; 🚌10) Downtown's best wine bar, this little nook combines a heritage mosaic floor and swanky white vinyl chairs that add a dash

of mod class. But despite the cool appearances, there's a snob-free approach that will have you happily taste-tripping through Old and New World delights, as well as some exciting BC wines: go for the citrusy Joie riesling. Add a cheese and charcuterie tasting plate.

Just a block from the party-hard madness (especially on weekends) of the Granville Strip, this is a great alternative to staggering around on the street wondering where you left your pants.

★MARIO'S COFFEE EXPRESS COFFEE

Map p266 (595 Howe St; ⏰7am-4pm Mon-Fri; Ⓜ Burrard) A java lover's favorite that only downtown office workers seem to know about. You'll wake up and smell the coffee long before you make it through the door here. The rich aromatic brews served up by the man himself are the kind of ambrosia that make Starbucks drinkers weep. You might even forgive the 1980s Italian pop percolating through the shop.

Hidden in plain view, this is arguably downtown's best for a cup of coffee.

FOUNTAINHEAD PUB GAY

Map p266 (www.thefountainheadpub.com; 1025 Davie St; ⏰11am-midnight Sun-Tue, to 1am Wed-Sat; 🚌6) The area's loudest and proudest gay neighborhood pub, this friendly joint is all about the patio, which spills onto Davie St like an overturned wine glass. Expect to take part in the ongoing summer evening pastime of ogling the passing locals or retreat to a quieter spot inside for a few lagers or a naughty cocktail: anyone for a Sicilian Kiss or a Slippery Nipple?

Perfect place to meet up before, during or after the Pride Parade.

BACCHUS LOUNGE BAR

Map p266 (www.wedgewoodhotel.com; 845 Hornby St; ⏰noon-midnight Sun-Wed, to 1am Thu-Sat; 🚌5) A roaring hearth on a chilly day is the main attraction at Bacchus, a decadent bar with a gentleman's club ambience on the lobby level of the Wedgewood Hotel & Spa. Sink into a deep leather chair, adjust your monocle and listen to the piano player as you sip a signature Red Satin Slip martini of vodka, raspberry liqueur and cranberry juice.

There's also a handy small-plate menu for the incurably hungry (go for the cheese).

CELEBRITIES GAY

Map p266 (www.celebritiesnightclub.com; 1022 Davie St; ⏰8pm-3am Wed, 10pm-3am Thu, 9pm-3am Tue, Fri & Sat; 🚌6) The city's fave gay club, Celebrities has recently undergone a long-overdue renovation, elevating its room to a new level of mood-lit cool. The club hosts a series of sparkling, sometimes sequined, event nights throughout the week, including a raucous Playhouse Saturday when everyone and his buddy seems to hit the dance floor. If you're on a budget, Tuesday is cheap-ass highball night.

LENNOX PUB PUB

Map p266 (www.lennoxpub.com; 800 Granville St; ⏰11am-midnight Sun-Thu, to 1am Fri & Sat; Ⓜ Vancouver City Centre) This narrow Granville St drinkery never seems to have enough tables to go around on weekends, when the noise levels prevent all but the most rudimentary of conversations. It's a different story during the week, when calm is restored and you can savor mostly standard import and domestic drafts from Belgium and beyond – try the Leffe or Big Rock Grasshopper.

The decor is reproduction old-school and the upstairs seating area is a popular couples nook. A good place to arrange a meet up if you're planning on launching yourself at the Granville Strip.

CAFFÈ ARTIGIANO COFFEE

Map p266 (www.caffeartigiano.com; 763 Hornby St; ⏰5:30am-9pm Mon-Fri, 6:30am-9pm Sat, to 8pm Sun; 🚌5) An international award winner for its barista skills and latte art, Artigiano has the locals frothing at the mouth with its satisfyingly rich java beverages. The drinks appear with leaf designs adorning their foam and there's a good side attraction of gourmet sandwiches and cakes. The small patio here is almost always packed – grab a table quickly if you see one.

This is one of the earliest-opening coffeehouses in town if you can't sleep and really need a java hit. The interior has a classy Tuscan look. There are several other outlets dotted around the city.

ROXY CLUB

Map p266 (www.roxyvan.com; 932 Granville St; ⏰7pm-3am daily; 🚌10) A raucous old-school nightclub that still has plenty of fans – including lots of partying youngsters who seem to be discovering it for the first time –

this brazen old timer is downtown's least pretentious dance space. Expect to be shaking your booty next to near-teenage funsters, kid-escaping soccer moms and UBC students looking for a bit of rough.

If you really want to dive into the Granville Strip club scene, this is where to do it.

VENUE CLUB

Map p266 (www.venuelive.ca; 881 Granville St; ⌚9pm-3am Thu-Sat; 🚌8) Redesigned from its previous incarnation as the Plaza Club, Venue has opened up with a much larger dance floor since the removal of the obtrusive central bar. The music is of the mainstream variety – party-hard WTF Fridays is best – and the crowd includes plenty of nonlocals in from Surrey and New Westminster for their weekly big night out.

It is also a live-music venue some evenings – check the website to see what's coming up.

West End

SYLVIA'S LOUNGE BAR

Map p270 (www.sylviahotel.com; 1154 Gilford St; ⌚7am-11pm Sun-Thu, to midnight Fri & Sat; 🚌5) Part of the permanently popular Sylvia Hotel, this was Vancouver's first cocktail bar when it opened in the mid-1950s. Now a comfy, wood-lined neighborhood bar favored by in-the-know locals (they're the ones hogging the window seats as the sun sets over English Bay), it's a great spot for an end-of-day wind down. Go for a 1954 vodka and Chambord cocktail.

The views and drinks are superior to the food here. And here's some scurrilous history for you: this is one of the bars Errol Flynn is reputed to have frequented during his booze-fueled final days, before dying in the city in 1959.

CARDERO'S MARINE PUB PUB

Map p270 (www.vancouverdine.com; 1583 Coal Harbour Quay; ⌚11:30am-midnight; 🚌19) Nestled between Coal Harbour's bobbing boats, Cardero's has a stellar waterfront location. The restaurant is fine, but the little pub on the side is better. With cozy leather sofas, a wood-burning fireplace and great views of the marina, it has a decent menu of comfort food (we recommend the oyster burger) and drafts from Strongbow to local Red Truck Lager.

There's also live singer-songwriter guitar music several times a week (usually after 8:30pm).

MILL MARINE PUB

Map p270 (www.millbistro.ca; 1199 W Cordova St; ⌚11am-10pm; Ⓜ Waterfront) The food here is nothing special but the waterfront alfresco panoramic views of Coal Harbour and the North Shore mountains more than make up for it. There's a small but drinkable beer selection – try Whistler Brewing's Black Tusk Ale – plus summer-friendly cocktail slushies.

It's one of the city's best spots to catch an evening Vancouver vista; arrive early or you'll be wrestling for a table.

1181 GAY

Map p270 (www.1181.ca; 1181 Davie St; ⌚6pm-3am; 🚌6) A popular gay bar if you like posing (or just looking), this loungy spot combines a sofa-strewn front space with a cozy back area that feels a lot more intimate. Separating the two is a side bar staffed by cooler-than-you servers: this is also where the singletons sit, so you can expect to be the subject of some flirty attention if you prop yourself here.

There's a good wine list and plenty of tempting cocktails, including the signature 1181 Margarita, made with Cointreau and lime-infused tequila. Davie's classiest gay bar.

PUMPJACK PUB GAY

Map p270 (www.pumpjackpub.com; 1167 Davie St; ⌚1pm-1am; 🚌6) Glancing through the open window as you walk past here on a summer night tells you all you need to know about this popular gay pub: it's a great place to meet leather-clad, often hairy locals ever-ready to make a new friend in town for a quick visit. Expect queues here on weekends as the local bears vie for a pick up or two. A long-time local favorite.

DELANY'S COFFEE HOUSE COFFEE

Map p270 (www.delanyscoffeehouse.com; 1105 Denman St; ⌚6am-9pm Mon-Thu, to 9:30pm Fri, 6:30am-9:30pm Sat & Sun; 📶; 🚌5) A laid-back, wood-lined neighborhood coffee bar that's the java-hugging heart of the West End's gay community, Delany's is a good perch from which to catch the annual Pride Parade, although you'll have to get here early if you want a front-row seat. The usual array of cookies and muffins will keep you fortified while you wait. A good spot to pick-up a takeout coffee for a stroll to nearby English Bay Beach.

MELRICHES COFFEEHOUSE COFFEE

Map p270 (www.melriches.com; 1244 Davie St; 🛜; 🚌6) With its mismatched wooden tables, hearty array of cakes and a crowd of journal-writing locals hunkered in every corner, this is an ideal rainy-day nook. Warm your hands on a pail-sized hot chocolate and press your face to the window to watch the Davie St locals bustling past. This is the kind of place where Morrissey would hang out on a wet Monday afternoon to check his emails. If you're hungry, the cookies are of the giant-sized variety here.

LOCAL KNOWLEDGE

ARCADE ATTRACTION

Strolling along the neon-winking Granville Strip, avoiding the cheap pizza joints and staggering drunks, it's easy to walk past one spot that hasn't changed much since the 1970s. **Movieland Arcade** (Map p266; 906 Granville St; ⏲10am-1am; 🚌10) is lined with dozens of mostly retro pinball machines and video games (anyone for Miss Pacman?). Here you can relive the days of blowing your paper-route money pumping the flippers on that Addams Family machine. Best of all, the games are just 25c a pop.

☆ ENTERTAINMENT

★COMMODORE LIVE MUSIC

Map p266 (www.commodoreballroom.ca; 868 Granville St; 🚌10) Local bands know they've made it when they play Vancouver's best mid-sized venue, a restored art deco ballroom that still has the city's bounciest dance floor – courtesy of tires placed under its floorboards. If you need a break from your moshing, collapse at one of the tables lining the perimeter, catch your breath with a bottled Stella and then plunge back in. The Commodore has been entertaining locals since 1929 and everyone from Count Basie to the Dead Kennedys has played here over the years (although they apparently weren't on the same bill).

★PACIFIC CINÉMATHÈQUE CINEMA

Map p266 (www.cinematheque.bc.ca; 1131 Howe St; tickets $11, double bills $14; 🚌10) This beloved cinema operates like an ongoing film festival with a daily-changing program of movies. A $3 annual membership is required – organize it at the door – before you can skulk in the dark with other chin-stroking movie buffs, who would probably name their children after Fellini and Bergman if they averted their gaze from the screen long enough to have a relationship.

The high point of the year for some is August's annual classic film noir season.

VANCITY THEATRE CINEMA

Map p266 (www.viff.org; 1181 Seymour St; tickets $11, double bills $14; 🚌10) The state-of-the-art headquarters of the Vancouver International Film Festival screens a wide array of movies throughout the year in the kind of auditorium that cinephiles dream of: generous legroom, wide armrests and great sight lines from each of its 175 seats. It's a place where you can watch a four-hour subtitled epic about a dripping tap and still feel comfortable.

Check the ever-changing schedule for shows and special events, and remember that a $12 annual membership is mandatory (but the fee includes one free ticket).

VANCOUVER CANUCKS SPECTATOR SPORT

Map p266 (www.canucks.com; Rogers Arena, 800 Griffiths Way; Ⓜ Stadium-Chinatown) The city's National Hockey League (NHL) team toyed with fans in 2011's Stanley Cup finals before losing Game 7 to the Boston Bruins, triggering riots and looting across Vancouver. But love runs deep and 'go Canucks go!' is still boomed out from a packed Rogers Arena at every game. Book your seat early or just head to a local bar for some raucous game-night atmosphere.

There's a large team merchandise shop at the stadium, which is open even when there are no games on: it's a good spot to pick up cool souvenirs for sporting kids (and adults) back home.

VOGUE THEATRE LIVE MUSIC

Map p266 (☎604-569-1144; www.voguetheatre.com; 918 Granville St; 🚌10) A 1940s heritage venue – check out the retro neon figure perched on top of the streamlined exterior – the Vogue was bought and refurbished a few years back. Happily the refurb didn't change

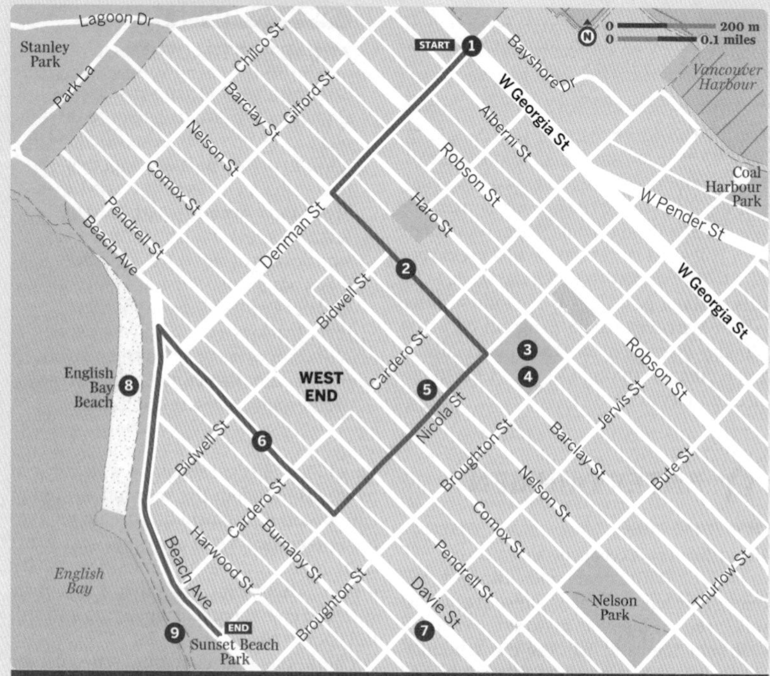

Neighborhood Walk
West End 'Hood & Heritage Stroll

START CORNER OF W GEORGIA AND DENMAN STS
END SUNSET BEACH
LENGTH 2KM; ONE HOUR

This urban walk takes you through one of Vancouver's most attractive residential areas, combining clapboard houses with art deco apartment buildings.

Start at the corner of W Georgia and Denman Sts and head south along **1 Denman St**. You'll pass dozens of mid-priced restaurants – choose one to return to for dinner – and plenty of enticing shops to attract your wallet.

Turn left on **2 Barclay St** and stroll through the residential heart of Vancouver's vibrant gay community. There are some smashing old heritage apartment buildings and wooden Arts and Crafts homes here.

Continue until you reach the well-preserved plaza of historic houses at **3 Barclay Heritage Square**, a reminder of how Vancouverites of yesteryear lived. Duck into what is perhaps the best-preserved of the bunch: lovely, antique-lined **4 Roedde House Museum** (p59) (even better if you time your visit for Sunday's afternoon tea).

Head southwest along Nicola St and you'll come across the lovely brick-built 1907 **5 Firehall No 6**. It's still in use but has the feel (and look) of a museum. There's often a shiny firetruck basking in the sun outside.

Continue on and turn right into **6 Davie St**, a teeming area lined with shops and cafes that's also the commercial hub of the gay community. It's a popular place at night as it has plenty of bars and clubs. If you need a coffee break, **7 Melriches** (p69) is nearby.

When you reach the end of Davie St at **8 English Bay Beach** (p59), turn left and stroll along Beach Ave. This becomes the main promenade for **9 Sunset Beach**, where you can sit on a grassy bank and watch the locals jog and rollerblade by, or you can catch a miniferry to Granville Island just across the water.

much and this is a great old-school venue to see bands. It's an all-seater, though, which sometimes means tension between those who want to sit and those of the mosh-pit persuasion.

The roster here is ecletic but it's usually a fave venue for visiting acts looking for a good-sized venue: a recent Friday to Sunday line-up included Billy Bragg, Nick Cave and Prince.

DANCE CENTRE — PERFORMING ARTS

Map p266 (www.thedancecentre.ca; 677 Davie St; 10) Vancouver's dance headquarters, this cleverly reinvented old bank building offers a kaleidoscopic array of activities that arguably makes it Canada's foremost dance center. Home to resident companies – Ballet BC is based here – it also hosts classes, workshops, performances and events throughout the year: check the website calendar to see what's coming up.

VANCOUVER FANCLUB — LIVE MUSIC

Map p266 (www.vancouverfanclub.ca; 1050 Granville St; 10) The newest Granville Strip live venue is also the most chilled. Attracting a crowd that would rather sip a nice bourbon than dive into a mosh pit, the acts are often of the smoky blues, roots or jazz variety. The space has a cool New Orleans–style feel to it with high-ceilings and a hardwood floor. There are acts every night and cover typically ranges up to $15.

If you're on a budget, drop by on Saturday afternoons at 2pm when there's a cover-free jazz-rock-blues showcase.

COMEDY MIX — COMEDY

Map p266 (www.thecomedymix.com; 1015 Burrard St, Century Plaza Hotel; shows 8:30pm Tue-Thu, 8:30pm & 10:30pm Fri & Sat; 2) It may be hidden in the basement of the Century Plaza Hotel, but this is arguably the city's best comedy venue; head here for some raucous belly laughs. Bigger acts strut their stuff here on weekends when it's typically packed, but consider early in the week for a more chilled-out visit: Tuesday's ProAm Night includes a plethora of newbies trying to make you laugh without wetting themselves.

There's tapas-style nosh available from the bar, as well as heartier dinner packages.

MALKIN BOWL — PERFORMING ARTS

(www.malkinbowl.com; Stanley Park; 19) Formerly just a summertime venue for musicals, this smashing Stanley Park stage has become an increasingly popular spot for alfresco live music. Elvis Costello, Franz Ferdinand and the Flaming Lips have had audiences (and those skulking around the fences outside) jumping up to punch the air here, often while partaking of a naughty BC cigarette or two.

Check the website for this year's Concerts in the Park menu and book ahead.

THEATRE UNDER THE STARS — PERFORMING ARTS

(604-734-1917; www.tuts.ca; Malkin Bowl, Stanley Park; tickets from $29; Jul & Aug; 19) The old-school Malkin Bowl is an atmospheric open-air venue in which to catch a summertime show. The season never gets too serious, usually featuring two enthusiastically performed Broadway musicals, but it's hard to beat the location, especially as the sun fades over the trees peeking from behind the stage. Increasingly the venue is also being used for live-music gigs.

This beloved local summertime fixture is a great way to meet the locals: many of them have been coming here for decades.

VANCOUVER'S THEATRICAL GRAND DAME

If you're lucky enough to catch a show at the **Orpheum Theatre** (Map p266; 604-665-3050; www.vancouver.ca/theatres; 884 Granville St; 4), be prepared to gasp when you enter the auditorium. Built in 1927 and now designated a national heritage site, the sumptuous Spanish baroque interior of multiple arches topped by an ornate painted dome harkens back to a time when theaters offered a fantasy escape from reality. But the beautiful old gal isn't just a well-preserved relic. In fact, she's steeped in theatrical history. Originally the Orpheum was part of a Chicago-headquartered chain of vaudeville houses. Stars who have hit the boards before the near-3000 seats have included Bob Hope, Shirley MacLaine and Harry Belafonte. Check out the commemorative wall plaques around the stage door out back and you'll find an A to Z of names from entertainment history.

MEDIA CLUB LIVE MUSIC

Map p266 (www.themediaclub.ca; 695 Cambie St; Ⓜ Stadium-Chinatown) This intimate, low-ceilinged indie space tucked underneath the back of the Queen Elizabeth Theatre books inventive local acts that mix and match the genres, so you may have the chance to see electro-symphonic or acoustic metal groups alongside power pop, hip-hop and country bands – although probably not on the same night. There are shows here several times a week.

An under-the-radar venue (except to those in the know), this is a great place for a loud night out...earplugs not supplied.

SCOTIABANK THEATRE CINEMA

Map p266 (www.cineplex.com; 900 Burrard St; tickets $12.50; 2) Downtown's shiny multiplex was big enough to attract its own corporate sponsor when it opened in 2005 and it's the most likely theater to be screening the latest must-see blockbuster. In contrast, it also shows occasional live broadcast performances from major cultural institutions such as London's National Theatre and New York's Metropolitan Opera. Note: there are no matinee or Tuesday discounts here.

For 3D movies, add an extra $5 to your ticket price.

SHOPPING

Downtown

Centered on lively Robson St – Vancouver's leading mainstream shopping promenade and the home of most major chains – the downtown core is a strollable outdoor mall of grazing shoppers moving between their favorite stores with an ever-growing clutch of bags. High fashion, shoes and jewelry are the mainstays here, and there are also plenty of coffee shops if you need to stop and count your money. Head south along Granville St from the intersection with Robson St for urban streetwear shops: this is where you can pick up those limited-edition Converse runners you've always wanted. For luxe labels such as Tiffany, Burberry and Louis Vuitton, head to the area around the Burrard and Alberni Sts intersection.

MACLEOD'S BOOKS BOOKS

Map p266 (455 W Pender St; 11am-6pm Mon-Sat, noon-5pm Sun; Ⓜ Granville) From its creaky floorboards to those skuzzy carpets and ever-teetering piles of books, this legendary locals' fave is the best place in town to peruse a cornucopia of used tomes. It's the ideal spot for a rainy-day browse through subjects from dance to the occult. Check the windows for posters of local readings and artsy happenings around the city.

A few steps in from the door, look out for the travel section. It's ideal for picking up a guidebook to 1987 New York, just in case you're a time-traveller planning a trip.

GOLDEN AGE COLLECTABLES BOOKS

Map p266 (www.gacvan.com; 852 Granville St; 10am-9pm Mon-Sat, 11am-6pm Sun; 10) If you're missing your regular dose of *Emily the Strange* or you just want to blow your vacation budget on a highly detailed life-sized model of Ultra Man, head straight to this Aladdin's cave of the comic-book world. While the clientele is unsurprisingly dominated by males, the staff is friendly and welcoming – especially to wide-eyed kids buying their first *Archie*.

There are occasional signings by artists here. This is also the best place to be in the city on the annual Free Comic Book Day (the first Saturday in May), when there's a party atmosphere and gratis goodies for all – whether or not you dress as Darth Vader (but don't expect to get anything if you wear your Jar Jar Binks costume).

HOLT RENFREW CLOTHING

Map p266 (www.holtrenfrew.com; 737 Dunsmuir St; 10am-7pm Mon, Tue & Sat, to 9pm Wed-Fri, 11am-6pm Sun; Ⓜ Granville) Vancouver's swankiest clothing and accessories department store. High-end-label lovers flock here to peruse the artfully presented D&G, Armani and Issey Miyake togs and accoutrements arrayed over several brightly lit floors. Service is personal from well-dressed staffers. The awesome end-of-season sales are recommended: racks of bargain clothes suddenly emerge on every floor, ripe for riffling.

Canada's answer to slick US chain Nordstrom, Holt Renfrew will finally get some competition soon: at the time of writing, downtown's giant old Sears department store was being renovated to house a sparkling new flagship Nordstrom. Let the battle commence.

MINK CHOCOLATES FOOD

Map p266 (www.minkchocolates.com; 863 W Hastings St; ⏲7:30am-6pm Mon-Fri, 10am-6pm Sat & Sun; Ⓜ Waterfront) If chocolate is the main food group in your book, follow your candy-primed nose to this designer choccy shop in the downtown core. Select a handful of souvenir bonbons – little edible artworks embossed with prints of trees and coffee cups – then hit the drinks bar for the best velvety hot choc you've ever tasted. Than have another.

It's always a good idea to pick up a few souvenir chocolate bars for home while you're here, although it's likely you'll scoff them before they make it into your suitcase: ganache-filled key lime and high-tea varieties are superb.

VANCOUVER PEN SHOP ACCESSORIES

Map p266 (512 W Hastings St; ⏲9:30am-5:30pm Mon-Fri, 10am-5pm Sat; Ⓜ Waterfront) There are two things about this store that are pleasingly old-fashioned: the staff greets you when you walk in and ask how to help you, and the items they're selling harken to a bygone age when fine pens and penmanship were important markers (no pun intended) of civilization. It's not all gold-nibbed fountain pens, though: there are writing tools for every budget here.

If you're a real aficionado of the modern-day quill, check out the monthly meetings of the Vancouver Pen Club, staged at venues across the city (www.vancouverpenclub.com).

SIKORA'S CLASSICAL RECORDS MUSIC

Map p266 (www.sikorasclassical.com; 432 W Hastings St; ⏲10am-7pm Mon-Sat, noon-5pm Sun; Ⓜ Granville) Sikora's blows away the classical inventory of mainstream music stores with its giant selection of more than 25,000 CD/DVD titles, plus hundreds of LPs for all those traditionalists out there. Opera, organ, choral, chamber and early music are well represented, as are New Age and spoken word, and there's also a section devoted to celebrated and lesser-known Canadian musicians.

The staff is highly knowledgeable and can point you to a hot Mahler or Rachmaninov recording at the drop of a hat.

BIRKS JEWELERY

Map p266 (www.birks.com; 698 W Hastings St; ⏲10am-6pm Mon-Fri, to 5:30pm Sat, noon-5pm Sun; Ⓜ Waterfront) A Vancouver institution since 1879 – hence the landmark freestanding clock outside – Birks crafts exquisite heirloom jewelry and its signature line of timepieces. It's an upscale place, similar to Tiffany & Co in the US, and ideal for picking up that special something in a classy, blue embossed box for a deserving someone back home.

If you're keen to splash your vacation spending money around, consider a little something accented with a Canadian diamond, laser-engraved with a tiny maple leaf.

ROOTS CLOTHING

Map p266 (www.canada.roots.com; 1001 Robson St; ⏲10am-6pm Mon-Fri, to 7pm Sat, to 5pm Sun; 🚌5) Basically a maple-leaf-emblazoned version of the Gap, Roots designs athletic, plaid-accented streetwear that's unmistakably Canadian. Its retro-styled jogging pants, hoodies and toques (if you don't know what that is, this is the place to find out) are ever-popular. There are additional outlets (usually in malls) throughout the city.

Check the sale rails here for end-of-season deals. You might even pick up an ironic fur-covered trappers hat for just a few bucks.

VANCOUVER CHRISTMAS MARKET MARKET

Map p266 (www.vancouverchristmasmarket.com; 650 Hamilton St; admission adult/child $5/2; ⏲11am-9pm late Nov–24 Dec; Ⓜ Stadium) Since starting in 2010, this German-style Christmas market has lured Yuletide-loving locals in their thousands. They come for dozens of stalls hawking arts and crafts (including lots of German Christmas ornaments), as well as hearty grub from baked apples to grilled bratwurst. Smile-triggering Christmas music and warm *glühwein* stoke the air of jollity.

Save money on the entry fee by coming during the day: weekday tickets from 11am to 4pm are reduced to $2.

VINYL RECORDS MUSIC

Map p266 (www.vinylrecords.ca; 321 W Hastings St; ⏲noon-6pm Mon-Sat, 1-5pm Sun; 🚌14) Recently relocated and now one of Vancouver's largest used (mostly) record shops. You'll need hours to sort through the higgledy-piggledy array of crates and cardboard boxes housing everything from polka to Pink Floyd. Make sure you know your prices since not everything is a bargain – most of the sale items are gathered near the front of the shop.

With one of the widest selections of albums available in the city, this is the spot to find that rare Nine Inch Nails record that always cheers you up.

PACIFIC CENTRE SHOPPING CENTRE

Map p266 (www.pacificcentre.ca; cnr Howe & W Georgia Sts; ⏲10am-7pm Mon, Tue & Sat, to 9pm Wed-Fri, 11am-6pm Sun; ⓂGranville) If rain threatens to curtail your shopping activities, duck inside downtown Vancouver's main mall. You'll find all the usual chain and department store suspects, plus highlights like H&M, Purdy's Chocolates and Harry Rosen. You can also check your email for free at the Apple Store. There's a large food court if you need a pit stop from all that retail therapy.

Check the mall's website for an up-to-the-minute listing of sales and deals at the stores and eateries here.

West End

Not only a vibrant district of restaurants and coffee shops, the West End has more than a few stores worth nosing around in. The majority of the most distinctive businesses are on Davie St and are tailored toward the area's large gay community, but you can also expect bookstores, bakeries, wine shops and just about everything else along the way. The western end of Robson St delivers some interesting Asian stores: the perfect place to pick up oddball Japanese candies and those essential cans of Pocari Sweat.

KONBINIYA JAPAN CENTRE FOOD

Map p270 (www.konbiniya.com; 1238 Robson St; ⏲11am-1am; 🚌5) Situated at a point on Robson St where the generic chain stores dry up and the Asian businesses begin, this is the kind of colorful, chaotic, even tacky store frequently seen in Tokyo's clamorous suburbs. It's the best place in town for Pocky chocolate sticks, wasabi-flavored Kit Kats and Melty Kiss candies, hence the homesick language students shuffling nostalgically around the aisles.

If your accommodation is self-catering, this is a good place to pick up cheap instant noodles and curry mixes – you can also buy some large bags of savory corn snacks for the road.

WEST END FARMERS MARKET MARKET

Map p270 (www.eatlocal.org; Nelson Park, btwn Bute & Thurlow Sts; ⏲9am-2pm Sat Jun–mid-Oct; 🚌6) The city's most urban alfresco farmers market is right in the heart of the West End. It runs for several of the sunniest months of the year (but doesn't stop for rain), and it's a great way to meet the locals. The strip of 30 or so stalls often includes baked treats, arts and crafts, and glistening piles of freshly picked, locally grown fruit and veg. Look out for seasonal blueberries, cherries, apricots and peaches, and expect a busker or two as you wander around gorging on your purchases.

LITTLE SISTER'S BOOK & ART EMPORIUM BOOKS, ACCESSORIES

Map p270 (www.littlesisters.ca; 1238 Davie St; ⏲10am-11pm; 🚌6) One of the only gay bookshops in western Canada, Little Sister's is a large bazaar of queer-positive tomes, plus magazines, DVDs and toys of the adult type. Proceeds of designated books support the store's long-running legal battle against Canada Customs for its seizures of imported items. If this is your first visit to Vancouver, it's a great place to network with the local 'gayborhood.'

Check the notice boards for events and announcements from the wider community. There are also occasional events in the store, including launches and author readings.

LULULEMON ATHLETICA CLOTHING

Map p270 (www.lululemon.com; 3118 Robson St; ⏲10am-9pm Mon-Sat, 11am-8pm Sun; 🚌5) The flagship downtown store of the Vancouver-based chain that made ass-hugging yoga wear a mainstream fashion, this is the shop for that archetypal West Coast look. Sporty tops and stretchy pants for women are the collection's backbone, but menswear is also in the mix for those blokes in touch with their yoga side. The range has recently expended to include cycling and jogging gear.

Ask the friendly staff about the warehouse sales that occasionally pop up around town: there are some serious bargains to be had.

MARQUIS WINE CELLARS WINE

Map p270 (www.marquis-wines.com; 1034 Davie St; ⏲11am-9pm; 🚌6) Small and friendly, this boutique wine shop has a down-to-earth approach to its products, which makes it a great place to hit if you can't tell the difference between a pinot noir and a pinot grigio. Expert staff and regular tastings are part of the mix – also check its website for a roster of enticing wine education events.

This is a good spot to dive into BC wine: ask for tips and you may be pleasantly surprised.

SIGNATURE BC LIQUOR STORE DRINK

Map p270 (www.bcliquorstores.com; 768 Bute St; ⏲10am-9pm; 🚌5) The 'Signature' in the name means this well-located shop – just off Robson St at Bute – is one of the larger-format BC government liquor stores. You'll find a big selection of pretty much anything you might want to imbibe, including a back wall of regional and international beers and a large array of wines from around the world. If you're a beer fan, make sure you peruse the BC craft beer selection. Many are available in (larger) single bottles, so you can sample a few without committing to a six-pack.

SPORTS & ACTIVITIES

VANCOUVER FOODIE TOURS GUIDED TOUR

Map p270 (☎877-804-9220; www.foodietours.ca; 1171 Alberni St; tour $69; ⏲2-5pm Mon, Fri & Sat; 🚌5) Of several culinary-themed strolls that have emerged in recent years, the Guilty Pleasures Gourmet Tour by Vancouver Foodie Tours is arguably the best. Your engaging host will lead you on a diverse sample-heavy stroll around downtown, taking in tastings at Chinese, Japanese and gourmet sandwich joints, plus a wine tasting and a finale finish at the city's best gelato shop.

There are also tours around the city's food-truck scene worth trying out ($49). Make sure you wait a couple of days to work up an appetite again.

ACADEMIE DUELLO SWORDPLAY

Map p266 (☎604-568-9907; www.academieduello.com; 412 W Hastings St; ⏲noon-8pm Mon-Fri, 10am-5pm Sat; 🚌9) The perfect spot to indulge your inner knight in ye olde Vancouver, this popular downtown sword-play school offers thrilling classes and workshops for kids and adults that show you how to wield everything from rapiers to broadswords. There's also a small on-site museum (entry by donation) covering the history of weapons, armor and heraldry.

CYCLE CITY TOURS GUIDED TOUR

Map p270 (www.cyclevancouver.com; 1798 W Georgia St, Spokes Bicycle Rentals; tours incl bike from $50; 🚌5) Vancouver is a good city for on-bike exploring, but if you're not great at navigating, consider a guided tour with this

RIOTOUS BEHAVIOR

When the 2010 Winter Olympics were staged in Vancouver, locals were surprised and delighted that the jam-packed nighttime streets never spilled over into trouble. So, when the Vancouver Canucks hockey team entered a play-off run in 2011, few were concerned that things might turn ugly – despite the distant memory of hockey riots here during a similar play-off run back in 1994.

On the night of 15 June 2011, however, just after the Canucks lost to the Boston Bruins, the downtown core rapidly descended into chaos. Hundreds of booze-fueled 'fans,' most of whom had been watching the game at an outdoor live-screening site, began rampaging through the city, smashing store windows, setting fire to police cars and looting dozens of shops, including the Bay and London Drugs. The police seemed unable to quell the rioters and control of the city center was lost for several hours. The region watched the unfolding events on their TV screens in horror.

The next day, after the violence had subsided, a different group of locals turned out on the streets. Armed with brooms and buckets, and rallied by a social media call-to-action that asked Vancouverites to show what the city was really all about, hundreds arrived to help with the massive clean-up. Interviewed on TV, many expressed their anger at what had happened the night before as well as their determination to help the recovery efforts.

As for the rioters, many were outed and eventually charged by the police after posting photos of themselves on social media during the evening's flame-licked shenanigans.

friendly operator. Meet at Spokes Bicycle Rentals and you'll soon be trundling around the city. Tours last from two to five hours and range from a grand city tour of local neighborhoods to a cool public-art trail.

If you're feeling peckish, the food tour is the way to go – it includes sample-heavy visits to food trucks, Chinatown and Granville Island Public Market. Bikes and helmets are provided, but if you have your own wheels you'll get a discount. Private tours are also available.

SECOND BEACH POOL SWIMMING

(www.vancouverparks.ca; cnr N Lagoon Dr & Stanley Park Dr, Stanley Park; adult/child $5.40/2.70; ⏲10am-8:45pm mid-Jun–Aug, reduced off-season; 👪; 🚌19) This smashing outdoor pool shimmers like an aquamarine gem right beside the ocean shoreline. It has lanes for laps but you'll be weaving past children on most summer days; the kids take over here during school vacations, making it very hard to get anywhere near the waterslide (we've tried). If you're travelling with under-10s, they'll love this place and the chance to hang with local kids.

Arrive early for a poolside towel spot. There's also a playground nearby and a concession stand if you need ice creams (who doesn't?).

SPOKES BICYCLE RENTALS BICYCLE RENTAL

Map p270 (www.vancouverbikerental.com; 1798 W Georgia St; adult per hr/7hr from $8.60/34.30; ⏲8am-9pm Jul & Aug, reduced off-season; 🚌5) On the corner of W Georgia and Denman Sts, this is the biggest of the bike shops crowding this stretch. Spokes can kit you and your family out with all manner of bikes, from cruisers to kiddie one-speeds.

Spokes also rents in-line skates and can hook you up with a guided bike tour if you fancy company.

ROBERT LEE YMCA GYM

Map p266 (www.robertleeymca.ca; 955 Burrard St; visitor pass $15; ⏲5:30am-10:30pm Mon-Fri, 7am-9pm Sat & Sun; 🚌22) A sparkling new YMCA facility crammed with just about everything you need to prevent those vacation double chins from forming, this centrally located spot includes a well-stocked gym, weight rooms, squash courts, yoga studio and a pool. It's very popular, so consider arriving off-peak. The staff is also friendly here, which is a huge plus over other gyms.

YWCA HEALTH & FITNESS CENTRE GYM

Map p266 (www.ywcahealthandfitness.com; 535 Hornby St; day pass $16; ⏲5:45am-10pm Mon-Fri, 8am-5:30pm Sat & Sun; Ⓜ Burrard) Despite its name, this excellent downtown gym is open to both women and men. It has three studios with wood-sprung floors, both combined and women-only weight rooms, a cardio room, steam room, meditation room and a 25m pool. There are also classes for kickboxing, cycling, pilates and other activities. A day membership provides you with access to all.

VANCOUVER AQUATIC CENTRE SWIMMING

Map p270 (www.vancouverparks.ca; 1050 Beach Ave; adult/child $5.40/2.70; ⏲6:30am-9:30pm Mon-Fri, 8am-9:30pm Sat, 10am-5pm Sun; 🚌6) Located at Sunset Beach beside the Burrard Bridge, this concrete monstrosity may look like a nuclear bunker but inside it is a busy aquatic center with a 50m pool, whirlpool, diving tank and sauna. There's also a gym if you want to continue your exercise purge.

There are lots of swimming, aquafit and family-friendly classes here throughout the week.

BAYSHORE RENTALS BICYCLE RENTAL

Map p270 (www.bayshorebikerentals.ca; 745 Denman St; per hr/8hr $6/23.80; ⏲9am-9pm May-Aug, to dusk Sep-Apr; 🚌5) One of several rival businesses taking advantage of their Stanley Park proximity, Bayshore will rent you just about anything to get you rolling around the nearby seawall. The 21-speed mountain bikes are its bread and butter, but it also rents in-line skates, tandems (you know you want one) and rugged toddler bike trailers so you can tow your kids like the royalty they are.

Bike helmets are the law in BC, and all rentals here include them for free.

YYOGA YOGA

Map p266 (☎604-682-3569; www.yyoga.ca; 888 Burrard St; drop-in sessions from $10; Ⓜ Burrard) This large and popular studio offers dozens of classes per week covering all manner of approaches. Spend some time figuring out which one would be best for you from a menu that includes Yoga Mechanics, ESL Yoga (for visiting students) and Yoga for Stiff Guys (don't ask). In addition to the stretching classes, there's a roster of additional wellness treats, from Thai massage to Shiatsu therapy.

SPA UTOPIA & SALON
SPA

Map p266 (☎604-689-7700; www.spautopia.ca; Pan Pacific Vancouver, 999 Canada Pl; ⏰9am-5pm Sat-Mon, to 9pm Tue-Fri; Ⓜ Waterfront) Welcome to the height of luxury. Spa Utopia is a perfect world of relaxation and pampering, specializing in 'spa suites,' where you hold court in a private, hotel-style room while various treatments and their practitioners come your way. There is a massive range of treatments; the deep hot-stone massage (from $149) is recommended.

FITNESS WORLD DOWNTOWN EXPRESS
GYM

Map p270 (www.fitnessworld.ca; 1185 W Georgia St; ⏰5am-11pm Mon-Thu, to 10pm Fri, 8am-8pm Sat & Sun; Ⓜ Burrard) Known as 'Fatness World' by locals, this West End 2nd-floor gym has long opening hours, so you can usually find some quiet time to work out. Hop on a running machine by the window and break a sweat while you look down over the unfit masses below. The company has several other city branches, many of them under the Steve Nash brand.

DAVID BUKACH / GETTY IMAGES ©

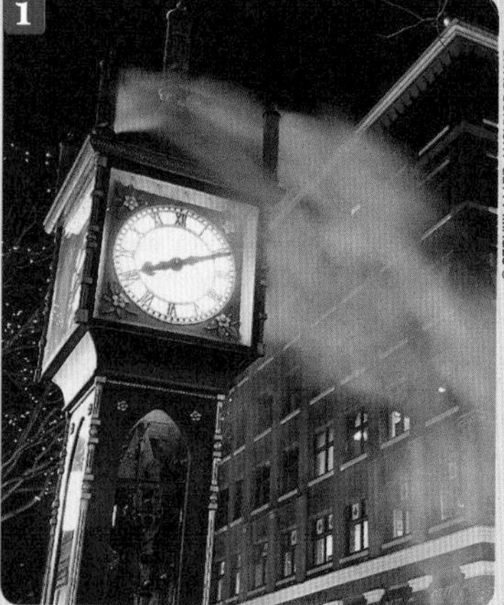

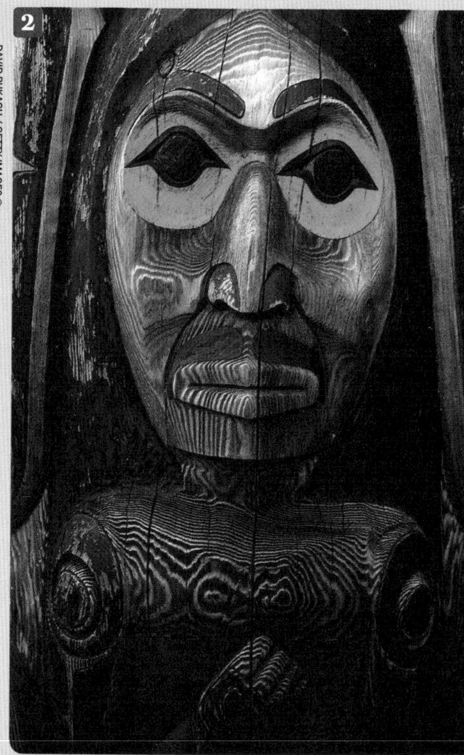

1. Steam Clock, Gastown (p82)
Gastown's most photographed landmark marks each hour with whistling symphonies.

2. North Vancouver
Across the Capilano Suspension Bridge (p179) you'll find historic exhibits, totem poles and nature trails.

3. Stanley Park (p52)
This 400-hectare woodland is revered for its forest-and-mountain oceanfront views.

4. English Bay
A boat trip on English Bay offers views of the Vancouver skyline to the mountains beyond.

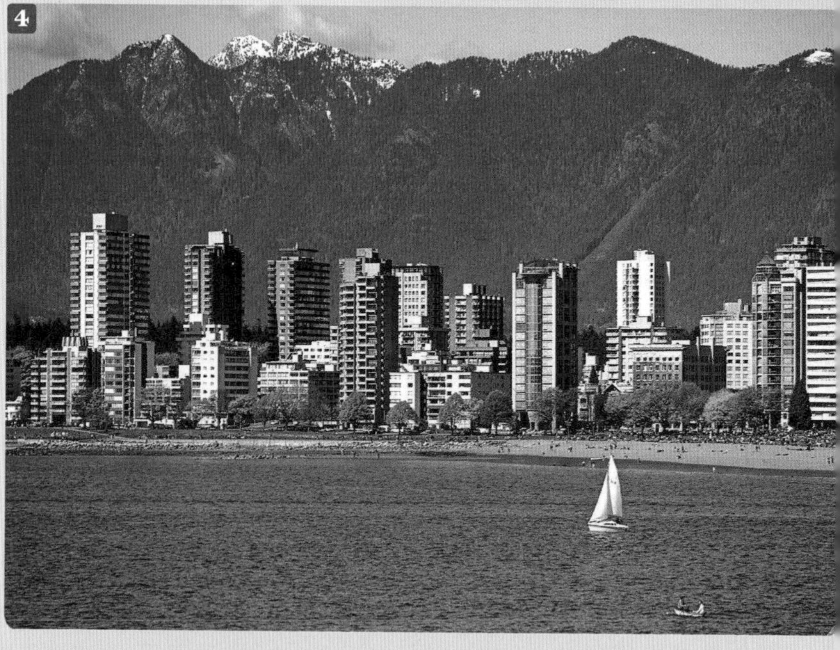

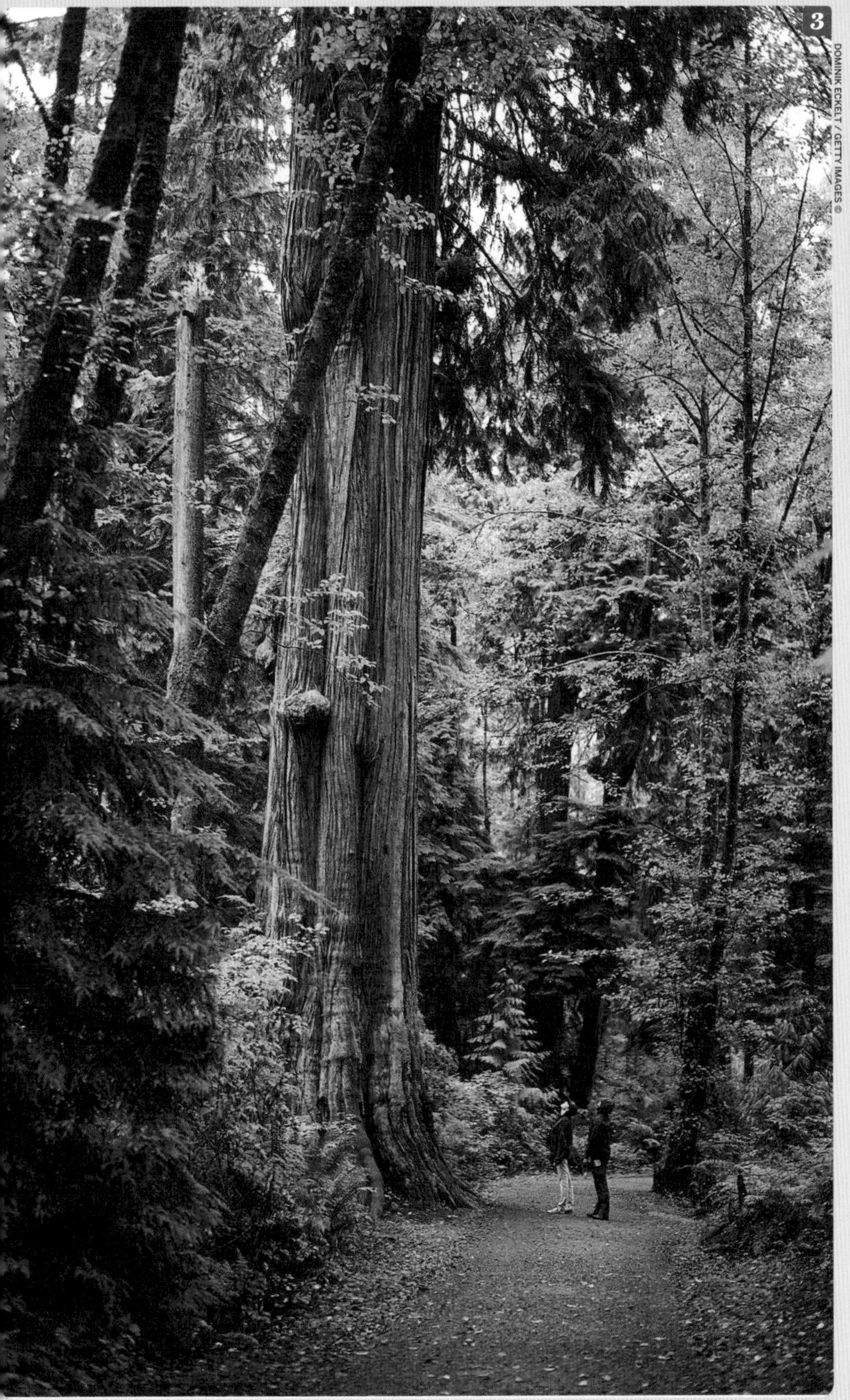

DOMINIK ECKELT / GETTY IMAGES ©

Gastown & Chinatown

GASTOWN | CHINATOWN

Neighborhood Top Five

❶ Tucking into top British Columbia (BC) craft beers at the **Alibi Room** (p89), preferably while rubbing shoulders with the locals at one of the long, candlelit tables.

❷ Sinking into a state of calm at the **Dr Sun Yat-Sen Classical Chinese Garden** (p83).

❸ Stuffing your face with Vancouver's best sandwiches at **Meat & Bread** (p84).

❹ Taking the eye-opening summertime Sins of the City walking tour at the **Vancouver Police Museum** (p82).

❺ Diving into the sights, sounds and aromas of the bustling **Chinatown Night Market** (p84).

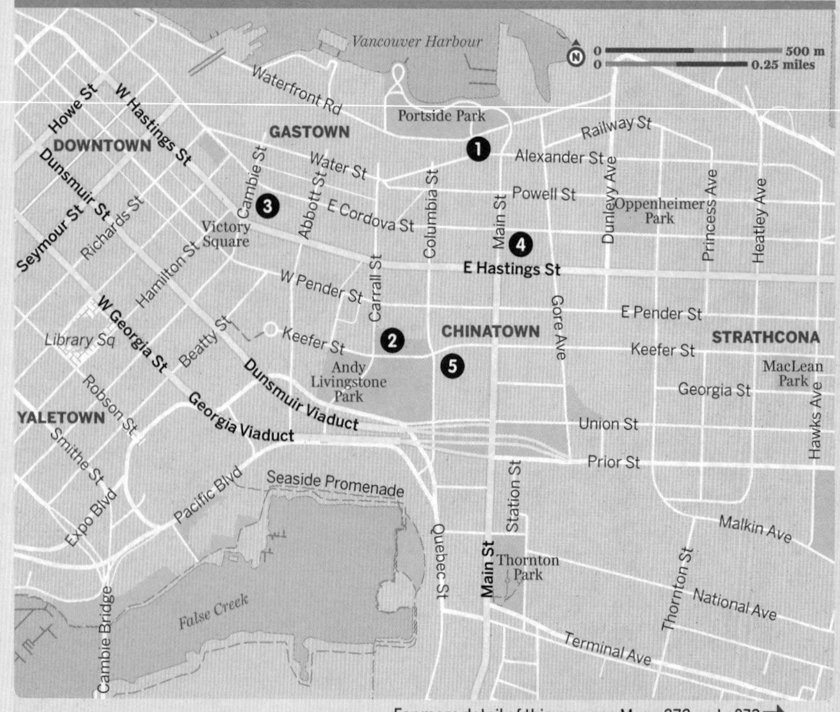

For more detail of this area see Map p272 and p273

Explore Gastown & Chinatown

Radiating from the 'Gassy' Jack statue in brick-paved Maple Tree Sq, the main thoroughfares of compact Gastown are Powell, Water, Carrall and Alexander Sts. You'll find plenty of shops and restaurants on Water, while Carrall is home to a more recent wave of hip bars, stores and coffee shops. Wandering south on this street, you'll enter the heart of the Downtown Eastside, where many of the neighborhood's poorest residents reside. Hastings St runs across Carrall and is the area's main drag, serviced by several bus routes. A block further south brings you to Chinatown, denoted by its flare-roofed buildings and dragon-topped street lamps. The entire Gastown and Chinatown district is easily explored on foot and makes for a fascinating afternoon of urban wandering. Couple this with an end-of-day drink or dinner in some of the city's best bars and restaurants. In summer, come back for the weekend Chinatown Night Market on Keefer St, between Columbia and Main Sts.

Local Life

➡ **Bars** Avoid downtown's Granville Strip drunks on a bar crawl of Gastown's top watering holes. You'll find hipster locals as well as more BC craft beer than you can shake a merry stick at.

➡ **Shops** Chinatown is teeming with traditional grocery stores, where looking is just as much fun as buying. You'll find interesting items such as lizards splayed on a stick. For a different scene, peruse the cool indie boutiques of Gastown.

➡ **History** Vancouver's best heritage buildings line this area, from tile-topped apothecaries to handsome century-old stone edifices repurposed as bars and restaurants.

Getting There & Away

➡ **Train** SkyTrain's Waterfront Station is at the western edge of Gastown, near the start of Water St. Stadium-Chinatown Station is on the edge of Chinatown and a 10-minute stroll south of Gastown.

➡ **Bus** Bus 14 heads northwards from downtown's Granville St along Hastings, which makes it handy for both Gastown and Chinatown. Buses 3, 4, 7 and 8 also service the area.

➡ **Car** There is metered parking throughout Gastown and Chinatown, with some nonmetered parking east of Main St.

Lonely Planet's Top Tip

Gastown and Chinatown are part of the Downtown Eastside, which some locals will tell you is a dangerous area. These are generally locals who haven't been here. The neighborhood certainly has many social challenges and a high proportion of residents with addiction or mental-health issues. You're far more likely, however, to be asked for 'spare change' while in the city center, and muggings in Downtown Eastside are exceptionally rare. Stay street smart and avoid back alleys and side streets (especially at night).

Best Places to Eat

➡ Bao Bei (p89)
➡ L'Abbatoir (p87)
➡ Rainier Provisions (p84)
➡ Campagnolo (p89)
➡ Meat & Bread (p84)

For reviews, see p84 ➡

Best Places to Drink

➡ Alibi Room (p89)
➡ Diamond (p91)
➡ Keefer Bar (p93)
➡ Brickhouse (p93)
➡ Guilt & Co (p91)

For reviews, see p89 ➡

Best Places to Shop

➡ Erin Templeton (p95)
➡ John Fluevog Shoes (p95)
➡ Orling & Wu (p96)
➡ Deluxe Junk (p96)
➡ Solder & Sons (p96)

For reviews, see p95 ➡

SIGHTS

Gastown

VANCOUVER POLICE MUSEUM — MUSEUM

Map p273 (☎604-665-3346; www.vancouverpolicemuseum.ca; 240 E Cordova St; adult/child $12/8; ⌚9am-5pm Tue-Sat; 🚌4) Illuminating the crime-and-vice-addled history of the region, this quirky museum is lined with confiscated weapons and counterfeit currency. It also has a former mortuary room where the walls are studded with preserved slivers of human tissue – spot the bullet-damaged brain slices. Consider a summertime Sins of the City walking tour to learn all about the area's old brothels and opium dens.

If you're really enthused, the museum also runs Forensics for Adults workshops; check ahead for schedules. One of Vancouver's hidden gem museums, it has plenty of exhibits and grainy photos covering a time when the city was rougher than a 1950s X-rated film noir movie.

STEAM CLOCK — LANDMARK

Map p272 (cnr Water & Cambie Sts; Ⓜ Waterfront) Halfway along Water St, this oddly popular tourist magnet lures the cameras with its tooting steam whistle. Built in 1977, the clock's mechanism is actually driven by electricity; only the pipes on top are fueled by steam (reveal it to the patiently waiting tourists and you might cause a riot). It sounds every 15 minutes, and marks each hour with little whistling symphonies.

Once you have the required photo, spend time exploring the rest of cobbled Water St. One of Vancouver's most historic thoroughfares, its well-preserved heritage buildings contain shops, galleries and resto-bars. Be sure to cast your gaze above entrance level for cool architectural features.

GASSY JACK STATUE — MONUMENT

Map p272 (Maple Tree Sq; 🚌4) It's amusing to think that Vancouver's favorite statue is a testament to the virtues of drink. At least that's one interpretation of the jaunty 'Gassy' Jack Deighton bronze, perched atop a whiskey barrel in Maple Tree Sq. Erected in 1970, it recalls the time when Deighton arrived here in 1867 and built a bar, triggering a development that soon became Vancouver.

Rivaling the nearby Steam Clock for most-photographed Gastown landmark, Gassy is popular enough to have his own Twitter account, where he spends his days whining about the indignities wrought by passing pigeons. The statue is roughly on the site of Deighton's first bar; he soon built a second, grander one nearby.

MAPLE TREE SQUARE — SQUARE

Map p272 (intersection of Alexander, Water, Powell & Carrall Sts; 🚌4) The intersection where Vancouver began was the site of 'Gassy' Jack Deighton's first bar, and the spot where the inaugural city-council meeting was held under a large maple tree. It drips with old-town charm. Snap a photo of the jaunty statue of Jack, plus the nearby, recently restored Byrnes Block, the oldest Vancouver building still in its original location.

Gastown was designated a national historic site in 2010, in the main because of this area. Stocked with historic buildings completed a few years after the 1886 Great Fire, Carrall St has some handsome architecture. Images from Vancouver's early days (just after it was renamed from the original moniker of 'Granville') show that the first 'city hall' was actually a sagging tent with a handwritten sign on it.

WOODWARD'S — NOTABLE BUILDING

Map p272 (149 W Hastings St; 🚌14) The project that catalyzed recent Downtown Eastside redevelopment, this former landmark department store was a derelict shell after closing in the early 1990s. Successive plans to transform it failed until, in 2010, it reopened as the home of new shops and condos, a trigger for what many have labelled neighborhood gentrification. Check out the monumental 'Gastown Riot' photo montage inside.

The Woodward's W-shaped red neon sign that stood atop the building for decades was replaced with a reproduction when the new development was completed; the old one is preserved in a glass cabinet at ground level near the Cordova St entrance. If you get the angle right (which might mean lying on the sidewalk), you can snap an image of both signs at the same time.

RETURN OF THE DOWNTOWN EASTSIDE

The Downtown Eastside was once Vancouver's primary business and shopping district. Radiating from the few blocks around the Main and Hastings Sts intersection, the area became a depressing ghetto of lives blighted by drugs and prostitution from the 1970s onwards. Nowadays, though, the neighborhood that time forgot is again on the rise.

Such change was triggered by the massive Woodward's redevelopment that opened in early 2010. What you'll find on your exploration of the area is a clutch of historic buildings that survived the era when similar structures in other neighborhoods were demolished. Now ripe for renovation, many are finally being reclaimed and restored, hence the sudden emergence of cranes in an area that developers once avoided. Check out the preserved copper-colored **Dominion Building** (Map p272; 205 W Hastings St) and the beautifully upgraded monumental **Flack Block** (Map p272; 163 W Hastings St), then nip into Woodward's. Don't stay too long outside the **Carnegie Centre** (Map p273; 401 Main St), where the milling crowds can be a little overwhelming, but look out for its stained-glass window of Shakespeare, Spenser and Milton.

Some of Vancouver's last remaining neon signs are also clinging on here, mostly along Hastings St. Look out for fine examples such as the Ovaltine Cafe and the Only Sea Foods Cafe signs. The latter was recently restored and returned to its original location, despite the closure of the business it once advertised.

Along with the preservation of historic sites, however, gentrification has also brought rising prices to the neighborhood, creating tension among the large number of homeless and underprivileged people who have called this area home for decades (see p229 for more).

It still pays to be street smart in the Downtown Eastside today. You likely won't be bothered by anyone on your walk, but avoid back alleyways and stay in busy areas after dark.

⊙ Chinatown

CHINATOWN MILLENNIUM GATE LANDMARK

Map p273 (cnr W Pender & Taylor Sts; Ⓜ Stadium-Chinatown) Inaugurated by Prime Minister Jean Chrétien in 2002, Chinatown's towering entrance is the landmark most visitors look for. Stand well back, since the decoration is mostly on its lofty upper reaches: an elaborately painted section topped with a terracotta-tiled roof. The characters inscribed on its eastern front implore you to: 'Remember the past and look forward to the future.'

The gate sits on the same site as a previous temporary wooden one that was built here for a royal visit in 1912. The lions on either side of the Millennium Gate once had polished granite balls in their mouths, but they mysteriously disappeared soon after the gate was unveiled and have never been found.

SAM KEE BUILDING NOTABLE BUILDING

Map p273 (8 W Pender St; Ⓜ Stadium-Chinatown) This structure, near the corner of Carrall St, made it into the *Guinness Book of World Records* as the world's narrowest office building. It's easy to miss it because it looks like the front of the larger building behind, to which it is attached. Check out the green glazing in the sidewalk – there used to be a public steam bath under the building.

It's interesting to note that this structure is only here as the result of a dispute. Chang Toy, the Sam Kee Co owner, bought land at this site in 1906, but in 1926 all but a 1.8m-wide strip was expropriated by the city to widen Pender St. Toy's revenge was to build anyway, and up sprang the unusual 'Slender on Pender' dwelling.

DR SUN YAT-SEN CLASSICAL CHINESE GARDEN & PARK GARDENS

Map p273 (www.vancouverchinesegarden.com; 578 Carrall St; adult/child $12/9; ⏲10am-6pm May–mid-Jun, 9:30am-7pm mid-Jun–Aug, 10am-6pm Sep, 10am-4:30pm Oct-Apr; Ⓜ Stadium-Chinatown) A tranquil break from clamorous Chinatown, this intimate 'garden of ease' reflects Taoist principles of balance and harmony. Entry includes a 45-minute guided tour, where you'll learn about the symbolism behind the placement of the gnarled pine trees, winding covered pathways and ancient limestone formations. Look out for the lazy turtles bobbing in the jade-colored water.

The adjacent **Dr Sun Yat-Sen Park** isn't as elaborate as its sister, but this free-entry spot is a pleasant oasis with whispering grasses, a large fish pond and a small pagoda. Check the website for summertime Friday-evening concerts.

CHINATOWN NIGHT MARKET MARKET

Map p273 (www.vancouverchinatownnightmarket.com; Keefer St, btwn Columbia & Main Sts; ⏲6-11pm Fri-Sun mid-May–early Sep; MStadium-Chinatown) Recently reinvented to compete with the success of larger night markets in Richmond, Chinatown's version is well worth a summer evening visit. Cheap and cheerful trinkets feature but the highlight here is the food – it's like a walk-through buffet of fish balls, bubble tea and tornado potatoes. Check ahead: there's an eclectic roster of live entertainment including alfresco movie screenings.

Expect ping-pong tournaments and hip-hop karaoke at the market's Columbia St, where Saturday nights are also reserved for food-truck meet-ups: several of the city's fave trucks roll in for the evening.

JIMI HENDRIX SHRINE NOTABLE BUILDING

Map p273 (207 Union St; ⏲1-6pm Mon-Sat Jun-Sep; 3) FREE Said to occupy the building that formerly housed Vie's Chicken and Steak House – the 1960s restaurant where Hendrix' grandmother cooked and the young guitarist frequently strummed – this spot is worth a quick look. A quirky, homemade attraction, the red-painted shack is lined with old photos and album covers and is staffed by a chatty volunteer or two.

Whether or not this is the real Vie's Chicken building has been hotly contested, but it was certainly around this area. And it's one of the last reminders of a neighborhood called Hogan's Alley that was Vancouver's black district for many years. You're not expected to pray at the shrine, but this is a good spot to indulge in some surreptitious air-guitar.

EATING

After years of offering little more than boring tourist-trap eateries, Gastown's handsome heritage buildings are now stuffed with innovative gourmet hangouts and convivial comfort-food haunts. Many of the area's watering holes are also high on the must-eat-here list. Things are changing rapidly, so keep your eyes peeled for new openings. In Chinatown, Pender and Keefer Sts (between Columbia St and Gore Ave) are your best bets for authentic Chinese dining, including some with contemporary fusion flourishes.

Gastown

★RAINIER PROVISIONS WEST COAST $

Map p272 (www.rainierprovisions.com; 2 W Cordova St; mains $8-12; ⏲11am-8pm Mon-Fri, 9am-8pm Sat & Sun; 4) Revitalizing a former Gastown hotel building, this great-value cafe-bistro is a perfect fuel-up spot. Drop in for Stumptown coffee or dive into a hearty menu ranging from hot sandwich specials served with soup or salad to a heaping roast with all the extras. The sausage and roast potatoes dish is the winner, though – complete with local-made bangers.

There's a deli counter with plenty of BC cheese and charcuterie treats if you want to gather up the makings of a fine picnic; a popular weekend brunch service; and a new streetside patio.

MEAT & BREAD SANDWICHES $

Map p272 (www.meatandbread.ca; 370 Cambie St; mains $7-9; ⏲11am-5pm Mon-Sat; 14) Arrive early to avoid the lunchtime queue at Vancouver's favorite gourmet sandwich shop and you might even snag one of the four tiny window perches. If not, you can hang with the hip locals at the chatty long table, tucking into the daily-changing special, which usually features slices of perfectly roasted local lamb, pork or chicken. The grilled cheese sarnie is ace, too.

Wash it all down with a $6 craft beer, and expect to come back: this place has an almost cult-like following. The daily special is announced on Meat & Bread's Twitter feed, so you'll know what's coming your way.

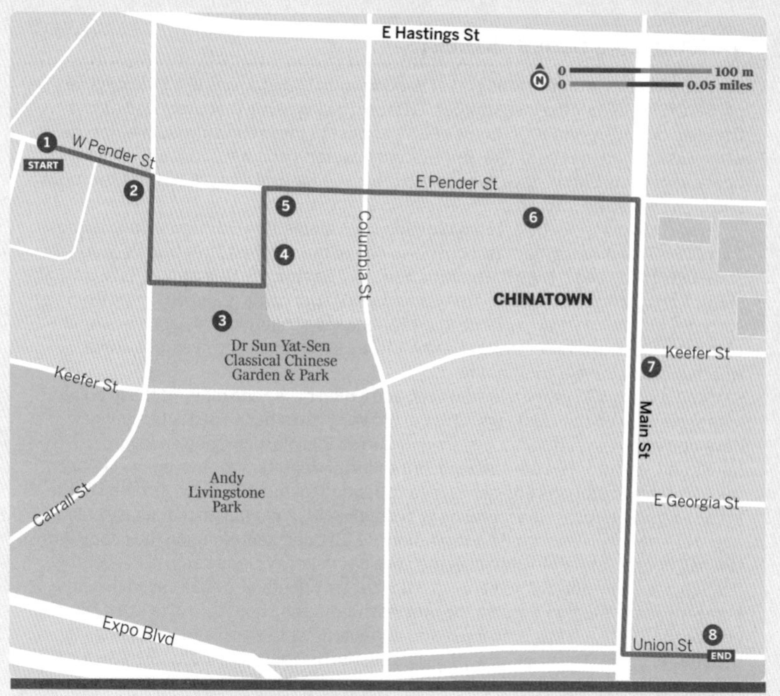

Neighborhood Walk
Chinatown Culture Crawl

START CHINATOWN MILLENNIUM GATE
END JIMI HENDRIX SHRINE
LENGTH 1.5KM; ONE HOUR

Stroll the streets of one of North America's largest Chinatown districts and immerse yourself in culture and heritage. Start near the intersection of W Pender and Taylor Sts, where the giant 1 **Chinatown Millennium Gate** (p83) dominates proceedings. Walk east under the gate and you'll come to the quirky 2 **Sam Kee Building** (p83), reputedly the world's narrowest office block. Peer in the windows and also notice the glass panels in the sidewalk, reminders of a subterranean public steam bath complex that once served area locals.

Turn right onto Carrall St. The entrance to the lovely, landscaped 3 **Dr Sun Yat-Sen Classical Chinese Garden** (p83) will soon be on your left. Inside the garden, check out tranquil pools, intriguing limestone formations and gnarly pine trees on a guided tour. When you exit, walk north towards Pender St noticing the 4 **bronze memorial** on the red tiles that commemorates the contribution of Chinese workers to building Canada's train system, and then the white-paneled 5 **alternative Chinatown gate** that was built for Expo '86.

Turn right onto Pender and stroll east for a couple of blocks. You'll pass rows of antique Chinatown buildings and several dragon-topped street lamps; you're now entering the heart of Chinatown. Time for a snack? Nip into 6 **New Town Bakery** (p88) for a takeout barbecued pork bun. Continue east on Pender, then cross over Main St. Explore the traditional Chinese grocery and apothecary stores that radiate a block or two east of Main, especially on Keefer St. Return to Main and walk south to Union St.

Turn left onto Union to find the 7 **Jimi Hendrix Shrine** (p84), reputedly on the site where Hendrix' grandmother used to work. Her grandson is said to have played in several area bars before he hit the big time.

VANCOUVER'S OLDEST STREET

Just a few weeks after renaming itself Vancouver in 1886 (no one liked the original name 'Granville,' nor the insalubrious 'Gastown' slang name that preceded it), the fledgling city of around 1000 homes burnt almost to the ground in just minutes in what was termed the Great Fire. But the locals weren't about to jump on the next boat out of town. Within days, plans were drawn up for a new city. And this time, brick and stone would be favored over wood.

The first buildings to be erected radiated from Maple Tree Sq, in particular along Carrall St. This thoroughfare (which is also one of the shortest streets in Vancouver) still exists today and it links the historic center of Gastown to Chinatown. Take a stroll south along Carrall from Maple Tree Sq and you'll spot some grand buildings from the early days of the city. Perhaps due to an abundance of caution, they are also some of the sturdiest structures around and will likely survive for many years to come, whether or not there's another fire.

If you'd visited 30 years ago, however, you would have seen many of these buildings seemingly on their last legs. This part of Vancouver hadn't attracted any new development or investment for years and Carrall St's old, paint-peeled taverns, hotels and storefronts were spiraling into skid-row degradation. Two things changed the inevitable: historians and heritage fans banded together to draw attention to the area's important role in the founding years of the city, a campaign that finally culminated in a national historic site designation in 2010; and gentrification took hold. With few neighborhoods left to enhance, the developers finally came back. While gentrification has many detractors here – particularly residents who have called this area home for years and don't want to be pushed out by rising housing costs – an undeniable positive is that it has preserved and protected Gastown's historic buildings for decades to come. The brick and stone landmarks that once lined Carrall have, for the most part, been sympathetically restored and renovated, giving the entire area a new lease on life beyond its heritage designation.

NELSON THE SEAGULL CAFE $

Map p272 (www.nelsontheseagull.com; 315 Carrall St; mains $6-10; ⏲9am-6pm Mon-Sat, 10am-5pm Sun; 🚌14) Gastown's hippest cafe, the mosaic-floored Seagull is also amazingly welcoming. Locals drop in to admire each other's MacBooks over lingering flat-white coffees and indulge in the kind of wholesome treats that might be made by a gourmet grandma. Start the day with poached eggs on house-baked bread, and return for the ploughman's lunch served on a board.

Grab a perch at the long table and you'll soon be in with the locals, or drop by for the Seagull's twice-weekly evening yoga classes – just $25 gets you a stretch and an organic dinner. Check the walls for locally created artworks, and take a peek at the open kitchen at the back: if you're here when the bread's being baked, you'll be in culinary heaven.

SAVE ON MEATS DINER $

Map p272 (www.saveonmeats.ca; 43 W Hastings St; mains $4-14; ⏲7am-10pm Mon-Wed, to midnight Thu-Sat, 8am-10pm Sun; 👪; 🚌14) A former old-school butcher shop, Save On Meats has been transformed into the Downtown Eastside's hipster diner of choice. But it's not just about looking cool. Slide into a booth or take a perch at the long counter and tuck into comfort dishes, including great-value all-day breakfasts and a menu of basic faves such as chicken pot pie, and mac and cheese.

The staff is among the friendliest in the city and there's even a kids menu – 'monkey sandwich' is recommended. Pick up a giant cookie for the road on your way out: it's the only way to wander. And also ask about the innovative feed-the-poor scheme: Save On sells food tokens that you can hand out on the streets instead of giving 'spare change' to people who ask for it.

CARTEMS DONUTERIE DONUTS $

Map p272 (www.cartems.com; 408 Carrall St; donuts $3; ⏲10am-6pm Mon-Fri, 11am-6pm Sat, to 5pm Sun; 🚌14) The irony of buying $3 gourmet donuts in Vancouver's poorest neighborhood doesn't seem to have stopped this tiny corner takeout from thriving. The friendly servers help, of course, but it's the treats that keep people coming back: a raft of fresh-made fusion donuts with irresistible flavors including earl grey, salted caramel and the truly spectacular bourbon bacon.

Check out the building while you're here. The recently restored **Pennsylvania Hotel** is a rare century-old structure with dozens of bay windows. Its restoration included a new heritage-style neon sign, echoing many that once lined this neighborhood. Just around the corner on Hastings St, you'll find an original one: the lovely, seahorse-themed **Only Sea Foods Cafe** sign.

JUDAS GOAT TABERNA — TAPAS $$

Map p272 (www.judasgoat.ca; 27 Blood Alley; plates $4-12; ⏲5pm-midnight Mon-Sat; 🚌4) Named after the goats that are used to lead sheep off slaughterhouse trucks, this tiny backstreet tapas nook has nailed the art of simply prepared small plates such as duck confit, beef brisket meatballs, and beet and goat cheese terrine. Like its Salt Tasting Room (p91) brother next door, it also has a good (although shorter) drinks list of wine and Spanish sherry.

Arrive off-peak to avoid long lineups. If you're intimidated by the choice of plates on offer, ask for a chef's menu selection ($20 to $30) and they'll do all the work for you.

ACME CAFE — DINER $$

Map p272 (www.acmecafe.ca; 51 W Hastings St; mains $9-13; ⏲8am-9pm Mon-Fri, 9am-9pm Sat & Sun; 👪; 🚌14) The black-and-white deco-style interior here is enough to warm up anyone on a rainy day – or maybe it's the comfy booths and retro-cool U-shaped counter. The hipsters have been flocking here since day one for hearty breakfasts and heaping comfort-food lunches flavored with a gourmet flourish: the meatloaf, chicken club and shrimp guacamole sandwiches are worth the trip.

A great spot for weekend brunch (if you can avoid the crowds), it's also perfect for afternoon coffee and a slab of house-baked fruit pie. For those traveling with youngsters, there's a good and healthy kids menu.

NUBA — MIDDLE EASTERN $$

Map p272 (www.nuba.ca; 207 W Hastings St; mains $8-25; ⏲11:30am-10pm Mon-Fri, noon-10pm Sat, 5-10pm Sun; 🌿; 🚌14) Tucked under the landmark Dominion Building, this hopping subterranean Lebanese restaurant attracts budget noshers and cool hipsters in equal measure. If you're not sure what to go for, try the minted pan-seared scallops (dinner only) or consider the $52 Grand Feast for two, which includes tiger prawns and juicy lamb and chicken skewers. There are also plenty of vegetarian options.

There's a real fresh-made feel to the food here and an atmosphere both welcoming and funky – due mainly to the staff who do a good job of keeping things lively. Consider taking a photo of the building on your way out: the copper-topped edifice is among the most iconic old buildings in the city and was once one of the tallest.

DEACON'S CORNER — DINER $$

Map p272 (www.deaconscorner.ca; 101 Main St; mains $6-13; ⏲8am-4pm Mon-Fri, 9am-5pm Sat & Sun; 🚌4) The ideal combination of Gastown development and old-school good value, this lively neighborhood diner lures Vancouverites to a grubby part of town they've previously avoided. They come for the hulking, hangover-busting breakfasts (biscuits with sausage, gravy and eggs is recommended if you want your weekly calorific intake in a single meal), while lunches include good-value grilled sandwiches and heaping fish and chips.

Avoid the peak weekend breakfast period; the place can be packed and finding a seat (even at the counter) can be hard. Weekdays you'll have the pick of the perches. This is the ideal spot to fill your belly and then walk it off with a wander around the neighborhood.

SEA MONSTR SUSHI — JAPANESE $$

Map p272 (www.seamonstrsushi.com; 55 Powell St; mains $7-15; ⏲11:30am-10pm Mon-Fri, 2-10pm Sat; 🚌4) This tiny Powell St spot comes with an almost equally diminutive menu. But despite its hipster popularity and cool exposed-brick room, there's no edge. This place would be right at home in a Tokyo back street. It's seriously committed to fresh, perfectly prepared sushi, and the under-$15 combos are a good deal.

Take a seat at the counter and watch the sushi masters at work. Don't expect bulging-but-boring California rolls: it's all about quality over quantity.

L'ABBATOIR — FRENCH $$$

Map p272 (☎604-568-1701; www.labbatoir.ca; 217 Carrall St; mains $26-45; ⏲5:30pm-midnight; 🚌4) Gastown's most romantic top-end

JAPANTOWN

The Chinese weren't the only group to arrive from Asia in the early days of Vancouver. A couple of blocks east of Chinatown, in an area that's now part of Strathcona, Japantown was once home to many residences, shops and businesses that served the fledgling city's Japanese community. Centered on an area around **Oppenheimer Park**, this intriguing historic district is worth a wander if you're in the vicinity. You'll find some of the city's oldest small wooden homes, many of them time-capsule reminders of a sometimes forgotten period in the city's history.

The best time to visit is in early August, when the park's unmissable weekend-long **Powell Street Festival** (www.powellstreetfestival.com) takes place in celebration of Japanese heritage and culture. One of Vancouver's most popular community festivals, and bound to be a highlight of your trip, this sensory extravaganza includes traditional music, performances and tasty nosh as well as a minimarket of arts and crafts. Arrive early to avoid the crowds at the highly popular food stands. Even more than the event's legendary Spam sushi tradition, the **Omikoshi shrine procession** is a festival standout. It's a camera-luring event that makes everyone stop what they're doing and rush over.

restaurant, this candlelit, brick-lined spot makes an art of attending to every detail. Be careful not to fill up on the warm bread before you tuck into a menu of French-influenced West Coast dishes. We recommend the roast scallops and pork belly. Reservations advised: ask for a table in the window-walled back room.

Whatever you end up eating, save some room for a perfect cocktail. The restaurant also encourages you to bring your own wine (one bottle per table; corkage costs $30).

WILDEBEEST WEST COAST **$$$**

Map p272 (www.wildebeest.ca; 120 W Hastings St; mains $13-42; ⏲5pm-midnight Tue-Sun; 🚌14) This moodlit, bi-level joint is a carnivore's dream dinner destination. In fact, they eat vegetarians here (just kidding; there are choices for you here, too). Find a table among the chattering classes – or better still at the communal long table downstairs – and tuck into short ribs, pork jowl or the juiciest roast chicken you'll ever eat.

Drop by on weekends for a meaty brunch that will fill you up for a week. And don't miss the drinks list: far from being an afterthought, there's an excellent array of well-made cocktails here.

BONETA WEST COAST **$$$**

Map p272 (☎604-684-1844; www.boneta.ca; 12 Water St; mains $15-24; ⏲from 5:30pm; 🚌4) Typifying Gastown's ever-moving transformation, this chichi but comfortable dining room relocated from just around the corner within a few years of opening. The new room is far warmer and the menu of international-influenced West Coast dining remains top-notch. This is the place to come for that delectable duck breast or velvet-soft lamb dish you've been craving.

Expect plenty of seasonal, locally sourced ingredients, and try one of the cocktails: the mixologists here really know their stuff. A good location for a romantic dinner date.

Chinatown

NEW TOWN BAKERY & RESTAURANT CHINESE **$**

Map p273 (www.newtownbakery.ca; 148 E Pender St; dishes $5-9; ⏲6:30am-8:30pm; 🌿; 🚌3) It's the glass cabinets of baked treats that lure most people through the door here. Even if you're just passing, pop in for a bargain-priced prawn turnover or barbecued pork steamed bun to go. If you're looking for more substantial fare, snag a table in the clamorous dining area and dive into a round of well-priced dim sum, including ever-popular shrimp dumplings.

There are several vegetarian steamed bun varieties, and lots of tempting sweet pastries to turn your head.

GAM GOK YUEN CHINESE **$**

Map p273 (142 E Pender St; mains $7-14; ⏲10:30am-8pm; 🚌3) Try to block out the faded 1980s decor in this unassuming Chinatown dining room: the carnivore-pleasing Hong Kong–style food is what keeps this place humming, especially the barbecued pork and duck dishes (the front window of roasted meats probably gives the game away). Order at will, but make sure you include a hearty bowl of noodle soup.

Don't expect any frills here; service can be perfunctory but the dishes are great value. It's cash only.

HOGAN'S ALLEY CAFE BREAKFAST, MEXICAN **$**

Map p273 (www.hogansalleycafe.com; 789 Gore St; mains $8-10; ⏲6:30am-5pm Mon-Fri, 8am-4pm Sat, to 2pm Sun; 🚌3) Part of the hipster reinvention of the Union St stretch between Main and Gore on the edge of Chinatown, this family-run corner nook adds a Mexican twist to its breakfast-cafe approach. As you tuck into your plate of sauce-smothered divorced eggs, you'll overhear plenty of debate about the area's gentrification: those beautifully restored, million-dollar heritage houses across the street were being sold for peanuts just 20 years ago.

This is a good spot for a Chinatown pit stop. Grab a latte and a free copy of *Discorder* magazine from the rack, and tuck into a cheesy chicken empanada as the sun streams through the windows. The viaduct across the street is scheduled to be removed or reinvented in the next few years, with many calling for a New York High Line–style garden. Watch this space.

★BAO BEI ASIAN **$$**

Map p273 (📞604-688-0876; www.bao-bei.ca; 163 Keefer St; small plates $9-18; ⏲5:30pm-midnight Mon-Sat; 🖉; 🚌3) Reinterpreting a Chinatown heritage building interior with funky flourishes, this hidden gem Chinese brasserie is the area's most seductive dinner destination. It enjoys a local cult following, bringing a contemporary edge to tapas-sized Asian dishes such as *shao bing* (stuffed Chinese flatbread), octopus salad and crispy pork belly. There's also a tasty commitment to inventive cocktails, so don't despair if you have to wait at the bar for your table.

Top-notch organic meat and sustainable seafood are used throughout, and the vegetarian options are never an afterthought. Reservations are not accepted so try to avoid peak 7pm to 9pm dining times. If you're looking to impress Vancouverites with your local knowledge, tell them you've been here.

CAMPAGNOLO ITALIAN **$$**

Map p273 (www.campagnolorestaurant.ca; 1020 Main St; mains $12-25; ⏲11:30am-2:30pm & 5-10pm; 🚌3) Eyebrows were raised when this contemporary Italian restaurant opened in a hitherto sketchy part of town. But intimate, minimalist Campagnolo has lured locals. And they've been rewarded with some of the city's best Italian cuisine: share some dishes and don't miss the truffle sausage rigatoni or the citrusy local octopus salad.

Save some room for a caramelized chocolate tart dessert, perhaps accompanied by a hit or two from the extensive grappa selection. There's a commitment to local produce here – Campagnolo cures its own meat. There are also regular wine-and-dine tasting dinners: check the website to see what's coming up.

PHNOM PENH VIETNAMESE, CAMBODIAN **$$**

Map p273 (244 E Georgia St; mains $8-18; ⏲10am-9pm Mon, to 10pm Tue-Sun; 🚌3) The dishes at this bustling joint are split between Cambodian and Vietnamese soul-food classics. It's the highly addictive chicken wings and their lovely pepper sauce that keep regulars loyal. Once you've piled up the bones, dive back in for round two: papaya salad, butter beef and spring rolls show just how good a street-food-inspired Asian menu can be.

Don't leave without sampling a steamed rice cake, stuffed with pork, shrimp, coconut and scallions, and washed down with an ice-cold bottle of Tsingtao. This is the kind of place that makes Vancouver Canada's most authentic ethnic-food city.

DRINKING & NIGHTLIFE

Home to many of the best bars in the city, Gastown's atmospheric old brick buildings have been revitalized with some distinctive watering holes in recent years, making this an ideal spot for an easy pub crawl. And don't forget about Chinatown, which also has a choice bar or two of its own.

Gastown

★ALIBI ROOM PUB

Map p272 (www.alibi.ca; 157 Alexander St; ⏲5-11:30pm Mon-Thu, to 12:30am Fri, 10am-12:30am

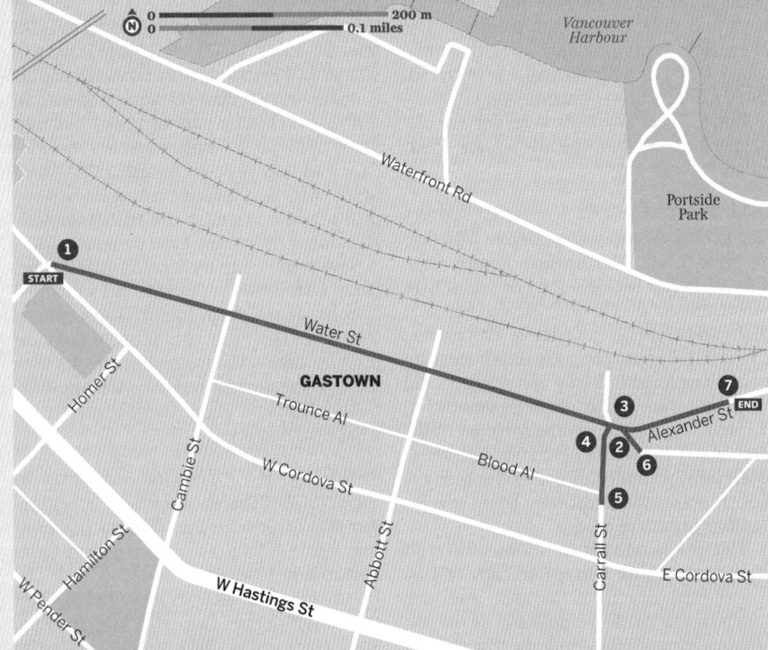

Neighborhood Walk
Gastown Barhop

START STEAMWORKS BREWING COMPANY
END ALIBI ROOM
LENGTH 1KM (TIME DEPENDS ON HOW FAST YOU DRINK...)

This short walk will take you on a merry weave around Gastown's best watering holes and give you a glimpse into the city's nightlife scene.

Start your crawl at the western end of Gastown (near the Waterfront SkyTrain station) with a Lions Gate Lager at **1 Steamworks Brewing Company** (p92), one of the city's only brewpubs. Enjoy the downhill slope east along Water St and you'll soon arrive at Maple Tree Sq. This is where 'Gassy' Jack triggered the city by building his first saloon – tip your hat at the **2 statue** (p82) of him here, then duck underground to **3 Guilt & Co** for a bottled beer and a board game. Back outside, nip across the square to **4 Six Acres**, one of the area's coziest hangouts. You'll be tempted to stick around, but the spirit of Gassy will be calling you back to the streets.

Stroll across Carrall St and duck into the **5 Irish Heather**. The best spot in town for a Guinness, it also has a hidden whiskey bar out back where you can indulge your love of some of the top spirits from Ireland, Scotland and beyond. If you're still walking by this stage, head back onto Carrall, walk north for a few seconds and turn right onto Powell St. The street sign will point you to the unassuming stairwell that leads to the lovely **6 Diamond**, a great spot to find Vancouver's best cocktails. You'll likely still be able to spot Gassy's statue through the window, smiling at you across the square. If he's also talking, you've probably had too much to drink.

But if not, head back out and take Alexander St eastwards. Within a couple of minutes you'll be at the **7 Alibi Room** (p89). This is the city's favorite craft-beer bar and the best place in Vancouver to end your evening with a beery flourish.

Sat, to 11:30pm Sun; 🚌4) Vancouver's best craft-beer tavern, Alibi has an exposed brick bar that stocks an ever-changing roster of around 50 drafts from celebrated BC breweries such as Phillips, Driftwood and Crannog. Adventurous taste-trippers – hipsters and veteran, red-nosed beer fans alike – enjoy the $9.50 'frat bat' of four sample tipples: choose your own or ask to be surprised. Be sure to check the board for guest casks.

Foodwise, go for a side order of skinny fries with chili garlic vinegar or the hearty barbecued pork-belly sandwich. There's a slender patio for alfresco summer quaffing, and the cave-like downstairs area is ideal for rainy-day hunkering and lingering taste-testing. The Alibi's communal tables are especially packed during Vancouver Craft Beer Week (www.vancouvercraftbeerweek.com) in May/June. Also ask about Brassneck, Alibi's new brewery on Main St.

DIAMOND — COCKTAIL BAR

Map p272 (www.di6mond.com; 6 Powell St; ⏲5:30pm-1am Wed & Thu, to 2am Fri & Sat, to midnight Sun; 🚌4) Head upstairs via the unassuming entrance and you'll find yourself in one of Vancouver's warmest little cocktail bars. A renovated heritage room studded with sash windows – try for a view seat – it's popular with local coolsters but is rarely pretentious. A list of perfectly nailed cocktails (from $9 to $14) helps, coupled with a tasty tapas menu.

Go for the Save On Meats sausage plate, coupled with some irresistible yucca fries. And expect to fight over the last bite. Check out the lovely crystal chandeliers here, too – antiques from a bygone age.

GUILT & CO — BAR

Map p272 (www.guiltandcompany.com; 1 Alexander St; ⏲7pm-1am Sun-Thu, to 2am Fri & Sat; Ⓜ Waterfront) This cave-like subterranean bar, tucked under Gastown's brick-cobbled sidewalks, has a cult following among the kind of under-30s crowd that love sipping Anchor Steam and playing Jenga at their tables (one of the many games available for imbibers to play). Avoid weekends when there are often lineups and the place is crammed – drop by on a chilled-out weekday instead.

Along with the beer, there's an array of inventive cocktails to keep things lively. Check ahead for live music of the singer-songwriter variety, too.

SIX ACRES — BAR

Map p272 (www.sixacres.ca; 203 Carrall St; 5pm-1am Mon-Sat; 🚌4) At Gastown's coziest tavern you can cover all the necessary food groups via the extensive, mostly bottled, beer menu. There's a small, animated summer patio out front but inside is great for hiding in a chatty, candlelit corner and working your way through the brews – plus a shared small plate or three (sausage platter recommended).

Along with trying one of the dozens of bottled ales, it seems right and proper to also have a whiskey here: that's 'Gassy' Jack's statue outside, perched atop a barrel, and he started the city with his first bar just a few steps from where you are now. If you frequent the upstairs bathrooms during your visit, be prepared for an unexpected audio soundtrack, which can range from 1930s Dixieland jazz to German-language recordings.

SALT TASTING ROOM — WINE BAR

Map p272 (☎604-633-1912; www.salttastingroom.com; 45 Blood Alley; ⏲noon-midnight; 🚌4) Tucked along a cobbled back alley reputedly named after the area's former butcher trade, this atmospheric little brick-lined wine bar offers dozens of interesting tipples, mostly available by the glass. From your communal table perch, peruse the giant blackboard of house-cured meats and regional cheeses, then go for a $16 tasting plate of three, served with piquant condiments including Brit-style piccalilli.

You can also extend the tasting approach to your wine: a three-glass flight is $15. And if you're a real grape aficionado, ask about the wine-tasting dinners staged regularly in the bottle-lined cellar: you'll think you're at a special event in an old-school European winery.

IRISH HEATHER — PUB

Map p272 (www.irishheather.com; 210 Carrall St; ⏲11:30am-midnight Mon-Thu & Sun, to 2am Fri & Sat; 🚌4) Belying the clichés about expat Irish bars (except for its reclaimed Guinness barrel floor), the Heather is one of Vancouver's best gastropubs. Alongside lovingly prepared sausage and mash, and steak and ale pie, you'll find top craft beers and some well-poured Guinness. Best time to come? The Sunday to Wednesday Long Table nights, which run for most of the year but usually take a break in summer. Dinner and a pint is around $18.

Whiskey fans will also be gobsmacked by the array of tipples in the back room **Shebeen** bar. It's the kind of place where you could hunker for hours and still be there a week later, as merry as a giddy kipper.

BITTER TASTING ROOM — BAR

Map p272 (www.bittertastingroom.com; 16 W Hastings St; 5pm-midnight; 14) Described by its owner as a taproom with not many taps (there are eight), this small, brick-walled bar has an impressive beer selection, mostly of the bottled variety. The drafts are usually excellent BC beers from the likes of Crannog or Howe Sound Brewing, while bottles roam from Belgium to California and beyond. Foodwise, it's gourmet pub snacks such as pretzels and Scotch eggs.

If you fancy trying a few brews, ask the server about the weekly changing tasting-flight offer. And take time to check out the grainy large-format black-and-white photos of the area on the walls: they recall a time when this was the center of the city, bustling with shops and businesses, and hatted locals.

BLACK FROG — PUB

Map p272 (www.theblackfrog.ca; 108 Cambie St; 11:30am-1am Mon-Thu, to 2am Fri, noon-2am Sat, to midnight Sun; M Waterfront) A few steps from the Steam Clock in a side-street blind spot, this bar – run by owners from Edmonton, Alberta – does everything right, from friendly staff to no-nonsense pub grub. In summer, aim to bask on the deck (it's covered against rain) with an array of Big Rock beers from across the border in Alberta. Foodwise, swap the burger route for the hearty ploughman's lunch.

Black Frog is a great place to catch a live ice hockey game on TV; you'll soon realize why the sport is often regarded as Canada's religion. In fact, this may be the only time you'll see locals openly weeping and plotting riots against the injustice of it all.

STEAMWORKS BREWING COMPANY — BREWERY

Map p272 (www.steamworks.com; 375 Water St; 11:30am-midnight Sun-Thu, to 1am Fri & Sat; M Waterfront) The signature beer at this huge brewpub on the edge of Gastown is Lions Gate Lager. It's a refreshing summer tipple, but the Empress IPA is even better. Popular with tourists and clocked-off office workers, Steamworks has an enticing pub-grub menu. The monthly Green Drinks night (www.greendrinks.org/bc/vancouver) is where chatty enviro-types flirt with each other.

Ask about special seasonal brews (the summer wheat beers and hardy winter ales are best). There are outdoor tables for summer drinkers, but the best views across the water are from inside on the main floor, where several tables face the mountain-framed Burrard Inlet. There's also a liquor store here if you fancy a takeout: Steamworks recently started bottling its beers for the first time.

GASTOWN TEA COMPANY — TEAHOUSE

Map p272 (www.gastowntea.com; 1 Gaolers Mews; noon-6pm Mon-Fri, 11am-6pm Sat & Sun; 4) Tucked down a back alley in a building that once housed a police-horse stable block, this large, lounge-like tearoom is an oasis from busy Gastown. Grab a seat in the windowed conservatory or nip upstairs to the second level. Indulge with afternoon tea (a bargain at just $12 for tea and scones) or choose from a menu of dozens of leafy varieties.

If you've been on your feet all day, go for the 'pure yerba mate tea,' a strong pick-me-up from South America – coupled with a cookie, of course.

CAMBIE — PUB

Map p272 (www.thecambie.com/pub; 300 Cambie St; 11am-1pm Sun-Thu, to 2am Fri & Sat; 14) While Gastown is increasingly gentrifying, it still has a few dive bars. The best of the bunch is sticky-tabled Cambie. It's a local legend that most Vancouverites fondly recall visiting at least once. Summer nights on the raucous patio are grungy fun, but perching at a bench inside with a cheap drink special is a good way to have a blast without busting your budget.

The Cambie has one of the best priced pub-grub menus in town, with burgers, fish and chips and the like all under $10 a pop.

CHILL WINSTON — BAR

Map p272 (www.chillwinston.ca; 3 Alexander St; 11am-1am; 4) Gastown's best summertime patio is the highlight of this large, brick-lined bar-restaurant. Snag a spot under a parasol and you're unlikely to move much for the rest of the day. Drinkswise, you'll find flirty cocktails plus a good boutique selection of beers from Quebec, Belgium, the UK and beyond. There's also a large menu of tapas plates and larger mains if it's time to fuel up.

EASTSIDE'S BEST FEST

Some locals claim that Vancouver doesn't have much of an arts scene. But if you're visiting in November and you know where to look, you'll have possibly the artiest weekend of your life. During the annual **Eastside Culture Crawl** (www.eastsideculture crawl.com), more than 300 local artists open their studios, houses and workshops for free to art-hugging visitors who wander from site to site, meeting the creators, hanging with artsy chums and even buying the occasional well-priced gem. Festival locations stretch from Main St to Commercial Dr, centering on the Strathcona area just east of Chinatown, and visitors spend their time walking the streets looking for the next spot, which is typically just around the corner.

You'll find full-time artists working on commissioned installations as well as artisans noodling away in their spare bedrooms. There's an almost party-like atmosphere to the streets during the weekend, especially if the rain holds off. Look out for the occasional street performer keeping things lively and incorporate a coffee-shop pit stop or two along the way. The event is a great opportunity to buy one-of-a-kind artwork souvenirs for that difficult person back home (you know the one).

Head to the website to plan your route, although we recommend just to wander and see what you find. Printed programs with maps are also available at most of the galleries involved in the event.

Chinatown

★BRICKHOUSE — PUB

Map p273 (730 Main St; 8pm-2am Mon-Fri, 7:30pm-2am Sat, 8pm-midnight Sun; 3) Possibly Vancouver's most original pub, this old-school hidden gem is a welcoming, windowless tavern lined with Christmas lights, fish tanks and junk-shop couches. It's like hanging out in someone's den, and is popular with artsy locals and in-the-know young hipsters. Grab a Storm Scottish Ale at the bar, slide onto a chair and start chatting: you're bound to meet someone interesting.

There's no food here (except chips) and the hours are eclectic – plus, the sign on the front door sometimes points you to the back-alley entrance. But the beloved Brickhouse is arguably the city's strongest claim to having its own Brit-style pub culture. Bicyle-shorts-wearing owner and barman Leo is committed to the idea that bars should be places where you hang out, socialize and connect. And play pool: there's a full-sized table here as well.

KEEFER BAR — COCKTAIL BAR

Map p273 (www.thekeeferbar.com; 135 Keefer St; 5pm-midnight Mon, to 1am Tue-Thu & Sun, to 2am Fri & Sat; M Stadium-Chinatown) A dark, narrow and atmospheric Chinatown bar that's been claimed by local cocktail-loving coolsters from day one. Drop in for a full evening of liquid taste-tripping and you'll have a blast. From perfectly prepared rosemary gimlets and Siamese slippers to an excellent whiskey menu and tasty tapas (go for the late-night Keefer dog), it offers up a great night out.

There are also cool extras here most nights, including Sunday's reggae turntable tunes and Thursday's happening burlesque shows ($10 cover charge). In summer, grab a perch on one of the wooden block stools outside and watch the Chinatown world go by. Couple the Keefer with dinner at the nearby Bao Bei (p89) and you'll have had the perfect Chinatown evening.

VANCOUVER URBAN WINERY — WINE BAR

(www.vancouverurbanwinery.com; 55 Dunlevy Ave; 11am-6pm Mon-Wed, to 11pm Thu & Fri, noon-5pm Sun; 4) Vancouver's only winery is actually a barrel-lined warehousing business storing tipples from BC and beyond. It has a large public tasting bar that's one of the city's hidden gems. Roll up for an afternoon tasting during the week (a five-glass tasting flight costs $12) or, better still, drop by on Friday night when the place is a hopping nightlife spot for those in the know.

Cheese and charcuterie are available if you're peckish (a combined wine and food pairing is $24). There's also a little on-site shop of wine trinkets and bottles.

UNION — BAR

Map p273 (www.theunionvancouver.ca; 219 Union St; 5pm-1am Mon-Thu, to 2am Fri & Sat, to midnight Sun; 3) If you can't find any hipsters on Chinatown's streets at night, that's because they're all at this contemporary Union St resto-bar just up from the Jimi Hendrix Shrine. The Union is ever-friendly, and it's a great spot to chill out at a communal bench. Excellent cocktails and Asian-influenced food at reasonable prices keep things lively.

It's often jam-packed on weekends; arrive early or come during the week to snag a seat.

PAT'S PUB — LIVE MUSIC

Map p273 (www.patspub.ca; 403 E Hastings St; 11am-midnight Sun-Thu, to 1am Fri & Sat; 14) Saved from gentrification annihilation by its grungy location, Pat's Pub started a century ago and has recently dusted off the jazz chops that saw Jelly Roll Morton play here back in the day. Saturday afternoon sees no-cover jazz shows from 3pm, while there are open mikes and other events throughout the month. The good-value beer menu includes house-brewed Pat's Classic Lager.

The food is a cut above typical pub fare – pulled pork sandwiches and yam fries, for example – and almost everything on the menu is under $10. Spot the beer tanks through the glass panel. Feel free to blow them a kiss.

FORTUNE SOUND CLUB — DANCE

Map p273 (www.fortunesoundclub.com; 147 E Pender St; Wed-Sat; 3) The city's best club has transformed a tired Chinatown spot into a slick space with the kind of genuine staff and younger, hipster-cool crowd rarely seen in Vancouver venues. Slide inside and you'll find a giant dance floor popping with party-loving locals just out for a good time. Expect weekend queues, and check out Happy Ending Fridays, when you'll possibly dance your ass off.

Reputedly home to one of the city's best sound systems, Fortune also hosts a roster of regular bands.

ELECTRIC OWL — BAR, DANCE

Map p273 (www.electricowl.ca; 926 Main St; from 7pm; 3) A nightlife social club for neighborhood cool kids, this brick-lined bar-resto-club combo always has something going on. The roster of happenings ranges from regular live acts to Tuesday-night eclectic karaoke. If you need to get your ping-pong on, head downstairs for Monday's table-tennis showdown. When you need to fill up, you'll find Asian-inspired tapas (go for the naughty *poutine* with teriyaki gravy).

Ask about the local beers on offer: there's usually something crafty and original available alongside the more generic factory stuff.

☆ ENTERTAINMENT

Gastown is more about the bars but Chinatown is home to some decent entertainment options, including a couple of local-fave live venues. Converse with a few Vancouverites and ask for recommendations about what's coming up and who's about to hit the stage.

RICKSHAW THEATRE — LIVE MUSIC

Map p273 (www.liveatrickshaw.com; 254 E Hastings St; 14) Revamped from its grungy 1970s incarnation, the funky Rickshaw shows that Eastside gentrification can be positive. The stage of choice for many punk and indie acts, it's an excellent place to see a band. There's a huge mosh area near the stage and rows of theater-style seats at the back.

PINBALL WIZARD

One of the neighborhood's greasiest dive bars for decades, **Pub 340** (Map p272; www.pub340.ca; 340 Cambie St, Gastown; 14) has cleaned up its act somewhat in recent years. But it's not the cosmetic paint job, revamped menu and new open-mike nights that have lured back many locals. It's the addition of arguably the city's best pinball room. A dozen or so shiny machines – from 1980s classics to new favorites – attract flipping fanatics. Regular tournaments welcome all-comers to show off their skills on machines including White Water, Terminator 2 and the Addams Family. Games cost $1, and if you lose everything you can cheer yourself up with a karaoke warble of that slightly well-worn Who song in the main bar area.

SHOE FRENZY

If you're in Vancouver sometime in early April you may find you start to get itchy feet. But rather than a sudden desire to hit the road and start traveling, your tingling toes will be telling you the city's biggest sartorial event for feet is about to take place. When the **Army & Navy** (Map p272; www.armyandnavy.ca; 36 W Cordova St, Gastown; 8) department store's annual 12-day shoe sale kicks off, there's always a long, excited queue of hundreds of locals ready to get in. Those who've waited in line for hours have the chance to hit – usually at maximum velocity – the shiny pyramids of deeply discounted designer footwear from the likes of Guess, Christian Dior and Jimmy Choo. Delighted shoppers stagger around with armfuls of must-have shoes, while on-lookers hang in corners, wondering how they can escape.

Check the schedule to see who's on: many nights there are several bands on the roster.

FIREHALL ARTS CENTRE THEATER

Map p273 (www.firehallartscentre.ca; 280 E Cordova St; 4) One of the leading players in Vancouver's independent theater scene, this intimate, studio-sized venue is located inside a historic former fire station. It presents culturally diverse contemporary drama and dance, with an emphasis on emerging talent. A key venue during the annual Dancing on the Edge festival (www.dancingontheedge.org), it also has a convivial licensed lounge on-site, where visiting drama fans can discuss the scene.

Check out the artworks lining the brick walls before you go in for your show: there's typically a focus on great local artists.

COBALT LIVE MUSIC, DANCE

Map p273 (www.thecobalt.ca; 917 Main St; 9pm-2am; 3) A favorite underground dive venue, the dark and shady Cobalt has transformed from being a grungy live venue to being a grungy live venue that's also a big part of the local gay scene. Alongside bands, you'll find an ever-changing menu of drag shows and raucous dance nights.

Tuesdays are great for drinks specials and free pinball; Cobalt stages regular pinball tournaments against local rivals Pub 340 (p94).

CINEPLEX ODEAN INTERNATIONAL VILLAGE CINEMA

Map p273 (www.cineplex.com; 88 W Pender St; Stadium-Chinatown) Incongruously located on the 3rd floor of a usually half-empty Chinatown shopping mall, this popular Vancouver theater combines blockbuster and art-house offerings and is often used for film festivals. Comfy stadium seating is the norm here, and it's ideal for sheltering on a rainy Vancouver day with a bottomless cup of coffee.

SHOPPING

Once lined with tacky souvenir stores, Gastown has been increasingly colonized by designer boutiques, making this area a downtown rival to Main St in the indie shopping stakes. While Chinatown's multisensory, ever-colorful streets used to be more for looking at than actually shopping – how many live frogs do you usually buy? – more and more it's home to its own cool indie stores, as well as the evocative night market, which is a summer highlight.

★ERIN TEMPLETON ACCESSORIES

Map p273 (www.erintempleton.com; 511 Carrall St; 11am-6pm Tue-Sat; Stadium-Chinatown) Known for recycling leather into hip, super-supple bags, belts, hats and purses, this eponymous store has a cult following. Erin herself is usually on hand and happy to chat about her creations (she trained in shoemaking at a London college). They're the kind of must-have, one-of-a-kind items that are hard to resist, no matter how many bags you already have back home.

The idea here is to marry form and functionality: locals rave about how long their purses last, and if anything does break, they're often fixed for free by Erin herself. Check the website for the full range and all her most recent designs.

JOHN FLUEVOG SHOES SHOES

Map p272 (www.fluevog.com; 65 Water St; 10am-7pm Mon-Wed, to 8pm Thu & Fri, to 7pm Sat, noon-6pm Sun; Waterfront) Like an art gallery for shoes, this alluringly cavernous store showcases the famed footwear of local designer Fluevog, whose men's and women's boots and brogues are what Doc Martens would have become if they'd stayed interesting and cutting-edge. Pick up that pair of thigh-hugging dominatrix boots you've always wanted or settle on some designer loafers that would make anyone walk tall.

Seasonal sales can be amazing and your new look will have everyone staring at your feet. Celebs such as Madonna have reputedly bought Fluevogs in the past.

ORLING & WU — HOMEWARES, ACCESSORIES

Map p272 (www.orlingandwu.com; 28 Water St; ⏲10am-6pm Mon-Wed, to 7pm Thu-Sat, 11am-6pm Sun; Ⓜ Waterfront) With an irresistible array of chichi trinkets presented in a gallery-like space, it's hard to browse here without falling for something. From Kusmi teas and handmade soaps to rubber stamp sets and wall clocks that will finally make you the coolest person in town; your credit card will be constantly under pressure here. Plus there's superbly friendly service.

Alternatively, just make a list of everything you want and circulate it to your friends and family before Christmas: if they really love you, they'll buy you that Russian-style glassware tea set. And if they don't, it's time cull your Christmas card list.

DELUXE JUNK — VINTAGE

Map p272 (www.deluxejunk.com; 310 W Cordova St; ⏲10am-6pm Mon-Thu, to 7pm Fri, 11am-7pm Sat, noon-5pm Sun; 🚌14) A treasure trove of antique glories, from flapper dresses to sparkly evening shoes, and even the occasional old-school wedding outfit, this is one of Vancouver's best vintage stores. Mostly serving discerning females, it also has essential outfits for passing blokes, from cummerbunds to Hawaiian shirts. Check out the vintage cigarette holders – perfect for that 1940s dinner party you're time-traveling back to.

Even if you don't plan to buy a full outfit, this is a great spot to accessorize with a crystal-beaded handbag or a must-have vintage wig that reminds you of a '70s Abba gig. The staff is great here, too: ask for tips and they'll point out some real finds dotted around the store.

SOLDER & SONS — BOOKS

Map p272 (247 Main St; ⏲10am-5pm Mon-Fri, noon-4pm Sat; 🚌3) Vancouver's smallest bookstore, this charming little nook has a cult following among locals. They drop in to peruse the shelves of used tomes (history, biography and contemporary fiction have the best selections), while indulging in an excellent cup of herbal tea or locally roasted coffee made by the store's friendly owner (he also makes great sandwiches). Sit in the window for the full effect.

There's often an artwork or two from a local on the walls and it's a comfortable spot to hang out in if it's raining heavily outside (have another java while waiting).

BLIM — ARTS & CRAFTS

Map p273 (www.blim.ca; 115 E Pender St; ⏲11am-9pm Mon-Thu, to 6pm Fri & Sat, noon-5pm Sun; 🚌14) This popular arts and crafts resource center is ideal if you need to scratch a creative itch. You'll find supplies and the space to make a design of your own – from buttons to knitted scarves – or you can just pick up something someone else has already labored over and tell people back home you made it yourself. Check ahead for workshops that include screen printing and soap making.

Blim also stages regular **craft markets** throughout the year at sites around the city, which are a great way to meet local artisans and pick up unique souvenirs. Check the website for event announcements, and also ask about other craft fairs around the city: these guys will point you in the right direction.

LYNN STEVEN BOUTIQUE — CLOTHING

Map p272 (www.lynnsteven.com; 225 Carrall St; ⏲11am-6pm Mon-Sat, noon-5pm Sun; 🚌4) An austere-looking white interior enlivened by a tower of paperbacks fashioned into a changing room, this excellent women's boutique is popular with an under-30s hip set looking for classic casual togs that stand the test of time. Tops and jeans from designers in Toronto, New York and LA dominate, but expect to also be tempted by the vegan bags from Montréal. Superfriendly service.

Look out for end-of-season sales where dramatic savings can make that new outfit seem like the bargain of the year.

BLOCK — CLOTHING

Map p272 (www.theblock.ca; 350 W Cordova St; ⏲11am-6pm Mon-Thu & Sat, to 7pm Fri, noon-5pm Sun; 🚌4) Colonizing this Gastown strip long before it was fashionable, this browse-worthy men's and women's boutique still offers plenty of reasons for a visit. Check out the ever-changing array of clothes and shoes by designers such as Nudie and Bloch London, and save time to peruse the ultracool jewelry, much of it crafted by local artisans.

Block also stocks an array of high-art footwear that triggers shoe fetishism in even the most conservative of shoppers.

HILL'S NATIVE ART — ARTS & CRAFTS

Map p272 (www.hills.ca; 165 Water St; ⏲9am-9pm; Ⓜ Waterfront) Launched in 1946 as a small trading post on Vancouver Island, Hill's flagship store has many First Nations carvings, prints, ceremonial masks and cozy Cowichan sweaters, plus traditional music and books of historical interest. Artists are often found at work in the 3rd-floor gallery. This is a great spot to pick up some authentic aboriginal artworks for savoring at home.

There are many souvenir stores on Water St with First Nations goods but this is the one if you want to find something special.

PEKING LOUNGE — HOMEWARES

Map p273 (www.pekinglounge.com; 83 E Pender St; ⏲11am-6pm Mon-Sat, to 5pm Sun; 🚌14) Presented like artworks in a cool, lounge-like contemporary setting, the Chinese repro antiques at this alluring modern boutique are difficult to resist. But if you don't have the luggage space for a floor-to-ceiling chest or flare-topped armoire, peruse the highly ornamental accessories instead: that decorative opium pipe would look great on your bookcase back home.

Check out the lovely silk and linen cushions at the back of the store as well. Now is the time to call your airline for a luggage restriction upgrade.

CANNABIS CULTURE HEADQUARTERS — ACCESSORIES

Map p272 (www.cannabisculture.com; 307 W Hastings St; ⏲10am-8pm Mon-Thu, to 10pm Fri & Sat, noon-8pm Sun; 🚌14) For arguments in support of legalization, duck into the friendly shop and offices of the BC Marijuana Party, in a small pocket of the city sometimes called 'Vansterdam.' With books, hemp clothing and associated paraphernalia, the store also houses a back room where (for $5) you can use the vaporizers to chill out with some new like-minded buddies.

If you like what you find, nip next door to the **New Amsterdam Cafe**, another popular herbal smoking room. You'll likely sometimes smell the aroma of 'naughty cigarettes' on streets around the city: it's still illegal here, but the police don't generally bother with small-scale home users.

TEN LEE HONG ENTERPRISES — FOOD, DRINK

Map p273 (500 Main St; ⏲11am-6pm Mon-Sat, noon-5pm Sun; 🚌3) This authentic Chinese tea and herb shop is a great place to buy supplies of good green, red, white and black teas. The friendly staff – women in cool pink pantsuits – are used to dealing with curious Westerners: they'll instruct you in the art of how to brew and may also serve you samples so you can find your favorite tipple.

It's one of several authentic tea and ginger shops in the area, so consider a giddy crawl to compare samples.

EASTERN GIFTS — TOYS

Map p273 (156 E Pender St; ⏲11am-6pm Mon-Sat, noon-5pm Sun; Ⓜ Stadium-Chinatown) This slender hole-in-the-wall is easy to miss, but if you can't live without buying that essential cellophane-wrapped anime-character soft toy or foot-high overly-detailed Gundam Wing figure, this is the shop for you. Don't expect friendly chitchat from the staff, who will mostly be eyeing you (and your backpack) in case you streak off down the street with a giant egg-shaped furry figure.

Not really a traditional toy shop, this is a good place to pick up a cool collectible for the kind of kid back home that likes to keep their possessions in the original store packaging.

CANADIAN MAPLE DELIGHTS — SOUVENIRS

Map p272 (www.mapledelights.com; 385 Water St; ⏲8am-7pm Mon-Fri, 10am-7pm Sat & Sun; Ⓜ Waterfront) It might seem like a chore but if you have to pick up souvenirs for all those greedy friends back home, this is an ideal one-stop shop. Canadian Maple Delights specializes in all manner of maple-syrup-flavored goodies (think maple sugar, maple tea, maple-leaf-shaped candy, maple-tree-growing kits etc). It also stocks vacuum-packed salmon for those who don't have a sweet tooth.

You'll find several additional large souvenir stores nearby if you want to get your list covered off in a single afternoon. Just don't buy the moose-dropping chocolate candies: they're not funny and they're not clever. Go for a T-shirt that makes jokes about beavers instead; that's much more sophisticated.

Yaletown & Granville Island

YALETOWN | GRANVILLE ISLAND

Neighborhood Top Five

❶ Wandering the deli stands at **Granville Island Public Market** (p100), gathering some goodies and then heading outside into the sun to catch a busker and watch the boats slide by.

❷ Weaving around the Granville Island artisan studios and picking up a pottery souvenir at the **Gallery of BC Ceramics** (p114).

❸ Dining with Yaletown's professional socialites at **Blue Water Café + Raw Bar** (p106).

❹ Catching a show with the locals at the **Granville Island Stage** (p112).

❺ Taking a beer-making tour and tasting at **Granville Island Brewing** (p103).

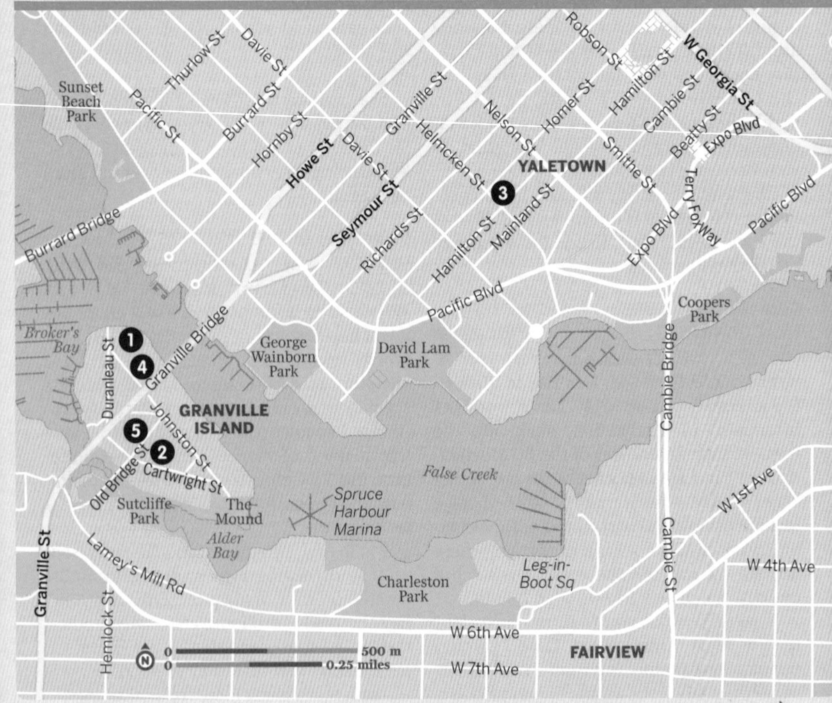

For more detail of this area see Map p274 and p275

Explore Yaletown & Granville Island

Yaletown and Granville Island lie on opposite banks of False Creek but it's easy to see both on the same day. Save most of your time for Granville Island with its unique shops and public market. Be sure to stroll the entire island, not just the market end. Poking around the back alleys, you'll find cool artisan studios, and you'll also escape the crowds that jam the market area in summer. Johnston St, Cartwright St and Railspur Alley are particularly worth exploring. The pedestrian and traffic entrance to Granville Island is under the south end of Granville Bridge. Here, Anderson St takes you right onto the island, just a few steps from the 'mainland'.

Yaletown is a miniferry ride away. Compact and easy to explore, it radiates a block or two either side of Hamilton St. There is some worthwhile shopping, and the city's renovated warehouse district is stuffed with dining options, a few of them among Vancouver's finest. Book ahead at fancier Yaletown joints and you'll nosh with some of Vancouver's VIPs.

Local Life

- **Produce** The Public Market (p100) is always stuffed with fruit and veg but the summertime farmers market – from June to October – is even better for fresh-picked local treats such as blueberries, peaches and cherries.
- **Beer** Most Granville Island Brewing (p103) beverages are now produced off-site, but locals know that the small-batch beers still made on the island are superior. Hit the brewery's liquor store and pick up a couple.
- **Theater** Granville Island is the heart of Vancouver's theater scene and hosts several theaters and festivals. Locals save money on main stage shows by checking the daily half-price deals at www.ticketstonight.ca.

Getting There & Away

- **Bus** The number 50 runs from downtown and stops near the entrance to Granville Island. Bus 10 stops on the south side of Granville Bridge – meaning a five-minute stroll under the bridge to reach the island.
- **Train** The Canada Line runs from downtown to Yaletown-Roundhouse Station, a short walk to all Yaletown's main attractions.
- **Car** There is metered parking in Yaletown. Free parking (up to three hours) is available on Granville Island but is severely limited at peak times.
- **Miniferries** Granville Island is accessible by miniferry from the West End and Yaletown side of False Creek.

Lonely Planet's Top Tip

Yaletown takes part in the city's annual **Dine Out Vancouver** (www.tourismvancouver.com) event, when local restaurants offer deals for midwinter dinners, and also hosts its own Taste of Yaletown for 10 days mid-October, when restaurants offer three-course menus for $25, $35 or $45. Check out www.yaletowninfo.com.

Best Places to Eat

- Flying Pig (p103)
- Edible Canada at the Market (p107)
- Blue Water Café + Raw Bar (p106)
- Rodney's Oyster House (p105)
- Go Fish (p106)

For reviews, see p103

Best Places to Drink

- Raw Canvas (p108)
- Granville Island Brewing Taproom (p110)
- Artisan Sake Maker (p110)
- George Lounge (p108)
- Yaletown Brewing Company (p108)

For reviews, see p108

Best Places to Shop

- Gallery of BC Ceramics (p114)
- Paper-Ya (p114)
- Granville Island Broom Company (p115)
- Goorin Bros Hat Shop (p113)
- Sport Gallery (p115)

For reviews, see p113

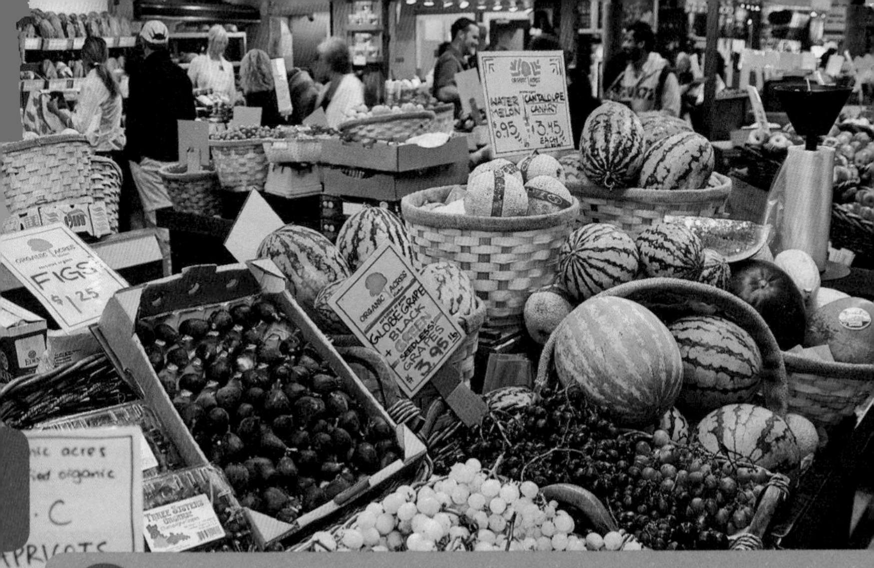

ALL CANADA PHOTOS RM / GETTY IMAGES ©

TOP SIGHT

GRANVILLE ISLAND PUBLIC MARKET

A foodie extravaganza specializing in gourmet cheese, deli treats, and pyramids of shiny fruit and vegetables, this is one of North America's finest public markets, and a chatty, visceral place to hang out with hungry locals. It's the perfect spot to while away an afternoon: snack on your goodies in the sun among the buskers outside or hunker from the rain with an entertaining guided market tour. You'll also find side dishes of (admittedly nonedible) arts and crafts.

DON'T MISS...

- Oyama Sausage Company
- Benton Brothers Fine Cheese
- Farmers Market
- Market Tour
- Day Vendors

PRACTICALITIES

- Map p275
- www.granvilleisland.com/public-market
- Johnston St
- 9am-7pm
- 50, miniferries

Taste-Tripping

Come hungry: there are dozens of food stands to weave your way around at the market. Among the must-see stands are **Oyama Sausage Company**, replete with hundreds of smoked sausages and cured meats; **Benton Brothers Fine Cheese**, with its full complement of amazing curdy goodies from British Columbia (BC) and around the world (look for anything by Farm House Natural Cheese from Agassiz, BC); and **Granville Island Tea Company** (Hawaiian rooibos recommended), with its tasting bar and more than 150 steep-tastic varieties to choose from. Baked goodies also abound: abandon your diet at **Lee's Donuts** and **Siegel's Bagels**, where the naughty cheese-stuffed baked bagels are not to be missed. In the unlikely event you're still hungry, there's also a small international food court: avoid off-peak dining if you want to snag a table and indulge in a good-value selection that runs from Indian curries to German sausages. And if you want to dive into some regional, seasonal produce, there's even a **farmers market** just outside the market building between June and October.

Arts & Crafts

Once you've eaten your fill, take a look at some of the market's other stands. There's a cool arts and crafts focus here, especially at the collection of **day vendors** that dot the market and which change every week. Hand-knitted hats, hand-painted ceramics, framed art photography and quirky carvings will make for excellent one-of-a-kind souvenirs – far better than the typical canned salmon and maple-sugar cookies. Further artisan stands are added to the roster in the run-up to Christmas, if you happen to be here at that time. For more information on the sorts of day vendors that appear at the market, visit www.gidva.org.

Insider's Tour

If you're an incurable foodie, the fascinating market tour organized by **Edible Canada at the Market** is the way to go. Taking about two hours to weave around the vendors, the $40 morning-only guided tour includes tastings of regional foods and chef-approved tips on how to pair and prepare local ingredients. A Public Market success story, Edible Canada started in the market as Edible BC and has grown so successfully that it now runs a Canadian-focused bistro and artisan food shop just across the street – the tour includes a 10% discount on goodies at the shop (organic Vancouver Island chocolate bars and jars of artisan ice cream are recommended). The company also runs Chinatown food-focused tours if you're hungry to compare the two scenes. Its old spot in the market has been taken by French-themed **L'Epicerie Rotisserie and Gourmet Shop**, which combines vinegars, olive oils and Barbapapa pop bottles with delicious, fresh-cooked picnic-friendly takeout chicken and sausages.

Forgotten Past

The Public Market is the centerpiece of one of Canada's most impressive urban regeneration projects – and the main reason it has been so successful. Built as a district for small factories in the early part of the last century, Granville Island – which has also been called Mud Island and Industrial Island over the years – had declined into a paint-peeled, no-go area by the 1960s. But the abandoned sheds began attracting artists and theater groups by the 1970s, and the old buildings slowly started springing back to life with some much-needed repairs and upgrades. Within a few years, new theaters, restaurants and studios had been built and the Public Market quickly became an instantly popular anchor tenant. One reason for the island's popularity? Only independent, one-of-a-kind businesses operate here.

PUBLIC MARKET TIPS

The market is the perfect place to wander around gathering the makings of a great picnic. But once you've filled your backpack with cured sausages, stinky cheeses, fresh bagels and a cake or three, where should you head? There's a hidden grassy knoll at the eastern tip of the island that's popular with picnickers, but even better is to hit the seawall westwards, just off the island. Within 10 minutes, you'll be in verdant Vanier Park (p165) with panoramic water-city-mountain views to accompany your dining.

If you're out enjoying the buskers on the market's waterfront exterior, you'll notice your False Creek view is sandwiched between two of Vancouver's most famous bridges. Opened in 1954, the ironwork Granville Bridge is the third version of this bridge to span the inlet here. The more attractive art deco Burrard Bridge, opened in 1932, is nearby. During its opening ceremony, a floatplane was daringly piloted under the bridge's main deck.

SIGHTS

Yaletown

BC PLACE STADIUM
STADIUM

Map p274 (www.bcplacestadium.com; 777 Pacific Blvd; MStadium-Chinatown) Recently renovated with a huge new crown-like retractable roof, Vancouver's main sports arena is home to two professional teams: the **BC Lions** Canadian Football League team and the **Vancouver Whitecaps** soccer team. It's also used for major rock concerts and consumer shows, and the prerenovated stadium hosted the opening and closing ceremonies for Vancouver's 2010 Winter Olympic Games.

Head into the Sports Hall of Fame & Museum to discover more about the Games.

BC SPORTS HALL OF FAME & MUSEUM
MUSEUM

Map p274 (604-687-5520; www.bcsportshalloffame.com; Gate A, BC Place Stadium, 777 Pacific Blvd; adult/child $15/12; 10am-5pm; ; MStadium-Chinatown) Inside BC Place Stadium, this small but perfectly formed attraction showcases top BC athletes, both amateur and professional, with galleries devoted to each decade in sports. There are medals, trophies and sporting memorabilia on display (judging by the size of their shirts, hockey players were much smaller in the old days), and there are tons of hands-on activities to tire the kids out.

You'll find plenty of info on the city's 2010 Winter Olympic Games in a dedicated gallery, plus stirring exhibits on Terry Fox and his Marathon of Hope run across Canada. Head outside the stadium for a cool **public artwork** by Douglas Coupland that also celebrates the nation's favorite hero.

ENGINE 374 PAVILION
MUSEUM

Map p274 (Roundhouse Community Arts & Recreation Centre, 181 Roundhouse Mews; MYaletown-Roundhouse) FREE In Vancouver's history, 23 May 1887 is an auspicious date. It was the day when Engine 374 pulled the first transcontinental passenger train into the fledgling city, symbolically linking the country and kick-starting the eventual metropolis. Retired in 1945, the engine was (after many years of neglect) finally restored and placed in this lovely pavilion. Drop by for a chat with the friendly volunteers.

Administered by the **West Coast Railway Heritage Park** in Squamish (a good excursion for rail buffs), the engine is kept in sparkling condition and is occasionally wheeled out onto the outside turntable, part of the beautifully restored roundhouse building that recalls Yaletown's gritty rail history.

ROUNDHOUSE COMMUNITY ARTS & RECREATION CENTRE
ARTS CENTER

Map p274 (www.roundhouse.ca; 181 Roundhouse Mews, cnr Davie St & Pacific Blvd; 9am-10pm Mon-Fri, to 5pm Sat & Sun; MYaletown-Roundhouse) Home of the Engine 374 Pavilion, Yaletown's main community gathering space colonizes the handsomely restored heritage railway roundhouse. It offers a full roster of events and courses for locals and visitors, including popular drop-in running classes and Philosopher's Cafe debating

CANADA'S HERO: TERRY FOX

The most poignant gallery at the BC Sports Hall of Fame & Museum is dedicated to national legend Terry Fox, the young cancer sufferer whose one-legged 1980 Marathon of Hope run across Canada ended after 143 days and 5373km, when the disease spread to the Port Coquitlam resident's lungs. When Fox died the following year, the funeral was screened live across the country and the government ordered flags to be flown at half-mast. A memorial was later constructed outside BC Place Stadium but it was replaced in 2011 by a new and much more impressive one created by Vancouver artist and writer Douglas Coupland, who had already penned his own celebrated book, *Terry*, in tribute to Fox. The new statue is a series of running figures showing Fox in motion during his cross-country odyssey. When Fox started his run, he received very little attention, but by the time he was forced to stop it felt like the entire country was behind him. Every year since his death, fundraising runs have been held across Canada and around the world to remember his bravery. The **Terry Fox Foundation** (www.terryfox.org) estimates that these have now raised more than $500 million for cancer research.

events. Check the website calendar to see what's on during your stay.

DAVID LAM PARK PARK

Map p274 (www.vancouverparks.ca; cnr Drake St & Pacific Blvd; Ⓜ Yaletown-Roundhouse) A crooked elbow of landscaped waterfront at the neck of False Creek, Yaletown's main green space is sometimes used for free alfresco summer movie screenings. It's an ideal launching point for a seawall walk along the north bank of False Creek to Science World; you'll pass intriguing public artworks and the glass condo towers that transformed the neighborhood in the 1990s.

Look out for birdlife along the route and ask the locals about the unexpected 2010 visit from a grey whale in these waters. It brought thousands of disbelieving Vancouverites to the shoreline.

Granville Island

GRANVILLE ISLAND PUBLIC MARKET MARKET

See p100.

GRANVILLE ISLAND BREWING BREWERY

Map p275 (GIB; ☎604-687-2739; www.gib.ca; 1441 Cartwright St; tours $9.75; ⏲tours noon, 1:30pm, 3pm, 4:30pm & 5:30pm; 🚌50) One of Canada's oldest microbreweries offers 30 minute tours where smiling guides walk you through the tiny brewing nook (production has mostly shifted to larger premises), before depositing you in the Taproom (p110) for three 4oz samples. This will likely include the company's lager and cream ale but if you're really lucky, you'll get a small-batch seasonal made right here on the island.

You'll spot many GIB brews in bars and restaurants around the city. You can also buy some takeout in the adjoining store – small-batch faves including Irish Red, Imperial IPA and Cloak & Dagger Cascadian Dark Ale are recommended.

RAILSPUR ALLEY STREET

Map p275 (btwn Old Bridge & Cartwright Sts; 🚌50) Seemingly far from the madding crowds of the Public Market – at least on summer days when every tourist in town seems to be there – this back-alley strip is a relaxing alternative. You'll find a string of unique artisan stores, from painters to jewelers. Be sure to check out the Artisan Sake Maker (p110). Sober up with coffee at Agro Café (p106) nearby. There's often a busker here on summer afternoons, so it's worth hanging around the alley for a bit.

KIDS MARKET MARKET

Map p275 (www.kidsmarket.ca; 1496 Cartwright St; ⏲10am-6pm; 👪; 🚌50) A nightmare if you stroll in by mistake, this two-story mini-shopping mall for under-10s is bustling with 30 kid-friendly stores, mostly of the toy variety. If your child's interests extend beyond Lego, there are also magic tricks, arts and crafts, and a menagerie of puppets for sale. Cool the sprogs down at the huge **Granville Island Water Park** (Map p275; ⏲10am-6pm mid-May–early Sep) FREE out back.

EATING

A favored haunt for conspicuously wealthy Vancouverites, Yaletown has some good, splurge-worthy dining options, especially along Hamilton and Mainland Sts. But not everything here is worth the price, so choose carefully. Many of this area's restaurants also have patios. Granville Island has plenty of places to eat, too, but you'll need to do a little digging if you want to avoid the tourist restaurants.

Yaletown

YOPO CAFE CHINESE $

Map p274 (www.yopocafe.com; 1122 Homer St; mains $5-11; ⏲11:30am-3pm & 4:30-9pm Mon-Fri, noon-3pm & 4:30-9pm Sat & Sun; Ⓜ Yaletown-Roundhouse) What passes for hole-in-the-wall budget dining in Yaletown, this tiny Chinese cafe is a handy pit stop if you've blown all your budget on chichi shopping. The typically huge menu covers all the standards, from wonton soups to *kung po* chicken. The lunch specials offer the best deals: two different dishes every day (you can also mix them half and half) for around $7.

Large combo feasts are available: get a huge takeout and sneak it back to your hotel room.

★FLYING PIG WEST COAST $$

Map p274 (www.theflyingpigvan.com; 1168 Hamilton St; mains $18-24; ⏲11:30am-midnight Mon-Fri, 10:30am-midnight Sat & Sun; Ⓜ Yaletown-Roundhouse) Yaletown's best midrange

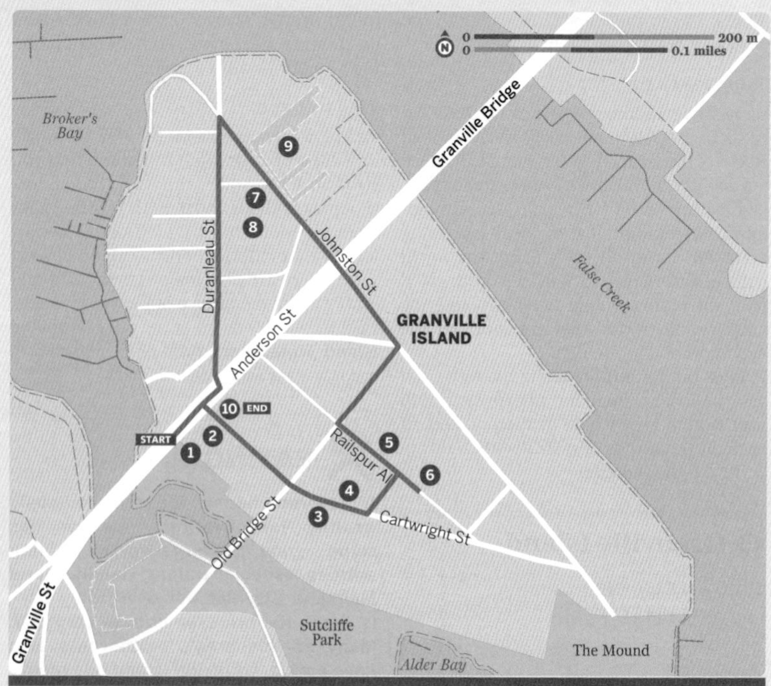

Neighborhood Walk
Granville Island Artisan Trawl

START UMBRELLA SHOP
END GRANVILLE ISLAND BREWING
LENGTH 1KM; ONE HOUR

This stroll takes you around some of Granville Island's favorite artisan studios and galleries, and ends with a well-deserved beer. Entering the island from the main entrance on Anderson St, nip into the **1 Umbrella Shop** (p115), especially if you need something to protect you from a deluge. Continue along Anderson to the corner of Cartwright St. Explore the **2 Kids Market** (p103) and consider one of the muppet-like puppets as a gift for a child.

Next weave eastwards along Cartwright. You'll start to see theaters and artisan shops along here. Take a look at two of the best artisan studios: **3 Crafthouse** (p115), which has plenty of regionally made arts and crafts to tempt your credit card; and, on the other side of the road, **4 Gallery of BC Ceramics** (p114), which offers even more to choose from among artisan pottery – consider a rustic teapot (maybe pick it up after you've finished your walk).

Duck along the little pathway beside the gallery and you'll hit the somewhat hidden **5 Railspur Alley** (p103). Peruse the excellent artsy stores here, including the **6 Artisan Sake Maker** (p110). Consider stopping for a three-glass tasting.

Continue on via Old Bridge St and turn left onto Johnston St. Here you'll find the **7 Net Loft**. It's lined with arts and crafts stores, including the ever-popular **8 Paper-Ya** (p114). Diagonally across the street from here is the entrance to the **9 Public Market** (p100). Dominating the area, it specializes in deli-style food stalls – cheese-filled bagels recommended. When you've had your fill, weave southwards from the market along Duranleau St. Within a couple of minutes you'll be at the intersection with Cartwright St and the entrance to **10 Granville Island Brewing** (p103). Take a tour or hit the Taproom for a pint.

LOCAL KNOWLEDGE

GRANVILLE ISLAND'S INDUSTRIAL EDGE

Many visitors spend their time on Granville Island at the Public Market end, nipping between the plentiful studios and shops. But heading a few minutes along Johnston St offers some reminders of the time when this human-made peninsula (since it's joined to the mainland, it's not actually an island) was home to dozens of hard-grating factories making everything from chains to iron hinges.

One million cubic yards of landfill was tipped into False Creek to create the island in the early 20th century, but almost all the reminders of its gritty first few years have been lost. Almost. The area's oldest tenant, **Ocean Construction Supplies**, is a cement maker that began here in 1917 and now cranks out enough product to build a 10-story tower block every week. Check out the ball-bearing-driven public artwork at the front of the facility and consider dropping by for its popular, family-friendly **open day** staged every spring.

Continue along Johnston a little further and you'll come to a second monument to the past: a landmark **yellow dock crane** that's been preserved from the old days. Nip across to the waterfront here for a final 'hidden' Granville Island view: a string of large and comfy-looking **houseboats** that many Vancouverites wish they lived in.

restaurant is a warm, woodsy bistro that has mastered the art of friendly service and excellent, savor-worthy dining. But since everyone knows how good it is, it's a good idea to dine off-peak to avoid the crowds. Dishes focus on seasonal local ingredients and are virtually guaranteed to make you smile: scallops and halibut are perfect but the roasted chicken is the city's best.

The Flying Pig offers an excellent and very popular weekend brunch (*croque madame* – grilled ham and cheese sandwich topped with a fried egg – is recommended), but the best deal is the afternoon happy-hour menu, when you can try a few tasty plates for around $5 a pop. Reservations are not accepted for dinner. A new Flying Pig has also recently winged it's way into Gastown – check it out; it promises to be bigger than its Yaletown sibling.

RODNEY'S OYSTER HOUSE SEAFOOD $$

Map p274 (☎604-609-0080; www.rohvan.com; 1228 Hamilton St; mains $16-32; ⏰11:30am-11pm; Ⓜ Yaletown-Roundhouse) Vancouver's favorite oyster eatery for many years, Rodney's always has a buzz about it. And it's not just because of the convivial room with its nautical flourishes: these guys really know how to do seafood. While the fresh-shucked oysters with a huge array of sauces (try the spicy vodka) never fail to impress, there's also everything from sweet mussels to superb Atlantic lobster available here.

Drop by from 3pm to 6pm weekdays for deals on oysters (usually as low as $1.50 each) or warm up in winter with possibly the best New England clam chowder in the city. Rodney's has also recently opened a branch in Gastown.

GLOWBAL GRILL STEAK & SATAY WEST COAST $$

Map p274 (☎604-602-0835; www.glowbalgrill.com; 1079 Mainland St; mains $18-38; ⏰11:30am-1am Mon-Thu, 10:30am-2am Fri & Sat, to 1am Sun; Ⓜ Yaletown-Roundhouse) Casting a wide net that catches the power-lunch, after-work and late-night-fashionista crowds, this hip joint has a comfortable, lounge-like feel and is a safe bet if you can't think of anywhere else to go: there's usually something on the menu for everyone here. The dishes range from steak and fish mains to pasta classics (try the lobster linguine). Save room for some spicy satay sticks.

CIOPPINO'S MEDITERRANEAN GRILL ITALIAN $$$

Map p274 (☎604-688-7466; www.cioppinosyaletown.com; 1133 Hamilton St; mains $32-40; ⏰5-10pm; Ⓜ Yaletown-Roundhouse) Not your standard Italian joint, this fine-dining Mediterranean eatery deploys the *cucina naturale* approach to cooking, which aims to reveal the delicate natural flavors of a range of regionally sourced ingredients. The warm wood and terracotta interior is the perfect surrounds for dipping into West

Coast dishes tweaked with Italian flourishes – try lobster and crab cannelloni or spit-roasted duck breast.

One of the best wine lists in town (60-plus pages) is at your disposal, with lots of rare vintages to keep your credit card fully deployed. In summer aim for a spot on the patio: it's often less clamorous with conversations than inside.

BLUE WATER CAFÉ + RAW BAR SEAFOOD **$$$**
Map p274 (☎604-688-8078; www.bluewatercafe.net; 1095 Hamilton St; mains $25-44; ⏰5pm-midnight; Ⓜ Yaletown-Roundhouse) Under expert chef Frank Pabst, this has become one of Vancouver's best high-concept seafood restaurants and is a highlight of Yaletown fine dining. Gentle music fills the brick-lined, blue-hued interior, while seafood towers, arctic char and BC sablefish grace the tables inside and on the patio. Consider the semicircular raw bar, and watch the whirling blades prepare delectable sushi and sashimi.

Service here is perfect: warm, gracious and ever-friendly. Reservations are required.

BRIX FRENCH **$$$**
Map p274 (☎604-915-9463; www.brixvancouver.com; 1138 Homer St; mains $23-29; ⏰5:30pm-1:30am Mon-Sat; Ⓜ Yaletown-Roundhouse) A charming and romantic heritage building setting with a courtyard that feels exactly like you've suddenly stepped into continental Europe, this lovely spot seems like a secret, despite having been here for years. The classy white-tablecloth setting is ideal for contemporary French approaches to dishes such as duck breast and Cornish game hen. And the wine list is large and impressive.

Unlike many fine-dining restaurants, there are dozens of tipples available by the glass here. In fact, check ahead for one of Brix' winemakers dinners, a social highlight for local oenophiles.

PROVENCE MARINASIDE FRENCH, SEAFOOD **$$$**
Map p274 (www.provencevancouver.com; 1177 Marinaside Cres; mains $20-37; ⏰8am-10pm Mon-Thu, to 10:30pm Fri, 9am-10:30pm Sat, to 10pm Sun; Ⓜ Yaletown-Roundhouse) There's a serious seafood fixation at this French-approach restaurant just across from Yaletown's False Creek waterfront, so if you're not in the mood for aquatic treats, this isn't the place for you. If you are, go for the huge, feast-tastic seafood platter, which includes everything from clams to crabs; it's simply prepared and delicious. Consider a patio table in summer.

At the weekend, this becomes one of Yaletown's fave brunch spots; try the crab and lobster omelet. Check the menu for dishes marked with the sustainable seafood symbol – sponsored by the Vancouver Aquarium.

Granville Island

★GO FISH SEAFOOD **$**
Map p275 (1505 W 1st Ave; mains $8-14; ⏰11:30am-6:30pm Tue-Sun, reduced hours in winter; 🚌50) A short stroll westwards along the seawall from the Granville Island entrance, this almost-too-popular seafood stand is one of the city's fave fish-and-chip joints, offering halibut, salmon and cod encased in crispy golden batter. The smashing (and lighter) fish tacos are also recommended, while ever-changing daily specials – brought in by the nearby fishing boats – often include scallop burgers or ahi (yellowfin) tuna sandwiches.

Expect long queues in summer and arrive as early as you can. There's not much of a seating area, so pack your grub and continue along the seawall to **Vanier Park** for a picnic with the ever-watchful seagulls.

PUBLIC MARKET FOOD COURT INTERNATIONAL **$**
Map p275 (1661 Duranleau St, Granville Island Public Market; mains $6-9; ⏰9am-7pm; 🚌50) A good budget option but also clamorously busy in summer; your table at the little Public Market food court can be auctioned off to the highest bidder when you're ready to leave (just kidding). Arrive off-peak to be sure of a seat and you'll have the pick of some excellent vendors hawking everything from Indian curries to German sausages.

Those on a health kick should consider the taco salad at the Mexican food stand: it's packed with fresh-chopped goodies.

AGRO CAFÉ CAFE **$**
Map p275 (www.agrocafe.org; 1363 Railspur Alley; mains $5-8; ⏰8am-7pm Mon-Fri, 9am-7pm Sat & Sun; 📶; 🚌50) This slightly hidden cafe on Railspur Alley is a smashing coffee stop but it also serves the best-value breakfast on Granville Island – go for the $7 eggs, hash browns and turkey sausage. Lunch delivers soups, salads, sandwiches and wraps, and there's a always a BC craft beer or two if you need to crank it up from coffee.

LOCAL KNOWLEDGE

FERRY-HOPPING

If you don't arrive or depart from Granville Island via one of the tiny miniferries operated by Aquabus Ferries (p246) or False Creek Ferries (p247), you haven't really conducted your visit correctly. But these signature little boats (the Aquabus vessels tend to be rainbow-hued while the False Creek Ferries are blue) don't only transport passengers from the north side of False Creek to the market on the south side. Both have several additional ports of call around the shoreline; if you have time, a 'cruise' of the area is a great way to see the city from the water. An all-day pass on each service costs $10 to $15 (unfortunately tickets are not interchangeable between the operators, who remain cutthroat rivals). There are several highlight stop-offs to consider along the way.

Aquabus can get you to Yaletown's David Lam Park (p103), a waterfront space that's ideal for watching the gently lapping waters of False Creek from a grassy promontory (preferably with a picnic). On the opposite shoreline, you can also step off at **Stamps Landing**, one of Vancouver's first urban waterfront housing developments: there's a pub here in the delightfully medieval-sounding **Leg-in-Boot Sq**. Back on the northern shoreline, there's a stop at the bottom of Davie St, which is a short stroll into the heart of Yaletown. You'll find the fascinating Engine 374 Pavilion (p102) here, home of the locomotive that pulled the first passenger train into Vancouver in 1887.

You can see how things have transformed around False Creek in recent years at one final stop. The south shoreline here used to be crammed with grungy industry but in 2010 the Olympic Village (p133) opened. Providing housing for the athletes at the 2010 Winter Games, this development is now a slick new city neighborhood. It's also just a short stroll from here to Science World (p133), one of Vancouver's most popular family-friendly attractions.

False Creek Ferries covers many of the same locations but also includes a unique stop at another popular – and appropriate – Vancouver attraction. From Granville Island, via a stop at the Aquatic Centre in the West End, it's a 25-minute voyage to the Vancouver Maritime Museum (p165). On the shoreline of verdant Vanier Park, it's a great spot to dive into the region's seafaring past, from historic vessels to scale models. And since you're now a veteran sea salt, you'll fit right in.

In summer, sip your Americano outside and watch the Granville Island world go by. It can be busy here, so grab your table before ordering at the counter.

TONY'S FISH & OYSTER CAFE SEAFOOD $$

Map p275 (www.tonysfish-granvilleisland.com; 1511 Anderson St; mains $8-23; ⏲11:30am-8:30pm Mon-Sat, to 8pm Sun, reduced hours in winter; 🚌50) A chatty spot where Vancouverites bring visitors to eat when they take them to Granville Island, this tiny checkered-tablecloth joint serves great fish and chips, along with generous dollops of house-made coleslaw and tartar sauce. The food is good value, and it's not just about fish and chips: the BBQ-sauced oyster burger is almost a local legend. Service is fast and friendly.

Those seafood fans not craving the deep-fried route will also find some good fresh alternatives here, from hearty clam chowder to fresh-shucked oysters and steamed mussels. Appropriately, the beer selection includes several from Granville Island Brewing, which is just across the street.

★EDIBLE CANADA AT THE MARKET WEST COAST $$

Map p275 (☎604-682-6681; www.ediblecanada.com/bistro; 1596 Johnston St; mains $18-29; ⏲11am-9pm Mon-Thu, to 10pm Fri-Sun, reduced hours in winter; 🚌50) Granville Island's most popular bistro (book ahead) delivers a short but tempting menu of seasonal dishes from across Canada, often including perfectly prepared Alberta beef, Newfoundland fish and several BC treats (look out for slow-roasted pork belly). Consider sharing some small plates if you're feeling adventurous, and perhaps top it off with a naughty maple-sugar pie for dessert and a glass of ice wine.

Service is warm and friendly here, and the 'best of Canada' approach that pervades the menu is extended to the drinks list: there's a tasty array of craft beers plus a great wine list featuring large and lesser-known wineries from across the country. Check out the shop of artisan food treats at the back of the restaurant before you leave and consider one of the tours of the nearby Public Market. Also a popular spot for weekend brunch; wild mushroom Benedict is recommended.

BRIDGES WEST COAST, SEAFOOD **$$**

Map p275 (www.bridgesrestaurant.com; 1696 Duranleau St; mains $18-45; ⏰11am-10pm; 🚌50) This bright-yellow waterfront bistro has one of Vancouver's best sunset patios from which to enjoy (slightly pricey) pub-style seafood such as chowder, halibut and chips, and thin-crust pizzas – the smoked-salmon variety is recommended. Accompany your dinner with a pitcher of Granville Island Iced Tea (if you have enough friends to finish it). There's also a fine-dining room upstairs if you want something a little fancier.

This upstairs white-tablecloth space cranks it up, with steaks and lamb racks added to the seafood (as well as higher prices). But the view is the same one enjoyed by the regulars chattering on the patio below.

SANDBAR SEAFOOD RESTAURANT SEAFOOD **$$$**

Map p275 (☎604-669-9030; www.vancouverdine.com; 1535 Johnston St; mains $15-35; ⏰11:30am-10pm Sun-Thu, to 11:30pm Fri & Sat; 🚌50) West Coast seafood dominates at this slick, high-ceilinged restaurant-with-a-view that's tucked under Granville Bridge's iron arches. The fresh oysters are popular and they're best sampled on the fireplace-warmed rooftop deck – there's also a sushi bar if your raw mood continues. Sandbar has a giant wine list, but the urban professionals crowding the U-shaped bar on weekends seem more interested in quaffing cocktails.

A good spot for a romantic dinner, but it can get clamorously crowded on weekends.

DRINKING & NIGHTLIFE

Yaletown is where the city's wealthy set come to sip martinis and exchange lap-dog stories. You're sure to find something worth checking out amid the warehouse renos. Granville Island offers several bars ideal for winding down in after a day spent weaving around the Public Market and artisan stores.

Yaletown

RAW CANVAS BAR

Map p274 (www.rawcanvas.com; 1046 Hamilton St; ⏰6-11pm Tue-Thu, to midnight Fri & Sat; Ⓜ Yaletown-Roundhouse) Possibly way too cool for Yaletown, this smashing communal-tabled lounge is perfect for a few glasses of wine and a plate or three of cheese and charcuterie. But the real reason to come here is to emulate the art lining the walls: head to the back-room studio and you can use the supplies to paint your own (perhaps slightly tipsy) masterpiece.

There's an instructor on hand to offer tips and you can even keep your drink with you for added inspiration. Smock provided.

YALETOWN BREWING COMPANY BREWERY

Map p274 (www.drinkfreshbeer.com; 1111 Mainland St; ⏰11:30am-midnight Sun-Wed, to 1am Thu, to 3am Fri & Sat; Ⓜ Yaletown-Roundhouse) There's a brick-lined brewpub on one side and a giant dining room on the other. Both serve pints of beer made on-site, but the restaurant adds a long menu of comfort foods. Check to see if there's an unusual small-batch beer on offer, and if there isn't, instead hit one of the mainstays: Brick & Beam IPA is recommended. Beer nuts should drop by at 4pm Thursdays for cask night.

If you really want to try something out of the ordinary, ask about the eye-popping Oud Bruin. It's guaranteed to put hairs on your chest, but only if you finish it. In summer the pub's tiny patio is a popular perch, but in winter a game of pool in the back of the bar is recommended.

GEORGE LOUNGE COCKTAIL BAR

Map p274 (www.georgelounge.com; 1137 Hamilton St; Ⓜ Yaletown-Roundhouse) One of hedonistic Yaletown's favorite haunts, George attracts the local glitterati with its perfectly executed high-concept cocktails – anyone for a Sazerac, featuring bourbon in an absinthe-washed glass? Work your way down the menu as you hone your chat-up lines on the locals, or just sink into a corner to figure out what that giant swirly glass thing above the bar is.

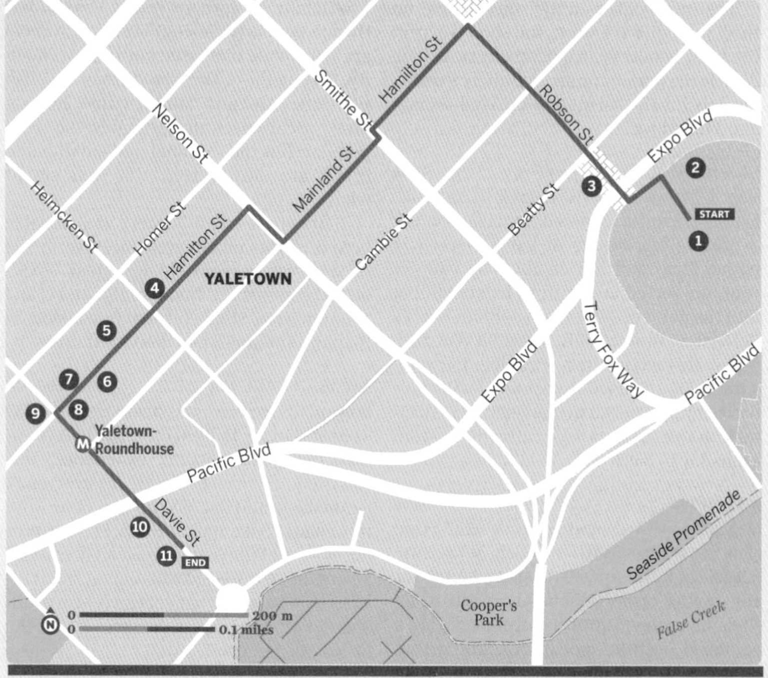

Neighborhood Walk
Yaletown: Sporting Life to Trainspotting

START BC PLACE STADIUM
END ENGINE 374 PAVILION
LENGTH 2KM; ONE HOUR

Start at the city's largest sports venue, ❶ **BC Place Stadium** (p102), checking out the ❷ **BC Sports Hall of Fame & Museum** (p102) located inside and the Douglas Coupland ❸ **public artwork** outside – it's a celebration of Canadian hero Terry Fox.

From here, head up Robson St and turn left onto Hamilton. This is your chance to scope out options for dinner later. You'll pass ❹ **Blue Water Café** (p106; seafood), ❺ **Cioppino's** (p105; Italian) and ❻ **Flying Pig** (p103; gourmet comfort grub). On your stroll, notice the elevated red-brick sidewalks and old rails embedded in the roads. These are remnants of the neighborhood's former incarnation as a train yard and warehouse district.

Latter-day Yaletown isn't just about dining. Along Hamilton, you'll come to a couple of stores that show how popular shopping is here, too. ❼ **Basquiat** (p113) dresses local women in top-notch labels while ❽ **Goorin Bros Hat Shop** (p113) is the perfect spot to add a trendy sunhat to your day.

When you reach Davie St, turn left. It's all downhill from here, but if it's time for a pit stop, pop into ❾ **Caffe Artigiano** (p110) for a restorative latte and a pastry or two. It's in the Opus Hotel building, one of the city's trendiest boutique sleepovers: spot the beautiful people gliding in and out of the lobby.

Continue your stroll along Davie, cross over Pacific Blvd and you'll spot the ❿ **Roundhouse Community Arts & Recreation Centre** (p102) just ahead of you. Check to see if there are any events or workshops you'd like to attend, then dig out your camera for the neighborhood's historic highlight. Attached to the side of the community center, ⓫ **Engine 374 Pavilion** (p102) houses the handsomely restored steam engine that pulled the first passenger train into the city in 1887.

The mixologists pride themselves on fresh ingredients here so you should expect the best. Foodwise, it's all about tasty side dishes; the pork buns are definitely worth a try. DJs hit the turntables on Wednesdays and Thursdays.

KILLJOY COCKTAIL TAVERN LOUNGE

Map p274 (www.donnellygroup.ca; 1120 Hamilton St; ⏲7pm-1am Sun-Wed, 5pm-1am Thu-Sat; Ⓜ Yaletown-Roundhouse) At Vancouver's only barber shop and bar combo, you can get your 'do' sorted at the front before sliding into the darkened bar room behind. But it's not just a gimmick (OK, it is a bit of a gimmick); this well-hidden, cave-like bar does a good job in moodlit cocktails, with gin-derived tipples a particular specialty. Turntable tunes keep things extra lively from Thursday to Saturday.

BAR NONE CLUB

Map p274 (www.donnellygroup.ca; 1222 Hamilton St; ⏲10pm-3am Fri & Sat; Ⓜ Yaletown-Roundhouse) Yaletown's favorite haunt for club-loving professionals who want to let their hair down after a hard week has a scrubbed beatnik appearance. But within its exposed-brick-and-beam shell the main topics of conversation are perfect cocktails and real-estate prices. It's only open on Fridays and Saturdays, but it's the best spot in Yaletown to sip, sway and wish you were richer.

CAFFE ARTIGIANO COFFEE

Map p274 (www.caffeartigiano.com; 302 Davie St; ⏲5:30am-9pm Mon-Fri, 6am-8:30pm Sat & Sun; Ⓜ Yaletown-Roundhouse) One of Vancouver's most popular local coffee chains serves up Yaletown's best java. Tucked into a corner of the Opus Hotel building, this ever-chatty spot takes pride in its drinks: go for a latte and they'll implant a nice little design into the foam (yes, we're easily pleased). There are also sandwiches and baked treats available if you need a fuel-up.

Granville Island

GRANVILLE ISLAND BREWING TAPROOM PUB

Map p275 (www.gib.ca; 1441 Cartwright St; ⏲11am-9pm; 🚌50) You can sample the company's main beers in this pub-style room – officially a taproom rather than a bar (hence the early closing) – although most are now made in a large out-of-town facility. Among these, the Island Lager, English Bay Pale Ale and summertime Robson Street Hefeweizen are arguably the most popular. But the seasonal and small-batch brews are even better: ask your server what's on tap.

Tours of the small brewery are available here and you might even meet Vern, the brewmaster responsible for great small-batch beers such as Imperial IPA and Chocolate Imperial Stout. Takeout is available in the souvenir and liquor store next door.

ARTISAN SAKE MAKER BREWERY

Map p275 (www.artisansakemaker.com; 1339 Railspur Alley; ⏲11:30am-6pm; 🚌50) A well-hidden daytime sipping experience, this tiny sake winery should be on everyone's Granville Island list. It's the first of its kind in Canada. Sake maker Masa Shiroki produces several tipples and you can dive in for a bargain $5 three-sake tasting. A small selection of Japanese bar snacks is also available. In summer, most drinkers sit on the little patio out front.

This place is a good way to learn all about sake; consider a takeout bottle of your fave. And, jumping on the locavore bandwagon, the company recently began producing sake from rice harvested just down the road in Abbotsford.

DOCKSIDE BREWING COMPANY BAR

Map p275 (www.docksidebrewing.com; Granville Island Hotel, 1253 Johnston St; ⏲11:30am-10pm; 🚌50) Often overshadowed by the other brewers in town (being stuck on the quiet end of Granville Island doesn't help), Dockside's beers that are made on-site include the tasty, hibiscus-toned Jamaican Lager. Sup on the waterfront patio for tranquil views of False Creek's boat traffic and the mountain-backed downtown skyline – this is what beer drinking in Vancouver should be all about.

If it's raining, stay indoors by the fireplace and sink into a leather couch. If you're not sure which beer to have, try a six-sample tasting flight ($14). There's also a large restaurant area – seafood recommended. Dockside has recently started offering free brewery tours (4:30pm Thursdays) for those who reserve ahead. Tours include a

WORTH A DETOUR

FALSE CREEK SEAWALL TRAIL

Stanley Park isn't the only stretch of seawall worth hitting. In fact, during summer when the park is crammed with tourists, other sections of Vancouver's waterfront trail are preferred by the locals. One such off-the-beaten-path area is **False Creek**. Running along the entire shoreline on both the north and south banks, the seawall trail is an excellent way to hang out with some Vancouverites.

Keep in mind that the northern bank walk is around 2.5km and the southern stretch around 3.5km. Rental bikes are available around the city as well if you'd rather take a two-wheeled approach instead of walking.

Start on the north side of False Creek at Yaletown's David Lam Park (p103) and head east alongside several intriguing public artworks. Look out for *Brush With Illumination*, which looks like a giant ray gun, and *Lookout*, which recalls the area's gritty industrial heritage. Continuing east, you'll pass under **Cambie Bridge**. The first version of this span was called the **Connaught Bridge**; the second had a swing mechanism so it could open for passing boats. This third version was opened in 1985. Continue on your weave and you'll pass into the area that housed **Expo '86**, the giant world exposition that put Vancouver on the international map and triggered the re-generation of this decaying industrial waterfront stretch. From here to Science World (p133), you'll pass several reminders of the big event: the **Plaza of Nations**, Science World itself and, in the distance, the **SkyTrain** Expo line.

From here, you can hop on the SkyTrain to downtown, take a miniferry to Granville Island or continue your walk by hitting False Creek's southern shoreline to Granville Island.

If you decide to keep strolling, follow the seawall trail past Science World to the Olympic Village (p133), the high-rise housing development on the southeast corner of False Creek. Home to around 3000 athletes during the 2010 Olympic and Paralympic Winter Games, it's now a new city neighborhood containing hundreds of condos plus shops, bars and restaurants. Depart from the seawall here for a nose around and make sure you take some snaps of the giant bird sculptures in the main pedestrian area. If you need a break for lunch, Tap & Barrel (p135) is a good pit stop and it has a great patio overlooking the water.

From here, continue west along the seawall, passing over a steel pedestrian bridge shaped like a canoe, and you'll soon come to an unlikely urban attraction. **Habitat Island** – an artificially constructed tree-and-shrub-lined creation – is a new inner-city sanctuary for passing cormorants and blue herons (plus the occasional falcon). Its rocky shoreline is also home to starfish and crabs. It's a reminder that although False Creek is in the heart of the city, the Pacific Ocean is on its doorstep.

From here, you'll pass under the Cambie Bridge again before reaching **Leg-in-Boot Sq**. The name reputedly comes from a limb that washed up in the area in the 1800s. The cozy-looking waterfront neighborhood here is worth a quick poke around. Built in the 1980s, the low-rise homes and condos are a stark contrast to the high-as-possible residential towers built within the last decade and now facing the area from the opposite shoreline.

Passing through the neighborhood and alongside **Charleson Park**, you'll next arrive at **Spruce Harbour Marina**, a live-aboard boat community. But, within a few minutes, Granville Island will appear on the shoreline ahead. You'll enter it from the hidden back route few visitors know about. Look out for the **totem pole** (Map p275) as you step onto the island. It was carved by hundreds of people and was erected in 1999, recalling the First Nations residents that once fished and lived in this area.

food-pairing talk with the brewer. There are no free samples, but the full range is available for purchase after the tour.

BACKSTAGE LOUNGE BAR

Map p275 (www.backstagelounge.com; 1585 Johnston St; noon-2am Mon-Sat, to midnight Sun; 50) This dark, under-the-bridge Granville Island hangout has winning patio views and live music of the local band variety. The bar is lined with more than 20 mostly BC microbrew taps from the likes of Dead Frog, Steamworks and Red Truck, and there's always a bargain $2.25 special on Tuesdays from Bowen Island Brewing. The pub-grub food menu includes good pizzas.

This is a popular spot for those attending the nearby theaters, and there's usually live entertainment by local bands every night.

ENTERTAINMENT

Granville Island is home to several theaters and a hotbed of performance art and theatrical festivals.

GRANVILLE ISLAND STAGE THEATER

Map p275 (www.artsclub.com; 1585 Johnston St; 50) Vancouver's leading theater company, the Arts Club, has two stages: the large Granville Island Stage hosts bigger productions – including musicals – while across the street the Revue Stage hosts smaller, more intimate plays, often by local playwrights. Either way, there's usually something worth seeing during the September to June main season. Be sure to check www.ticketstonight.ca for day-of-show half-price tickets.

If you're curious about West Coast theatrics, look out for plays by Morris Panych, one of BC's favorite playwright sons.

BC LIONS FOOTBALL

Map p274 (www.bclions.com; BC Place Stadium, 777 Pacific Blvd; tickets $32-112; Jun-Nov; M Stadium-Chinatown) The Lions are Vancouver's team in the Canadian Football League (CFL), which is arguably more exciting than its US NFL counterpart. They've had some decent showings over the past few years, winning the all-important Grey Cup championship most recently in 2011. Tickets are easy to come by – unless the boys are laying into their arch enemies, the Calgary Stampeders.

The team relies on its jump-out-of-your-seat offense, and catching a game at the stadium includes plenty of schmaltzy razzamattaz, from cheerleaders to half-time shows. It's family friendly and a lot cheaper than catching an NHL hockey game.

VANCOUVER WHITECAPS SOCCER

Map p274 (www.whitecapsfc.com; BC Place Stadium, 777 Pacific Blvd; tickets $25-150; Mar-Oct; M Stadium-Chinatown) Now using BC Place Stadium as its home, Vancouver's leading soccer team plays in North America's top-tier Major League Soccer (MLS) arena. They've struggled a little since being promoted to the league in 2011, but have been finding their feet (useful for soccer players) in recent seasons. A game makes for a fun couple of hours. Save time for a souvenir

GRANVILLE ISLAND'S BEST FEST

It might feel like an invasion but it's probably more accurate to call the 11-day **Vancouver International Fringe Festival** (www.vancouverfringe.com) an energetic occupation of Granville Island. Running every September, the event includes a multitude of enthusiastic performers from Canada and around the world staging approximately 800 shows – from comedy reviews to poignant dramas – at venues large and small. Naturally the island's surfeit of theaters is well utilized, but shows are also frequently staged in less conventional venues, from floating miniferries to pop-up stages on every street corner. Tickets hover around the $10 mark but deals are plentiful and free shows are common. Book ahead for shows before you arrive, but note that just strolling the island during the event can be entertaining, as buskers and flyposting performers try to catch your attention. Finally, consider hanging out with the performers themselves: usually one bar is set aside during the festival for the thesps to chill out with audience members between shows – it's the perfect opportunity for you to dust off that searing reinterpretation of *Death of a Salesman* you've written and that just needs a producer (and a lyricist for the musical numbers).

soccer-shirt purchase to impress everyone back home.

A good family-friendly activity that's also better value than taking everyone to a Vancouver Canucks game.

VANCOUVER THEATRESPORTS LEAGUE COMEDY

Map p275 (☎604-738-7013; www.vtsl.com; The Improv Centre, 1502 Duranleau St; ⊙Wed-Sun; 50) The city's most popular improv group stages energetic romps – sometimes connected to themes such as Shakespeare or *Star Trek* – at this purpose-fitted theater. Whatever the theme, the approach is the same: if you're sitting near the front, expect to be picked on. The 11:15pm Friday and Saturday shows are commendably ribald.

If you fancy your skills as a performer, try not to rush the stage. Theatresports offers regular drop-in Saturday afternoon workshops ($15) for those keen to give improv a try – you'll likely find out it's much harder than it looks.

CAROUSEL THEATRE THEATER

Map p275 (www.carouseltheatre.ca; Waterfront Theatre; ; 50) Performing at Granville Island's Waterfront Theatre, this smashing child-focused drama company stages some great, wide-eyed productions that adults often enjoy just as much as their kids. Adaptations of children's classics such as *The Wind in the Willows* have featured in the past, with clever versions of Shakespearen works added to the mix for older children.

It also hosts an excellent kids theater school in summer if you're traveling with a young thesp.

SHOPPING

Colonizing the area's evocative old brick warehouses, the chichi Yaletown shopping scene has some interesting indie stores and designer boutiques. But for arts and crafts fans, it has to be Granville Island. It's teeming with studios where artisans throw clay, blow glass and silversmith jewelry. A tempting array of shopping nooks are housed in former industrial buildings. Head to the Net Loft, Railspur Alley or Granville Island Public Market if you're lacking direction, but make sure you explore as much as possible and duck down the back alleys to see artists at work in their studios. Buskers also hang out here on summer afternoons, making this Vancouver's most convivial shopping area.

Yaletown

GOORIN BROS HAT SHOP HATS

Map p274 (www.goorin.com; 1188 Hamilton St; ⊙11am-7pm Mon-Thu, to 8pm Fri & Sat, to 6pm Sun; MYaletown-Roundhouse) This highly welcoming hat emporium can transform your tired old look in an instant. An outlet of a funky US family-run business, it caters to men and women, and the store feels like an old-fashioned haberdashers. Styles mix the classics with the latest looks; you can't go wrong with a straw fedora, and you'll be up there with Yaletown's fashionable blokes when you step outside.

CROSS HOMEWARES

Map p274 (www.thecrossdesign.com; 1198 Homer St; ⊙10am-6pm Mon-Sat, 11am-5pm Sun; MYaletown-Roundhouse) A large store with an entirely irresistible array of goodies for your home – from perfect wine glasses to cool linen sheets – Cross has a continental, vintage-chic feel to much of its collection. It's ideal for a rainy afternoon browse, but be careful: you'll almost certainly find something you want to buy, which could mean blowing your baggage allowance on the way home.

Aside from furnishings and kitchenware, you'll also discover some cool interior design books here.

COASTAL PEOPLES FINE ARTS GALLERY ARTS & CRAFTS

Map p274 (www.coastalpeoples.com; 1024 Mainland St; ⊙10am-7pm Mon-Sat, 11am-6pm Sun; MYaletown-Roundhouse) This museum-like store showcases an excellent array of Inuit and Northwest Coast aboriginal jewelry, carvings and prints. On the high-art side of things, the exquisite items here are ideal if you're looking for a very special souvenir for someone back home. Don't worry: they can ship the totem poles if you can't fit them in your suitcase.

BASQUIAT WOMEN'S CLOTHING

Map p274 (www.basquiat.ca; 1189 Hamilton St; MYaletown-Roundhouse) A minimalist clothing joint where you might need more than

VANCOUVER'S BRICK-BUILT SOHO

Aesthetically unlike any other Vancouver neighborhood, Yaletown has a trendy warehouse district appearance today because it was built on a foundation of grungy, working-class history. Created almost entirely from red bricks, the area was crammed with railway sheds and goods warehouses in the late 1800s after the Canadian Pacific Railway (CPR) relocated its main western Canada operation from the British Columbia (BC) interior town of Yale. Along with the moniker, the workers brought something else with them: a tough-as-nails, hard-drinking approach that turned the waterfront area into one where the taverns usually served their liquor with a side order of fist-fights. But at least the rough-and-ready workers kept the area alive: when the rail operations were closed down a few decades later, Yaletown descended into a half-empty mass squat filled with rats and homeless locals. But that wasn't the end of the story.

When plans were drawn up for Vancouver to host the giant **Expo '86** world exposition, there were few areas of town with the empty space – and the absence of other businesses – to host it. But Yaletown fit the bill. The area became part of the planned Expo grounds along the north shoreline of False Creek, and was cleared, refurbished and given a new lease on life. After the summer-long fair, its newly noticed historic character made Yaletown the ideal spot for urban regeneration. Within a few years, the old brick warehouses had been repaired, scrubbed clean and recolonized with a sparkling array of boutiques, fancy restaurants and swish bars – serving tipples that are a far cry from the punch-triggering beers that used to be downed here.

one credit card to buy that perfect outfit. Service is excellent and the carefully curated selection of international labels is top-notch: look out for Ian, Preen, Humanoid and beyond. Since fashion is followed closely here, the end-of-season sales are often fantastic.

BROOKLYN CLOTHING CLOTHING

Map p274 (www.brooklynclothing.com; 418 Davie St; ⌚11am-9pm; Ⓜ Yaletown-Roundhouse) Proving that Yaletown men are just as aesthetically focused as women, this hipster menswear boutique is the perfect spot to upgrade your style from that New Romantic look you've been sporting since 1982. Local designers are well represented – check out the achingly cool T-shirts – and there are dozens of jeans styles so you can finally nail that perfect fit.

Drop by on Sunday night when it's quiet and you can try on everything in the store.

Granville Island

★GALLERY OF BC CERAMICS ARTS & CRAFTS

Map p275 (www.bcpotters.com; 1359 Cartwright St; ⌚10:30am-5:30pm; 🚌50) The star of Granville Island's arts-and-crafts shops and the public face of the Potters Guild of BC, this excellent spot exhibits and sells the striking works of its member artists. You can pick up one-of-a-kind ceramic tankards or swirly painted soup bowls; the hot items are the cool ramen noodle cups, complete with holes for chopsticks. It's well-priced art for everyone.

The handmade honey pots (honey included) and unique mugs are ideal for local-made souvenirs at reasonable prices. There were some tempting puffer-fish-shaped teapots on our visit. Before you leave, peruse the corner gallery space with its ever-changing exhibits of eye-catching creations.

PAPER-YA ARTS & CRAFTS

Map p275 (www.paper-ya.com; Net Loft, 1666 Johnston St; ⌚10am-7pm; 🚌50) A magnet for slavering stationery fetishists (you know who you are), this treasure trove of writing-related ephemera ranges from natty pens to quirky, hand-crafted greeting cards. In between, you'll find an intriguing undercurrent of kitsch-cool Japanese journals and reams of sumptuous washi paper. It's a store that makes you long for the return of traditional letter writing.

There's also a back wall of seals and sealing wax if you happen to be corresponding with someone from the Middle Ages.

CRAFTHOUSE — ARTS & CRAFTS

Map p275 (www.craftcouncilbc.ca; 1386 Cartwright St; ⏲10:30am-5:30pm; 🚌50) At this bright and friendly nonprofit gallery run by the Craft Council of British Columbia (CCBC), the shelves hold everything from glass goblets and woven scarves to French butter dishes and lathe-turned arbutus wood bowls – all produced by dozens of artisans from across the region. It's a great place to pick up something different.

On your way out, check the flyers near the door for more info on local gallery and art-scene happenings.

SPORT GALLERY — CLOTHING, GIFTS

Map p275 (www.thesportgallery.com; 1551 Johnston St; ⏲11am-6pm; 🚌50) With its cool array of retro sportswear and art-gallery selection of historic sports photography, this is the perfect pit stop for traveling sports nuts. Pick up a 1940s-style Boston Celtics jacket or a T-shirt proclaiming the old Vancouver Baseball Club and you'll be the coolest dude at the next sports bar you head into.

Class it up a little with some cuff links made from sections of old baseballs or hockey pucks used in professional games. You'll find Sport Gallery tucked in a (nameless) alley of shops under the bridge.

★GRANVILLE ISLAND BROOM COMPANY — HOMEWARES

Map p275 (www.broomcompany.com; 1406 Old Bridge St; ⏲10am-5pm; 🚌50) Ever since Harry Potter arrived on the scene, locals and visitors have been entranced by this Granville Island fave, which makes its own beautifully handcrafted straw brooms right in the store (you can watch the mesmerizing process in action). But these gnarly handled lovelies aren't just for decoration. You can pick up cobwebbers, golf-shoe brushes and car whisks that will easily fit in your luggage.

And just in case you're wondering, the brooms – which can take anywhere from 20 minutes to several hours to produce – are all made from broom corn, which grows in Mexico.

UMBRELLA SHOP — ACCESSORIES

Map p275 (www.theumbrellashop.com; 1550 Anderson St; ⏲10am-6pm; 🚌50) It may be that the only outdoor gear you need in Vancouver is a sturdy brolly to fend off the relentless rain. This family-run company started in 1935 and has just the thing, with hundreds of bright and breezy designs that should put a smile on the face of any torrentially drenched visitor. Duck inside, choose a great umbrella, then launch yourself back into the tempest.

In summer, the window is taken over by parasols – it's your duty to bring this old-school approach to sunny weather back into vogue. Make sure it's as frilly as possible.

CIRCLE CRAFT — ARTS & CRAFTS

Map p275 (www.circlecraft.net; Net Loft, 1666 Johnston St; ⏲10am-7pm; 🚌50) This 40-year-old cooperative hawks 100% BC arts and crafts, including sculptures from found objects, quirky oversized ceramics and sleek jewelry, with hand-sewn puppets and dolls thrown in (not literally) for good measure. Prices vary considerably but there's usually something here to suit most budgets and just looking around the gallery-like space is fun.

AINSWORTH CUSTOM DESIGN — ARTS & CRAFTS

Map p275 (www.ainsworthcustomdesign.com; 1243 Cartwright St; ⏲10am-6pm Mon-Fri, noon-6pm Sat & Sun; 🚌50) Ostensibly a metal-design studio working to commission, the Ainsworth's front-of-shop area showcases a kaleidoscopic array of arts and crafts by mostly local artists. It's an amazing selection, with bright-colored cartoon monster paintings competing for your attention with cute, handmade greetings cards. You'll get lots of ideas for furnishing rooms that belong to the kind of cool kids who like Roald Dahl.

Prices are good on many of the paintings. Save time to nip upstairs to the mezzanine so you can check out even more.

NEW-SMALL & STERLING STUDIO GLASS — ARTS & CRAFTS

Map p275 (www.hotstudioglass.com; 1440 Old Bridge St; ⏲10am-6pm Mon-Sat, 11am-5pm Sun; 🚌50) Peer through the windows at this family-run artisan glass studio and you can watch the team blow and twirl their stuff. There are plenty of works to purchase in the adjoining store. And you don't have to just watch: for $35 you can create your own spangly flower masterpiece under the guidance of experts.

Additional intensive classes are offered if you're more serious, or you can take the easy route: buy something in the shop and tell everyone back home that you made it yourself.

ROGER'S CHOCOLATES FOOD

Map p275 (www.rogerschocolates.com; 1571 Johnston St; ⏱10am-6pm; 🚌50) This classy West Coast chocolate emporium is based across the water in Victoria, but this is their flagship Vancouver store. Try not to lick the dark wood shelves as you peruse boxes of delectable treats that will never make it back home as souvenirs (and you know it). The rich Victoria Creams are the signature here: maple, coconut and maraschino cherry are highly recommended.

You'll likely be offered a sample or two (especially if you look like you need cheering up) and there's also icecream if you want to pick up a cone for the road.

MICHAEL DEAN JEWELLERY JEWELLERY

Map p275 (www.michaeldeanjewellery.com; 1808 Boatlift Lane; ⏱11am-5pm; 🚌50) Pearls and Canadian diamonds feature prominently in the rings created by local artisan Michael Dean, who works on his shiny trinkets at this cozy little island studio. Wife Carole also creates her own jewelry and has a sparkling range of abstract designs on silver necklaces. If you're looking for something extra special, start here.

SILK WEAVING STUDIO CLOTHING

Map p275 (☎604-687-7455; www.silkweavingstudio.com; 1551 Johnston St; ⏱10am-5pm; 🚌50) Almost hidden in a back alley maze of shops, this little spot turns out luxurious, hand-dyed silk dresses, blouses, scarves, shawls, lingerie, belts and hats in a rainbow of colors. Visitors are welcome to wander through the small waterfront studio and watch the weaving process in action. Silk yarns and fabrics are sold, too. If you're here in June, check out the annual exhibition of top weaving work.

You'll find the studio tucked down a nameless alley under the bridge.

SPORTS & ACTIVITIES

SKOAH SPA

Map p274 (☎604-642-0200; www.skoah.com; 1007 Hamilton St; ⏱10am-8pm Mon-Fri, 9am-7pm Sat & Sun; Ⓜ Yaletown-Roundhouse) 'No whale music and no bubbling cherubs,' as they say at this tongue-in-cheek, trying-hard-not-to-be-pretentious spa. Come for deep-cleansing masks, facial massages, scalp massages, foot 'facials' and muscle stimulation treatments, all done by your 'personal skin-care trainer.' Skoah also sells its own line of all-natural products, and it's one of the locals' fave spa operators.

If you can't make it to this their flagship spa, you'll also find branches in Kitsilano and South Granville.

ECOMARINE PADDLESPORT CENTRES KAYAKING

Map p275 (☎888-425-2925, 604-689-7575; www.ecomarine.com; 1668 Duranleau St; 2/24hr $39/94; ⏱9am-6pm Sun-Thu, to 9pm Fri & Sat Jun-Aug, 10am-6pm Sep-May; 🚌50) Headquartered on Granville Island, the friendly folks at Ecomarine offer guided kayak tours (from $65) as well as kayak and stand-up paddle board (SUP) rentals. At the center's **Jericho Beach branch** (Map p282; ☎604-222-3565; Jericho Sailing Centre, 1300 Discovery St; ⏱9:30am-dusk late Apr-early Sep; 🚌4), events and seminars are organized where you can rub shoulders with local paddle nuts. And from June to September, you'll also find these guys renting kayaks on English Bay beach.

If you have time for just one guided kayak tour, take one of the cool sunset paddles for a memorable experience you'll be telling everyone about when you get back home.

RECKLESS BIKE STORES CYCLING

Map p275 (www.reckless.ca; 1810 Fir St; per 1/5hr $8.25/29.50; ⏱10am-6pm Mon-Fri, to 5pm Sat, 11am-5pm Sun; 🚌50) The team at Reckless have been big players in the city's bike community for years, sponsoring events and supporting initiatives across the region. You'll find a good selection of rental cruisers and mountain bikes, and staff can provide maps of regional road routes. It's located in a no-man's-land of mismatched businesses near the Granville Island entrance; there's also a handy **Yaletown branch** (Map p274; 110 Davie St; ⏱9:30am-7pm Mon-Sat, 10am-6pm Sun).

Commercial Drive

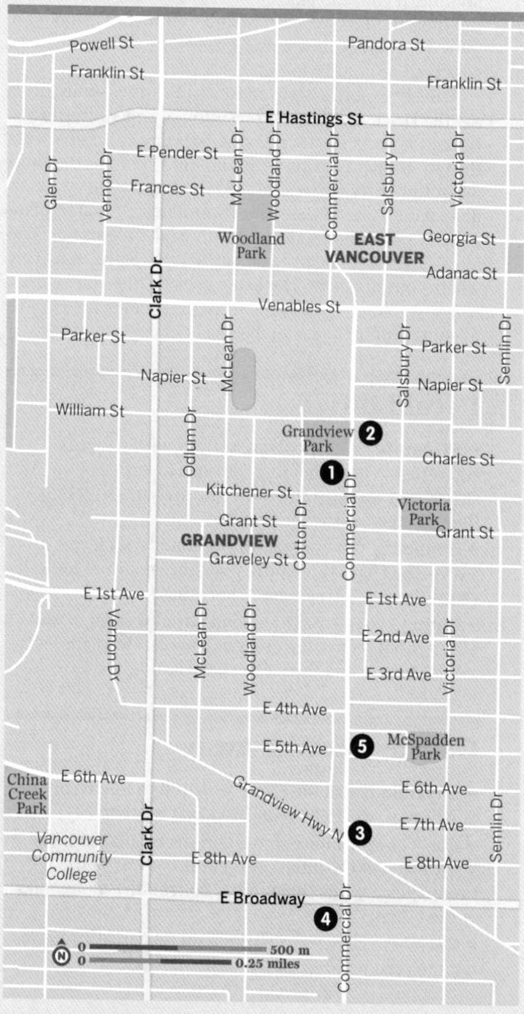

For more detail of this area see Map p276

Neighborhood Top Five

❶ Slurping creamy cappuccinos and watching the world go by at several Italian-run coffee bars, including perky, new **Renzo's** (p124).

❷ Spending a summer evening drinking and dining on a patio at **Havana** (p122).

❸ Diving tongue-first into BC's craft-beer scene with a piquant tasting flight at **St Augustine's** (p122).

❹ Hanging with the locals at a late-night cult movie screening at the **Rio** (p126).

❺ Taking the stage (after a few beers) for poetry slam night at **Cafe Deux Soleil** (p124).

Lonely Planet's Top Tip

When you walk north along Commercial Dr from the SkyTrain station, look out for the sidewalk book vendors that often ply their trade here. There are typically some good deals to be had and you'll have something to read when you pull into your first coffee shop – which will likely be just a couple of minutes away.

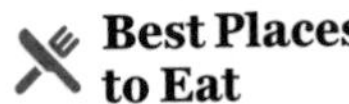

Best Places to Eat

- Cannibal Cafe (p120)
- Kishimoto Japanese Kitchen + Sushi Bar (p120)
- Carthage Cafe (p121)
- Via Tevere (p121)
- Prophouse Cafe (p119)

For reviews, see p119

Best Places to Drink

- Storm Crow Tavern (p122)
- St Augustine's (p122)
- Biercraft Tap & Tapas Bar (p124)
- Renzo's (p124)
- Café Calabria (p124)

For reviews, see p122

Best Places to Shop

- Barefoot Contessa (p128)
- Attic Treasures (p128)
- Licorice Parlour (p128)
- People's Co-Op Bookstore (p128)
- Audiopile (p128)

For reviews, see p128

Explore Commercial Drive

Take SkyTrain's Expo or Millennium line from downtown and when you hop off at Commercial-Broadway station a few minutes later the Drive will be just around the corner. Walk north towards the mountains and everything will unfold in a linear fashion: the Drive's main stores, restaurants and bars run on either side of the street for about 17 blocks until the intersection with Venables. If it's too far to walk, bus number 20 trundles along much of the Drive's main drag so you can jump aboard when you feel tired. Better still, just take a coffee-shop pit stop and you'll be back on your feet in no time. If you're exploring both of East Vancouver's two top thoroughfares – Main St and Commercial – take the 99B-Line express bus along Broadway: it links the two streets in around 10 minutes.

A lively, colorful strip most of the time, some locals say the Drive is at its best on sunny summer afternoons. In fact, it's a perfectly relaxing half-day excursion from the city center. For others, it's languid summer evenings when the Drive thrives. This is the time when its abundant patios are at their most animated. If you're planning to eat here, make sure you wander along the strip for a few blocks before you settle on a place that truly whets your appetite. The same goes for the chatty bars, where you'll meet everyone from pixie-chick bohemians to chin-stroking poets and old-school dope smokers.

Local Life

- **Streetlife** From locals passing by with naughty cigarettes to hand-holding tattooed lovers strolling into stores, just taking a sidewalk cafe seat and watching the Drive go by is recommended.
- **Shopping** The opposite of Robson St's slick chain stores, the Drive is teeming with one-of-a-kind indie shops that are always worth perusing.
- **Dining** Like a far tastier, food-based version of the UN, it often seems like every cuisine on the planet is available here and the locals tuck right in.

Getting There & Away

- **SkyTrain** Board the Expo/Millennium line from downtown to Commercial-Broadway station.
- **Bus** The 99B-Line express and the regular number 9 both stop at the intersection of Broadway and Commercial, while the number 20 trundles along much of the Drive.
- **Car** There is metered parking on the Drive and some nonmetered parking on its residential side streets.

SIGHTS

GRANDVIEW PARK
PARK

Map p276 (Commercial Dr, btwn Charles & William Sts; 20) The Drive's alfresco neighborhood hub is named after the smashing views peeking between its trees: to the north are the North Shore mountains, while to the west is a cityscape vista of twinkling towers. Teeming with buskers, dreadlocked drummers and impromptu sidewalk sales, the park is a big summertime lure for nearby locals.

It originally housed the drill hall of the local Irish Fusiliers and is now home to a slender granite war memorial. Wreaths are still laid here on Remembrance Day.

EATING

The Drive is a strollable smorgasbord of independent and adventurous dining. Combining ethnic soul-food joints, cheap-but-good pizza spots, chatty streetside cafes and the kind of convivial pub-style hangouts that give the concept of 'neighborhood bar' a very good name, this is the city's most sociable dine-out district. It's also Vancouver's patio capital, so if the weather's good, drop by for an alfresco meal.

★ PROPHOUSE CAFE
CAFE $

Map p276 (www.prophousecafe.com; 1636 Venables St; main $7-9; 8am-8pm; ; 20) Just around the corner from the Drive, this is the neighborhood's most original cafe. Next to the unassuming coffee counter at the front, trip up the stairs and you'll enter a funky Aladdin's cave teeming with rentable vintage movie-set props, from tiki masks to leopard-skin chairs. Food-wise, its housemade cookies, sandwiches and a popular veggie burger, while there's live music and performances most nights.

Local musician CR Avery has been known to tickle the keys on the 1950s piano here, while comedy evenings, book launches and folk music also make frequent appearances – check the board of Post-It notes at the front for current happenings. It's opposite the owner's prize possession:

DIPPING INTO THE DRIVE'S PAST

Strolling along bustling Commercial Dr today it's easy to imagine that the counterculture bohemians have ruled this strip forever. But the street has an unexpected past as one of the city's most historic neighborhoods. Once part of the main transportation link between Vancouver and the city of New Westminster, streetcars trundled down the middle of the Drive from the 1890s, triggering many of the storefronts and housing developments that are still here today. Many of these shops were later colonized by European families (mostly Italian as well as some Portuguese) emigrating across the Atlantic in the 1950s. The number of old-school, Euro-style coffee shops still here shows that this period in the Drive's history has never been forgotten.

But the Italians were a later addition to the Drive. While main-drag storefronts catch the eye here today, make sure you take a peek down the side streets. They're lined with gabled, wood-built homes constructed for Canadian Pacific Railway (CPR) workers in the first few years of the last century, and many have been restored in recent decades to their bright-painted clapboard glory. In fact, this neighborhood is home to one of the largest collections of **heritage homes** in Vancouver. Architecture fans will likely spot some well-known styles, including Edwardian, Queen Anne, Craftsman and Arts and Crafts.

In recent years, locals have begun to celebrate the area's rich past and a volunteer organization calling itself the **Grandview Heritage Group** (www.grandviewheritagegroup.org) has formed to help preserve the Drive's architectural treasures. Meeting monthly, the organization's annual **Centenary Birthday Signs** initiative sees houses and buildings in the area that are more than 100 years old recognized with cool plaques. Walkers can then trawl the neighborhood spotting the best examples. There's a map of the included houses on the website, where you'll also find some evocative vintage images of the area's past.

a steampunk-like espresso machine that recalls an old-school diving helmet. If you're on a budget, food is 25% off between 5pm and 7pm.

UPRISING BREADS BAKERY CAFE BAKERY $

Map p276 (www.uprisingbreads.com; 1697 Venables St; mains $6-10; ⏲7am-7pm Mon-Fri, 7am-6pm Sat & Sun; 🚌20) Vancouver's favorite bakery minichain has been satisfying the bread and cake cravings of the locals for 30 years, but this East Side rustic-chic storefront is where it all started. Perfect for coffee and treats any time of day (don't miss the ginger cookies), it's also a great lunch spot for a soup and sandwich, especially if it's warm enough to snag an outdoor table.

This is a good spot to pick up some fresh-baked takeout croissants or a loaf of bread – go for the hearty Finnish loaf.

FRATELLI BAKING BAKERY $

Map p276 (☎604-255-8926; www.fratellibakery.com; 1795 Commercial Dr; baking from $2; ⏲7:30am-5:30pm Tue-Sat, 9am-4pm Sun; 🚌20) An authentic holdover from the Drive's Italian immigrant years, this ever-busy bakery is teeming with fresh-made treats – from loaves of warm asiago cheese bread to more cakes and pastries than you could possibly sample in a lifetime. No harm in trying, though: you might be surprised how far you get. Whatever you go for, don't miss a creamy Neapolitan slice (or two).

Consider starting the makings of a great picnic here and then combining it with some cheese and charcuterie at the Italian deli next door. Once your ad hoc lunch is fully gathered, weave north a few blocks and find a picnic perch in Grandview Park.

BELGIAN FRIES FAST FOOD $

Map p276 (1185 Commercial Dr; mains $5-12; ⏲11am-10pm Mon-Wed, 11am-midnight Thu-Sat; 🚌20) The flagship location of this irresistible local minichain flies the deep-fried flag for what may be Canada's national dish. Originating in Quebec, poutine is a naughty pile of crispy fries topped with gravy and cheese curds. And it's seriously delicious. There are lots of additional treats and toppings – plus larger dishes – but fries (and a beer) is the main reason for coming here.

Check the roster of local craft beers: if there's anything from Storm Brewing, snap it up (its ales are made right here on the Drive).

LA CASA GELATO ICE CREAM $

(www.lacasagelato.com; 1033 Venables St; single scoops $4.50; ⏲11am-11pm; 🚌20) If you've been skiing, cycling, kayaking or just on your feet all day exploring the neighborhoods, it may be time to cool down with an ice-cold treat. A visit to Vancouver's fave ice-cream joint should hit the spot, although you'll likely get brain-freeze trying to choose from the bewildering kaleidoscope of flavors – 518 at last count.

SWEET CHERUBIM VEGETARIAN $

Map p276 (www.sweetcherubim.com; 1105 Commercial Dr; mains $6-12; ⏲10am-10pm Mon-Sat, 11am-10pm Sun; 🖉; 🚌20) Many Drive restaurants offer vegetarian options but Sweet Cherubim – attached to a wholefood grocery store – goes the whole hog with a full-on vegan and veggie menu of hearty, well-priced comfort foods. There's an Indian feel to much of the menu, with pakoras and chapati wraps proving justifiably popular. Go for the great-value thali combo to fuel up for the day.

The desserts are also worth dropping in for. Consider a mid-afternoon pit stop on the woodsy patio with a cheeky Nanaimo bar or a not-quite-so-cheeky raw hemp and blueberry smoothie.

★CANNIBAL CAFÉ BURGERS $$

Map p276 (www.cannibalcafe.ca; 1818 Commercial Dr; main $12-15; ⏲11:30am-midnight; 👪; 🚌20) This is a punk-tastic diner for fans of seriously real burgers. Made with love (and the service here is ever-friendly), you'll find an inventive array from classics to the highly recommended Korean BBQ burger. Top-notch ingredients will ensure you never return to a fast-food joint. Check the board outside for daily specials and keep in mind that there's a good kids menu here, too.

KISHIMOTO JAPANESE KITCHEN + SUSHI BAR JAPANESE $$

Map p276 (2054 Commercial Dr; combo mains $9-14; ⏲11:30am-2:30pm & 5-9:45pm Tue-Sun; 🚌20) Reservations are not accepted at the Drive's best Japanese restaurant, so arrive early to snag a table or expect to join a long line. Even if you have to queue, it'll be worth it: the sushi here uses fresh ingredients with exquisite presentation and attentive service. The salmon and OMG rolls are recommended but they also do an excellent *okonomiyaki* (Japanese pancake).

The menu is generally good value, but consider a combo bento box for the full stomach-stuffing effect. And if the pine mushroom soup is available, slurp it up immediately: it's a seasonal house specialty.

CARTHAGE CAFE FRENCH $$

Map p276 (www.carthage-cafe.com; 1851 Commercial Dr; main $15-32; ⏲5-11pm Mon, 11:30am-3pm & 5-11pm Tue-Sat, 5-10pm Sun; 🚌20) This hidden gem is the Drive's most romantic European-style restaurant. Hunker in a candlelit corner with your date and stare lovingly at a menu of French-Tunisian dishes that come to your table perfectly prepared. You can't go wrong with the spicy lamb shank on couscous, but consider the mussels, too (coconutty Asian-style recommended). This is also a great spot to sample a tapas plate of escargot. They're served in traditional style, drenched in garlic butter. Expect excellent, old-school service.

VIA TEVERE PIZZA $$

Map p276 (www.viateverepizzeria.com; 1190 Victoria Dr; mains $12-19; ⏲5-10pm Tue-Thu, 5-11pm Fri & Sat, 5-9pm Sun; 🚌20) Just two blocks east from the Drive, it's worth the five-minute walk for what may well be East Van's best pizza. Which is saying something, since the Drive is studded like an over-packed pepperoni pie with good pizza joints. Run by a family with true Neapolitan roots, check out the mosaic-tiled wood-fired oven, then launch yourself into a feast: capricciosa highly recommended. There's a focus on simple, but supremely well-made classic pizzas here, which means even the margherita is the perfect example of how amazing pizza should taste.

There's a respectable wine list as well, or you can bring your own bottle for a $20 corkage fee.

LA MEZCALERIA MEXICAN $$

Map p276 (1622 Commercial Dr; ⏲5pm-midnight; 🚌20) The upmarket Mexican brother of Vancouver's beloved La Taqueria mini-chain. Expect superb little soft tacos topped with delectable ingredients like pork confit, zarandeado fish and braised beef cheeks. Take a perch at the long bar and you can also chat with the kind of servers that give friendliness a good name. And don't miss the drinks list: the eyebrow-raising mezcal and tequila menu is serious.

Handily, you can do tastings here so you can sip on Mexico's finest booze creations without your head swimming too much.

PALKI RESTAURANT INDIAN $$

Map p276 (www.palkirestaurant.com; 1130 Commercial Dr; mains $13-23; ⏲11:30am-2:30pm & 4:30-10pm Mon-Fri, 11:30am-10pm Fri & Sat, 4:30-10pm Sun; 🚌20) Don't be discouraged by the drab, gray-brick exterior of this popular Indian restaurant: inside, it's cozy and welcoming with a swish, contemporary look. Budget-huggers should check out the weekday all-you-can-eat buffet ($10.95), but it's worth coming back in the evening for a more considered approach. Start with a mixed platter of samosas and pakoras then graduate to the excellent lamb rogan josh.

It's a good idea to share a few dishes here – note that there's a Northern Indian feel to much of the menu.

FALCONETTI'S EAST SIDE GRILL PUB $$

Map p276 (www.falconettis.com; 1812 Commercial Dr; mains $10-22; ⏲11:30am-1pm Sun-Thu, 11:30am-2am Fri & Sat; 🚌20) A local legend that's expanded far beyond its grungy, hole-in-the-wall start, Falconetti's is still famed for its house-made sausage hot dogs. You'll come here for a beer – Storm Scottish Ale (made just down the street) recommended – but it's a crime not to sink your teeth into a Hot Italian with fries. In summer, aim for a rooftop patio perch.

The menu, like the establishment, has expanded in recent years, with burgers, steaks and a popular weekend brunch added to the mix. There's live music here most nights but consider Tuesday's trivia quiz, which shows that Falconetti's still has a pubbish approach to a great night out. If you like what you scoff, there's also an adjoining take-home sausage deli counter.

MERCHANT'S OYSTER BAR SEAFOOD $$

Map p276 (www.merchantsoysterbar.ca; 1590 Commercial Dr; small plates from $7-14; ⏲5-11pm daily, 10:30am-2:30pm Sat & Sun; 🚌20) This classy little corner joint seems like it would be more at home in chichi Yaletown, but it's developed a loyal following among Drive locals looking for a romantic night out. There are a few additional small plates (including bison tartare), as well as a weekend brunch, but the freshly shucked bivalves in a candlelit setting are what most come here for.

Check the website before you come for buck-a-shuck specials and happy hours. And ask about BC wines: there are usually several top tipples to choose from here.

TIMBRE PUB $$

Map p276 (www.timbrerestaurant.com; 2068 Commercial Dr; mains $12-19; ⏲4pm-1am Mon-Thu, 4am-2pm Fri, 11am-2am Sat, 11am-1am Sun; Ⓜ Commercial-Broadway) This buzzy, wood-lined neighborhood resto-bar is a popular weekend brunch spot (live bluegrass music included), while its dinner menu focuses on the usual range of comfort grub: burgers, sandwiches and steaks. The beer list offers some good BC craft brews – if there's a Driftwood Farmhand or fat Tug IPA, snap it up.

On summer evenings, aim for a perch on the tiny porch and you can watch the Drive's happy locals strutting by.

HAVANA LATIN AMERICAN $$

Map p276 (www.havanarestaurant.ca; 1212 Commercial Dr; mains $14-27; ⏲5-10pm Mon-Thu, 10am-midnight Fri, Sat & Sun; 🚌20) The granddaddy of Drive dining buzzes on summer evenings when its patio – the area's largest – is animated with clamorous chatter. With a couple of counterculture holdovers (check the graffiti-scratched walls inside and the back gallery/theater combo), it's all about mojito pitchers and a comfort menu combining tacos, 'Cuban sandwiches' and jerk chicken wraps. Go for the jambalaya.

Expect to wait for a park-view patio perch on peak summer evenings. And if you get one, hold onto it for dear life – or at least until the next round of drinks turns up.

REEF CARIBBEAN $$

Map p276 (www.thereefrestaurant.com; 1018 Commercial Dr; mains $10-19; ⏲11am-10pm Mon-Fri, 10am-11pm Sat & Sun; 🚌20) The funkily bright interior and Caribbean soul-food menu at this cheery joint can almost chase away the city's rainy-day blues. Stomach-lagging dishes like St Barts lamb shank and eye-poppingly spicy curries help, but don't ignore the saltfish Jamaican patties, which will have you returning for more. Cocktails are also a specialty (try the Dark & Stormy) and all are also available booze-free.

DRINKING & NIGHTLIFE

If you like your drinks served with a frothy head of ever-chatty locals, the Drive's friendly neighborhood bars are hard to beat – especially on a sunny day with a patio seat to be had. And don't forget: this is the best neighborhood in town for java fans, so you'll find a tasty surfeit of coffeehouse options as well.

★STORM CROW TAVERN PUB

Map p276 (www.stormcrowtavern.com; 1305 Commercial Dr; ⏲4pm-1am Mon-Thu, 11am-1am Fri & Sat; 🚌20) Knowing the difference between Narnia and *Neverwhere* is not a prerequisite for enjoying this smashing Commercial Dr nerd pub. But if you do, you'll certainly make new friends. With displays of *Dr Who* figures and steampunk rayguns – plus a TV that seems to be always screening *Game of Thrones* – dive into the craft beer here and settle in for a fun evening.

There's a small but perfectly formed menu of BC brews (plus some knowingly named cocktails like Romulan Ale and Release the Kraken), while the grub is of the cheap-and-cheerful sandwiches and shepherd's pie variety. There are also role-play books and a wall of board games for the so-inclined (if you know what Elfenland is, that means you), while live events, including comedy nights, were just being introduced on our visit. A warm and friendly spot for a night out with some quirky locals.

ST AUGUSTINE'S PUB

Map p276 (www.staugustinesvancouver.com; 2360 Commercial Dr; ⏲11am-1am Sun-Thu, to 2am Fri & Sat; Ⓜ Commercial-Broadway) Looking like a regular neighborhood sports bar from the outside, step inside St Aug's and you'll find more than 40 on-tap microbrews – one of the largest selections in the city. Most are from BC – look out for highlights from Russell Brewing, Storm Brewing and Howe Sound Brewing – but there's also an intriguing selection from south of the border as well.

Drop by for Monday evening's cask night and you'll find a special-guest tipple on offer, often a seasonal brew like winter ale or a springtime IPA. And if you're just not sure what to order, ask for the four-glass tasting flight. The food is of the standard pub-grub variety. Check the website to see

Neighborhood Walk Commercial Drive Drink & Dine

START ST AUGUSTINE'S
END PROPHOUSE CAFE
LENGTH 1KM; AN HOUR OR THREE (DEPENDING ON DRINKING)

From the Commercial-Broadway SkyTrain station, walk north one block to **1 St Augustine's** (p122), a large local bar. You'll find one of the city's biggest array of draft, mostly BC microbrews (four-beer tasting flights recommended). If you haven't indulged too much, continue north on Commercial – don't worry, it's a straight line – and sober up with a coffee at **2 Prado Café** (p124). If you're packing your laptop, there's free wi-fi here. And if it feels like time for a rest, continue north and lay back in the grass at **3 Grandview Park** (p119) – but not before you've checked out the handsome vistas to the north (the mountains) and west (the downtown cityscape).

Peel yourself from the park and nip next door to Euro-style **4 Biercraft Tap & Tapas Bar** (p124). Play it safe with a whiskey or work your way down the amazing menu of local and imported microbrews. Even better, forsake the booze and try a fortifying bowl of Belgian-style mussels.

If you didn't eat at Biercraft, head across the road and drop into the cheery Caribbean-themed **5 Reef** (p122). The hearty soul food here is nicely spicy. And if you're keen to stay on an even keel, the tropical cocktails also come in handy nonalcoholic versions.

If it's still open, stroll a few doors along to salivate over the eclectic little **6 Licorice Parlour** (p128). Aside from the dozens of imported varieties, it sells handmade hula-hoops (an ideal purchase unless your head is still reeling from the beer earlier).

Finally, sober-up with a coffee around the corner on Venables St at the quirky **7 Prophouse Cafe** (p119). There may even be an act or two in the tiny corner performance space. And if it's open-mike night, you may be tempted to recite that epic poem you've been working on: 'Ode to Beer'.

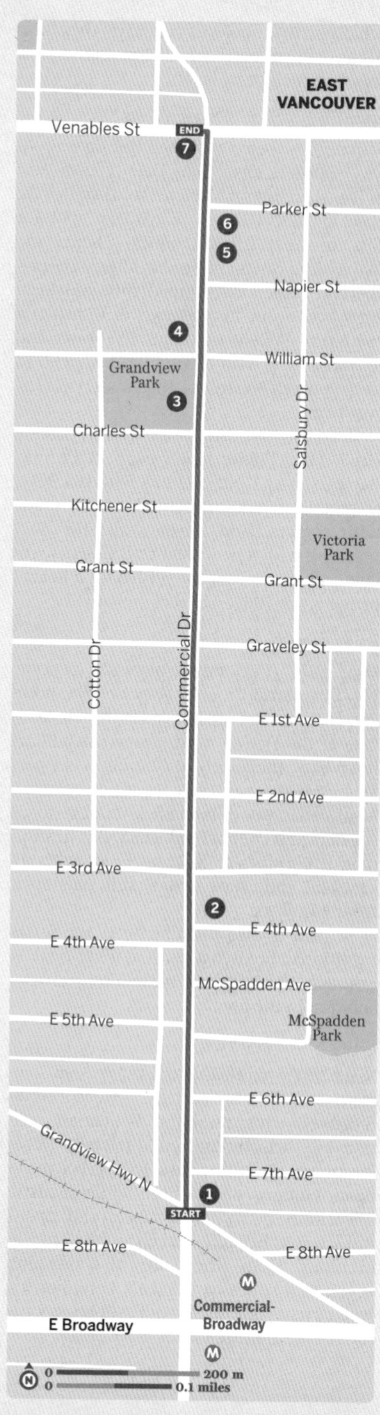

what's on draft before you arrive: they have a clever 'live' beer menu that shows how much of each brew is left.

BIERCRAFT TAP & TAPAS BAR

BAR

Map p276 (www.biercraft.com; 1191 Commercial Dr; ⌚10am-11:30pm Sun, 11am-11:30pm Mon & Tue, 11am-midnight Wed & Thu, 11am-1am Fri, 10am-1am Sat; 🚌20) A pilgrimage spot for fans of great Belgian brews – hence the astonishing menu of dozens of rare beers – Biercraft has also jumped into the local craft-beer scene in recent years. Consider a taste-test of Belgian versus BC brews and accompany it with a few plates of grub to keep yourself coherent – the mussels are the way to go.

Belgian-wise, the brews here include fruity Mort Subite Kriek, coppery Chimay Rouge, strong Golden Draak and dark X.O., a brooding, end-of-the-night beer made with cognac. And if you wake the next morning with a head that feels like a medicine ball on a toothpick, return for a hearty brunch (eggs Benedict recommended).

CHARLATAN

PUB

Map p276 (www.thecharlatanrestaurant.com; 1447 Commercial Dr; ⌚4pm-1am Mon-Thu, noon-2am Fri, 11am-2am Sat, 11am-midnight Sun; 🚌20) One of the Drive's most popular neighborhood bars, the darkly lit Charlatan is a perfect rainy-day hunker spot if you want to head to the wood-lined back room for beer specials and comfort pub grub. But in summer, it becomes a different beast with its excellent and ever-popular patio plus open front windows.

Brunch is also popular here: the $9.95 traditional breakfast with Caesar deal is arguably the best hair-of-the-dog recovery solution in the area.

CAFE DEUX SOLEILS

CAFE

Map p276 (www.cafedeuxsoleils.com; 2096 Commercial Dr; ⌚8am-midnight; Ⓜ Commercial-Broadway) This rambling bohemian cafe is a hip, healthy and child-friendly Drive landmark. On sunny days, folks relax at the open windows with a beer, while acoustic musicians, performance poets and open-mike wannabes often take the stage in the evenings. There are plenty of good-value vegetarian snacks and meals here, but it's just a great spot to chill out and hang with the counterculture locals.

Poetry slams are held on Monday nights ($6 cover charge) and shows start at 8pm (doors open 7pm). This is your big chance to regale the locals with your modern retelling of 'The Rhyme of the Ancient Mariner', perhaps while playing a lute.

ROYAL CANADIAN LEGION

BAR

Map p276 (2205 Commercial Dr; noon-10pm Mon-Thu, noon-12:30pm Fri & Sat) Local hipsters have claimed this typically basic Legion social club as their own, congregating outside to smoke, then nipping back in for cheap beers and a chatty ambience. The old timers seem to be happy that the place is still being used and the darts board hasn't seen so much action in years; there's also free ping-pong and shuffleboard, plus Tuesday-night Scrabble. The perfect spot for a budget-friendly night out.

RENZO'S

COFFEE

Map p276 (1301 Commercial Dr; ⌚9am-8pm; 📶; 🚌20) Showing that not all the Drive's Italian coffee shops are traditional old haunts, this bright, perky and relatively new corner spot is a breath of fresh air. Overlooking Grandview Park, expect a jazzy soundtrack and tables topped with little airplants – plus some excellent java made on a shiny machine that looks like the sibling of a Vespa.

Check out the local artworks studding the walls and consider a food fuel-up: there are cakes, treats and $8 made-to-order pannini sandwiches available. Cash only.

CAFÉ CALABRIA

COFFEE

Map p276 (1745 Commercial Dr; ⌚6am-10pm Mon-Thu, 6am-midnight Fri & Sat; 🚌20) When Vancouverites tell you the Drive is the city's best coffee street, this is one of the places they're thinking about. It tops a healthy mug-full of cafes founded here by Italian immigrants. Don't be put off by the chandeliers-and-statues decor (not everyone likes a side order of statuesque genitalia with their drink): just order an espresso, sit outside and watch the Drive slide by.

PRADO CAFÉ

COFFEE

Map p276 (www.pradocafe.com; 1938 Commercial Dr; ⌚7am-8pm; 📶; 🚌20) Eschewing the kitsch-heavy interiors of some Commercial Dr coffee shops, the comparatively austere Prado is the kind of place where minimalists sup in peace. But it's not just about aesthetics: the baristas here are serious about

WORTH A DETOUR

EASTSIDE MICROBREWERY CRAWL

If you're a true beer nut, consider checking out a round of little, off-the-beaten-path East Vancouver microbreweries that even some locals don't know about. Stay on the Drive and continue walking north for about 10 minutes past the intersection with Venables St and into an old industrial part of town (it's perfectly safe). You'll come to **Storm Brewing** (☎604-255-9119; www.stormbrewing.org; 310 Commercial Dr; 🚌20), a local legend beermaker that's been crafting great ales since 1995. Call ahead for an impromptu tour (Wednesday is brewing day, so that's the best time to come). With any luck, you'll be able to sample their excellent Black Plague Stout. Continue north for two blocks and turn right onto Powell St. A few minutes along, you'll find the lovely **Powell Street Craft Brewery** (www.powellbeer.com; 1830 Powell St; ⏲1-7pm Wed-Sat; 🚌4). This art-lined, gable-roofed nanobrewery is one of the city's smallest beer producers. Consider a sample of the lip-smacking Dive Bomb Porter, and pick-up a takeout growler to go. Despite its diminutive stature, this producer stunned beer fans across the country in 2013 when its Old Jalopy Pale Ale was named the nation's Beer of the Year at the annual Canadian Brewing Awards. Continue east on Powell, turn right onto Victoria Dr and then left on Triumph St. Within a couple of minutes, you'll hit the storefront of **Parallel 49 Brewing Company** (www.parallel49brewing.com; 1950 Triumph St; ⏲noon-9pm; 🚌14). Nip into the tasting room here and sample the array of quirky tipples, including Hoparazzi India Pale Lager and Gypsy Tears Ruby Red Ale.

their fair-trade coffee, which – don't tell the Italians down the street – may be the best on the Drive.

Recent new owners have altered very little here and this is still the hippest coffee spot on the Drive, beloved of MacBook-wielding regulars quietly updating their Facebook status.

BUMP N GRIND — COFFEE

Map p276 (www.bumpngrindcafe.com; 916 Commercial Dr; ⏲7am-7pm Mon-Fri, 8am-7pm Sat & Sun; 📶; 🚌20) Showing that Drive locals can never get enough good java, this more recent addition to Commercial's coffeehouse culture deploys a comfy modern lounge approach. But there's still a strong commitment to great brews – which is not always the case among the area's highly competitive scene. It also uses beans from popular 49th Parallel: the current Vancouver 'it' roaster.

Friendly service is a byword here and there's also an array of good-value cakes, cookies, wraps and sandwiches if you can't live by coffee alone.

JJ BEAN — COFFEE

Map p276 (www.jjbeancoffee.com; 2206 Commercial Dr; ⏲6am-10pm; Ⓜ Commercial-Broadway) Many Vancouver coffee bars close their doors too early for those who want to hang out at night but don't want to drink booze. This JJ Bean, one of the oldest outlets of a popular citywide minichain, subverts that by opening into the wee hours (of 10pm). There's a cozy, almost neighborhood-pub, feel to this friendly joint and, befitting its Drive location, there's a chatty patio for summertime sipping.

With quality house-roasted beans on sale, consider picking up an apposite souvenir for coffee-loving friends back home: a bag of rich, earthy Eastside Blend. No wi-fi.

CAFFE ROMA — COFFEE

Map p276 (1510 Commercial Dr; ⏲8am-8pm; 🚌20) The best place to be in Vancouver when the FIFA World Cup tournament is on, this grungy neighborhood coffee spot is like a social club for old Italian dudes, who sit scanning the TVs and watching sports all day. It hasn't changed for decades and that's its main charm. Expect good coffee plus some handy pizzas slices: that other Italian food group.

A great spot to imagine yourself in a backstreet, no-nonsense coffee bar in Italy. You'll likely hear plenty of chatter of the soccer-related variety and if you drink enough espresso here, you might even begin to understand it.

ENTERTAINMENT

★CULTCH (VANCOUVER EAST CULTURAL CENTRE) THEATER

Map p276 (www.thecultch.com; 1895 Venables St; ⏲varies; 🚌20) This once-abandoned 1909 church has been a gathering place for performers and audiences since being officially designated as a cultural space in 1973. Following a comprehensive recent renovation, the beloved Cultch (as everyone calls it) is now one of Vancouver's entertainment jewels with a busy roster of local, fringe and visiting theatrical shows from spoken word to touring Chekov productions.

Check the online calendar to see what's on stage during your visit. And, after the show, hang around in the lobby wine bar to meet the locals and check out the exhibition in the on-site art gallery – it changes every three weeks. While you're here, ask the staff about the nearby **York Theatre**, a renovated studio performance space the Cultch plans to open soon.

RIO THEATRE CINEMA, THEATER

Map p276 (www.riotheatre.ca; 1660 E Broadway; ⏲varies; Ⓜ Commercial-Broadway) A recently restored 1980s movie house with very comfy seats, the Rio is like a community rep theater staging everything from blockbuster and art-house movies to live music (there's an excellent sound system), spoken word and saucy burlesque nights. Check the calendar to see what's on: Friday night's midnight cult movies (from *Donny Darko* to *The Rocky Horror Picture Show*) are always popular.

GRANDVIEW LANES BOWLING CENTRE BOWLING

Map p276 (www.grandviewbowling.com; 2195 Commercial Dr; ⏲10am-11pm Mon-Wed, to midnight Thu, to 1am Fri & Sat, to 10pm Sun; Ⓜ Commercial-Broadway) For many, the Drive's best night out is to be had slipping on some rented shoes and hitting the lanes at this family-run, old-school gem. But it's not the regular 10-pin lanes upstairs that get everyone excited. Downstairs is home to a local nightlife legend: five-pin, glow-in-the-dark bowling that's as much fun as anyone can handle on a big night out.

WISE HALL MUSIC, CABARET

Map p276 (www.wisehall.ca; 1882 Adanac St; ⏲varies; 🚌20) This comfortably grungy former church hall is a friendly neighborhood spot that's close to the heart of in-the-know locals who flock here to catch live ska, salsa, improv shows and the occasional hip-hop DJ night. Check the schedule for events or just hang out in the lounge (ask the bartender to sign you in as a guest).

It's a great place to mix with cool East Vancouverites; the bouncy floor here brings out the mosh-pit desires in the most reluctant of dancers. Regular monthly events include the quirky Taboo Revue burlesque show and the **Eastside Flea**, a community market of vintage togs and artisan bits and bobs.

THE DRIVE'S BEST FESTS

In addition to the Pacific National Exhibition (p127) a few blocks away, consider celebrating Commercial Drive's rich Italian heritage at the annual **Italian Day** (www.italianday.ca) festival, a street party of music, bocce ball and plenty of food. Expect to see generations of Italian families flocking to the neighborhood to hold court at sidewalk cafes during this day-long event, mingling with street vendors and fostering a festive atmosphere that welcomes all. Check the website for dates and information.

June's family-friendly **Car Free Day** (www.carfreevancouver.org) sees the street closed to traffic and turned into a huge fiesta of food, music, face-painting and stands selling or demonstrating artsy creations. In August, feel free to support or join in the annual **Dyke March** (www.vancouverdykemarch.com), which has been a East Van tradition for years.

Also look out for the city's fave Halloween happening if you're here at that time of year: staged by Vancouver's Public Dreams Society, the **Parade of Lost Souls** (www.publicdreams.org) invites locals to dress up in their most alluringly ghoulish attire, stroll *en masse* with lanterns along a route that usually includes Commercial Dr and congregate (often in Grandview Park) for a spot of flaming shrine building. It's as much fun as any self-respecting zombie-wannabe could ever hope for.

WORTH A DETOUR

VANCOUVER'S SUMMER FAIR

Some of Vancouver's summer events and festivities have been around for several decades, but only one is still going strong after more than a century. Started in 1912, the **Pacific National Exhibition** (PNE; www.pne.bc.ca; Hastings Park, East Vancouver) – known simply as the PNE by locals – is held just a few blocks from the northern end of Commercial Dr (hop on the Hastings St bus number 14 for faster access) and it's an August tradition for generations of Vancouverites. Starting life as an agricultural fare and community festival, the fair has done a good job of updating itself over the years. It continues to be a popular, family-friendly day out, and a great way for visitors to rub shoulders with locals; it's hard to imagine an event that caters so well to such a diverse range of interests.

Plan ahead for a successful visit: check the website to see what entertainment you'd like to catch, then arrive as close to opening time as you can in the morning. This helps beat the crowds but also gives you the chance to see as much as possible. The parkland site is crammed with **exhibition halls** and **arenas**; take time to check out the market halls lined with vendors selling 'miracle' made-for-TV products. Then head to the **livestock barns**: the PNE is an important agricultural show for regional farmers, and the barns are lined for the duration with prize horses, cows, goats and sheep. To keep things lively, there are also **piglet races** that get the crowds roaring. There are **horse shows** in the domed stadium, which also give a you a chance to take a seat and plot the rest of your day using the printed program.

Included with your admission (typically around $20) are a wide array of performances running all day. In recent years, these have often included **Chinese acrobats**, **motorcycle stunts** and – the star attraction – the **SuperDogs** show. These talented mutts perform races and stunts for hollering crowds in what has become a PNE tradition. But they're not the only ones showing off: there's **live music** on alfresco stages throughout the day, especially in the evening when nostalgic acts like Olivia Newton-John and ABBA tribute bands add to the party atmosphere.

Not everyone wants to stick around and watch their parents dance, though, and there are other attractions. The **Playland fairground** offers more than 50 rides from dodgems to horror houses, but the top lure for thrill-seekers is the 1950s-built wooden **rollercoaster**. Coaster aficionados from across North America frequently eulogize this scream-triggering bone-shaker, which reaches speeds of up to 75km/hour. It's usually a good idea to go on it before indulging in the final big attraction.

This is the one time of year when Vancouverites forget about their yoga-and-rice-cakes regimen, happily loosening their pants and stuffing themselves silly. The midway here is jam-packed with treats from **giant barbecued turkey legs** to **two-foot-long hotdogs**. Deep-fried everything is also a recent trend (from Oreo cookies to ice-cream) while older culinary traditions still lure: you'll see plenty of older visitors munching on scones from one of the Tudoresque stands, while just about everyone else will be sticking their hands into warm paper bags of **minidonuts**, fresh-fried at several family-run stands around the site.

Don't spend all your money on food, though, because you'll need some for the big **lottery**. Take a walk through the show home, then enter the draw; you might win a brand new house, furnishings included. Try fitting that in your suitcase.

LIBRA ROOM JAZZ

Map p276 (www.libraroom.com; 1608 Commercial Dr; ⌚3:30pm-1am Mon-Thu, 3:30pm-2am Fri, 10am-2am Sat, 10am-1am Sun; 🚌20) This glowing, brick and art-lined long room is a cozy, loungelike spot for a relaxing, chatty dinner over a martini or three. Even better is the roster of nightly live music – typically of the smooth jazz variety – when two hopping house bands hit the stage (not at the same time, luckily) to deliver a mellow, toe-tapping side dish.

The kind of place you'd happily stay into the wee hours (they'll probably kick you out around 1am), the Libra Room is one of the Drive's most popular live venues. Consider dropping by on Tuesday for the $11 burger and beer night.

VANCOUVER POETRY SLAM PERFORMING ARTS

Map p276 (www.vancouverpoetryhouse.com; Cafe Deux Soleils, 2096 Commercial Dr; 8pm Mon; Commercial-Broadway) If you thought poetry was a tweedy, soporific experience, check out the events organized by the Vancouver Poetry House at Cafe Deux Soleils for a taste of high-speed, high-stakes slamming. The expert performers will blow your socks off with their verbal dexterity, which often bears more than a passing resemblance to rap. Every fourth Monday is also Youth Slam.

The venue itself offers vegetarian eats and local craft beers (down some Storm Brewing ales and you'll soon be considering your own on-stage appearance).

SHOPPING

Like a counterculture department store stretched along both sides of one street, the Drive is Vancouver's 'anti Robson.' You'll find dozens of eclectic, independent shops here, ranging from ethical clothing stores to intelligent-minded bookshops. If the area sounds a little too earnest, keep in mind that Commercial also has plenty of frivolous shopping outlets where you can pick up handmade chocolates and pop-culture gifts for your friends back home. Coffee-shop central, the Drive is a great place to shop and sup on a lazy afternoon.

BAREFOOT CONTESSA CLOTHING

Map p276 (www.thebarefootcontessa.com; 1928 Commercial Dr; 11am-6pm; 20) Vintage-look dresses and sparkling costume jewelry – plus a 1920s-style flapper hat or two – are the mainstays of this popular women's-wear boutique aimed at those who never want to be a clone of a chain-store mannequin. You'll find cute tops and accessories from Canadian and international designers, plus extras like artsy-craftsy purses and laptop bags trimmed with lace.

The staff here are famously friendly with plenty of suggestions for the perfect new look.

ATTIC TREASURES VINTAGE

Map p276 (www.attictreasuresvancouver.com; 944 Commercial Dr; 11am-6pm Tue, Thur-Sat, noon-5pm Sun; 20) One of Vancouver's favorite antiques stores, this retro-cool double-room shop specializes in mid-century furniture and treasures. Peruse the candy-colored coffee pots and cocktail glasses and save time for the clutter room at the back, where bargains sometimes live. Much of the furniture has a Danish modern feel and there are also collections of German pottery and Finnish glassware.

Ask the front-desker to turn on the revolving display of salt and pepper pots on the counter: from poodles to mini toilet bowls, it's amazing what people used to buy to put on their dinner tables.

★LICORICE PARLOUR FOOD

Map p276 (1002 Commercial Dr; 11am-6pm; 20) Just when you think you'll never find that combination licorice and hula-hoop store you've been searching for all your life, here it is. A perky little spot with a serious commitment to the love-it-or-hate-it candy, there are 65 varieties here – including an entire row of salt licorice. Work off your candy belly with a hula-hoop: they'll even teach you a few moves.

There's also a carefully curated array of nostalgic candy, including ruby-red Wax Lips and a few treats that only those from the Netherlands will ever have heard of. And if licorice doesn't meet all your nutrient requirements, pick up some quinoa waffle cookies: they make them in the kitchen out back.

PEOPLE'S CO-OP BOOKSTORE BOOKS

Map p276 (www.peoplescoopbookstore.com; 1391 Commercial Dr; noon-6pm Mon-Thu, noon-8pm Fri & Sat, noon-5pm Sun; 20) A Commercial Dr fixture for more than 70 years and a loud echo of the Drive's counterculture heyday, this is the bookshop to pick-up the latest copy of *Proletarian* magazine. But it's not all revolutionary fervor. The sky-blue stacks include art and cookery tomes – with new and used volumes mixed together – alongside their 'Labour' and 'Philosophy & Political Economy' sections.

AUDIOPILE MUSIC

Map p276 (www.audiopile.com; 2016 Commercial Dr; 11am-7pm Mon-Sat, noon-6pm Sun; 20) This little local-fave record store takes a no-nonsense approach with its basic racks of well-priced new and used vinyl and CD recordings. Perfect for that rare Velvet Underground (or not-so-rare Suzi Quatro) album you've always wanted, make sure you check the bargain CDs near the entrance where there are plenty of tempting steals for just $2.99 a pop.

This is the perfect location for a rainy-day rummage and the staff really knows their stuff: quiz them on Half Man Half Biscuit albums and see if they flinch.

CANTERBURY TALES — BOOKS

Map p276 (2010 Commercial Dr; ⏲11am-5:30pm Mon-Sat, noon-5pm Sun; 🚌20) Serving the area's well-read bohemians, this used (and occasionally new) bookstore is one of several literary nooks along the Drive. It's a mini-labyrinth of floor-to-ceiling stacks bulging with titles, including some quirky staff picks near the entrance – sci-fi and fantasy nuts should also check the ever-growing sections at the back of the store. Also a good spot to buy your new Moleskin journal.

There's a well-curated literary travel section near the center of the stacks. And consider picking up a Bukowski anthology or two: the infamous American author and poet gave a few notorious live readings on the Drive back in the day.

LA GROTTA DEL FORMAGGIO — DELI

Map p276 (1791 Commercial Dr; ⏲9am-6pm Mon-Thu & Sat, 9am-7pm Fri, 10am-5:30pm Sun; 🚌20) If you insist on eating something other than chocolate or ice cream, drop into this legendary old-school deli, a family-run holdover from the days when this was Vancouver's 'Little Italy.' Peruse the lip-smacking cheese and charcuterie selections then check out the wall of marzipan, antipasti, olive oil and balsamic vinegar. Almost everything here has been imported from the mother country.

A good spot to gather the makings of a mighty fine picnic – prosciutto and smoked ricotta recommended – you can scoff the lot in nearby Grandview Park. But before you leave the store, check out the ceiling: it's painted with clouds just like the Sistine Chapel (but better).

MINTAGE — VINTAGE

Map p276 (www.mintagevintage.com; 1714 Commercial Dr; ⏲10am-7pm Mon-Sat, 11am-6pm Sun; 🚌20) The store where Vancouver hipsters come to add a little vintage glam to their look, Mintage is a great spot for an afternoon of browsing. Some new lines add to the mix, but it's mostly about uncovering that 1960s prom dress that will make you the envy of your next retro cocktail house party. There are togs for both men and women here.

Don't miss the funky costume jewelry selection and check out the array of cleverly reworked clothes that give new life to old, otherwise unfashionable pieces.

WOMYNS' WARE — ADULT SHOP

Map p276 (www.womynsware.com; 896 Commercial Dr; ⏲11am-6pm; 🚌20) Unlike any other sex shop, this friendly, ultrawelcoming spot is dedicated to female sexual empowerment. There's an eye-popping menu of sex toys and the helpful staff is happy to explain the workings of everything from the 'family jewels harness' to 'nun's habit flogger.' There's also a good array of books and games to put the fun back into your sexual shenanigans.

Fair-trade committed, the store is a great place for first-timers looking for tips and encouragement in a nonseedy, nonjudgmental setting.

MIS'CEL'LA'NY FINDS — VINTAGE

Map p276 (www.miscellanyfinds.ca; 1029 Commercial Dr; ⏲10am-6pm Mon-Sat, 11am-5pm Sun; 🚌20) Like an explosion at a garage sale, this rambling used and vintage store invites serious perusing. The front room is packed with racks of mostly women's togs (plus some kids clothing and menswear) and the back area is crammed with just about everything else. From gravy boats to velour paintings, this is a fun place for treasure hunting. There's also an intriguing used-book section.

RIOT CLOTHING — CLOTHING

Map p276 (www.riotclothing.ca; 1395 Commercial Dr; ⏲11am-6pm Mon-Sat, noon-5pm Sun; 🚌20) Arguably the Drive's coolest clothing and accessories store, Riot curates an ever-changing array of mostly locally made fashions (although you'll also find choice labels from other parts of the world). Mostly for hipster women, there are also some natty togs for men here if you need to change your (or your partner's) look in a hurry.

It's not all new, though: check out the well-chosen vintage racks for that unique addition to your wardrobe. And have a chat with staffers: they'll give you the low-down on what's in (or not) with local coolsters.

URBAN EMPIRE — ACCESSORIES

Map p276 (1108 Commercial Dr; ⊙11am-5:30pm Mon-Sat, noon-5pm Sun; 🚌20) This wacky, all-out, kitsch trinket shop is just the kind of place you can pick up that Crazy Cat Lady action figure you've always wanted. Other must-haves include bacon-strip sticking plasters and dog-butt flavored chewing gum – you'll have plenty of ideas for souvenirs for your friends back home.

It's surprising how easy it is to squander an hour browsing the quirky gifts and knicknacks here. But it's also easy to spend more than you planned, so keep an eye on the prices.

PULPFICTION BOOKS EAST — BOOKS

Map p276 (www.pulpfictionbooksvancouver.com; 1830 Commercial Dr; ⊙11am-7pm; 🚌20) The smallest of Pulpfiction's mini-empire of three Vancouver bookstores, this spartan-looking shop has little decoration beyond its wood floors and well-stocked wooden bookshelves. And what that shows, of course, is that it really is all about the books here. An easy spot to while away an hour of browsing, it's almost impossible not to find something you want to buy here.

And, if you're a fast reader, you can try to resell it back to the store before you leave for home: they have an active book-buying program here (although they're apparently not very keen on anything by Dan Brown).

WONDERBUCKS WONDERFUL LIVING — HOMEWARES

Map p276 (www.wonderbucks.com; 1803 Commercial Dr; ⊙10am-6pm; 🚌20) Dedicated to cut-price chic for homes that don't have million-dollar budgets, you can find everything here from bargain art prints to mod tablecloths. It's worth a peruse, especially if you have room in your luggage for that floor-to-ceiling vase. There's an ever-changing array of goods so it's worth revisiting, and there are often excellent sales.

DREAM DESIGNS — HOMEWARES

Map p276 (www.dreamdesigns.ca; 956 Commercial Dr; ⊙10am-6pm Mon-Sat, 11am-6pm Sun; 🚌20) 🍃 Visiting greenies will enjoy dipping into this mini eco-department store that sells everything from yoga mats to linen pajamas and bamboo-fiber sheets. Check out the clothing section at the front of the store for hemp and organic cotton togs and save time to peruse the range of natural soaps and bath treatments.

A good place to rub shoulders with local eco-chic Vancouverites, the staff is also savvy about their all-natural product lines and happy to point you to other ethical businesses around the city.

KALENA'S SHOES — FOOTWEAR

Map p276 (www.kalenashoes.com; 1526 Commercial Dr; ⊙10am-6pm Mon-Fri, 10am-5:30pm Sat, noon-6pm Sun; 🚌20) True to Commercial Dr's Italian heritage, Kalena's imports handsome top-quality leather shoes and boots from the old country. Well-crafted men's and women's styles can be had for reasonable prices and there's also a big area devoted to sale items. This is the kind of place where you'll pay $200 for a pair of brogues and they'll last you for a couple of decades.

There's not really any attempt to follow North American shoe fashions here: it stocks classics as well as following dressy fashions from Europe.

SPORTS & ACTIVITIES

BRITANNIA COMMUNITY CENTRE — ICE SKATING

Map p276 (www.britanniacentre.org; 1661 Napier St; adult/child/senior $5.65/3/4, skate rental $2.90; ⊙8am-9pm Mon-Thu, 8:30am-7pm Fri, 9am-5pm Sat, 10am-4pm Sun; 🚌20) Handily open for skaters all year round, this popular community center rink offers skate lessons and regular events, including women-only drop-in hockey, late-night co-ed drop-in hockey and evening adults-only skating (the perfect place to meet your new ice-dance partner). There's also a gym, a pool and even an on-site art gallery.

A hub for the locals, this popular and well-used facility is open to drop-in visitors.

Main Street

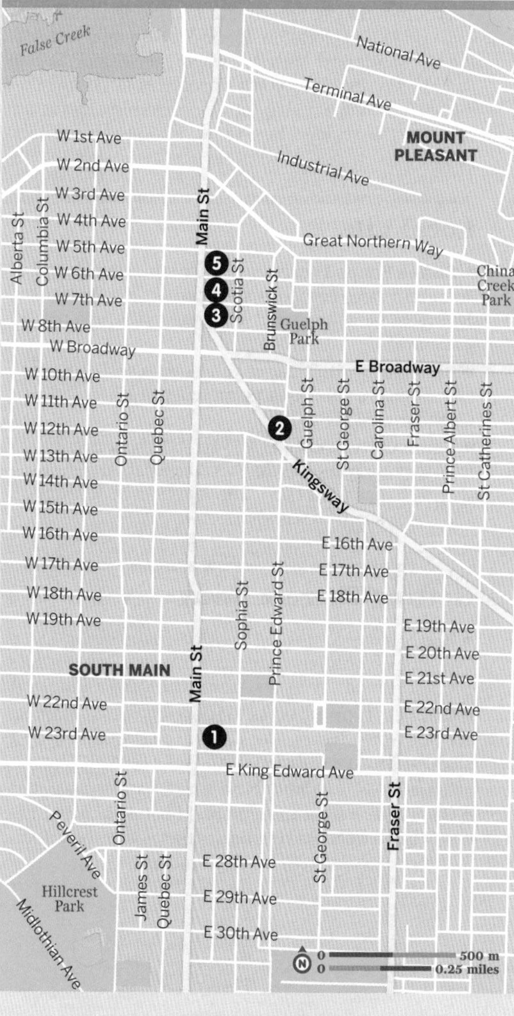

For more detail of this area see Map p278

Neighborhood Top Five

1. Composing missives to your loved ones on vintage typewriters at the legendary monthly letter-writing club at **Regional Assembly of Text** (p142).
2. Catching a live show and moshing to your heart's content at **Biltmore Cabaret** (p139).
3. Sipping coffee in the sun on a wood-block perch outside **Gene Cafe** (p139).
4. Catching a quirky gallery opening at **Hot Art Wet City** (p134) and buying some cool-ass local art.
5. Lounging on the little patio at **Whip** (p137) with a Sunday afternoon guest cask beer.

Lonely Planet's Top Tip

Locals like to keep the community suppers at **Holy Trinity Ukrainian Orthodox Church** (Map p278; www.uocvancouver.com; 154 East 10th Ave; ⏲1st Fri every month 5-8pm; 🚌3) a secret. The reason? The queues, forming well before its 5pm opening, are long enough already. It's worth the wait for home-cooked pierogy, borscht and cabbage rolls. Budget for $15 and you won't need to eat for days.

Best Places to Eat

➡ Tap & Barrel (p135)
➡ Burgoo Bistro (p136)
➡ Sun Sui Wah Seafood Restaurant (p136)
➡ Budgie's Burritos (p135)
➡ Acorn (p136)

For reviews, see p135➡

Best Places to Drink

➡ Whip (p137)
➡ Shameful Tiki Room (p138)
➡ Narrow Lounge (p138)
➡ Portland Craft (p138)
➡ 49th Parallel Coffee (p139)

For reviews, see p137➡

Best Places to Shop

➡ Regional Assembly of Text (p142)
➡ Smoking Lily (p142)
➡ Bird on a Wire Creations (p142)
➡ Neptoon Records (p142)
➡ Mountain Equipment Co-op (p142)

For reviews, see p140➡

Explore Main Street

After the north-end hub of Science World and the nearby Olympic Village, the main action on Main takes place further south in two key areas: around the intersection with Broadway and then south from 18th Ave: these are the twin hearts of Vancouver's hipster scene. The first, the center of the Mount Pleasant neighborhood, is lined with independent bars and coffee shops, while the Riley Park area past 18th is perfect for airing your credit cards: it's full of one-of-a-kind fashion, arts and accessories stores. Consider an afternoon of window shopping here, followed by dinner and a few beers in either area. Bus 3 runs along Main from the Main St-Science World SkyTrain station, but make sure you hop off regularly for some on-foot exploration. If you're still hungry, stay on the bus south past 48th Ave where you'll find the Punjabi Market district. Known by some as Little India, it's a colorful, compact strip of Asian clothing stores and some of the region's best-value, all-you-can-eat curry restaurants.

Local Life

➡ **Coffee Shops** Locals spend more time hunched over laptops in cafes here than anywhere else in the city. Join them for a glimpse of what makes the area tick (ie good java).

➡ **Bars** Lined with some of Vancouver's best watering holes, this is a good area for an independent-minded neighborhood night out.

➡ **Community Events** From yarn-bombing to craft fairs to pop-up book exchanges, the locals are always staging happenings here – check notices at libraries and coffee shops to see what's on.

Getting There & Away

➡ **Bus** Number 3 runs the length of Main St. The 99B-Line express bus connects Main and Commercial Dr along Broadway, as does the much slower number 9.

➡ **Train** SkyTrain connects to bus 3 services at Main St-Science World Station. But if you're on the Canada Line, alight at Broadway-City Hall and take the 99B-Line along Broadway to Main St.

➡ **Car** There is some metered parking on Main St, plus lots of side-street parking the further south you drive.

SIGHTS

SCIENCE WORLD
MUSEUM

Map p278 (www.scienceworld.ca; 1455 Quebec St; adult/child $22.50/15.25; ⌚10am-5pm Mon-Fri, 10am-6pm Sat & Sun; 👪; Ⓜ Main St-Science World) Under Vancouver's favorite geodesic dome (okay, its only one), the recently revamped science-and-nature showcase has added tons of new exhibition space and a cool outdoor park crammed with hands-on fun (yes, you *can* lift 2028kg). Inside, there are two floors of educational play from a walk-in hamster wheel to an air-driven ball maze and, of course, a karilloscope.

Alongside the permanent galleries, there are ever-changing visiting exhibitions and regular, entertaining demonstrations of scientific principles for those who like to watch – the giant Omnimax Theatre takes that one step further. And if you fancy exploring without the kids (you know you do) check out the regular adults-only **After Dark** events, combining bar drinks and some live entertainment. These regular socials are one of the city's cool nightlife secrets. And there's even a teen version if you need something to entertain a sullen adolescent during your stay.

SOUTH FALSE CREEK SEAWALL
WATERFRONT

Map p278 (cnr Quebec St & Terminal Ave; Ⓜ Main St-Science World) Starting a few steps from Science World, this popular waterfront trail alongside False Creek's southern shoreline is about 3km long and takes you all the way to Granville Island. You'll pass the giant **Olympic Village**, **Habitat Island** – a minisanctuary for passing birdlife – and the dockside **Stamps Landing** area before reaching the back entrance to the island (it's actually a peninsula).

Stay on Granville Island for lunch and, if you need to return to your point of origin, pick up a miniferry for a relaxing False Creek 'cruise' back to Science World. It's a cool way to enjoy the Vancouver skyline, framed by water and a mountain-fringed backdrop.

OLYMPIC VILLAGE
NEIGHBORHOOD

Map p278 (Athletes Way; Ⓜ Main St-Science World) Built as the home for 2800 athletes during the 2010 Olympic and Paralympic Winter Games, this glassy waterfront development became the city's newest neighborhood once the sporting-types went home. It's taken a while to make the area feel like a community, but shops and restaurants – plus some cool public art – have helped. Worth a look on your seawall stroll.

Don't forget to photograph the gigantic **bird sculptures** – preferably with the mountains behind them. And keep an eye on the hulking, red-sided **Salt Building** in the middle of the plaza: at time of writing, what promises to be Vancouver's largest craft-beer pub was close to opening in this building.

WINSOR GALLERY
GALLERY

Map p278 (www.winsorgallery.com; 258 E 1st Ave; ⌚10am-6pm Tue-Sat; 🚌3) FREE Large-format contemporary photography is a specialty at this expansive, double-room space. Each room usually runs its own exhibition and recent shows have included works by local popular artists such as Attila Richard Lukacs and Brian Howell.

MAIN STREET POODLE

Many locals were up in arms when a new neighbor arrived unannounced at Main St's 18th Ave intersection in early 2013. But the unnamed new resident wasn't a typical transplant. Created by Montreal artist Gisele Amantea – and soon known by locals as the Main Street Poodle – the 2m porcelain sculpture of a dog sitting atop a 7.6m pole irked many who thought it didn't reflect the area's hip, counterculture sensibilities. And others were upset that the thousands of dollars spent on the installation could have been better devoted to artists who actually live in the area. The mayor weighed in on the debate, sending out a message on his Twitter account that he was 'not a fan.' But as the locals became used to the poodle, a strange thing happened: many started to like it. Some took to Twitter to defend the mutt. And the pooch himself – kind of – got in on the act by setting up his own Twitter account to talk about his love of sausages, his hatred of cats and squirrels and his failed attempts to get served in area bars. Perhaps the poodle may turn out to be a Main St mainstay after all.

LOCAL KNOWLEDGE

GALLERY HOPPING THE FLATS

Vancouver's newest gallery district, known as the Flats, is still a secret to many locals. But if you're a contemporary art fan, hop off the number 3 bus around Main and 2nd Ave (which joins to Great Northern Way) and you'll find more than a dozen cool spaces colonizing the area's former industrial units. Among the highlights, check out the Winsor (p133), Equinox and Catriona Jeffries.

This district is rapidly changing, with new college and university campuses altering the feel, but the galleries initially began opening here because spaces were large and rent was cheap. Many of them have relocated in the last couple of years from South Granville's Gallery Row area, where their spaces were much smaller and generally far pricier.

The galleries have recently banded together to produce a free map of the area's arty hot spots – you can pick this up for free from any of them. Plan ahead and you can also partake of an exhibition opening night (so make sure you pack your tweed jacket and black polo-neck). Be sure to check online before you visit: more galleries are opening down here all the time. At time of research a new **First Thursdays** (www.firstthursdayvancouver.com) initiative was also launching in this area, with galleries staying open late on the first Thursday of every month.

EQUINOX GALLERY — GALLERY

Map p278 (www.equinoxgallery.com; 525 Great Northern Way; ⏲10am-5pm Tue-Sat; 🚌3) FREE One of Vancouver's oldest-established private galleries, Equinox pioneered this area's arty new credentials by being one of the first big names to move here. Look out for ever-changing works by local and national artists – and if there's a show by Fred Hertzog, make sure you visit. His brightly colored yesteryear photos of vintage Vancouver are spectacular.

MONTE CLARK GALLERY — GALLERY

Map p278 (www.monteclarkgallery.com; 525 Great Northern Way; ⏲10am-6pm Tue-Sat; 🚌3) FREE Joining its arty brethren here in 2013, the new Monte Clark is well worth a look. Past exhibitors have included photography by local-boy-made-good Jeff Wall, while works by celebrated artists like Roy Arden and Douglas Coupland have also graced the walls.

MACAULAY & CO FINE ART — GALLERY

Map p278 (www.mfineart.ca; 293 E 2nd Ave; ⏲noon-6pm Wed-Sat; 🚌3) FREE One of the area's top smaller galleries represents a stable of brilliant, newer artists that may be the next big thing. Look out for eye-popping photography plus First Nations works combing traditional and startlingly modern themes.

CATRIONA JEFFRIES — GALLERY

Map p278 (www.catrionajeffries.com; 274 E 1st Ave; ⏲11am-5pm Tue-Sat; 🚌3) FREE Transforming a former auto-parts warehouse, this is another migrant from a different part of town. The move has enabled more artworks to be displayed, but there remains a very strong focus on internationally renowned artists who reflect the city's rich conceptual art heritage.

HOT ART WET CITY — GALLERY

Map p278 (www.hotartwetcity.com; 2206 Main St; ⏲noon-5pm Wed-Sat; 🚌3) FREE Possibly the most fun you can have at a private gallery in Vancouver, trip up the stairs at this funky little space and you're guaranteed some eye-popping art to look at. Mostly local artists are showcased and there's a new exhibition every month. Past themes have ranged from bizarre paintings of dolls heads to art on beer bottles.

Check the retail space in the corner for quirky souvenir ideas and peruse the calendar before you arrive: there's a lively roster of artist talks, workshops and show openings. Or just pick up an artwork to go – most shows have some highly affordable goodies.

PUNJABI MARKET — NEIGHBORHOOD

(🚌3) Located on Main St (past 48th Ave) and also known as 'Little India,' this enclave of sari stores, bhangra music shops and Vancouver's best-value curry buffet restaurants is worth a quick visit – especially if you're hungry. Bus number 3 takes you right here, and makes for an easy escape once you've bought some traditional Indian candies for the road.

There's been talk in recent years of building a Chinatown-style Little India Gate here – ask about the plans on your visit, unless you're too busy stuffing your face at the all-you-can-eat curry joints.

EATING

Renowned for alternative shopping options plus its independent bar and coffeehouse scene, Main is also an intriguing area for eclectic, one-of-a-kind dining experiences. Most radiate from the intersection with Broadway, with additional pockets of tasty treats southwards as far as 48th Ave, where the city's Little India area offers cheap-and-cheerful curry buffets. Make sure you also peruse the local bar listings since many of the area's drinkeries also have worthwhile dining menus.

★BUDGIE'S BURRITOS MEXICAN $

Map p278 (www.budgiesburritos.com; 44 Kingsway; mains $6-8; ⏲11am-midnight; 🌶; 🚌8) It's a rare vegetarian eatery that has a loyal clientele of carnivores, but the bulging burritos at this quirky, well-hidden neighborhood haunt keep locals coming back for a seat among the velour artworks. First time here? Go for the Mr Jones and a glass of local R&B Sun Gold Wheat Ale.

If you're still hungry, chase it with a bowl of house-made broth. Vegan options are also available. Finally, pick-up a takeout menu on your way out and plan you next meal – you'll likely be back within a day or two, if only to confirm that sad-eyed clown painting on the wall is actually real rather than something you had a nightmare about.

FRENCH MADE BAKING BAKERY $

Map p278 (www.frenchmadebaking.com; 81 Kingsway; mains $4-9; ⏲noon-6:30pm Mon, 10am-6:30pm Tue-Sat, 11am-4:30pm Sun; 🚌8) You know that feeling when you're walking around and you're suddenly struck by a maddening craving for macaroons as well as the creeping realization that you're thousands of miles from Paris? Don't worry, this tiny cafe has your back (and your bake). The delectable (and well-priced) treats are made to perfection here, along with an array of perfectly naughty pastries.

Stick around for coffee and a croissant (you may have to fight over the handful of seats) or return for a $9 lunch deal (quiche, dessert and beverage). The fresh-made crepes here are also excellent and everything is highly authentic: hence the French-speaking staff.

HAWKERS DELIGHT ASIAN $

Map p278 (4127 Main St; mains $4-10; ⏲11am-9pm Mon-Sat; 🚌3) It's easy to miss this cash-only hole-in-the-wall, but it's worth retracing your steps for a taste of authentic Malaysian and Singaporean street food, all made from scratch at this family-run favorite. Peruse the photo-menu, with dishes such as aromatic coconut-milk curry or yellow noodles with tofu and spicy sweet potato sauce, then top your table with shareable dishes.

Dining here is supercheap, making this one of the city's best and most enduring budget eats. But there's not much room, so consider arriving off-peak – unless you're planning a takeout picnic.

ARGO CAFE DINER $

Map p278 (www.argocafe.ca; 1836 Ontario St; mains $6-12; ⏲7am-4pm Mon-Fri; 🚌3) One of Vancouver's last genuine diners, friendly Argo is tucked away in a light industrial part of town. It's easy to get to, though, and you'll soon be comfy (especially in a vinyl booth). Superior to your average greasy spoon, fresh-made breakfasts are recommended while comfort grub options throughout the day include tasty burgers and bulging fruit-pie slices.

Check the daily specials board and expect to find anything from salmon burgers to Dijon lamb chops. It's the kind of place that was built for the area's tough-ass working men and is now frequented by coolsters, and it isn't fazed by either.

TAP & BARREL WEST COAST $$

Map p278 (www.tapandbarrel.com; 1 Athletes Way; mains $12-19; ⏲11:30am-midnight; Ⓜ Main St-Science World) In the heart of the Olympic Village, this warm and welcoming neighborhood haunt is the area's best spot for gourmet comfort nosh like blackened chicken clubhouse or wild mushroom and smoked mozzarella pizza. Its regionally made beer and wine list is also superb: ask about seasonal craft brews or check out the great menu of British Columbia (BC) wines by the glass.

It's an ideal destination for a patio brew with a view: ales from Driftwood, Crannóg and Howe Sound Brewing are recommended as you drink in the False Creek vistas and work on your tan. And don't worry about those giant bird statues nearby: they hardly ever peck at people.

BURGOO BISTRO — WEST COAST $$

Map p278 (www.burgoo.ca; 3096 Main St; mains $10-18; 11am-11pm; 3) Hit the patio in summer or hunker in the woodsy interior on those frequent Vancouver rainy days – either way, Burgoo has mastered the art of gourmet comfort dining. Always check the seasonal specials, then dive into a tasty fall-back position of Irish stew, butter chicken or irresistible cheddar-packed mac-and-cheese. End with a glass of BC-made mead.

This is also a great spot for brunch: arrive early on weekends to beat the crowds and go for the croque monsieur. And if you really like this place, keep your eyes peeled around the city: there are additional Burgoo branches lurking around and each has a couple of distinctive specialties to keep things interesting.

SUN SUI WAH SEAFOOD RESTAURANT — CHINESE $$

Map p278 (www.sunsuiwah.com; 3888 Main St; mains $8-22; 10:30am-3pm & 5-10:30pm Mon-Fri, 10am-3pm & 5-10:30pm Sat & Sun; 3) One of the best places in the city for dim-sum, this large, chatty Hong Kong–style joint has been a deserved local favorite for years. Order an array of treats, then sit back for the feast, although you should expect to be fighting over the Lazy Susan to see who gets the last mouthful. Seafood is a huge specialty here (hence the live tanks).

If it's a special occasion and you want to push out the boat, gorge on some king crab legs.

RUMPUS ROOM — BURGERS, BREAKFAST $$

Map p278 (www.rumpusroom.ca; 2680 Main St; mains $7-15; 11am-1am Mon-Thu, 11am-2am Fri, 10am-2am Sat, 10am-1am Sun; 3) Peering through the open windows on a sunny evening here is like looking at a Brueghel painting teeming with hipsters. Don't let that put you off, though. Like a rec-room of mismatched garage-sale tables, this cozy joint welcomes everyone, no-matter what T-shirt you're wearing. Tuck into calorie-packed comfort food (grilled cheese sandwich recommended) and you'll forget all about looking cool.

And if it's really sunny, bask on the patio – alongside an honor guard of plastic, beady-eyed pink flamingos that will have you wondering what's in your drink.

TOSHI SUSHI — JAPANESE $$

Map p278 (181 E 16th Ave; mains $8-16; 5pm-9:30pm Tue-Sat; 3) There are no reservations and the place is tiny, but this unassuming-looking sushi joint just off Main is the best place in the neighborhood for Japanese dining. Expect to line-up (try your best to arrive off-peak) before tucking into outstanding fresh-made dragon rolls, crunchy tempura and succulent sashimi platters: order a selection and everyone at the table will be delighted.

The service can be hit-and-miss – they're sometimes overwhelmed by the crowd – but this family-run joint is usually all smiles.

ACORN — VEGETARIAN $$

Map p278 (www.theacornrestaurant.ca; 3995 Main St; mains $17-19; 5:30pm-1am Tue-Thur, 5:30pm-2am Fri & Sat, 5:30pm-midnight Sun; ; 3) Quickly becoming one of Vancouver's hottest vegetarian restaurants soon after its 2012 opening – hence the sometimes long wait for a table – the Acorn has since settled into being a dependable, dineresque joint for vegetarians looking for something more upscale than a mung-bean soup kitchen. Consider artfully presented dishes like beet ravioli and the excellent, crunch-tastic kale caesar salad.

Vegan and gluten-free dishes are also available here and they're never just an afterthought. And consider dropping by late Friday or Saturday to shoot the breeze with local veggie-types: the bar is open until 2am and there's a special late-night, tapas-style menu.

EL CAMINO'S — LATIN AMERICAN $$

Map p278 (www.elcaminos.ca; 3250 Main St; dishes $7-14; 5-11pm Mon-Thu, 5pm-midnight Fri, 10am-midnight Sat, 10am-10pm Sun; 3) The booze (think beer, cocktails and tequila) is just as important as the food (South American street nosh) at this buzzing little streetside spot. But more important than both, is to snag a summer spot on the tiny patio. It's the perfect place to dive into shareable dishes of lime prawns, coconut mussels and a good array of tacos and arepas.

There are some great drink or dine specials here throughout the week (Thursday is a beer and a tequila shot for $8), so make sure you quiz your server about the day's deals.

BOB LIKES THAI FOOD — THAI $$

Map p278 (www.boblikesthaifood.com; 3755 Main St; mains $11-13; ⊙11:30am-2:30pm, 5-9pm; 3) Take a seat beneath the giant wooden spoon on the wall at this laid-back joint and tuck into some satisfying, home-style Thai comfort grub. The papaya salad and green curry with chicken mains are ever-popular staples, but consider the exotic *miang kham* (six bites) starter dish, a cornucopia of flavors from peanut and ginger to lime and coconut shavings, all wrapped up in vine leaves.

And don't bother asking who Bob is. He's a made-up person and the staff is well-used to explaining 'he's not here' without rolling their eyes too much.

EAST IS EAST — MIDDLE EASTERN $$

Map p278 (www.eastiseast.ca; 4413 Main St; mains $9-18; ⊙11am-10pm; ; 3) Locals craving Indian and Middle Eastern comfort food plus a side dish of live music and international dance love this aromatic and spicy little haven. Avoid weekends when it can be overcrowded and you'll have a much more pleasurable meal – especially with some roti rolls followed by the Silk Road tasting menu. End with a round of the city's best chai.

There are lots of vegetarian options here if you're that way inclined. And don't bother leaving your sprogs with the hotel babysitting service – there's a surprisingly good kids menu here as well.

CHUTNEY VILLA — INDIAN $$

Map p278 (www.chutneyvilla.com; 147 E Broadway; mains $15-22; ⊙11:30am-3pm & 5-10pm Mon-Fri, 11am-10pm Sat, 11am-9pm Sun; ; 9 or 99B) This warmly enveloping South Indian restaurant lures savvy Vancouverites with its lusciously spiced curries (the lamb poriyal is a favorite), best served with fluffy dosas to mop them up. There are some excellent vegetarian options, but make sure you end your meal with a hot Indian coffee, a house specialty.

Come hungry with a group of friends and expect to share everything on the table – then buy a cool reusable steel tiffin container here to take home the leftovers.

FOUNDATION — VEGETARIAN $$

Map p278 (2301 Main St; mains $8-18; ⊙noon-1am Mon-Thu, noon-2am Fri & Sat; ; 3) This lively vegetarian (mostly vegan) noshery is beloved of local coolsters, but it's sometimes too busy for its own good. Arrive off-peak for attentive service – they're sometimes rushed off their feet otherwise – and you'll have your pick of the retro-cool mismatched Formica tables. Among the hearty house-made soups and veggie burgers, the heaping Utopian Nachos is the standout.

Perfect for sharing (but hard not to be one that hogs it all), it's best accompanied by a jug of Storm Brewing beer, made on Commercial Dr.

CRAVE — WEST COAST $$

Map p278 (www.craveonmain.com; 3941 Main St; mains $12-30; ⊙11am-10pm Tue-Fri, 9am-10pm Sat, 9am-9pm Sun; 3) The hidden back patio here is ideal for a drowsy late breakfast on the weekend – go with the apple and goat cheese omelet. Alternatively, drop by in the evening for all the Main St local gossip (and a good-value pitcher of BC-made beer) at a candlelit table. Starving? Go for the velvety slow-cooked lamb shank.

There's also a surprisingly large wine list here – ask your server for a few top made-in-BC recommendations.

DRINKING & NIGHTLIFE

Combining excellent independent bars and cozy coffeehouse hangouts, Main St is the kind of area you can nurse a drink all afternoon while you type your latest epic blog entry on your MacBook. At time of writing, the hotly anticipated new Craft Beer Market (www.craftbeermarket.ca) pub was also preparing to kick-off in the Olympic Village area. It promises 100-plus draft taps; check the website for the latest details.

★WHIP — PUB

Map p278 (www.thewhiprestaurant.com; 209 E 6th Ave; ⊙10am-1am Mon-Thu, to 2am Fri, 9am-2am Sat, to 1am Sun; 3) The laid-back, wood-floored Whip fuses the best in pub

RETURN OF BREWERY CREEK

Mainland Brewery, Red Star Brewery, San Francisco Brewery and, of course, Vancouver Brewery. The names of the city's long-gone beer producers recall a time when Brewery Creek – an area radiating from Main St around 7th Ave – was responsible for concocting the suds quaffed by many beer-loving Vancouverites. The area is named after a rolling creek that originally ran roughly alongside part of what's now called Main St – and was formerly called Westminster Ave. The creek powered water wheels in the area and helped local producers fuel their beer-making operations. Those in-the-know can still spot reminders of the neighborhood's ale-making golden age – including two former brewery buildings still standing just off Main St at East 7th and East 6th. But the best is yet to come for thirsty nostalgia buffs: around 125 years after the first brewery set up shop in this area in 1888, Brewery Creek is making a beer-tastic comeback.

Several brand-new breweries have opened or are on the cusp of opening in this area: **33 Acres Brewing Company** (www.33acresbrewing.com), **Main Street Brewing** (www.mainstreetbrewingcompany.com) and **Brassneck Brewery** (www.brassneck.ca), the latter a hotly anticipated new project from the co-owners of Gastown's Alibi Room (p89), Vancouver's favorite craft-beer bar. Marks James Group, owners of Yaletown Brewing Company (p108), were also planning to open a new Red Truck Brewery nearby on Great Northern Way. Check their websites to see if they're up and running by the time you arrive. And be sure to raise a glass or three to the historic area that started it all.

and lounge approaches. Hit the martini list with some yam *frites* on the side or indulge in the excellent local beer list – check the specials board or order a Central City ESB. Better still, drop by at 4pm Sundays when they crack open a guest keg: perfect for a patio bask in the sun.

Arrive early on weekend nights when this spot can often be heaving: you don't want to be lining up outside watching everyone else drink. And check out the artworks on the walls: the Whip has a strong commitment to showcasing local artists and the exhibitions are changed every few months.

★SHAMEFUL TIKI ROOM — BAR

Map p278 (www.shamefultikiroom.com; 4362 Main St; ⏲5pm-midnight Wed-Mon; 🚌3) Slip through the curtains into this windowless snug and you'll be instantly transported to a Polynesian beach. The lighting – including glowing puffer fish lamp shades – is permanently set to dusk and the walls are lined with tiki masks and rattan coverings under a straw-shrouded ceiling. But it's the drinks that rock: seriously well-crafted classics from Zombies to Scorpion Bowls.

Arrive early on weekend nights: there's only space for around 50 people. And check ahead for events: a local surf band was playing the tiny corner stage on our visit and more are planned, along with a promised Movie Monday night of apposite B-flicks. Food-wise, you'll find simple skewer-type menu items. And the worse thing about this perfect little tiki bar? When someone opens the door and lets the light in from outside.

NARROW LOUNGE — BAR

Map p278 (www.narrowlounge.com; 1898 Main St; ⏲5pm-1am Mon-Fri, 5pm-2am Sat & Sun; 🚌3) Push through the door on 3rd Ave – the red light tells you if it's open or not – then descend into Vancouver's coolest small bar. Little bigger than a train carriage and lined with junk-shop pictures, it's an atmospheric nook that always feels like midnight. In summer, try the hidden tiki bar out back for a Dark & Stormy or three.

Mac-and-cheese is the fuel-up dish of choice here, or you can just have another whiskey and hope for the best – but if the mangy bear head on the wall starts talking to you, it's probably time to call it a night. Popular with Main St hipsters, this is a great location to spot local lads and their attempts to grow full-on Noah beards.

PORTLAND CRAFT — BAR

Map p278 (www.portlandcraft.com; 3835 Main St; ⏲4pm-1am Mon-Thu, 11:30am-2am Fri, 10am-2am Sat, 10am-midight Sun; 🚌3) With its unique-for-Vancouver 20-strong draft list of mostly Western US beers, this convivial new resto-bar is tapping into the popularity of craft brews from Portland and beyond. You'll find Rogue, Hopworks, Elysian and Deschutes well represented here, so if you're a fan of superhoppy IPAs, you'll soon be puckering your lips with pleasure. Arrive early on weekend evenings to snag a table.

Life isn't just about booze, though. Absorb some of that beer with a flatbread pizza or two – there's often one on the daily specials board.

CASCADE ROOM BAR

Map p278 (www.thecascade.ca; 2616 Main St; ⌚5pm-1am Mon-Thu, 5pm-2am Fri & Sat, 5pm-midnight Sun; 🚌3) The perfect contemporary reinvention of a trad neighborhood bar, this is arguably Mount Pleasant's merriest watering hole. The top-drawer craft-beer list runs from Fullers to Phillips and includes own-brand Main Street Pilsner, soon to be produced in a nearby new brewery building. Indulge in Main's best Sunday roast or hang with the locals at Monday's funtastic quiz or Name that Tune night.

Along with the beer, there's an excellent 50-strong cocktail menu here – check the board above the bar for the week's fresh sheet, then decamp to a back table to sip your prize. It won't help you answer the quiz questions any faster but it may make you call out the answers by mistake.

49TH PARALLEL COFFEE COFFEE

Map p278 (www.49thparallelroasters.com; 2901 Main St; ⌚7am-10pm Mon-Sat, 8am-9pm Sun; 📶; 🚌3) Attesting to Main's status as one Vancouver's independent coffeehouse capitals, when this large corner cafe opened in 2012 it was soon crammed with locals. It roasts its own coffee so the quality is high and you can also faceplant into a full selection of lovely Lucky's Doughnuts. Avoid peak times: this place is often full to bursting point.

The perfect place to check out the local cool set, there's also plenty of outdoor seating here. Consider topping up your tan and watching the local streetscene with a macchiato and a naughty orange honey pistachio doughnut.

GENE CAFE COFFEE

Map p278 (2404 Main St; ⌚7:30am-7pm Mon-Fri, 8:30am-7pm Sat & Sun; 📶; 🚌3) Colonizing a flatiron wedge of concrete floors and expansive windows, slide onto a chunky cedar bench here with your well-thumbed copy of *L'Etranger* and you might catch the eye of an available local. If not, console yourself with a perfectly made cappuccino and a chunky homebaked cookie (the fruit pies are recommended for additional consolation).

On sunny afternoons, bask on a wood-block perch in the sun outside and watch the Mount Pleasant locals strolling around the neighborhood like they own the place. They might look serious, but they just need a hug. And if you're lucky, you'll spot a regular: a little dog transported around by its owner in a tiny bicycle sidecar that looks like the cockpit of a WWI German fighter plane (complete with fake machine gun).

KAFKA'S COFFEE

Map p278 (www.kafkascoffee.ca; 2525 Main St; ⌚7am-9pm Mon-Fri, 8am-8pm Sat & Sun; 📶; 🚌3) With more MacBooks than an Apple Store, Main St locals fill the tables here, silently updating their Facebook statuses as if their lives depended on it. But despite appearances, this is a warm and welcoming hangout for all. The single-origin coffee is excellent and there's a serious commitment to local artworks on the walls.

All the art is for sale – making this the perfect spot to pick-up a unique local souvenir that beats anything you'll find in the usual places. And if you're lucky, you might even meet the artist supping an espresso in the corner and trying to look nonchalant.

☆ ENTERTAINMENT

The Biltmore is Main's favorite nightlife joint, but at time of research a new venture – Fox Cabaret (www.foxcabaret.com) – was getting ready to compete for the favors of local hipsters. Check ahead to see if it's open.

★BILTMORE CABARET LIVE MUSIC

Map p278 (www.biltmorecabaret.com; 2755 Prince Edward St; 🚌9) One of Vancouver's best alt venues, the Biltmore is a firm favorite on the local indie scene. A low-ceilinged, good-vibe spot to mosh to local and touring musicians, there are also regular event nights: check their online calendar for upcoming happenings or hit the eclectic monthly Talent Time, Wednesday's rave-like dance night or Sunday's ever-popular

MAIN'S BEST FEST

Stroll the streets here most days and you'll likely think that everyone who lives in this area is achingly hip, from their de rigueur plaid shirts to their ubiquitous Apple laptops. But if you make it to June's annual **Car Free Day** (www.carfreevancouver.org) – staged in the heart of Mount Pleasant radiating south from the Broadway intersection – you'll realize there's much more diversity to Main than you thought. Taking over the streets for this family-friendly community fest, you'll find live music, craft stalls, steaming food stands and a highly convivial atmosphere that makes for a party-like afternoon with the locals. And if you miss it? Consider checking out September's **Autumn Shift Festival** as well. It's just as much fun and has a sustainability theme.

Kitty Nights burlesque show (www.kittynights.com), which ends with a full-on DJ dance party.

If you want to socialize with the Main St locals in all their plaid-shirted glory, this is the place to be (and not just at the wildly popular monthly Ping Pong Club). It's also a great spot to meet area musos and swap record collection war stories.

ANZA CLUB — MUSIC, CABARET

Map p278 (www.anzaclub.org; 3 W 8th Ave; 9) This wood-built community hall – which has the aesthetics of a workers club without the edge – is popular with local cool kids as well as old-school hippies who've been coming here for years. Staging an eclectic roster of weekly events (many of them in the upstairs tiki lounge) there are also regular live shows and DJ nights.

Check the calendar before you arrive and look out for highlights like open mikes, bluegrass nights and the ever-popular Celluloid Social Club that lures local movie makers and cinephiles from across the city.

CELLULOID SOCIAL CLUB — FILM

Map p278 (www.celluloidsocialclub.com; ANZA Club, 3 West 8th Ave; 7:30pm Wed, mid-month; 9) Visiting movie nuts with a penchant for making their own flicks – or just chewing the fat with those who do – should unspool their film at one of Vancouver's coolest underground hangouts. Held every month at the ANZA Club community hall, the club is a drop-in for local filmmakers and video artists who like showing their shorts to anyone who turns up.

The results – seven mini-epics are shown over the course of a couple of hours – are always interesting, and the screenings are followed by a few beers and a chance to rub shoulders and chat with local auteurs.

PACIFIC BLUEGRASS JAM NIGHT — FOLK & WORLD MUSIC

Map p278 (www.pacificbluegrass.bc.ca; ANZA Club, 3 W 8th Ave; 7:30pm Mon; 9) A weekly public jam session for local bluegrass nuts staged upstairs at the ANZA Club, everyone is welcome to watch or join in here. A great way to meet Vancouver fiddle-huggers, this foot-stomping night out is staged throughout the year, with a summer break to rest those weary plucking fingers.

The group also stages concerts throughout the year – check their website for upcoming events.

VANCOUVER UKULELE CIRCLE — FOLK

Map p278 (www.vcn.bc.ca/vanukes; Our Town Cafe, 245 E Broadway; 7:30pm, third Tues of the month; 9) Even if you haven't packed your ukulele, you can still drop by this monthly strum-fest at **Our Town Cafe** to enjoy dozens of locals performing at all skill levels. It's hard not to smile as they work through their songs and jam along to each other, often spilling out on to the street on summer evenings. Suggested donation: $5.

Arrive early for dinner and you'll also have the pick of the tables for when showtime rolls around – the menu is of the hearty soup and sandwiches variety.

SHOPPING

The neighborhood's retail lure lies in its unique clothing and accessories boutiques: this is Vancouver's must-see area for locally owned independent stores. Many showcase the exciting creative skills of hot regional designers, but there's also some tasty treats to scoff along the way, plus some perfect spots to buy that souvenir that no-one

Neighborhood Walk Main Street Shop Hop

START NEPTOON RECORDS
END SHAMEFUL TIKI ROOM
LENGTH 1KM, ONE TO THREE HOURS

Vancouver's hippest strip is ideal for those who like to browse in some of the city's coolest indie stores.

Hop off southbound bus number 3 around 18th Ave. Start at indie-favorite **1 Neptoon Records** (p142) for some cool vinyl that's way more hip than you are. Then, nip across the street to the smashing little designer shop **2 Smoking Lily** (p142) – especially if you're an intellectual clotheshorse. The staff here is ever-friendly and they'll have plenty of additional suggestions for what to see on your walk.

Further south, you can can dip into the vintage clothing racks at **3 Front & Company** (p143). If you've always wanted a 1950s crushed-velvet smoking jacket to wear with your jeans, this is the place to find it. But it's not only togs: the store does a cool line in kitsch giftware, too. At this point, you should also begin to notice your surroundings: check the painted wall murals on the sides of many buildings just off Main and look out for the steaming coffee cup motifs emblazened in the sidewalk concrete.

From here, re-cross to the west side of the street and if it's time to eat, join the throng at the popular neighborhood restaurant **4 Crave** (p137). Consider a seat on the hidden patio.

Across the street you'll find one of the city's most eclectic stores, the **5 Regional Assembly of Text** (p142), where you can indulge your fetish for sumptuous writing paper, old-fashioned typewriters and all manner of stationery items. Pick the right day for your visit and join the hipsters at the monthly letter-writing social club.

Continue south to the area's other top indie record shop **6 Red Cat Records** (p143). Peruse the CDs and vinyl and ask the staff for tips on who to see in town – tickets are available here for area shows. End your crawl with a cocktail at the delightful **7 Shameful Tiki Room** (p138).

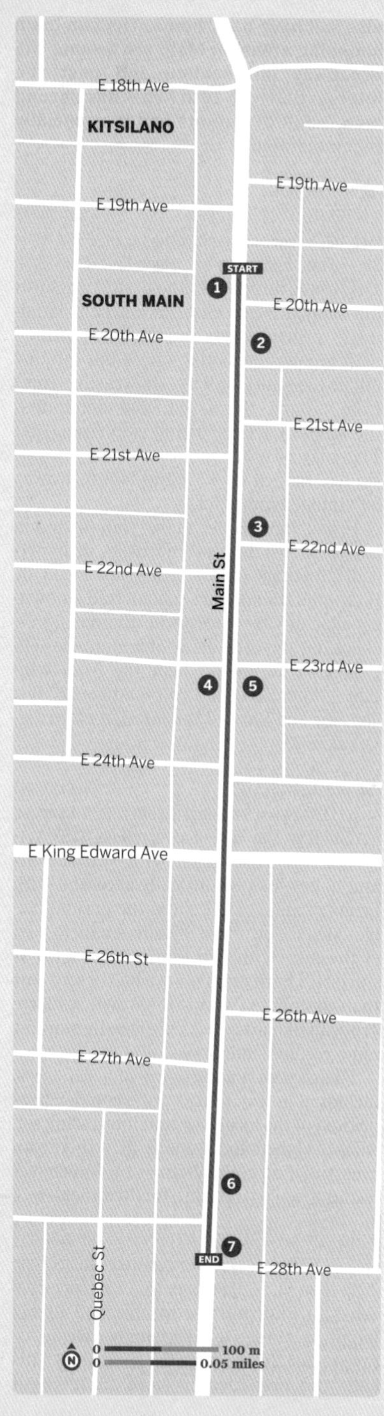

else will have back home. The two main shopping areas on Main are around the Broadway intersection and past the intersection with 18th Ave – this second area is full of options and is especially recommended.

★REGIONAL ASSEMBLY OF TEXT — ARTS & CRAFTS

Map p278 (www.assemblyoftext.com; 3934 Main St; ⏲11am-6pm Mon-Sat, noon-5pm Sun; 🚌3) This ironic antidote to the digital age lures ink-stained locals with its journals, handmade pencil boxes and T-shirts printed with typewriter motifs. Check out the tiny under-the-stairs gallery showcasing zines from around the world, and don't miss the monthly letter-writing club (7pm, first Thursday of every month), where you can sip tea, munch cookies and hammer away on vintage typewriters.

If you have time, make your own pin badge or just browse the racks of hyper-cool greetings cards mostly fashioned by the store's friendly, art-school-grad co-owners. One of Vancouver most original stores, check out the little array of handmade self-published minibooks near the front window – where else can you read *One Shrew Too Few* and *Secret Thoughts of a Plain Yellow House*?

★SMOKING LILY — CLOTHING

Map p278 (www.smokinglily.com; 3634 Main St; ⏲11am-6pm Mon-Sat, noon-5pm Sun; 🚌3) Art-school cool rules here, with skirts, belts and halter-tops whimsically accented with prints of ants, bicycles and the periodic table. Men's clothing is also (a smaller) part of the mix, with fish, skull and tractor T-shirts. It's hard to imagine a better souvenir than the silk tea cozy printed with a Pierre Trudeau likeness – ask the friendly staff for more recommendations.

There's also a great array of accessories, including quirky purses and shoulder bags beloved of the local pale and interesting set. All is designed and made in BC – there's an even tinier store in Victoria on Vancouver Island if you're traveling further afield.

BIRD ON A WIRE CREATIONS — ARTS & CRAFTS

Map p278 (www.birdonawirecreations.com; 2535 Main St; ⏲10am-6pm Mon-Sat, noon-5pm Sun; 🚌3) Eminently browsable and highly tempting, there's a surprisingly diverse array of tasteful handmade goodies at this cute and ever-friendly store. Your credit cards will start to sweat as you move among the printed purses, flower petal soaps, artsy T-shirts and grinning monster kids' toys (that adults always want, too). But it's not just for show: there are regular craft classes here too.

You can learn how to brush up your knitting skills (at classes as well as Friday night's hipster knitting group) or see regular artist talks and presentations. And if you're wondering where the store is on Main: just look out for the permanently yarn-bombed tree right outside.

★MOUNTAIN EQUIPMENT CO-OP — OUTDOOR GEAR

Map p278 (www.mec.ca; 130 W Broadway; 🚌9) Grown hikers weep at the amazing selection of clothing, kayaks, sleeping bags and clever camping gadgets at this cavernous outdoors store: MEC has been encouraging fully fledged outdoor enthusiasts for years. You'll have to be a member to buy, but that's easy to arrange for just $5. Equipment – canoes, kayaks, camping gear etc – can be rented here.

There's also a good selection of regional and international maps and guidebooks, plus a climbing wall to test your new gear. And when it comes to Swiss Army Knives: this is the place for that triple-blade-ice-pick-toaster combo. Check the notice board at the front of the store: it's a great place to see what the local hiking/biking brigade are up to.

★NEPTOON RECORDS — MUSIC

Map p278 (www.neptoon.com; 3561 Main St; ⏲11am-6:30pm Mon-Sat, noon-5pm Sun; 🚌3) Vancouver's oldest independent record store is still a major lure for music fans, with its *High Fidelity* ambience and time-capsule feel. But it's not resting on its laurels here: you'll find a well-priced array of new and used vinyl and CD recordings and some serious help with finding that obscure Ska-Boom recording you've been looking for.

Unlike some record stores, there's no attempt to be hip here, making it arguably the most comfortable spot in town for a browse, whether or not you're a geeky muso.

REFIND — ANTIQUES

Map p278 (www.refindhomefurnishings.com; 1849 Main St; ⏲noon-6pm Wed-Sun; 🚌3) From Bakelite clocks to 1970s cocktail shakers (plus a table topped with kitch pin badges), this highly browsable, retro-loving shop is the star of a three-business row of stores on this corner, each dedicated to funky trinkets and furnishings of the mid-century era. Expect lots of nostalgic discoveries as you spot that phone you used to have when you were a kid.

This store is a local fave, so expect to be squeezing past others as you nose around the main room and the additional hideaway rooms out back.

VANCOUVER SPECIAL — HOMEWARES

Map p278 (www.vanspecial.com; 3612 Main St; ⏲11am-6pm Mon-Sat, noon-5pm Sun; 🚌3) An irresistible, white-walled, double-sized store that appeals to design-minded individuals with its carefully chosen array of Tivoli radios, molded plastic side tables and glossy architecture books. It's the kind of place you can easily spend an hour just browsing: the problem is you'll almost certainly find something – an Alessi bottle opener perhaps? – that you just can't live without.

RED CAT RECORDS — MUSIC

Map p278 (www.redcat.ca; 4332 Main St; ⏲11am-7pm Mon-Thu, to 8pm Fri & Sat, to 6pm Sun; 🚌3) The ideal destination to hang out on a Main St rainy day, Red Cat's wooden racks are home to a well-curated collection of new and used CDs and vinyl records in what is one of the coolest record stores in the city. It helps that it's co-owned by musicians – ask them for tips on who to see live on the local scene.

You can also buy local show tickets here and listen to your possible purchases before you buy. There are occasional in-store performances – announced ahead of time via the store's website.

FRONT & COMPANY — CLOTHING, ACCESSORIES

Map p278 (www.frontandcompany.ca; 3772 Main St; ⏲11am-6:30pm; 🚌3) A triple-fronted store where you could easily spend a couple of hours, the largest section here contains trendy consignment clothing (where else can you find that vintage velvet smoking jacket?). Next door houses new, knowingly cool housewares, while the third area includes must-have gifts and accessories such as manga figures, peace-sign ice trays and nihilist chewing gum (flavorless, of course).

The ideal store to pick up a quirky souvenir for that difficult person back home who hates maple syrup (does such a person exist?); make sure you buy something cool for yourself as well.

MUCH & LITTLE — ACCESSORIES

Map p278 (www.muchandlittle.com; 2541 Main St; ⏲11am-6pm Mon-Sat, noon-5pm Sun; 🚌3) Proving that not all of Main St's best boutiques are clustered past 18th Ave, this smashing little store is a must for artsy, indie types. With a perfectly curated array of superbly designed but ever-functional household goods, accessories and women's clothing, there's an artisan flare and a focus on small designers here. Your challenge: to look without falling in love with something.

The staff is also superfriendly and more than happy to offer tips and suggestions for that difficult-to-buy-for friend back home.

GIVING GIFTS & COMPANY — ANTIQUES, ARTS & CRAFTS

Map p278 (www.givinggifts.ca; 4570 Main St; ⏲11am-6pm Tue-Sat, noon-5pm Sun; 🚌3) Despite the twee name, this pop-up shop-turned-permanent is an eclectic and browse-worthy co-operative of 11 vendors in five little rooms. From Bakelite antiques to artisan chocolate bars and handmade kids wear, it's well worth a browse if you're in the neighborhood. The vendors are changed every few months to keep things lively, so there's almost always something tempting to buy.

Keep your eyes peeled for vintage postcards of yesteryear Vancouver – then mail them home to show your friends that the city is still locked in 1947.

NINETEEN TEN — HOMEWARES

Map p278 (www.nineteenten.ca; 4366 Main St; ⏲10am-6pm Mon-Sat, noon-5pm Sun; 🚌3) There's a highly tempting array of must-have's at this whimsical, wood-floored homewares shop. From crafty candle-holders to wood-block printing sets, you have to really take your time to browse everything here. But when you spot the ironwork rams-head bottle openers, it's time to get your credit card ready. There's also a brilliant array of quirky greetings cards on display.

Check out the sale shelf, too – it's well hidden but worth a look.

PULPFICTION BOOKS — BOOKS

Map p278 (www.pulpfictionbooksvancouver.com; 2422 Main St; ⏲10am-8pm Mon-Wed, 10am-9pm Thu-Sat, 11am-7pm Sun; 🚌3) One of the city's best used bookstores (there are also plenty

LOCAL KNOWLEDGE

PORTOBELLO WEST

The Portobello West weekend-long arts, crafts and fashion **market** (Map p278; www.portobellowest.com; Creekside Community Recreation Centre, 1 Athletes Way; adult/under 12yr $2/free; ⏲11am-5pm weekends, 4 times a year; 👪; Ⓜ Main St-Science World) runs four times a year – one for each season – in the cavernous Creekside Community Centre in the Olympic Village. Expect to find an eclectic blend of handmade, one-of-a-kind goodies and locally designed togs to take back home, or just enjoy the live music and fresh-made bakery and lunch treats.

While you're here, be sure to ask the locals and vendors about other craft fairs in the city: Vancouver is packed with them, so long as you know where to look.

of new tomes, especially in the front room), this is the ideal haunt for the kind of serious browsing where you forget what time it is. You'll find good literature and biography sections, as well as a handy travel area at the back for planning your next big trip.

They also buy used books here so if you happen to be traveling with your personal library in several steamer trunks, this is the place offload it and cash it in for dinner. And if they don't buy, just hang around the stacks for a few more hours looking morose.

CHOCOLATERIE DE LA NOUVELLE FRANCE — FOOD

Map p278 (www.chocolaterienouvellefrance.ca; 198 E 21st Ave; ⏲11am-6pm Wed-Sun; 🚌3) With its old-school pine shelves and blackboard menu, you'll feel like you are stepping into a village store in France here. Try to peruse the chocolate squares and dainty truffles without salivating – they're all made in the kitchen through the hatch – then content yourself with a bag of butter-soft sea-salt caramels to go. Grinning and eating has never been easier.

If it's cold outside, also consider a cup of possibly the best hot chocolate you'll ever have: rich, creamy and velvet smooth; you'll be back the next day for seconds.

MAIN STREET STATION FARMERS MARKET — MARKET

Map p278 (www.eatlocal.org; Thornton Park, 1100 Station St; ⏲3-7pm Wed Jun-Sep; Ⓜ Main St-Science World) Transforming the south side of the small park that fronts Pacific Central Station, this convivial, summer-season little farmers market is also handily located across from a SkyTrain station. Drop by for artisan bread, food-cart treats and many stalls selling freshly picked produce from farms dotted around the region: seasonal fruit is the main lure.

From crisp, fresh-crop apples to juicy blueberries, it's not hard to overindulge here.

BREWERY CREEK LIQUOR STORE — DRINK

Map p278 (www.brewerycreekliquorstore.com; 3045 Main St; ⏲11am-11pm; 🚌3) The staff sometimes seems indifferent, but there's no denying the bottled beer selection at this private liquor store (ie not run by the government like most throughout the city) is among the best around. Alongside seasonal and stalwart favorites from celebrated BC brewers like Driftwood and Hoyne, there's a jaw-dropping array of Belgium brews to keep you merry. There's also a good boutique selection of BC and international wines.

A local favorite, the store is often busy with Main Streeters stocking up for their house parties (stick around and look alluring and you might even get an invite).

EUGENE CHOO — CLOTHING

Map p278 (www.eugenechoo.com; 3683 Main St; ⏲11am-6pm Mon-Sat, noon-5pm Sun; 🚌3) Behind the blue-painted exterior of this Main St favorite beats the heart of a store that pioneered the emergence of this area as Vancouver's hip-wear capital. Once a grungy vintage-clothing shop, it's now a hotbed of local designer duds for the city's slim-fit set – both men and women. And if you're looking for shoes, try the footwear annex next door.

They can't guarantee to make you cooler here, but they'll certainly have a good try.

TWIGG & HOTTIE — CLOTHING

Map p278 (www.twiggandhottie.com; 3671 Main St; ⏲11am-6pm Mon-Sat, noon-5pm Sun; 🚌3) Named after owners Glencora Twigg and Christine Hotton, this wood-floored nook showcases distinctive garments (plus idiosyncratic jewelry) for women from Canadian designers: it's *the* place to find something that nobody else is wearing back home. If you're in a budgeting mood, peruse the Steals and Deals rack at the back.

There's also a real interest in using sustainable materials here, so feel free to ask about how those shoes you're salivating over were made.

SPORTS JUNKIES OUTDOOR EQUIPMENT

Map p278 (www.sportsjunkies.com; 102 W Broadway; ⌚10am-6pm Mon-Wed & Sat, 10am-7pm Thur & Fri, 11am-5pm Sun; 🚌9) Along with the shelves of used boots and shoes near the door of this outdoor gear and sports equipment consignment store, you'll find racks of end-of-range new togs. Upstairs is a cornucopia of new and used equipment, from skis to snowshoes. If you know your prices, you can save a bundle here.

If you're inspired to take to the city's surfeit of cycling lanes on your visit but don't want to rent, there's always a good selection of well-priced used bikes on offer here, including some good-value mountain bikes.

SPORTS & ACTIVITIES

CLIFFHANGER CLIMBING ROCK CLIMBING

Map p278 (www.cliffhangerclimbing.com/vancouver; 670 Industrial Ave; ⌚10am-11pm Mon, noon-11pm Tue-Thu, 10am-10:30pm Fri, 10am-9:30pm Sat & Sun, reduced off-season; Ⓜ Main St-Science World) This popular indoor climbing center has a chatty, welcoming vibe and offers tons of courses for beginners and more advanced climbers alike. The popular two-hour intro course ($69) is ideal if you're a climbing virgin. The facility has 15,000 sq ft of terrain and 53 top ropes and now also offers outdoor courses so you can apply your skills to some real faces.

These outdoor events are typically one or two-day courses held in Squamish, a popular spot near Whistler – it's about an hour's drive away – for climbers throughout the region.

Fairview & South Granville

FAIRVIEW | SOUTH GRANVILLE

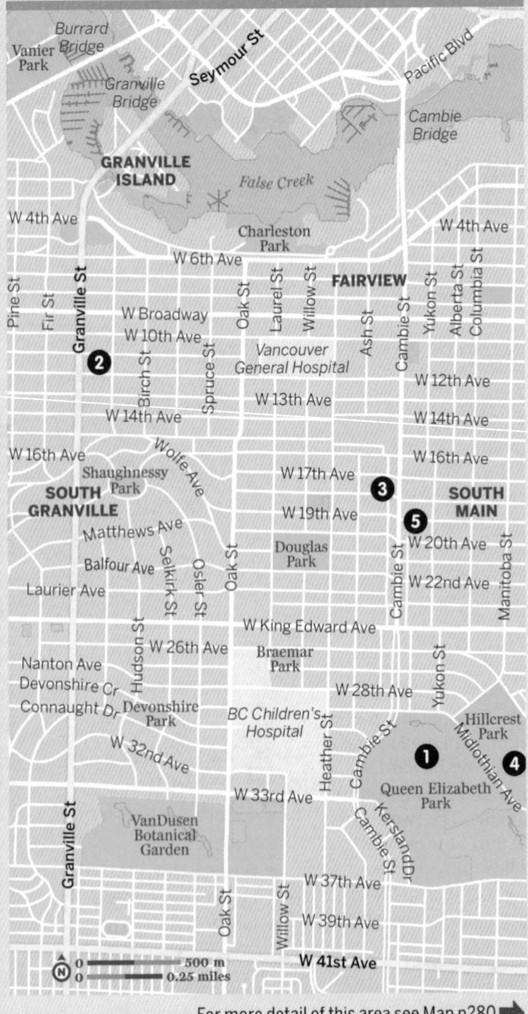

For more detail of this area see Map p280

Neighborhood Top Five

❶ Weaving uphill to the summit of **Queen Elizabeth Park** (p148) to takes snaps of the mountain-backed cityscape, before ducking into jungly **Bloedel Conservatory** (p148) to hang with the exotic birdlife.

❷ Scoffing Vancouver's best fine-dining Indian food at **Vij's** (p153).

❸ Hanging out with a Belgian beer on the street-side patio at **Biercraft Bistro** (p153).

❹ Basking in the sun with a beer at a **Vancouver Canadians** (p156) baseball game at Nat Bailey Stadium.

❺ Catching a foot-stomping flamenco show at **Kino Cafe** (p155).

Explore Fairview & South Granville

Start your exploration of Fairview's Cambie St (also called Cambie Village) by taking the Canada Line to Broadway-City Hall station. From here, you can nose south along Cambie on foot, ducking into the independent shops and restaurants lining the strip (especially between 15th and 21st Aves). This is not a heavily touristed district, so you'll get a good glimpse of local life. You can continue walking along Cambie to Queen Elizabeth Park or catch bus 15 if you're in a hurry.

Bus number 10 from downtown runs right through the busier South Granville neighborhood. Jump off the bus on the south side of Granville Bridge (coming from downtown) for an uphill stroll via several galleries on Granville St. It flattens out around Broadway which is also where the majority of the shops start. It's full of browseable fashion boutiques and homewares stores, and there are also a couple of high-end restaurants that rank among Vancouver's best.

Each area makes for a leisurely couple of hours, but it's a 30-minute walk between the two along Broadway. The 99B-Line express bus covers the same ground in under 10 minutes if you want to easily hit both neighborhoods on the same day. Not a nightlife hot spot, the handful of local bars here are a good way to escape the crowded city-center scene.

Local Life

- **Shops** South Granville is busy with locals buzzing between boutiques and chatty coffees.
- **Dinner and movie** Fairview's Cambie Village is popular for dinner at a local restaurant before a flick at one-screen Cineplex Park Theatre (p155).
- **Parklife** Summertime cooling-down means Queen Elizabeth Park (p148) where you can picnic on the grass and feel as if you're far away from the city.

Getting There & Away

- **Train** Farview's main Cambie St shopping and dining area is sandwiched between the Canada Line SkyTrain stations at Broadway-City Hall and King Edward.
- **Bus** The number 15 service runs along Cambie St; the number 10 runs along South Granville. The two streets are linked along Broadway by the 99B-Line express service and the slower number 9 bus.
- **Car** There is metered parking on Cambie and South Granville, with some limited street parking available throughout both areas.

Lonely Planet's Top Tip

The **Bloedel Conservatory** (p148) in Queen Elizabeth Park helps Vancouverites escape their winter blues. It's hard to avoid the city's gray-skied cold season without jetting off to sunnier climes (which many locals do) but this glass-roofed, climate-controlled garden is a much cheaper alternative. Step inside on a chilly day (expect your spectacles to fog up) and you'll find tropical flowers, a balmy climate and bright-plumed birds strutting about as if they're in a far warmer region.

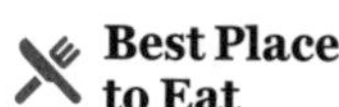

Best Places to Eat

- Vij's (p153)
- La Taqueria Pinche Taco Shop (p149)
- West (p153)
- Pied-a-Terre (p151)
- Salmon n' Bannock (p150)

For reviews, see p149

Best Places to Drink

- Biercraft Bistro (p153)
- Pekoe Tea Lounge (p154)
- Kino Cafe (p155)
- Elysian Coffee (p154)
- Marquis (p154)

For reviews, see p153

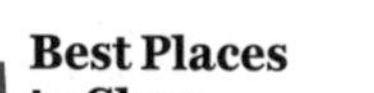

Best Places to Shop

- Oscar's Art Books (p156)
- Walrus (p156)
- Oliver + Lilly's (p158)
- Lusso Verde (p158)
- Ian Tan Gallery (p159)

For reviews, see p156

SIGHTS

VANDUSEN BOTANICAL GARDEN GARDENS

Map p280 (www.vandusengarden.org; 5251 Oak St; adult/child $10.75/5.75; ⏲9am-9pm Jun-Aug, reduced off-season; 🚌17) The city's favorite green space, this 22-hectare, 255,000-plant idyll featurs a web of paths weaving through many small, specialized gardens: the Rhododendron Walk blazes with color in spring, while the Korean Pavilion is a focal point for a fascinating Asian collection. Great views of the Vancouver cityscape provide photo-ready vistas. Free tours are offered daily at 2pm April to October.

In addition, there's a fun Elizabethan maze and an intriguing menagerie of marble sculptures here. VanDusen is also one of Vancouver's top Christmastime destinations, complete with thousands of twinkling fairy lights illuminating the dormant plant life. Check the website for the dates and also to see what's in bloom seasonally.

QUEEN ELIZABETH PARK PARK

Map p280 (www.vancouverparks.ca; entrance cnr W 33rd Ave & Cambie St; 🚌15) FREE The city's highest point – it's 167m above sea level and has panoramic views of the mountain-framed downtown skyscrapers – this 52-hectare park claims to house specimens of every tree native to Canada. Sports fields, manicured lawns and two formal gardens keep the locals happy, and you'll likely also see wide-eyed couples posing for their wedding photos.

Check out the synchronized fountains at the park's summit (home to the Bloedel Conservatory), where you'll also find a hulking Henry Moore bronze called *Knife Edge – Two Piece*. If you want to be taken out to the ball game, the park's recently restored Nat Bailey Stadium is also a popular summer hangout for baseball fans.

BLOEDEL CONSERVATORY GARDENS

Map p280 (☎604-257-8584; www.vancouverparks.ca; Queen Elizabeth Park; adult/child $6.50/3.25; ⏲9am-8pm Mon-Fri, 10am-8pm Sat & Sun May–mid-Sep, reduced off-season; 🚌15) Cresting the hill in Queen Elizabeth Park, this lovely triodetic domed conservatory – an ideal indoor warm-up spot on a rainy day – is the area's green-fingered centerpiece. Its climate-controlled zones are home to 500 plant species, many koi carp and dozens of free-flying tropical birds, including parrots and macaws: ask for a free brochure to help you identify the exotic flora and fauna.

You'll spot the birds dotted around the branches (although you'll likely hear many of them before you see them). Some seem permanently camera shy and may turn their backs to you but others are happy to strut around showing you who runs the show. Once you've circled the pathway, you'll likely want to double back to make sure you haven't missed any flighty friends.

CITY HALL HISTORIC BUILDING

Map p280 (www.vancouver.ca; 453 W 12th Ave; ⏲8:30am-5pm Mon-Fri; Ⓜ Broadway-City Hall) FREE Architecture fans should save time

KING OF CITY HALL

The Great Depression caused major belt-tightening among the regular folks of 1930s Vancouver. But despite the economic malaise, mayor Gerry McGeer spared no expense when it came time to build a new **City Hall** in 1936 (50 years since Vancouver was incorporated as a city). Defending the grand art-deco edifice he wanted as a make-work project for the idled construction industry, the $1 million project (a very large sum for the time) was completed in just 12 months.

But while the work was appreciated by some, McGeer showed no additional sympathy for the local working class. Believing that radicalism was taking hold among out-of-work locals, he ordered police officers to crack down on protests whenever they emerged. When hundreds gathered to call for jobs in East Vancouver's Victory Sq, McGeer turned up to personally read them the riot act. A few weeks later, police and an estimated 1000 protesters fought a three-hour street battle with rocks, clubs and tear gas. Rumors at the time said the police were preparing to use machine guns against the crowd when it began to disperse. The most famous incident in Vancouver labor history, it was later called the **Battle of Ballantyne Pier**.

for a stroll through the marble-lined lobby of one of Vancouver's best art-deco buildings. Completed in 1936, its highlights include a mirrored ceiling, streamlined signs, cylindrical lanterns and embossed elevator doors. Duck inside one of the elevators to peruse their intricate inlaid wood design, then check out the handsome heritage homes on surrounding Yukon St and W 12th Ave.

Exit the building on the north side and you'll find a statue of captain Vancouver, not a superhero but rather the historic seafarer the city is named after. This is the spot to take your photo, with City Hall in the background. Glance at the far less elegant 1960s addition to the complex here, then check out the rest of the neighborhood: many of the grand wooden heritage homes nearby were built for early mayors and merchants. If you're on a deco roll, you should also hit downtown's lovely Marine Building (p58).

EATING

The Fairview area has some welcoming casual eateries where the neighbors drop by to chill out, while higher-end South Granville is home to a couple of the city's best fine-dining restaurants – Vij's and West. Linking the two is Broadway which is lined on both sides with good-value restaurants of every variety, from steaming *pho* (Vietnamese noodle soup) spots to fresh-serve sushi joints.

Fairview

★LA TAQUERIA PINCHE TACO SHOP — MEXICAN $

Map p280 (www.lataqueria.ca; 2549 Cambie St; four tacos $7-9.50; 11am-8:30pm Mon-Sat; ; Broadway-City Hall) Vancouver's fave taco spot expanded from its tiny Hastings St location (which is still there) to this much larger storefront. It's just as crowded but, luckily, many of the visitors are going the take-out route. Snag a brightly-painted table, then order at the counter from a dozen or so meat or veggie soft tacos (take your pick or ask for a selection), washed down with a cheap-ass beer.

Service is warm and friendly and the prices and quality ingredients are enough to keep you coming back: the tacos are $2.50 each or four for $9.50 (or $7 if you take the vegetarian option). The braised beef cheeks variety is ever-popular and there are bottles of house-made salsa to keep things lively. Before you order, check the specials board: there's usually something intriguing worth trying.

SOLLY'S BAGELRY — BAKERY $

Map p280 (www.sollysbagelry.com; 268 W 7th Ave; 7am-7pm Mon-Fri, 8am-7pm Sat & Sun; Broadway-City Hall) The main branch of a family-run Jewish bakery minichain, Solly's is the city's best bagel spot. Drop by for a breakfast schmear of cream cheese and smoked salmon on a toasted, fresh-made sesame and you'll likely leave an hour later with an armful of unanticipated treats for later in the day: potato knishs, chocolate babkas and deep-fried potato latkas recommended.

With a deli cabinet filled with tubs of cream cheese and jars of pickles, this is a great spot to create a picnic (there's a small park two blocks east). But if it's raining, stick around for lunch: chicken matzo ball soup and a pastrami on rye sandwich is the way to go. So you don't look like a tourist, copy the locals by ordering from the right-hand end of the counter then paying at the left-hand end before picking up your order.

BENTON BROTHERS FINE CHEESE — SANDWICHES $

Map p280 (www.bentonscheese.com; 3423 Cambie St; sandwiches $7-8; 11am-7pm Mon-Fri, 10am-6pm Sat, noon-6pm Sun; 15) Step inside this deliciously pungent gourmet cheese emporium and you'll be transported to a world of curdy treats. But it's not just about looking: you have two dining options here. Check out the fresh-made crusty sandwiches in the cabinet near the door (we love the chunky meatloaf) or create your own cheesy picnic from the dozens of available varieties before decamping to nearby Queen Elizabeth Park.

The available cheeses come from all over the world but there are always several tasty BC varieties if you want to keep things local. Add a loaf of crusty bread or a box of crackers – plus a jar of Turkish fig and walnut wine preserve from BC farm Vista D'oro – and you'll be set for a tasty al fresco lunch.

APERTURE COFFEE BAR — CAFE $

Map p280 (243 W Broadway; mains $5-7; 7am-6pm Mon-Fri, 8am-6pm Sat & Sun; ; 9)

URBAN WILDLIFE

Vancouver's urban green spaces are home to a surprising array of critters. Many of them roam the city's streets after dark foraging for extra food. During your visit, you'll see **black squirrels** everywhere, but don't be surprised to also spot **racoons**. Common in several parks, they are often bold enough to hang out on porches and root through garbage bins. Don't attempt to pet them, though: they carry rabies. **Skunks** are almost as common, but the only time you'll likely see them is after an unfortunate roadkill incident (a fairly common occurrence around area parks). But while squirrels, raccoons and skunks are regarded as urban nuisances, some animals are more dangerous.

Every spring, one or two neighborhoods post notices of **coyote** spottings (there are an estimated 3000 living in metro Vancouver). This is the time of year when the wolf-like wild dogs build dens and raise pups, often in remote corners of city parks, and they become more protective of their territory in the process. This can lead to problems with domesticated pets. Vancouverites are warned to keep pets inside when coyotes are spotted in their neighborhoods, and report any sightings to authorities. Most locals will tell you they've only seen a coyote once or twice in their lives – the animals are mostly very adept at avoiding humans.

Animal encounters are a bigger problem for areas that back directly on to wilderness regions. The North Shore is shadowed by a forest and mountain swathe that's long been a traditional home for **bears** – mostly black bears. Residents in North Vancouver and West Vancouver know how to secure their garbage so as not to encourage bears to become habitualized to human food. But every year – often in spring when the hungry furballs are waking from hibernation – a few are trapped and relocated from the area.

At the other end of the scale, Vancouver is a great city for bird spotters. In Queen Elizabeth Park, keep your eyes peeled for **bald eagles** whirling overhead. **Northern Flicker woodpeckers** (known for their red cheeks and black-spotted plumage) are worth looking out for, although they're harder to see than **yellow warblers**, **American robins** and **Steller's jays**, a blue feathered friend that's also BC's provincial bird. if you have trouble spotting any birds – sometimes, they're as hard to catch sight of as the elusive but lovely local **Rufous hummingbird** – head into the Bloedel Conservatory (p148). Here, you can take photos of a host of birds who are perfectly happy to be snapped.

For more information on wildlife in Vancouver's parks – and beyond – check out www.stanleyparkecology.ca.

More than just a coffee bar, this neighborhood cafe is a perfect haunt for a rainy day hangout – especially if you dip into the impressive wall of loaner books ranging from JD Salinger to Stephen King. Coffee is good while the light meals include fresh-made wraps and chunky sandwiches plus servings of quiche or mac-and-cheese served with olives and potato chips.

Warm and friendly (despite the animal-skull artworks on the whitewashed walls), it's a local hipster haunt without the too-cool edge that some cafes have.

SALMON N' BANNOCK WEST COAST **$$**

Map p280 (www.salmonandbannock.net; 1128 W Broadway; mains $14-24; ⏰11am-3pm & 5-9pm Mon-Thu, to 5-11pm Fri, 5-11pm Sat; 🚌9)

Vancouver's only First Nations restaurant is a delightful little art-lined bistro among an unassuming strip of Broadway shops. It's worth the bus trip, though, for fresh-made aboriginal-influenced dishes made with local ingredients. If lunching, tuck into the signature (and juicy) salmon 'n' bannock burger, made with the popular aboriginal flat bread, a thick flatbread introduced by Scottish settlers and now a staple of First Nations dining in BC. But if you're planning dinner, go for the velvet-soft braised deer shank.

There's also a third option for groups of four or more: from $30 per head, you can have a choice of four multicourse feasts (including salmon or elk) offering an adventurous way to explore modern First Nations cuisine. Whatever you decide to have, wash it down with a bottle Nk'mip, from BC's only First Nations winery.

SHIZEN YA JAPANESE **$$**

Map p280 (www.shizenya.ca; 1102 W Broadway; mains $8-16; ⊙11:30am-10pm Mon-Sat; ✎; 🚌9) A cut above the area's humdrum cheap-and-cheerful sushi shops, the prices here are just as good but the quality and service make a huge difference. Only organic brown rice is used and there's a healthy approach which includes crispy fresh salads and quinoa specials. And while vegetarians are well looked after, the sushi is top-notch and the beef terriyaki is a local favorite.

It can get crowded here on weekend evenings, so consider dropping in for lunch; the well-priced combo curry-rice or udon noodle deals (both usually under $10) are recommended.

LANDMARK HOTPOT HOUSE CHINESE **$$**

Map p280 (4013 Cambie St; mains $8-22; ⊙5pm-2am; MKing Edward) Pull up a black-laquered chair and dive into the menu at this Hong Kong–style hot-pot spot. It's a surprisingly large, long-established place that is often bustling with locals from the Chinese-Canadian community – usually a good sign of authenticity – and they're mostly here for plates of meat and veggies that you cook yourself at your table via a pot of boiling broth.

A good place to come for a feast, this is also an accessible introduction to the city's traditional Chinese dining scene.

DUTCH WOODEN SHOE CAFE BREAKFAST **$$**

Map p280 (☎604-874-0922; 3292 Cambie St; mains $8-14; ⊙8am-2:30pm Mon-Fri, 8am-4pm Sat & Sun; 🚌15) Get your clogs on for what may be the neighborhood's kitchest (and certainly Vancouver's most Dutch) home-style eatery. Nothing has changed at this family-run joint in years: you'll still find faded photos of Netherlands' farm scenes and feel like you're at your grandma's house. But the food – especially the perfect *pannekoek* (Dutch pancake) – is comfort-grub defined. Tuesday has buy-one-get-one-half-price pancakes.

PIED-A-TERRE FRENCH **$$$**

Map p280 (☎604-873-3131; www.pied-a-terre-bistro.ca; 3369 Cambia St; 3-course prix-fixe $39; ⊙5-10:30pm Mon-Sat & noon-2:30pm Fri, 5-9:30pm Sun; 🚌15) Cambie's most romantic and intimate restaurant is this charmingly classic French bistro. Slide into a candlelit banquette for a leisurely three-course dinner of perfectly executed dishes and excellent service. The menu changes to reflect the seasons but if mussels are available, snap 'em up. Book ahead, especially on weekends, as there are just 30 seats.

There's no attempt to reinvent the wheel here: it's just an excellent little room that does everything right. And that includes one of the city's best French-only wine lists, with a dozen or so available by the glass.

TOJO'S JAPANESE **$$$**

Map p280 (☎604-872-8050; www.tojos.com; 1133 W Broadway; mains $28-45; ⊙5-10pm Mon-Sat; 🚌9) Hidekazu Tojo's legendary skill with the sushi knife launched Vancouver's Japanese dining scene and his sleek restaurant is still a pilgrimage spot for many. Among his exquisite dishes are favorites such as lightly steamed monkfish, sautéed halibut cheeks and fried red tuna wrapped with seaweed and served with plum sauce. A sophisticated night out; book ahead for a seat at the *omakaze* sushi bar.

If Tojo is there on your visit, consider asking him about his Tojo tuna roll. Created to introduce 1970s North American audiences to the pleasures of eating raw fish, local legend says that his creation later became known as the California Roll. And the rest, of course, is sushi history.

South Granville

★BEAUCOUP BAKERY & CAFE BAKERY **$**

Map p280 (www.beaucoupbakery.com; 2150 Fir St; cakes and sandwiches under $10; ⊙7am-6pm Tue-Fri, 8am-5pm Sat & Sun; 🚌10) Vancouverites used to content themselves with humdrum croissants and lame French pastries that would be laughed off the counter in Paris – until this hidden-gem bakery opened. Now, it's the pilgrimage spot of choice for eye-rollingly amazing treats from apricot almond scrolls to completely irresistible peanut butter sandwich cookies. And as for the croissants? They're the best in the city: shatteringly crisp with chewy-soft interiors.

This is a great place to make up a little brown box of treats to go (the prices are surprisingly reasonable). But if it's not too

LOCAL KNOWLEDGE

SHAUGHNESSY SWANK

If you're coming in from the airport along Granville St, watch for some extremely large heritage mansions hidden behind the towering hedges. When you're later ambling up South Granville checking out the shops, continue south past W 16th Ave and turn left up McRae Ave. Within a couple of minutes, you'll be in the leafy heart of **Shaughnessy Heights**. Planned as a fat cats' neighborhood for the wealthiest Vancouverites in the early 1900s, it's still lined with magnificent old piles that make it a wanderable museum of architectural styles. Look out for everything from revivalist Tudor and Georgian to colonial Dutch and Spanish. Then buy a lotto ticket so you can move right in.

crowded (which is unlikely) claim a perch at the window and sip a locally roasted 49th Parallel coffee with your *pain au chocolat*. They also make sandwiches here: try the vegetarian variety, complete with avocado and Asian pear in a croissant.

PAUL'S OMELETTERY — BREAKFAST $

Map p280 (www.paulsomelettery.com; 2211 Granville St; mains $8-14; ⏲7am-3pm; 🚸; 🚌10) You'll be jostling for space with chatty moms at this unassuming breakfast and lunch joint near the south side of Granville Bridge. But it's worth it: this cozy, superfriendly place is far superior to most bacon-and-eggs spots. The menu is grounded on signature omelettes but they also do great eggs Benedict and there are house-made burgers and sandwiches at lunch.

It's a perfect place to start the day before you wander down to nearby Granville Island. Be sure to arrive early on weekends when there's often a line-up of bleary-eyed locals looking for a hearty end-of-the-week breakfast feast.

RANGOLI — INDIAN $$

Map p280 (www.vijsrangoli.ca; 1488 W 11th Ave; mains $9-15; ⏲11am-10pm; 🍷; 🚌10) The good-value alternative to queuing next door for the full fine-dining experience at Vij's, this small, bistro-style satellite is preferred by many. Service is brisk and friendly and if you snag a table on the patio, you'll soon be enjoying the hum of conversation around you as you tuck into top-notch dishes like lamb in cumin and cream curry.

There's always a cool microbrew bottle or two to keep your grub company (IPAs are a great curry accompaniment) and the coconut pudding dessert is enough to make anyone smile. If you like what you've had (and you're staying in a place with a kitchen) you can also pick up ready-to-eat meals to go from the cabinets near the front.

SUIKA — JAPANESE $$

Map p280 (www.suika-snackbar.com; 1626 W Broadway; main $8-18; ⏲11:30am-2pm & 5:30pm-midnight Sun-Thu, to 1am Fri & Sat; 🚌9) A contemporary *izakaya* (Japanese neighborhood pub) with a playful edge, Suika is all about sliding alongside a moodlit table under the sake-bottle chandelier and sharing dishes of rice balls, deep-fired tori-yako chicken (highly recommended) and the naughty-but-delicious Chinese *poutine* – fries topped with mozzarella and spicy ground pork gravy. Drinks-wise, try a smashing oolong tea cocktail.

If you're a fan of Japanese pop culture, make sure your seat faces a TV screen so you can watch classic episodes of Ultraman to your heart's content – don't worry, your date will understand (or maybe not).

HEIRLOOM VEGETARIAN — VEGETARIAN $$

Map p280 (www.heirloomrestaurant.ca; 1509 W 12th Ave; mains $14-18; ⏲11am-3:30pm Mon-Fri, 9am-3:30pm Sat & Sun, 5-10pm daily; 🍷; 🚌10) With a modern cafeteria-meets-rustic artisan feel (yes, those are old farm tools on the wall), this is Vancouver's trendiest vegetarian restaurant. But it's not just about appearances. With mostly local and organic ingredients fused with international influences, you'll find repeat dishes like chickpea curry and spicy Cuban black bean chilli popping up on the menu. Stay for a drink after dining: the bar is open late.

This the kind of place you can bring carnivores (and vegans) and everyone will be happy.

OUISI BISTRO — CAJUN $$

Map p280 (www.ouisibistro.com; 3014 Granville St; mains $12-24; ⏲5pm-2am Mon-Fri, 11am-2am Sat & Sun; 🚌10) Vancouver's most authentic Creole and Cajun dining in a casual, bar-style setting, Ouisi (as in 'Louisiana') serves up adventurous dishes like habanero coconut chicken, cornmeal-crusted trout and vegetarian étouffée for those who like a taste-tripping dinner. For a hearty lunch, consider one of the New Orleanian sandwiches, while the weekend brunch offers hot fusion riffs on traditional breakfast dishes.

The large menu of accompanying malts and bourbons plus regular live jazz spices things up. Drop back on Sunday evening for the $10 burger-and-beer deal.

VIJ'S INDIAN **$$$**

Map p280 (www.vijsrestaurant.ca; 1480 W 11th Ave; mains $24-30; 5:30-10pm; 10) Just off South Granville St, this Vancouver favorite is the high-water mark of contemporary East Indian cuisine, fusing regional ingredients, subtle global flourishes and classic ethnic flavors to produce an array of innovative dishes. The unique results range from signature wine-marinated 'lamb popsicles' to savor-worthy meals like halibut, mussels and crab in a tomato-ginger curry. Reservations are not accepted, which sometimes means a very long wait.

You can avoid the queues (or a meal that stretches all night) in a couple of handy ways: next door's bistro-style Rangoli (p152) is also part of chef Vikram Vij's local empire, while his **Railway Express** food truck can often be spotted downtown or at festivals serving tasty Indian takeout.

WEST WEST COAST **$$$**

Map p280 (604-738-8938; www.westrestaurant.com; 2881 Granville St; mains $27-49; 11:30am-2:30pm Mon-Fri, 11am-2:30pm Sat & Sun, 5:30-11pm daily; 10) This sleek but never snobbish fine-dining favorite is committed to superb West Coast meals with ultra-attentive service and a great wine selection. Ideal for a classy night out, seasonally changeable menu highlights often include Queen Charlotte halibut and Pemberton Valley striploin, while the pastry chef delivers some of Vancouver's best desserts. Arrive early for a seat at the bar and sup some excellent cocktails.

Before you leave, ask to try the sliding ladder attached to the wine shelves: they usually (okay always) say no. And if you're looking for a romantic dinner destination – and maybe a place to pop the question – West is ideal: you likely won't be the first to propose here.

DRINKING & NIGHTLIFE

Not renowned for its big-night-out credentials, there are still a couple of spots here that are perfect for parking your boozy thirst, so long as you know where to look. Java-wise, there are some excellent neighborhood coffeehouses dotted on the main drags of Cambie and South Granville, plus some hidden spots just off the beaten path.

Fairview

★BIERCRAFT BISTRO WEST COAST

Map p280 (www.biercraft.com; 3305 Cambie St; 11:30am-midnight Mon-Thu, 11:30am-1am Fri, 10am-1am Sat, 10am-midnight Sun; 15) With a wood-lined interior dominated by an imposing stag painting and with two very popular street-side patios, this is a one of the city's best spots for beer aficionados. Dive into the astonishing array of Belgium tipples and excellent BC and US craft brews: a $10 four-flight tasting sampler is a good start. Save time for food: the menu covers both Belgian and West Coast gastropub fare.

You'll see many of the same locals back here on weekend mornings, salving their hangovers with brunch: eggs Benedict and huevos rancheros are the perfect medicine. And if you're a shellfish fan, this is also a popular spot for mussels and fries, with several piquant varieties to choose from.

ROGUE KITCHEN & WET BAR BAR, WEST COAST

Map p280 (www.roguewetbar.com; 602 W Broadway; 11am-11pm Sun-Thu, to midnight Fri & Sat; 9) Divided between a casual West Coast restaurant on one side and a funky lounge bar on the other, the main reason to visit this new kid on the Broadway block is the excellent craft beer selection. Expect to find drafts from celebrated BC brewers like Parallel 49 and Howe Sound Brewing as well as US tipples by Oregon-based Elysian, among many others.

Ask your server for the day's beer specials – there's usually a good deal or two on craft brews – and consider accompanying your quaff with a tiger prawn pesto pizza.

ELYSIAN COFFEE COFFEE

Map p280 (www.elysiancoffee.com; 590 W Broadway; ⌚7am-7pm; 🚌9) Just to show that not all the hipsters hang out on Main St, this chatty neighborhood joint lures every skinny-jeaned local in its vicinity. They come for the excellent coffee (it's not just about looking cool here) plus a small array of baked treats and some very tempting home coffee making paraphernalia. Take a perch at the front window and watch Broadway bustle past.

A handy pit stop if you're walking between South Granville and Cambie, you won't be the only one flicking through a copy of the *Georgia Straight* and planning your weekend here. In fact, there's a box just outside where you can pick up your free copy.

PEKOE TEA LOUNGE TEAHOUSE

Map p280 (www.pekoetealounge.com; 895 W Broadway; ⌚8am-7pm Mon-Fri, 11am-6pm Sat & Sun; 🚌9) A welcoming and restorative respite from clamorous Broadway, this smashing locals' favorite is ideal for visiting tea nuts. Choose from dozens of varieties from around the world (the nutcracker oolong recommended) then sink into a coveted sofa seat at the back of the store. Better still: go for the $6.75 pie and tea deal, which includes a bulging housemade slice (the strawberry and rhubarb is the best).

It's just 75c to add ice-cream to your warmed pie choice, and most slices are vegan and gluten-free. If you enjoy your brew, consider a takeout tin for the road.

CAFFE CITTADELLA COFFEE

Map p280 (www.caffecittadella.com; 2310 Ash St; ⌚7am-7pm Mon-Fri, 8am-7pm Sat, 8am-6pm Sun; 📶; Ⓜ Broadway-City Hall) Don't tell anyone you found this place, since the regulars will be very upset. A cute, two-floored cafe tucked into a restored heritage home, this is an easy spot to spend a morning reading the papers and supping perfect java. Aim for the single table on the tiny upstairs patio (there's a larger ground level area on the side of the building).

If you're still here by lunchtime, extend your stay by ordering from the panini sandwich menu. There is also an array of housemade cakes and bakery treats including some gluten-free varieties. It can get packed here so to ensure access to a table it's best to avoid peak times.

South Granville

MARQUIS BAR

Map p280 (www.themarquis.ca; 2666 Granville St; ⌚5am-2am Mon-Thu, 4pm-2am Fri & Sat, 4pm-midnight Sun; 🚌10) Don't blink or you'll miss the entrance to this cozy hidden nook that's popular with locals meeting to start their night out or dropping in for a nightcap before bed. Find a perch at the high tables facing the bar and tuck into a menu of classic martinis and flirty cocktails (plus a couple of nice European bottled beers).

If you're in an adventurous mood, try a beer cocktail: regular beers mixed with Belgium's Fruli fruit beer. There's also a small gastrobar-style food menu here: the succulent lamb shank osso buco is recommended.

DOSE ESPRESSO BAR COFFEE

Map p280 (www.dosedosedrink.com; 1517 W Broadway; 📶; 🚌9) The neighborhood's trendiest coffee nook isn't just about looking cool. Roasting their beans on Granville Island, there is a serious commitment to quality java here and it's a great place to savor a proper espresso while scribbling an ode to coffee in your journal. Take inspiration

WHAT'S IN A NAME?

In 1870, the Earl of Granville – otherwise known as George Leveson-Gower – generously lent his grand title to the search for a new name for the fledgling community that had grown up around Gassy Jack Leighton's bar on the banks of the Burrard Inlet (in what's now known as Maple Tree Sq). The locals had begun calling it 'Gastown' but the colonial administration wanted something of its own. Virtually no-one used the name 'Granville' to describe the settlement and it was abandoned after a year and replaced with 'Vancouver,' after the seafaring British captain who had set foot on the forested shoreline in 1792. 'Granville Street' was later adopted for the moniker of one of the city's busiest thoroughfares.

from the funky artwork on the walls, or just have another caffeine hit to get the juices flowing.

PHOSCAO CAFE COFFEE

Map p280 (3007 Granville St; ⌚6am-7pm Mon-Fri, 7am-7pm Sat & Sun; 🚌10) It's easy to walk obliviously past this near-hidden coffeeshop. But step inside and you'll feel like you've been transported to continental Europe. The fireplace, wood floors and vintage posters help, but it's the serious approach to coffee that seals the deal: you'll get the best cappuccino on South Granville here. There are also light meals available if you're peckish.

Sadly, there's only one table outside if you want to try emulating Europe's street-cafe culture. And if you're curious, the cafe's name comes from the moniker of a classic old drinking chocolate company from France.

ENTERTAINMENT

This area offers some laid-back entertainment options away from the crowds of downtown. You're much more likely to meet the locals at these events and there are plenty of nearby dining options if you want to add a meal to your big night out.

STANLEY THEATRE THEATRE

Map p280 (www.artsclub.com; 2750 Granville St; 🚌10) Popular musicals are a large part of the program at this beloved heritage theater, but there's also often a contemporary international or Canadian play added to the mix. Officially called the Stanley Industrial Alliance Stage (a moniker that not a single Vancouverite uses), the Stanley is part of the Arts Club Theatre Company, Vancouver's biggest.

The 1200-seat theater was opened as a movie house and live venue in 1931, and its interior is an unusual mix of the era's architectural fashions, from Moorish to art deco. And if you're reading this in 2107, it's time to open the time capsule of contemporary street photographs that was recently buried outside the theater.

PACIFIC THEATRE THEATRE

Map p280 (www.pacifictheatre.org; 1140 W 12th Ave; 🚌10) This unusual and well-hidden fringe-style venue stages an ever-eclectic roster of shows during its September to June season. There's usually a different one every month, ranging from contemporary retellings of Shakespeare to new or classic dramas. The intimate setting – the seats are configured 'alley style' on either side of the stage – often makes for especially involving performances.

Tickets are around the $30 mark (discounted for weekdays and matinees) while the Christmas show is usually the busiest of the year: it's typically an uplifting affair with plenty of Yuletide cheer.

CINEPLEX PARK THEATRE CINEMA

Map p280 (www.cineplex.com; 3440 Cambie St; 🚌15) Last holdout of a popular Vancouver independent movie theater chain, the Park succumbed to a takeover by the big boys in 2013. So far, little has changed at this one-screen charmer (except the missing home-baked cookies) and this is a still a great, never-packed spot to catch a flick with the locals. Arthouse and blockbusters are still part of the mix.

Keep in mind that they only screen one film per week (and frequently that film can be here for a few weeks at a time). Despite the age of the theater, everything is well maintained and the screening equipment is state-of-the-art: there are often 3D movies shown here. Be sure to check out the cool deco-esque neon sign on top of the building.

KINO CAFE CABARET

Map p280 (www.kinocafe.ca; 3456 Cambie St; 🚌15) Vancouver's only flamenco cafe, this popular haunt is a great place to chill on a summer evening. If it's really warm, bask in the sun with a beer at a table outside. But be sure to trip back in when the show starts: there's live dancing on the little wooden stage from Wednesday to Sunday, with world music on Monday and live comedy on Tuesday.

Whether or not you think you like flamenco, it's hard not to be caught up in the energy of the performances and you'll likely be tapping your own toes on the hardwood floor within minutes. Order some tapas for your table to keep everyone in the mood (the Spanish meatballs are recommended). If you're here on Friday and Saturday, expect a crowd: this room can really buzz on weekends.

LOCAL KNOWLEDGE

TAKE ME OUT TO THE BALL GAME

If you can't get tickets to a Vancouver Canucks game, there's another option if you want to scratch your itch for spectator sports. It's a tradition for many Vancouverites to catch a summertime baseball game with the minor league **Vancouver Canadians** (Map p280; www.canadiansbaseball.com; Nat Bailey Stadium, 4601 Ontario St, Fairview; tickets $10-22; ⌚Jun-Sep; Ⓜ King Edward, then 🚌33). A farm-team affiliate of the Toronto Blue Jays, it's a bargain $12.50 to catch a game at the lovely, nostalgic **Nat Baily Stadium** – an idyllic, 1950s-built wooden stadium venue (capacity around 5000), with adjoining Queen Elizabeth Park adding a verdant side dish to the sunsets. Naturally, nosh is a big draw – especially if the action flags a little – and, for many, that means sitting in the stands munching on an impressive foot-long corn dog and gulping a few Granville Island Lagers. This being Vancouver, sushi is also available. Adding to the fun are the nonbaseball shenanigans, from kiss cams trained on the crowd to mascot races. And, several times during the season, the nighttime action ends with a fun **fireworks** display. Cathching a game here is arguably the most fun you can have at a spectator sport in Vancouver – and it's also one of the most budget-friendly options (depending on how many foot-long corn dogs you can put away).

YUK YUK'S COMEDY CLUB COMEDY

Map p280 (www.yukyuks.com; 2837 Cambie St; ⌚Thu-Sat; Ⓜ Broadway-City Hall) Although there are other comedy nights in bars and theaters around the city, Yuk Yuk's is one of Vancouver's only dedicated stand-up venues. Check ahead to see what's on: amateur nights are the best deal but there's also a roster of journeyman comedians rolling in from across Canada and the US. A small, windowless venue, it can feel a bit crowded on busy nights.

Don't be put off by the unassuming exterior, which resembles the stage door at the back of a regular theater. Food-wise: stick to the drinks.

SHOPPING

The main retailing activity here is along South Granville, which – especially between Broadway and 16th Ave – recalls a boutique-packed English high street in a well-to-do town. It makes for a pleasant hour or two of strolling as you nose around fashion stores and slick homeware emporiums. Art fans should also check out the handful of private galleries on Granville north of Broadway. Cambie Village is also worth a poke around, with some cool indie stores nestled between the restaurants and coffeehouses.

★OSCAR'S ART BOOKS BOOKS

Map p280 (www.oscarsartbookstore.com; 1533 W Broadway; ⌚9am-9pm Mon-Fri, 10am-6pm Sat & Sun; 🚌9) A drool-triggering array of gorgeous art, fashion, architecture and graphic-design books (especially the large-format ones near the front) dominates the stacks here and it's worth some leisurely browsing if you have time to spare. There's an ongoing 20% reduction off catalog prices, which includes the back wall of Taschen tomes which are almost impossible to walk past.

There's also a good Moleskine journal selection here. On your way out, check the rack of art-happening flyers and magazines near the front door and have a quick poke through the bargain box outside.

WALRUS HOMEWARES, GIFTS

Map p280 (www.walrushome.com; 3408 Cambie St; ⌚10am-7pm Mon-Fri, 10am-5pm Sat, noon-5pm Sun; 🚌15) A small but perfectly curated store that's teeming with superbly designed homewares and accessories that are almost impossible to resist. Form meets function with everything on the shelves here, including excellent travel clocks, mod coffee pots with a knowing nod to the 1970s and must-have magnetic keychains from New York's Museum of Modern Art. Your credit card will soon be sweating.

Along with the usual designery suspects – that means you, Alessi – there are many lesser-known creators showcased here, including several contemporary

Neighborhood Walk South Granville Shop Hop

START IAN TAN GALLERY
END MEINHARDT FINE FOODS
LENGTH 1KM; ONE HOUR

Hop on bus number 10 from downtown. While you're on the Granville Bridge, pull the bell and alight at the first stop after the bridge. Take the first pedestrian street crossing to the other side of Granville and nip into the **1 Ian Tan Gallery** (p159) for a chin-rubbing look at some modern Canadian art. Don't buy anything too large or you'll have to carry it on the uphill southbound stretch of Granville St accurately known as South Granville Rise. Re-cross Granville at the intersection with 8th Ave, slip into **2 Tilley Endurables** (p159) to try on a few of their signature travel hats.

Continue south up to the intersection with Broadway. Turn right and within a few steps you'll come to **3 Oscar's Art Books** (p156). Salivate over the glossy art and design tomes before retracing your steps along Broadway back to Granville and heading south. You're now in the heart of South Granville's shopping district. Stay on the right side of Granville and nose into **4 Restoration Hardware** (p159), where you can pick up some design tips for your apartment.

Continue walking south a couple more blocks until you reach the intersection with W 11th Ave. On the corner you'll find Vancouver's favorite home-grown chocolate purveyor **5 Purdy's Chocolates** (p159). Consider stopping for a well-deserved ice-cream bar, or save your appetite for lunch.

Cross over and head east on W 11th Ave for half a block. On your right, you'll see **6 Rangoli** (p152), the perfect pit stop for a tasty Indian curry lunch. Once you've had your fill, rejoin Granville St and continue south. At the end of the block, you'll come to **7 Bacci's** (p158); nip inside to peruse the funky homewares and trendy fashions. A couple more blocks delivers you to **8 Meinhardt Fine Foods** (p158) where you can peruse the tempting deli treats.

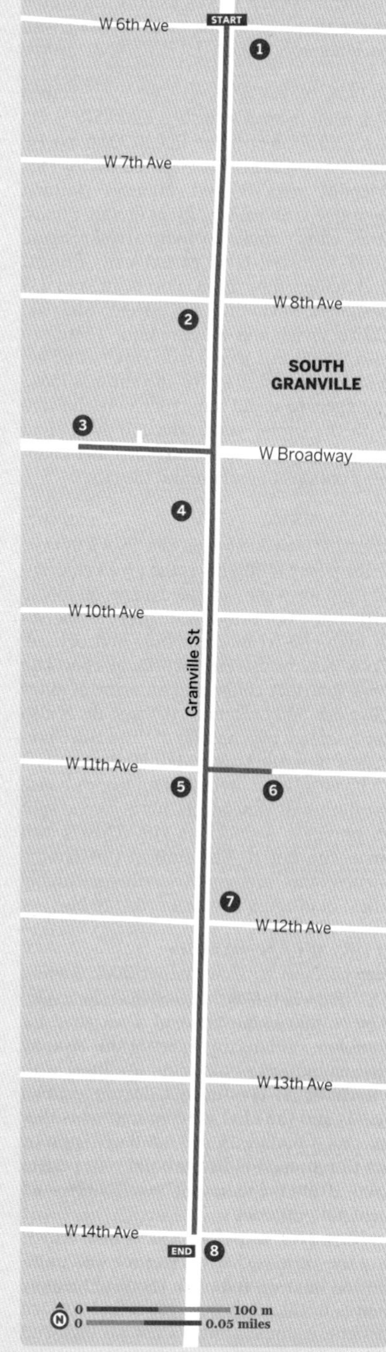

Canadian designers. Be sure to check out the available art: there's usually something clever that would look great on your wall back home.

OLIVER + LILLY'S CLOTHING

Map p280 (www.oliverandlillys.com; 1575 W 6th Ave; ⏲10:30am-6pm Mon-Thu, 10:30am-7pm Fri, 10:30am-5pm Sat, 11:30am-5pm Sun; 🚌10) This friendly, wood-floored women's clothing boutique is an oasis of great designer duds, from classic looks to more frivolous fun. You'll find stylish but casual jeans, dresses and halter tops from European and US designers, including APC, Heidi Merrick, Claire Vivier and Steven Alan. There are also often some local-made jewelry and accessory flourishes to accent your new look.

Expect to spend some time here chatting with the smiley staff, who are more than happy to offer suggestions for other shopping options in and around the city.

LUSSO VERDE FOOD, GIFTS

Map p280 (www.lussoverde.com; 1523 W 8th Ave; ⏲10am-7pm; 🚌10) This is the area's chic, go-to shop for when you need a special foodie gift or just want to salivate over the shelves of high-end treats from Italy and beyond. Look out for Baratti & Milano chocolate bars, gourmet coffee and an array of fancy olive oils and balsamic vinegars. BC is also represented: pick up a jar of Vista D'oro preserves from the Lower Mainland.

If you've been invited to someone's house for dinner in Vancouver, this is a good spot to purchase a delicious gift. There's also an onsite florist. The staff at this family-owned store are superfriendly and highly adept at offering advice on what to buy.

MEINHARDT FINE FOODS FOOD

Map p280 (www.meinhardt.com; 3002 Granville St; ⏲8am-9pm Mon-Sat, 9am-8pm Sun; 🚌10) The culinary equivalent of a sex shop for food fans, the narrow aisles at this swanky deli and grocery emporium are lined with international condiments, luxury canned goods and the kind of tempting treats that everyone should try at least once. Drop by for Christmas goodies or build your perfect picnic from the tempting bread, cheese and cold-cuts selections.

It's worth spending some time browsing the close-packed shelves for that unexpected item: Meinhardt's is one of the only places in the city where you'll find Turkish delight, example. But it's not all high-end prices: treat yourself to a $2.95 smiley-face cookie and savor it as you stroll down the street.

SHOP COCOON CLOTHING, ACCESSORIES

Map p280 (www.shopcocoon.com; 3345 Cambie St; ⏲11am-7pm Mon-Sat, 11am-6pm Sun; 🚌15) An idyllic little white-painted store showcasing the carefully curated dresses and jewelry of local designers and artisans; some Vancouverites are fully addicted to this Cambie Village nook. There's also a serious line in handmade soap, artfully presented on antique bookcases. Famously friendly, ask the staff for tips on other stores to check out around the city.

BACCI'S HOMEWARES, CLOTHING

Map p280 (www.baccis.ca; 2788 Granville St; ⏲9:45am-5:45pm Mon-Sat; 🚌10) Combining designer women's (and some men's) clothing on one side and a room full of hard-to-resist trinkets piled high on antique wooden tables on the other, Bacci's is a dangerous place to browse. Before you know it, you'll have an arm full of chunky luxury soaps, embroidered cushions and picture-perfect coffee pots to fit in your suitcase.

It's hard to miss the store from the outside: it has more stripes than a Paul Smith dress shirt. But note the bulls-eye target on the south side: it marks the spot where several cars have crashed into the store over the years.

UMBRELLA SHOP OUTDOOR EQUIPMENT

Map p280 (www.theumbrellashop.com; 1106 W Broadway; ⏲10am-6pm Mon-Sat; 🚌10) If you've lived for more than a few months in Vancouver (or if you've been unlucky with the weather on your visit), you'll know the value of a good umbrella. This family-owned local company does, too. This is their factory store and they make and repair their own brands here but also sell a wide selection of imported umbrellas.

Now's the time to stop buying a different umbrella every year, and leaving it in crumbled heap of broken spokes after a few months. Expect to pay a few dollars more and also ask the friendly staffers for some handy tips about longevity (it's all about how you put it away).

FABTABULOUS THRIFT VINTAGE

Map p280 (3190 Cambie St; ⏲11am-5pm Tue-Sat; 🚌15) A modern-day neighborhood thrift store that's not trying to be an antique shop, everything is bargain-priced to go here. Which means that alongside the $3 T-shirts and $5 shoes, there are often finds to be uncovered. Check out the used DVDs and well-thumbed books at the back and always check for late-breaking sales announced on the board out front.

It's always worth dropping back here a couple of times during your stay in the city: the selection (and the sales) are ever-changing.

PURDY'S CHOCOLATES FOOD

Map p280 (www.purdys.com; 2705 Granville St; ⏲10am-6pm Mon-Sat, noon-5pm Sun; 🚌10) Like a beacon to the weary, this purple-painted chocolate purveyor stands at the corner of Granville and W 11th Ave calling your name. It's a homegrown BC business with outlets dotted like candy sprinkles across the city, and it's hard not to pick up a few treats: go for chocolate hedgehogs, mint meltie bars or sweet Georgia browns (pecans in caramel and chocolate).

A great spot to pick up distinctive, Vancouver-made souvenirs for your friends and family back home, check out the sales racks after Christmas and Valentine's Day for dramatic bargains. And on sunny days, drop in and treat yourself: the nut and chocolate-covered ice-cream bars are a local legend.

RESTORATION HARDWARE HOMEWARES

Map p280 (www.restorationhardware.com; 2555 Granville St; ⏲10am-8pm Mon-Fri, to 7pm Sat, 11am-6pm Sun; 🚌10) Filled with furnishings and interior flourishes that you wish you had in your house, this upmarket favorite also carries some kitsch-tastic reproduction toys and old-school gadgets, especially at Christmastime. Nothing is cheap here, except the bargain pile of dinged goods shamefully hidden near the washrooms at the back. Even if you don't buy anything, it's a great place to poke around and get some ideas.

BOOK WAREHOUSE BOOKS

Map p280 (www.bookwarehouse.ca; 632 W Broadway; ⏲9am-9pm Mon-Wed & Sat, 9am-10pm Thu & Fri, 10am-6pm Sun; 🚌9) When Vancouver's beloved discount book chain announced its closure a couple of years back, locals were sad to see the end of an era. But at the last minute, the final store was rescued and revived by another company (Black Bond Books). They kept the old name and the same approach: stacks of new books (best-sellers included) at discounted prices.

You'll find good selections of fiction and travel guides here. It is also a great spot to pick-up tomes covering local history (if your baggage limits allows go for *The Chuck Davis History of Metropolitan Vancouver*) at the best price in the city.

IAN TAN GALLERY ARTS & CRAFTS

Map p280 (www.iantangallery.com; 22013 Granville St; ⏲10am-6pm Mon-Sat, noon-5pm Sun; 🚌10) While some private galleries can look intimidating from the outside (perhaps purposely), this newer entry in the city's one-time gallery-row area is the opposite. The storefront of windows help, enabling you to view many of the works without going in. But step inside and check out the rest. Bold, often bright contemporary works dominate with Canadian artists the main focus.

There's usually an intriguing mix of styles and approaches on display, including large paintings, smaller-scale photography (Vancouver is renowned for its contemporary photoconceptualism) and a plinth or two of ceramics or sculpted figures.

BAU-XI GALLERY ARTS & CRAFTS

Map p280 (www.bau-xi.com; 3045 Granville St; ⏲10am-5:30pm Mon-Sat, 11am-5:30pm Sun; 🚌10) One of the long-established galleries responsible for the city's artistic renaissance in recent years, Bau-xi – pronounced 'bo-she' – showcases the best in local artists and generally has prices to match its exalted position. The main gallery selection changes monthly and the focus is usually on original paintings – although prints, drawings and sculpture are also added to the mix on occasion.

Look out for works by favored Vancouver contemporary painters like Jack Shadbolt, one of Canada's most collectible modern artists.

TILLEY ENDURABLES CLOTHING

Map p280 (www.tilleyvancouver.com; 2401 Granville St; ⏲10am-5:30pm; 🚌10) The flagship BC store of this family-owned Canadian outdoor-clothing company, this is the kind of place where you can pick up that safari jacket for your next trip into the Amazon rainforest. But while the hardy clothing lines haven't changed much over the years, the company's signature is its classic Tilley Hat, an ever-popular travel sun hat for men and women that comes in many variations Go for the natty camouflage variety, then check out the bags, belts and other accessories here, all designed to make traveling a lot more comfortable.

SPORTS & ACTIVITIES

MIRAJ HAMMAM SPA SPA

Map p280 (☎604-733-5151; www.mirajhammam.com; 1495 W 6th Ave; ⊙noon-6pm Mon, 11am-7pm Tue & Wed, noon-8pm Thu & Fri, 10am-6pm Sat, noon-6pm Sun; 🚌10) One of Canada's only hammams is based on the real Middle Eastern deal. Step into the arched and tiled interior for a steam followed by *gommage* (full-body scrub with authentic black Moroccan soap, starting at $115). Men are only admitted from 4pm to 8pm Thursday while couples are catered to on Sundays; the rest of the time it's women only.

SUKI'S SALON & SPA SALON, SPA

Map p280 (☎604-738-7713; www.sukis.com; 3157 Granville St; ⊙8am-7pm Mon & Tue, Sat & Sun, 8am-8pm Wed, 8am-9pm Thu & Fri; 🚌10) If you're jealous of all those stunningly coiffed people you keep seeing in the clubs here, don't get mad, get even. They often get their 'dos and colors at Suki's, the city's fave salon minichain. There are three other Suki's around the region and this one also offers a good range of spa services.

Kitsilano & University of British Columbia (UBC)

KITSILANO | UBC

Neighborhood Top Five

❶ Immersing yourself in UBC's magnificent **Museum of Anthropology** (p163), preferably on a free tour that brings to life the institution's wealth of First Nations art and artifacts.

❷ Shopping for yoga gear and fancy teas with the cool locals on **West 4th Avenue** (p166).

❸ Stepping back into nostalgic yesteryear Vancouver at Vanier Park's **Museum of Vancouver** (p165).

❹ Tucking into locally sourced farm-to-table comfort dishes at **Fable** (p168).

❺ Strolling (or jogging) the fern-lined, tree-shaded trails in **Pacific Spirit Regional Park** (p167).

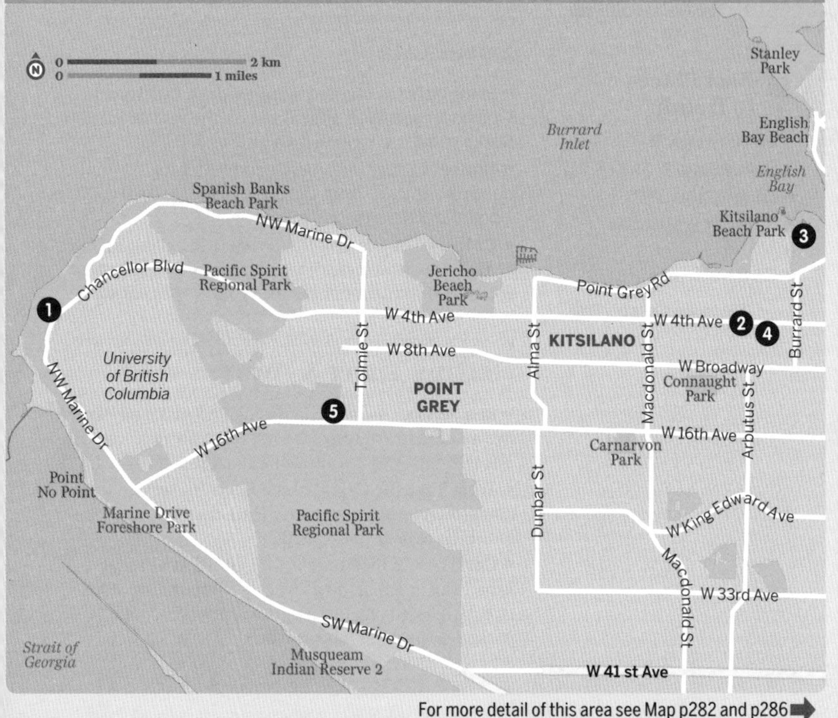

For more detail of this area see Map p282 and p286

Lonely Planet's Top Tip

Many of Kitsilano's best restaurants are packed on weekends and finding a table can be a problem. Consider dining off-peak or coming on a weekday when you'll have your pick of the best options. Breakfast and brunch is almost as popular as dinner among weekending locals so follow the same rule for your first meal of the day: come early or late or wait for a weekday.

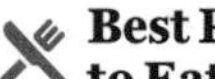

Best Places to Eat

- Fable (p168)
- Bishop's (p170)
- Maenam (p168)
- Naam (p170)
- Sophie's Cosmic Café (p170)

For reviews, see p168

Best Places to Drink

- Corduroy (p171)
- Galley Patio & Grill (p171)
- Fringe Café (p171)
- 49th Parallel Coffee (p173)
- O5 Rare Tea Bar (p173)

For reviews, see p171

Explore Kitsilano & UBC

Kitsilano and UBC occupy the same peninsula, but you'll hit Kits first when traveling from downtown. The number 4 bus will take you along West 4th Ave, which is Kitsilano's best shopping district (especially on the stretch west of Cypress St). Walk five blocks north from West 4th and you'll come to Broadway, the other main Kitsilano thoroughfare. West of Trafalgar St this major Vancouver artery takes on a village-like ambience and is well stocked with restaurants and stores (including some excellent bookshops). A fun fusion of groovy patchouli and slick retail therapy, Kits is great for a spot of easy urban exploring – add the three museums in Vanier Park plus dinner on West 4th and you'll have a full day out.

From Kits, you can hop back on a westbound-bus (4, 9 or 99B-Line) and you'll soon arrive at the end of the peninsula on the sprawling UBC campus. An excellent half-day hangout, UBC has some great attractions, including museums, galleries and ornamental gardens. It's also a tranquil break from the busy downtown streets and there are live music and theater venues here if you fancy extending your visit – there are plenty of buses to and from UBC's main bus loop to get you back downtown.

Don't forget the beaches here, either: the peninsula is lined with great sandy spots, from summertime-packed Kits Beach to UBC's naturist Wreck Beach.

Local Life

- **Hangouts** On languid summer days, everyone in Vancouver seems to be soaking up the rays at Kitsilano Beach (p165). Arrive early to find a good spot.
- **Sunsets** Snagging a perch and watching the multi-hued evening sky from the Galley Patio & Grill (p171) is a popular Kits-area pastime.
- **Culture** The Bard on the Beach (p173) Shakespeare festival is a local legend: watch a show in a huge tent, with the hulking mountains as your scenic backdrop.

Getting There & Away

- **Bus** Services 4 and 9 run through Kitsilano on West 4th Ave and Broadway respectively, eventually reaching UBC. The 99B-Line express also runs along Broadway to UBC.
- **Train** Take the Canada Line SkyTrain service from downtown to Broadway-City Hall, then hop the 99B-Line express bus to UBC.
- **Car** There is metered parking on West 4th and Broadway in Kitsilano as well as surrounding side streets. There is metered parking plus six public parkades (parking lots) at UBC.

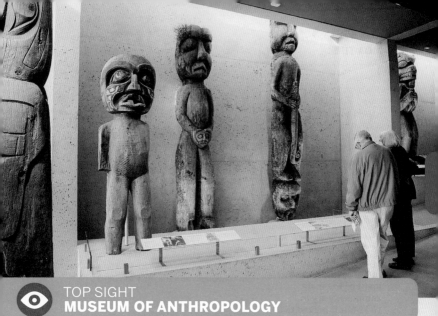

TOP SIGHT

MUSEUM OF ANTHROPOLOGY

After a comprehensive multimillion-dollar renovation a few years back, Vancouver's best museum cemented its reputation as the main reason to lure visitors to the UBC campus. Even before the makeover, the Museum of Anthropology (MOA) was already home to one of Canada's finest and most important collections of Northwest Coast aboriginal art and artifacts. But that's just the start: the ambitious collection here goes way beyond local anthropological treasures.

DON'T MISS...

- Great Hall
- Free tour
- Multiversity Galleries
- Live performances
- MOA gift shop

PRACTICALITIES

- Map p286
- www.moa.ubc.ca
- 6393 NW Marine Dr
- adult/child $16.75/14.50
- 10am-5pm Wed-Sun, to 9pm Tue
- 99B-Line

MOA 101

The highlight of the Arthur Erickson–designed museum, the grand **Great Hall** is a forest of dozens of towering totem poles plus a menagerie of carved ceremonial figures, house posts and delicate exhibits – all set against a giant floor-to-ceiling window facing the waterfront and mountains. Many of the ornate carvings here are surprisingly vibrantly colored: look out for some smiling masks as well as a life-sized rowing boat containing two figures that look ready to head straight out to sea on an adventure. The Great Hall is everyone's introduction to the museum – it's the first part you stroll into after paying your admission – and it's also where the hour-long **free tours** depart from several times a day: these are highly recommended since they provide an excellent overview of what else there is to see here.

Getting Lost

If you miss the tour or just want to go at your own pace, this is also a good museum in which to get lost. And, despite its reputation for only showcasing aboriginal culture, there is much more to be seen than you'd imagine. The renovation enabled more of the university's immense collection to be displayed in the jam-packed **Multiversity Galleries**.

MOA TIPS

Admission to the MOA is pretty good value, especially if you include a free tour and maybe a lecture, but you can stretch your budget even further by rolling in after 5pm on Tuesday evenings, when admission is cut to $9. Arrive at 5pm and you have four full hours to see as much as possible.

The museum was founded in the basement of the main campus library in 1949 but it moved to its current purpose-built space in 1976. Architect Arthur Erickson's design was inspired by traditional post and beam structures built by regional Northwest Coast aboriginal communities. Since moving to its own space and undergoing two major renovations, the museum has almost doubled in size. Appropriately, the museum stands on traditional Musqueam land.

There are more than 10,000 fascinating and often eye-popping ethnographic artifacts from cultures around the world, closely packed into display cabinets. A sensory immersion, you'll find everything from Kenyan snuff bottles and Maori stone knives to ancient Greek jugs and Navajo blankets. A selection of ornate, brightly hued Asian opera costumes is also a highlight.

There's so much to see in this part of the museum that it can be a little overwhelming, but you can calm your brain in the soothing **European Ceramics Gallery**. Sometimes overlooked by visitors clambering to see the totem poles, it's a subtle stunner, created from a private collection of hundreds of pieces of delicately beautiful pottery and porcelain made between the 16th and 19th centuries. This gallery is rarely crowded, so you can usually peruse in relative tranquillity: look out for detailed porcelain figures, ornate tea sets and a hulking tile-covered oven that once graced a busy kitchen.

Before You Leave

Aside from the regular permanent galleries, there are some diverse **temporary exhibitions** here during the year. Do not leave before you've checked these out. Recent visiting shows have included Buddhist art, Peruvian silverware and First Nations treasures from across BC and beyond. Check the MOA's website calendar before you arrive and you'll also find **lectures**, **movies** and **presentations**, as well as occasional **live music** performances, which are often staged in the grand Great Hall. Some shows and presentations are included with your admission, for others you'll have to pay extra.

But the final part of anyone's visit here – aside from a coffee-and-carrot-cake pit stop at the courtyard cafe – should be the **gift shop**. While many museum stores are lame afterthoughts offering cheesy trinkets at inflated prices, the MOA's version is far superior. And while you can certainly pickup postcards and T-shirts here, the best purchases are the authentic aboriginal arts and crafts created by local artisans. Look out for rare and unique carved masks as well as intricately engraved gold and silver jewelry. There is also delicate Japanese pottery as well as intricate Tibetan paintings and South American beaded necklaces. In fact, you could start your own anthropology museum when you get back home.

SIGHTS

Kitsilano

KITSILANO BEACH BEACH

Map p282 (cnr Cornwall Ave & Arbutus St; 22) Facing English Bay, Kits Beach is one of Vancouver's favorite summertime hangouts. The wide, sandy expanse attracts buff Frisbee tossers and giggling volleyball players, and those who just like to preen while catching the rays. The ocean is fine for a dip, though serious swimmers should consider the heated Kitsilano Pool, one of the world's largest outdoor saltwater pools.

Perch on a log on a summer afternoon and catch the breathtaking view here. One of Vancouver's signature panoramas, you'll be treated to shimmering seafront backed by the twinkling glass towers of downtown and the North Shore mountains beyond. It's one of those vistas that will have your considering your emigration options.

MUSEUM OF VANCOUVER MUSEUM

Map p282 (MOV; www.museumofvancouver.ca; 1100 Chestnut St; adult/child $12/8; 10am-5pm Fri-Wed, 10am-8pm Thu; ; 22) The recently rebranded MOV has upped its game with cool temporary exhibitions and regular late-opening parties for adults. It hasn't changed everything, though. There are still colorful displays on local 1950s pop culture and 1960s hippie counterculture – a reminder that Kits was once the grass-smoking center of Vancouver's flower-power movement.

There's plenty of hands-on stuff for the history-minded kids here, including weekend scavenger hunts and fun workshops. The museum is hoping to relocate to a downtown site in future years, so check the website for progress reports.

HR MACMILLAN SPACE CENTRE MUSEUM

Map p282 (www.spacecentre.ca; 1100 Chestnut St; adult/child $15/11; 10am-5pm daily Jul & Aug, 10am-3pm Mon-Fri, 10am-5pm Sat, noon-5pm Sun Sep-Jun; 22) Popular with schoolkids – expect to have to elbow them out of the way to push the flashing buttons – this slightly dated science center illuminates the world of space. There's plenty of fun to be had battling aliens, designing spacecraft or strapping yourself in for a simulator ride to Mars – plus movie presentations on all manner of spacey themes.

SAVE YOUR DOSH

The **Vanier Park Explore Pass** costs $30/24 per adult/child and covers entry to the Museum of Vancouver, Vancouver Maritime Museum and HR MacMillan Space Centre. It's available at each of the three attractions and can save you around $10 on individual adult entry. You can also save with the **UBC Museums and Gardens Pass**. It costs $33/28 per adult/child and includes entry to the Museum of Anthropology, Botanical Garden, Nitobe Memorial Garden and Beatty Biodiversity Museum. Available at any of these attractions, it also includes discounts for the Greenheart Canopy Walkway, plus deals on campus parking, dining and shopping.

Drop by on Saturday evenings for a date with a difference: a planetarium presentation, a mini-lecture on a hot space topic and a visit to the observatory to peek at the stars – all for $11.

VANCOUVER MARITIME MUSEUM MUSEUM

Map p282 (www.vancouvermaritimemuseum.com; 1905 Ogden Ave; adult/child $11/8.50; 10am-5pm Tue-Sat, noon-5pm Sun; 22) The Vancouver Maritime Museum combines dozens of intricate model ships, detailed re-created boat sections and some historic vessels, including the *St Roch*, a 1928 Royal Canadian Mounted Police Arctic patrol sailing ship that was the first vessel to navigate the legendary Northwest Passage in both directions.

The A-frame museum building was actually built around the *St Roch* (evocative free tours of the vessel are offered). The museum has struggled slightly in recent years, with its non-city-center location making it hard to keep admission numbers up. But it is adding some interesting temporary exhibitions to lure the locals – a recent one covered sailors' tattoos and naughty scrimshaw carvings.

VANIER PARK PARK

Map p282 (west of Burrard Bridge; 22) Winding around Kitsilano Point towards Kits Beach, waterfront Vanier Park is more a host than a destination. Home to three

NEON STROLL

During your visit to the Museum of Vancouver (p165), ask about their cool (and free) **Visible City app**. It allows you to stroll around Vancouver, point your phone at buildings and see the neon signs that once existed on them. The app includes 57 signs around the city that recall a time when Vancouver was a twinkling metropolis of winking adverts proclaiming everything from cinemas and drug stores to restaurants and vaudeville theaters. At the time of writing, the app included two neighborhoods – Granville St and the Hastings St area around Chinatown – and users were able to view stills from the 1950s to the 1970s, along with 40 audio and video stories.

museums, it's also the venue for the tents of the annual Bard on the Beach Shakespeare festival (p173). It's also a popular picnic spot: bring takeout from Granville Island (a 10-minute stroll away via the seawall) and watch the kite flyers.

If you want to avoid the sweaty crush in English Bay during the Celebration of Light fireworks event, bring your blanket and spread it out here. You'll have great views of the aerial shenanigans among a far more convivial and family-friendly crowd.

OLD HASTINGS MILL STORE MUSEUM — MUSEUM

Map p282 (☎604-734-1212; www.hastings-mill-museum.ca; 1575 Alma St; admission by donation; ⏲1am-4pm Tue-Sun mid-Jun–mid-Sep, reduced hours in winter; 🚌4) Built near Gastown in 1865, this wooden structure is Vancouver's oldest surviving building. Originally a store for sawmill workers, it survived the Great Fire of 1886 and was used as a make-shift morgue that fateful day. Saved from demolition by locals, it was floated here in the 1930s and now houses an eclectic array of pioneer-era and First Nations exhibits.

Staffed by volunteers, this charming little neighborhood museum is well worth a visit if you're in the area. Ask about the old kitchen chair: it also survived the Great Fire and is still on display.

VANCOUVER COMPOST DEMONSTRATION GARDEN — GARDEN

Map p282 (www.cityfarmer.info; 2150 Maple St; ⏲9am-4pm, reduced hours off-season; 🚌4) FREE Don't be put off by the name: this verdant city garden is an oasis among the backstreets of Kits. A rustic plot with a cob shed, compost toilet and wild and cultivated areas of flowers and vegetables, it's a great place for gardeners to visit. You can chat to the staff and volunteer to pull a few weeds yourself. Check out the fledgling monkey puzzle tree and also peruse the cool beehive.

JERICHO BEACH — BEACH

Map p282 (north foot of Alma St; 🚌4) Jericho is great if you just want to putter along the beach, clamber over driftwood and catch stunning views of downtown. It's popular with locals on summer evenings; expect impromptu but civilized beach gatherings where discreet coolers of beer may appear. Talk nicely to them with your novelty foreign accent and they'll likely invite you over.

WEST 4TH AVENUE — NEIGHBORHOOD

Map p282 (🚌4) This strollable smorgasbord of stores and restaurants may have your credit cards whimpering for mercy after a couple of hours. Since Kits is now a bit of a middle-class utopia, shops that once sold cheap groceries are now more likely to be hawking designer yoga gear, hundred-dollar hiking socks and exotic (and unfamiliar) fruits from around the world.

There are also some excellent bookstores and coffeehouses here, as well as the ever-present menagerie of well-maintained wooden heritage homes along almost every side street. The neighborhood is definitely worth a lazy afternoon of anyone's time – and you're never far from the beach if you need to cool off.

⊙ UBC

MUSEUM OF ANTHROPOLOGY — MUSEUM

See p163.

UBC BOTANICAL GARDEN — GARDENS

Map p286 (www.ubcbotanicalgarden.org; 6804 SW Marine Dr; adult/child $8/4; ⏲9:30am-5pm, reduced hours in winter; 🚌99B-Line, then C20) You'll find a giant collection of rhododendrons, a fascinating apothecary plot and a winter green space of off-season bloomers in this 28-hectare complex of themed gardens. Save time for the attraction's **Greenheart Canopy Walkway** (Map p286; www.greenheartcanopywalkway.com; adult/child $20/6; ⏲9am-5pm), which lifts visitors 17m above the forest floor on a 308m guided eco-tour. Walkway tickets include garden entry.

Check the garden's website calendar before your visit: free tours are available on select days and they provide a great introduction to the various garden areas. And make sure you drop into the gift shop before you leave for green-thumbed books and goodies.

BEATY BIODIVERSITY MUSEUM MUSEUM

Map p286 (www.beatymuseum.ubc.ca; 2212 Main Mall; adult/child $12/8; ⏲10am-5pm, closed Mon off-season; 🚌99B-Line) UBC's newest museum is also its most family-friendly. Showcasing two million natural history specimens that have never before been available for public viewing, there are fossil, fish and herbarium galleries here. The highlight is the 25m blue-whale skeleton, artfully displayed in the museum's two-story main entrance. Check the schedule for regular free tours and kids activities. Many of the museum's exhibits are in high-tech pullout drawers, which means you can spend hours here poking around seeing what's in the next one. There's also a cafe if you need to sit down and rest your trigger finger.

NITOBE MEMORIAL GARDEN GARDEN

Map p286 (www.nitobe.org; 1895 Lower Mall; adult/child $6/3; ⏲9:30am-5pm mid-Mar–mid-Nov, reduced hours off-season; 🚌99B-Line, then C20) Exemplifying Japanese horticultural philosophies, this tranquil oasis includes a Tea Garden – complete with ceremonial teahouse – and a Stroll Garden that represents a journey through life, with little waterfalls and languid koi (carp). It's named after Dr Inazo Nitobe, a scholar whose mug appears on Japan's ¥5000 bill. Consider a springtime visit for the florid cherry-blossom displays.

MORRIS AND HELEN BELKIN GALLERY GALLERY

Map p286 (www.belkin.ubc.ca; 1825 Main Mall; ⏲10am-5pm Tue-Fri, noon-5pm Sat & Sun; 🚌99B-Line) FREE This excellent little gallery specializes in contemporary and often quite challenging pieces – which explains the billboard-style depiction of an Iraqi city outside, complete with the caption 'Because there was and there wasn't a city of Baghdad.' Inside, you can expect a revolving roster of traveling shows plus chin-stroking exhibits from a permanent collection of Canadian avant-garde works.

Although the gallery only opened in 1995, it replaced the UBC Fine Arts Gallery, which opened in 1948 and for many years was the only place where Vancouverites could view contemporary art.

PACIFIC SPIRIT REGIONAL PARK PARK

(www.pacificspiritparksociety.org; cnr Blanca St & W 16th Ave; 🚌99B-Line) FREE This stunning 763-hectare park stretches from Burrard Inlet to the North Arm of the Fraser River, a green buffer zone between the campus and the city. It's a smashing spot to explore with 70km of walking, jogging and cycling trails; you'll also find **Camosun Bog wetland** (accessed by a boardwalk at 19th Ave and Camosun St), a bird and plant haven.

Some of the denser forest trails here give an indication of what Vancouver would have looked like before it was developed: a rich, verdant jungle of huge ferns, unencumbered birdlife (including bald eagles) and towering trees arching overhead.

SPANISH BANKS BEACH

Map p286 (cnr NW Marine Dr & Blanca St; 🚌44, then C19) This tree-backed public beach is a popular locals' hangout – they're the ones jogging past in Lululemon outfits – and is a good spot to unpack a picnic and perch on a log to enjoy some sigh-triggering waterfront vistas. It was named after English Bay's 1792 meeting between British mariner Captain George Vancouver and his Spanish counterpart Dionisio Galiano.

While the two captains parted amicably, it was Vancouver's name that would eventually grace the city that he almost certainly did not imagine would rise out of the area's dense wilderness. As for Galiano, posterity remembered the Spaniard by naming a tiny Gulf Island after him.

WRECK BEACH BEACH

Map p286 (www.wreckbeach.org; via Trail 6; 🚌99B-Line, then C20) Follow Trail 6 into the woods and down the steep steps to find Vancouver's only official naturist beach, complete with a motley crew of counterculture locals, independent vendors and sunburned regulars. The pants-free bunch are in a battle with the university over the building of residential towers that threaten their privacy, so be sure to offer your support as you peel off.

Time your visit well and you can take part in the annual Bare Buns Fun Run. And if you fancy connecting with other local naturists during your stay, check in with the Van Tan Nudist Club for events, including regular swimming meets at local pools.

EATING

Kitsilano's two main arteries – West 4th Ave and Broadway – offer a healthy mix of eateries: it's well worth the trek here to lounge on a beach or stroll the shopping areas then end your day with a rewarding meal. The neighborhood's hippie past has left a legacy of vegetarian-friendly restaurants, but Kits' more recent wealth means there are also some top-notch high-end options worth a splurge. Although UBC has a few places to eat – including its ever-popular SUB building food court – we recommend a quick bus hop to Kits for a far superior selection.

SERANO GREEK PASTRY — BAKERY $

Map p282 (3185 W Broadway; pastries $2-6; ⏲9:30am-6pm Mon-Sat, noon-6pm Sun; 🚌9) You'll find it impossible to pass this fancy-free little Greek bakery; the aromas call to you like a siren song. Step inside and the temptation increases exponentially. Naturally, the spanakopita is fantastic, but this family-run joint is really all about traditional desserts: the cream-filled korne makes the art of smiling and eating at the same times suddenly seem easy.

Try to make this your first call of the day if you're exploring Kits. Every local in the area knows about this place and some treats quickly sell out on any given day.

TERA V BURGER — VEGETARIAN $

Map p282 (www.teravburger.com; 2961 W Broadway; mains $6-9; ⏲11:30am-8pm Mon-Wed, 11:30am-8:30pm Thu & Sun, 11:30am-9pm Fri & Sat; 🖉; 🚌9) Aiming to convert meat-eaters into herbivores is the stated aim of this modern vegetarian burger bar. Which means hearty, meat-esque dishes like veggie 'chicken' strips and grilled Tofurkey sandwiches. The burgers are the way to go, especially the barbecue tempeh burger with yam fries. Most dishes are available in vegan options and a fruit smoothie is the perfect accompaniment.

There's not much seating here – it echoes the layout of meatarian fast-food joints – so if you can't snag a perch, pack your burger and head north. If you hotfoot it, you can be on the Kitsilano waterfront in 15 minutes.

★FABLE — WEST COAST $$

Map p282 (☎604-732-1322; www.fablekitchen.ca; 1944 W 4th Ave; mains $18-28; ⏲11:30am-2pm Mon-Fri, 5:30-10pm Mon-Sat, brunch 10:30am-2pm Sat & Sun; 🚌4) One of Vancouver's favorite farm-to-table restaurants is a lovely rustic-chic room of exposed brick, wood beams and prominently displayed red rooster logos. But looks are just part of the appeal. Expect perfectly prepared bistro dishes showcasing local seasonal ingredients, such as duck, chicken and halibut. It's great gourmet comfort food with little pretension, hence the packed room most nights. Reservations recommended.

The lunch menu – including a grab 'n' go takeout option – is invitingly priced and usually includes two or three excellent gourmet sandwiches for under $10 each. And if you're lucky enough to snag a table for weekend brunch, go for the pulled pork johnny cakes: the perfect hangover cure.

MAENAM — THAI $$

Map p282 (☎604-730-5579; www.maenam.ca; 1938 W 4th Ave; mains $15-19; ⏲noon-2:30pm Tue-Sat, 5-10pm Mon-Thu & Sun, 5-11pm Fri & Sat; 🖉; 🚌4) A contemporary reinvention of the Thai-restaurant, where subtle and complex traditional and international influences flavor the menu in a room with a modern lounge feel. You can start with the familiar (although even the pad Thai is eye-poppingly different), but save room for something new: the *geng pa neua* beef curry is a sweet, salty and nutty treat.

The halibut cheek green curry is also a local favorite. The mains here are generally good value, but why not go the banquet route: for $32.50 per person the five-selection chef's menu will have the whole table feasting like kings.

MODERNE BURGER — DINER $$

Map p282 (www.moderneburger.com; 2507 W Broadway; mains $8-16; ⏲noon-8pm; 🚌9) This is possibly Vancouver's best-looking retro diner – slide into a green vinyl booth and tuck into comfort-food heaven (but not

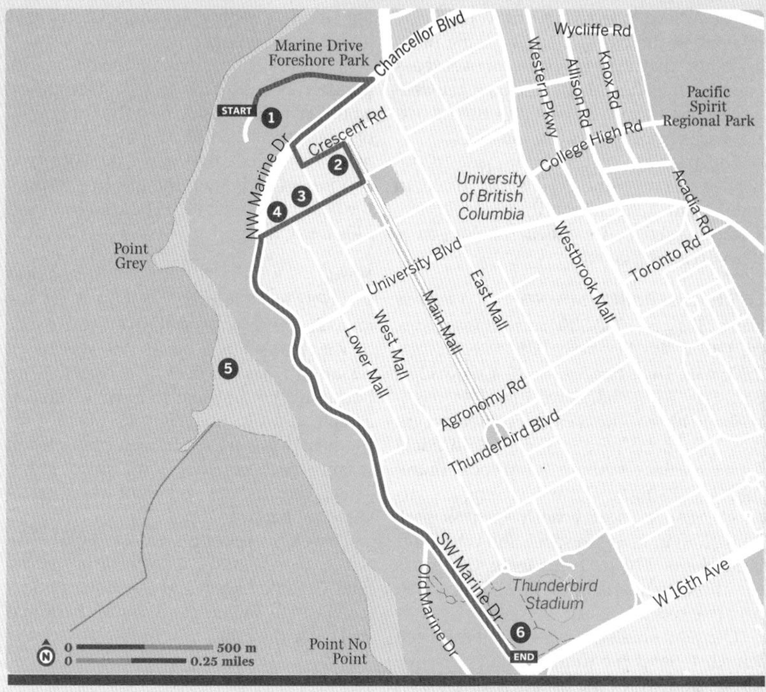

Neighborhood Walk
UBC Campus & Gardens Walk

START MUSEUM OF ANTHROPOLOGY
END UBC BOTANICAL GARDEN
LENGTH 3KM; 1.5 HOURS

This walk introduces you to UBC's leading cultural attractions and celebrated gardens. Keep your eyes peeled – and your camera ready – for the many public artworks that dot the campus.

Start at Vancouver's best museum, the **1 Museum of Anthropology** (p163), where you'll gain an appreciation for the culture and artistry of the region's original First Nations residents. Save time for the ceramics and make sure you take some photos of the towering main gallery totem poles.

Cross NW Marine Dr and head down West Mall, turning left on Crescent Rd then right onto Main Mall. On your left is the free-entry **2 Morris and Helen Belkin Gallery** (p167), which houses an impressive modern-art collection.

Continue southwards along Main Mall, then turn right onto Memorial Rd. Continue downhill until you come to the rock garden of the **3 UBC Asian Centre**, on your right. The boulders here are inscribed with Confucian philosophies.

Continue along Memorial and ahead you will see the entrance to the oasis-like, Japanese-themed **4 Nitobe Memorial Garden** (p167). Spend time here immersing yourself in the site's subtle yet meaningful design. Tours are often available and are highly recommended.

Return to NW Marine Dr and continue southeastwards for about 1km. If you're feeling adventurous, look for the signs for Trail 6. Follow the trail to the waterfront, where you can disrobe – you're on **5 Wreck Beach** (p167), Vancouver's official naturist beach. It's the only one in the region.

Continue your walk along NW Marine Dr until it becomes SW Marine Dr. Near the intersection with W 16th Ave, you'll find **6 UBC Botanical Garden** (p166). Wander through the garden areas and save time for the Greenheart Canopy Walkway, an illuminating elevated walk through the trees.

before you've selected a track from the jukebox in the corner). Unlike some burger joints, they haven't gone for weird-ass combinations here. Instead, you'll get well-made classics such as beef and turkey patties with cheese and bacon toppings.

The fries are of the fresh-made, plate-heaped variety and this is the place to indulge in that naughtily calorific ice-cream-packed coffee mocha shake you've been dreaming about.

LA CIGALE FRENCH BISTRO — FRENCH **$$**

Map p282 (☎604-732-0004; www.lacigalebistro.ca; 1961 W 4th Ave; mains $15-27; ⌚11:30am-2:30pm Tue-Fri, 5-11pm Tue-Sun, 10:30am-2:30pm Sat & Sun; 🚌4) A charming, snob-free neighborhood bistro with a casual contemporary feel. The menu here combines traditional French recipes with seasonal local ingredients and simple, flavor-revealing preparations. Expect hearty nosh such as pork tenderloin in mustard sauce and velvet-soft lamb shank. The best way to go, though, is the three-course Sunday to Thursday $30 prix-fixe special.

There's a small but well-curated French wine list, but if you want to bring your own bottle, they waive the usual corkage fee on Tuesdays.

ZAKKUSHI — JAPANESE **$$**

Map p282 (www.zakkushi.com; 1833 W 4th Ave; tapas $4-8; ⌚5:30pm-1am; 🚌4) Dive into a retro-feel *izakaya* (Japanese neighborhood pub) at this wood-cocooned hole-in-the-wall. Stay for a few hours and you'll be so immersed in your Tokyo fantasy that stumbling back onto West 4th with be decidedly discombobulating. The main approach here is to order an array of grilled yakitori sticks, from chicken thigh to duck breast, and a jug of ice-cold Sapporo.

Asahi Black, plus a good array of sake and shochu-based cocktails, is also available for more discerning quaffers.

SOPHIE'S COSMIC CAFÉ — DINER **$$**

Map p282 (www.sophiescosmiccafe.com; 2095 W 4th Ave; mains $9-16; ⌚8am-2:30pm Mon, 8am-8pm Tue-Sun; 👪; 🚌4) Slide between the oversized knife and fork flanking the entrance and step into one of Vancouver's favorite retro-look diners, with a cornucopia of kitsch lining the walls. Burgers and big-ass milkshakes dominate the menu, but breakfast is the best reason to come. Expect weekend queues as you await your appointment with a heaping plate of eggs and chorizo sausage.

To avoid lineups, soak up the decor with an afternoon window seat – although you won't see much outside past the windowsill of junk-shop bowling trophies – coupled with a pyramid-sized apple pie slice (you can jog up and down the hill to and from the beach to work it off). There's also a good kids menu here.

NAAM — VEGETARIAN **$$**

Map p282 (www.thenaam.com; 2724 W 4th Ave; mains $9-16; ⌚24hr; 🖉; 🚌4) An evocative relic of Kitsilano's hippie past, this vegetarian restaurant has the feel of a comfy farmhouse. It's not unusual to have to wait for a table at peak times, but it's worth it for the hearty stir-fries, Mexican platters and sesame-fried potatoes with miso gravy. This is the kind of veggie spot where carnivores are happy to dine.

There's an eclectic array of nightly live music, good beers (go for a bottle of Natureland Organic Lager) and a popular patio – it's covered, so you can cozy up here and still enjoy the rain.

ABIGAIL'S PARTY — FUSION **$$**

Map p282 (☎604-739-4677; www.abigailsparty.ca; 1685 Yew St; mains $14-20; ⌚5:30pm-2am Mon-Sat, 9am-2:30pm Sat & Sun; 🚌22) A romantic little tapas and wine haunt that creates its own atmosphere depending on the crowd filling its small, candlelit tables. The idea here is to sit back, order some tapas and explore the wine list. The duck confit and buttermilk fried chicken dishes are great if you're starving, but the bruschetta and creole mussels are ideal for sharing.

There's a good array of bottled craft beers alongside the blackboard wine list, but save room for an end-of-night whiskey: there are a few dozen to choose from. A short uphill stroll from Kits Beach, this is a good spot to cool down your tan and grab dinner after your day in the sun.

BISHOP'S — WEST COAST **$$$**

Map p282 (☎604-738-2025; www.bishopsonline.com; 2183 W 4th Ave; mains $32-44; ⌚5:30-11pm; 🚌4) A pioneer of West Coast cuisine long before 'locavore' was a word, legendary chef-owner John Bishop is still at the top of his game in this small, art-lined charmer. Served in an elegant white-tableclothed room, the seasonally changing menu can include stuffed rabbit loin, steamed smoked

KITSILANO: WHAT'S IN A NAME?

Kitsilano was named after **Chief Khatsahlano**, leader of the First Nations village of Sun'ahk, which occupied the area now designated as Vanier Park. In 1901 the local government displaced the entire community, sending some families to the Capilano Indian Reserve on the North Shore and others to Squamish. The first Kits streetcar service in 1905 triggered an explosion of housing development, but by the 1960s many of these homes had been converted for university students, sparking the 'beatnik ghetto' that soon defined Kits. Fueled by pungent BC bud, counterculture political movements mushroomed – including a little group of antinuclear protesters that a few years later became Greenpeace. But Khatsahlano has not been completely forgotten: every July, the neighborhood's biggest community festival is a day-long street party with 50 live bands. The area's most popular (and well-attended) event, it's called the **Khatsahlano! Music + Art Festival**. For details see www.khatsahlano.com.

sablefish and succulent veggies that taste like they've just been plucked from the ground.

The service here is pitch-perfect, so stay a little longer and indulge in dessert: if you're lucky, it'll be sweet fried fig empanada with brown sugar ice cream. And look out for the man himself: he'll almost certainly drop by your table to say hi.

DRINKING & NIGHTLIFE

You can only hang out at the beach and wander the shops in Kits for so long. After a while, the bars will start calling your name. Don't be afraid to listen. UBC has a couple of watering holes, which are great if you need a drink on campus, but there are better options a short bus ride away.

★CORDUROY — BAR

Map p282 (www.corduroyrestaurant.com; 1943 Cornwall Ave; 5:30pm-2am Mon-Sat; 22) Handily located near the first bus stop after the Burrard Bridge (when coming from downtown), this tiny spot is arguably Kitsilano's best haunt. Slide onto a bench seat and peruse the oddball artworks – junk-shop pictures and carved masks – then order a house beer from the shingle-covered bar: if you're lucky, it'll be served in a boot-shaped glass.

Tempting cocktails are also offered at this quirky spot and there are often live events, including open-mike and comedy nights.

GALLEY PATIO & GRILL — PUB

Map p282 (www.thegalley.ca; Jericho Sailing Centre, 1300 Discovery St; 9am-10pm Jun-Aug, reduced hours off-season; ; 4) A terrific perch at sunset: plop down in one of the plastic patio chairs then eyeball the sailboats steering toward shore as the pyrotechnic sky unfolds. There are usually a couple of BC wine offerings, along with tasty local beers from R&B Brewing (the Sun God Wheat Ale is recommended in summer). Grub is of the fish-and-chips variety.

This is a family-friendly joint where you'll mostly meet locals. They're always up for a chat and you can quiz them about other sunset-viewing spots around the city (they'll likely mention Third Beach in Stanley Park).

FRINGE CAFÉ — PUB

Map p282 (3124 W Broadway; 3pm-1am Mon-Thu, 3pm-2am Fri & Sat; 9) An ever-friendly hangout, the tiny Fringe is a reminder of Kitsilano's counterculture heritage, from its funky memorabilia-lined walls to its chatty bar-propping regulars. Russell Brewing beers – here called Ugly Boy Lager and Dirty Girl Pale Ale – are usually on special, but there's also a surprising array of international bottled brews that usually includes everything from Tyskie to Tuborg.

If you're hungry, try the Sherpa's Pie, the best of several hearty house-cooked meals on the one-page menu. And by the way, you can't dial out on the rotary phone lamps on the tables, no matter how drunk you are. This is a great spot to meet the locals; you'll overhear plenty of gossip about house prices and the bohemian good old days.

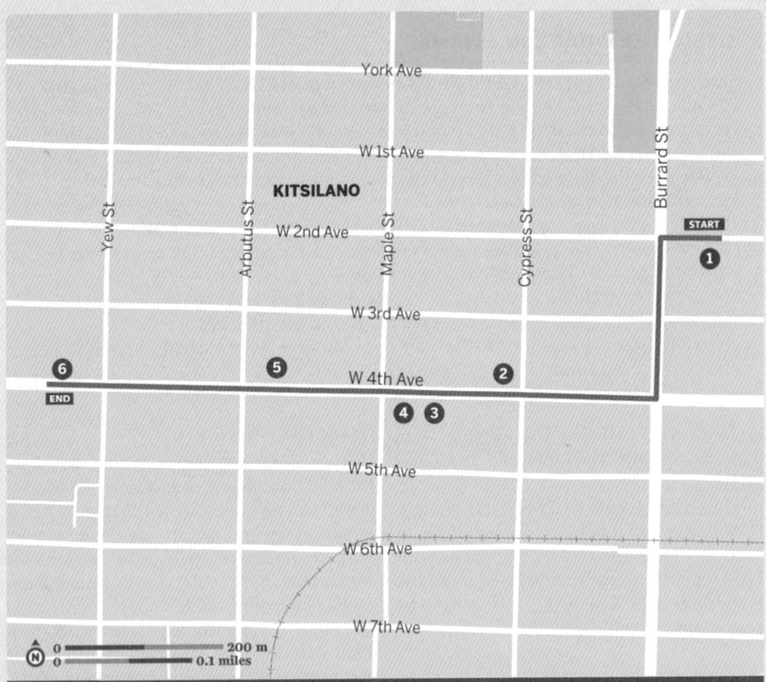

Neighborhood Walk
Kitsilano's Food-for-Thought Hop

START BARBARA-JO'S BOOKS TO COOKS
END GRAVITY POPE
LENGTH 1KM; 1.5 HOURS

This walk will introduce you to the Kitsilano neighborhood and two of its main obsessions: shopping and dining.

Kick things off on West 2nd Ave (near the intersection with Burrard St) at the recipe-and-chef-themed bookshop **1 Barbara-Jo's Books to Cooks** (p175). You can pick up a tome or two from famed local star chefs such as Vikram Vij and Rob Feenie.

Stroll west to Burrard St, turn left and walk two blocks south until you reach West 4th Ave. Cross over and head up West 4th until you come to the city's biggest travel book store, **2 Wanderlust** (p175). Duck inside for some inspiring travel tomes and a can of mosquito repellant – not something you'll usually need in Vancouver.

Cross over and you'll be in front of one of the city's favorite indie shops, **3 Zulu Records** (p174). It's well worth a few minutes to browse the vinyl among the local musos here. You should also ask the all-knowing staff to recommend some Vancouver bands.

You're in the heart of the Kits shopping district here, so spend some time checking out what's on offer. Once you've had your fill, continue westwards on West 4th and within a few steps you'll come to **4 Fable** (p168), one of the city's best farm-to-table restaurants. Consider nipping in here to make a dinner reservation for later in the day: it's usually the only way to avoid a long evening wait for a table. But if you're hungry now, cross to the other side of West 4th and slide into **5 Sophie's Cosmic Café** (p170), a retro diner with a great line in heaping brunches and hearty comfort-food lunches.

After your fuel-up, continue west on the same side and salve your appetite for fashion at **6 Gravity Pope** (p175). Women and men are treated as clothes-loving equals here, but it's the shoes that stand out: buy a pair and work them in with some more strolling.

WOLF & HOUND

PUB

Map p282 (www.wolfandhound.ca; 3617 W Broadway; ⏲4pm-midnight Mon, noon-midnight Tue-Thu, noon-1am Fri & Sat, 11am-11pm Sun; 🚌4) The nearest good pub to UBC and one of Vancouver's best Irish watering holes, you'll find plenty of students avoiding their assignments here. They come to watch sports in the den-like back room or catch free live Celtic music on Friday and Saturday nights. Harp and Kilkenny join Ireland's fave stout on the beer list alongside some good BC craft brews.

Go for the Driftwood Fat Tug IPA; made in Victoria, it's arguably BC's best India Pale Ale. Or, if you're intent on taking the dark route, try Storm Brewing's Black Plague Stout – arguably superior to the Guinness.

BIMINI

PUB

Map p282 (www.donnellygroup.ca; 2010 W 4th Ave; ⏲11:30am-1am Mon-Thu, to 2am Fri, 11am-2am Sat, to 1am Sun; 🚌4) It's packed on weekends with more of a nightclub feel, but this is a good pub to visit on weekday afternoons for a sly ale and some fries in a darkened corner (of which there are many). There's a pretty good array of craft beers, often including ales from BC darlings Driftwood and Phillips, and there are specials most days.

Tuesday is best: craft-beer sleeves are $3 and there's also an $11 beer-and-burger deal. They also have their own liquor store next door if you're craving takeout.

49TH PARALLEL COFFEE

COFFEE

Map p282 (www.49thparallelroasters.com; 2152 W 4th Ave; ⏲7am-7pm Mon-Sat, 8am-6pm Sun; 🚌4) Nip into Kitsilano's favorite independent coffeehouse to hang out with the cool locals. Grab a perch in the spartan, cafeteria-style room, and sip on a sky-blue cup of great java. This company roasts its own beans, which means you're unlikely to be disappointed – except if you're craving a Lucky's Doughnut (only the Main St branch serves them).

It's busy here during peak hours, with the tables dominated by fashionable young mothers and their strollers, so consider an off-peak visit or a takeout for your stroll along shop-lined West 4th. At the time of research plans were afoot to move to a larger location just along the street: check the website before you drop by.

O5 RARE TEA BAR

TEAHOUSE

Map p282 (www.o5tea.com; 2208 W 4th Ave; ⏲9:30am-11pm Mon-Sat, 10:30am-6pm Sun; 🚌4) A sign of the modern-day renaissance of tea bars, this lounge-like hipster spot is ideal for fans of that other hot caffeine beverage. Perch on a metal stool at the counter – which has the feel of a communal long-table – and prepare for a tea-based voyage of discovery. Single cups cost $5 to $7, while tasting flights are up to $17.

Be aware that the top-end teas here can be very expensive and it's easy to drop $50 on a couple of nice ones to take home. There are also regular evening tasting events that are always fun and revealing: check ahead before your visit to see what's coming up.

☆ ENTERTAINMENT

★BARD ON THE BEACH

PERFORMING ARTS

Map p282 (☎604-739-0559; www.bardonthebeach.org; Vanier Park; ⏲Jun-Sep; 🚌22) Watching Shakespeare performed while the sun sets against the mountains beyond the tented stage is a Vancouver summertime highlight. There are usually three Bard plays, plus one Bard-related work (*Rosencrantz and Guildenstern are Dead,* for example) to choose from during the run. Q&A talks are staged after Tuesday-night performances, along with regular opera, fireworks and wine-tasting nights throughout the season.

Expect Christopher Gaze – the festival's effervescent artistic director and public figurehead (and popular local actor) – to hop up on stage to introduce the show. He's the kind of old-school actor-manager that Shakespeare himself would have recognized.

CELLAR JAZZ CLUB

CABARET

Map p282 (☎604-738-1959; www.cellarjazz.com; 3611 W Broadway, Kitisilano; ⏲doors open 6:30pm; 🚌9) A serious muso venue where you're required to keep the noise down and respect the performers on the tiny corner stage, this subterranean 70-seat club is as close as you'll get in Vancouver to a classic jazz venue. Known for showcasing hot local performers and great touring acts, the atmospheric spot lures aficionados from across the region.

UBC'S BEST FEST

From Jonagold and Honey Crisp to Blushing Susan and Cox' Orange Pippins, fans of the real king of fruit have plenty to bite into at the autumnal, weekend-long **UBC Apple Festival**. Staged at the UBC Botanical Garden (p166), it's one of Vancouver's most popular community events. Along with live music and demonstrations on grafting and cider-making, there are lots of smile-triggering children's activities. But the event's main lure is the chance to nibble on a vast array of BC-grown treats that make most supermarket apples taste like hockey pucks. The best way to sample as many as possible is to pay an extra $5 and dive into the **Tasting Tent**. Here, 60 locally grown heritage and more recent varieties are available for considered scoffing, including rarities such as Crestons and Oaken Pins. Before you leave, follow your nose to the sweet aroma of perhaps the best apple pie you'll ever taste. A highlight of the festival, the deep-dish, golden-crusted slices for sale here are an indulgence you could happily eat until you explode – with an apple-flavored smile on your face.

Depending on the night, the calendar runs from mainstream to edgier fare. Keep in mind that, on top of your ticket charge, there's a minimum $10 food/drink charge ($15 on Friday and Saturdays). Keep your cost down by turning up on Tuesdays when there's no cover and beer specials all night.

JERICHO FOLK CLUB WORLD MUSIC

Map p282 (www.discoverysailing.org/folksong.html; Jericho Sailing Centre, 1300 Discovery St; 7:30pm Tue May-Sep; 4) Hosted by the Jericho Folk Club in a convivial beachfront sailing center, local folkies start their regular Tuesday-night event with a fun drop-in jam session. The evening then progresses to an open-mike hour – make sure you bring your tambourine – and concludes with a headline act that's guaranteed to have your toes tapping and your beard growing.

It's $10 for an evening's worth of entertainment and the definition of folk includes anything from Celtic and bluegrass to guitar-wielding singer-songwriters.

CINEPLEX FIFTH AVENUE CINEMAS CINEMA

Map p282 (www.cineplex.com; 2110 Burrard St; 44) Kitsilano's biggest movie house, popular Fifth Avenue screens indie, foreign flicks and blockbuster Hollywood schlock (those locals might look like intellectuals, but they enjoy *Iron Man* as much as anyone else). Also check out the loveseats, where you can lift the padded divider and snuggle up with your movie buddy.

SHOPPING

West 4th Ave is one of Vancouver's best strollable shopping strips, especially on the stretch west of Cypress St. Nip five blocks south to Broadway for another round of good local stores and bookshops, especially west of Trafalgar St. Wherever you wander, there are coffee shops and restaurants to keep you well-fueled.

ZULU RECORDS MUSIC

Map p282 (www.zulurecords.com; 1972 W 4th Ave; 10:30am-7pm Mon-Wed, to 9pm Thu & Fri, 9:30am-6:30pm Sat, noon-6pm Sun; 4) It's easy to spend a rainy afternoon at Kitsilano's fave indie music store sifting through the racks of new and used vinyl and hard-to-find imports (including some of those new-fangled CDs). There's an old-school *High Fidelity* ambiance here – the scuffed blue carpet and Death Race vintage video game help – but ask the music-nerd staff for tips on the local live scene: they know their stuff.

Tickets are sold here for local shows and there's also a back corner DVD section if you need something to pop in your laptop for the flight home.

STEPBACK HOMEWARES

Map p282 (www.stepback.ca; 3026 W Broadway; 11am-5:30pm Tue-Fri, 10am-6pm Sat, noon-5pm Sun; 9) This quirky store combines an inventory of trendy retro knickknacks – 1970s whiskey glasses, vintage suitcases, school exercise books etc – with reproduction items that look just as old. Among all the furniture, homewares and accessories, look out for enamel kitchenware, leather journals and classic books (including some legendary children's titles that will take you right back to your childhood).

A great place to pick up a weird and wacky alternative souvenir.

★KIDSBOOKS BOOKS

Map p282 (www.kidsbooks.ca; 3083 W Broadway; ⌚9:30am-6pm Mon-Thu, to 9pm Fri, to 6pm Sat, 11am-6pm Sun; 👪; 🚌9) Like a theme park for bookish kids, this huge child-friendly store – reputedly Canada's biggest kids' bookshop – has thousands of novels, picture books, history titles and anything else you can think of to keep your sprogs quiet. There are also regular readings by visiting authors and a selection of quality toys and games if they need a break from all that strenuous page-turning.

Along with the usual classics and vampire-themed young adult novels, there's a cool array of First Nations books to flick through.

WANDERLUST BOOKS, ACCESSORIES

Map p282 (www.wanderlustore.com; 1929 W 4th Ave; ⌚10am-7pm Mon-Fri, 10am-6pm Sat, noon-5pm Sun; 🚌4) Divided between guidebooks, maps and travel literature on one side and an array of travel accessories on the other, this store has been inspiring itchy feet for years. While the book selection is among Vancouver's best, it's the gadgets that are most intriguing. Peruse the money belts and mosquito nets, then wonder how you ever got by without quick-drying underwear.

The staff of seasoned travelers is super-knowledgeable if you just want to talk up your next big adventure. This is a good spot to pick up that plug adapter you mistakenly left at home.

THOMAS HAAS FOOD

Map p282 (www.thomashaas.com; 2539 W Broadway; ⌚8am-5:30pm Tue-Sat; 🚌9) This independent chocolatier is often bursting with locals purchasing their regular supplies of gourmet treats, such as caramel pecan squares and chili-suffused bon-bons. But the stars of the glass cabinet are the choc-encased fruit jellies (raspberry ganache recommended). A good spot for Vancouver-made souvenirs like chunky chai and espresso chocolate bars.

And since you're buying treats for everyone back home, you deserve one yourself: a huge slab of 'dark bark' chocolate brittle topped with nuts and dried fruit should do the trick. There are also a few tables (although they're often fully occupied) if you want to stop for a hot chocolate and a pastry treat.

BARBARA-JO'S BOOKS TO COOKS BOOKS

Map p282 (www.bookstocooks.com; 1740 W 2nd Ave; ⌚9:30am-6pm Tue-Sat, noon-5pm Sun & Mon; 🚌4) Traveling epicureans will salivate over to this popular bookstore, specializing in finger-licking food and wine tomes. There are book-reading events and cooking classes in the demonstration kitchen – if you fancy rubbing shoulders with a culinary maestro, check the website schedule. There are also dinner events with chefs and writers around the city: book ahead since they usually sell out.

KITSILANO FARMERS MARKET MARKET

Map p282 (www.eatlocal.org; Kitsilano Community Centre, 2690 Larch St; ⌚10am-2pm Sun mid-May–mid-Oct; 🚌4) Kitsilano's best excuse to get out and hang with the locals, this seasonal farmers market is one of the city's most popular. Arrive early for the best selection and you'll have the pick of freshly plucked local fruit and veg, such as sweet strawberries or spectacularly flavorful heirloom tomatoes. You'll likely never want to shop in a mainstream supermarket again.

Save some tummy room for the baked treats and peruse the arts and crafts: there may be something here of the handmade variety that will serve as a perfect souvenir of your West Coast visit.

GRAVITY POPE SHOES

Map p282 (www.gravitypope.com; 2205 W 4th Ave; ⌚10am-9pm Mon-Fri, 10am-7pm Sat, 11am-6pm Sun; 🚌4) This unisex temple of footwear is a dangerous place to come if you have a shoe fetish – best not to bring more than one credit card. Quality and designer élan are the keys here and you can expect to slip into Vancouver's best selection of fashion-forward clogs, wedges, mules and classy runners.

Next door, there's an adjoining fashion-forward clothing store. Called **Gravity Pope Tailored Goods**, it's stuffed with stylish must-have men's and women's clothing.

TRAVEL BUG BOOKS

Map p282 (www.travelbugbooks.ca; 3065 W Broadway; ⌚10am-6pm Mon-Sat, noon-5pm Sun; 🚌9) Lined with maps, guidebooks and travel literature (plus on-the-road accessories), this place is a treat for those planning a trip or those who just like to imagine afar from a comfy armchair. Check the website for readings from sinewy travel writers just back from navigating the Amazon equipped only with a toothpick. A good spot to browse and decide on your next adventure, there are always a few like-minded individuals browsing the stacks: consider saving on the single supplement by vacationing together.

SPORTS & ACTIVITIES

KITSILANO POOL SWIMMING

Map p282 (www.vancouverparks.ca; 2305 Cornwall Ave; adult/child $5.38/2.67; ⌚7am-8:30pm Mon-Fri, 10am-8:45pm Sat & Sun Jun-Aug, reduced hours off-season; 🚌22) This giant, heated 137m saltwater outdoor pool provides one of the best dips in town. It has a designated kids' area, where young families often teach their sprogs to swim, plus some lanes so you can practice your laps.

DIVING LOCKER DIVING

Map p282 (☎604-636-2681; www.divinglocker.ca; 2745 W 4th Ave; rentals from $60, dives from $30; ⌚10am-6pm Mon-Fri, 10am-5:30pm Sat, 10am-4pm Sun; 🚌4) A long-established favorite with local snorkelers and scuba divers, the Diving Locker is not just for experienced practitioners. Along with its regular series of PADI training courses, there's a great introductory course ($100, including equipment) for first-timers. There are also specialist kids courses for aquatically inclined youngsters.

WINDSURE ADVENTURE WATERSPORTS WATERSPORTS

(☎604-224-0615; www.windsure.com; 1300 Discovery St; ⌚9am-8:30pm Apr-Sep; 🚌4) For those who want to be at one with the sea breeze, Windsure specializes in windsurfing, skimboarding and stand-up paddleboarding (SUP) rentals and courses for a variety of skill levels. Prices are reasonable (for example, one-day skimboard rental is under $25) and the venue is inside the Jericho Sailing Centre, home of the city's recreational aquatic community.

Novices are more than welcome here: the two-hour windsurfing introductory group lesson ($55) is recommended. There are also lots of classes and activities for kids.

MAC SAILING BOATING

Map p282 (☎604-224-7245; www.macsailing.com; 1300 Discovery St; rental per hr $35-50; ⌚9am-7pm Mon-Fri, noon-6pm Sat & Sun, reduced hours off-season; 🚌4) This excellent operation at the Jericho Sailing Centre caters to sailing veterans and newbies who want to learn the ropes. The are several boats available for rent – the super-fast and easy-to-sail *Hobie Getaway* is fun – and lessons (including weekday evening introductory courses) are also offered, some tailored specifically for kids.

UBC AQUATIC CENTRE SWIMMING

Map p286 (www.aquatics.ubc.ca; 6121 University Blvd; adult/child $6/3.25; ⌚7:30am-10pm Mon-Fri, 10am-9pm Sat, 10:30am-9pm Sun, reduced hours off-season; 🚌99B-Line) One of the city's best indoor pools is on the UBC campus. It's a bit of a hike from downtown and students take precedence in the water, so you'll have to plan your visit around them – check the website for schedules. If you negotiate those obstacles, you'll find a 50m pool, saunas and exercise areas for public use.

UNIVERSITY GOLF CLUB GOLF

Map p286 (☎604-224-1818; www.universitygolf.com; 5185 University Blvd; green fees $40-69; ⌚dawn-dusk; 🚌99B-Line) Tucked inside UBC's giant Pacific Spirit Regional Park, this popular and attractive course has been luring locals of all skill levels for 90 years. The tree-lined 13th hole will have you reaching for your camera, and there's a driving range and an excellent clubhouse restaurant – as well as the cool BC Golf Museum behind the 17th tee.

Book at least one week ahead to be sure of a spot.

JERICHO SAILING CENTRE SAILING

Map p282 (☎604-224-4177; www.jsca.bc.ca; 1300 Discovery St; 🚌4) The salty heart of Vancouver's aquatic community, this bustling center is home to several operators that can teach or rent equipment for those interested in everything from surfing to sailing. There's also an on-site resto-bar (with a great water-view patio) for relaxing at the end of the day and exchanging stories about your ocean-going shenanigans.

North Shore

NORTH VANCOUVER | WEST VANCOUVER

Neighborhood Top Five

❶ Inching gingerly, with ever-increasing jelly legs, over the **Capilano Suspension Bridge** (p179), especially early or late in the day when few others are around.

❷ Skiing or snowboarding at **Grouse Mountain** (p185), particularly on a floodlit winter evening.

❸ Sliding across the glassy, mountain-shadowed waters of **Deep Cove** (p186) in a kayak.

❹ Careening down the North Shore mountain-bike trails on an **Endless Biking** (p186) tour.

❺ Stuffing your face with a bulging Skookum Chief burger at **Tomahawk Restaurant** (p181).

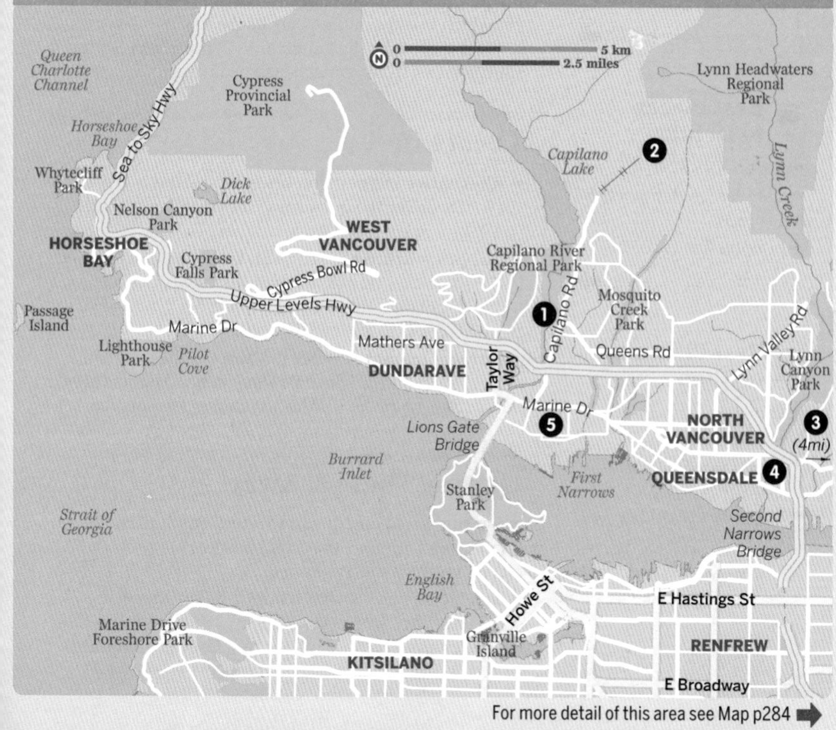

For more detail of this area see Map p284

Lonely Planet's Top Tip

Buy a transit day pass (adult/child $9.75/7.50), which includes travel by SeaBus, when coming from downtown. You'll be able to hit Lonsdale Quay Public Market, Capilano Suspension Bridge and Grouse Mountain without having to think about making the next bus before your ticket expires.

Best Places to Eat

- Tomahawk Restaurant (p181)
- Fraiche (p182)
- Artisan Bake Shoppe (p181)
- Savary Island Pie Company (p182)
- Salmon House on the Hill (p183)

For reviews, see p181

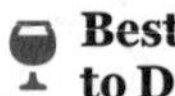

Best Places to Drink

- Raven (p183)
- Cafe for Contemporary Art (p183)
- Buddha-Full (p183)

For reviews, see p183

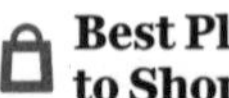

Best Places to Shop

- Lonsdale Quay Public Market (p184)
- Mountain Equipment Co-op (p184)
- Shipyards Night Market (p184)

For reviews, see p184

Explore North Shore

The North Shore area comprises North Vancouver and West Vancouver. Most visitors arrive here from downtown via the SeaBus ferry from Waterfront Station. You'll have an easy couple of hours of on-foot exploration straight off the boat: the Lonsdale Quay Public Market is just a few steps from the dock, and the waterfront on the market's eastern side has been reclaimed from its grungy shipyard past and now sports pleasant shoreline boardwalks. You'll also be well situated at the bottom of Lonsdale Ave, North Van's main thoroughfare. The avenue has loads of restaurants for when you get peckish: there are several at the waterfront end and more as you head up towards the mountains. Keep in mind this street is quite steep.

Once you're done with the market and Lower Lonsdale, hop on a bus from Lonsdale Quay. The 236 will take you to (and from) the region's two main attractions: the Capilano Suspension Bridge (about 20 minutes from the Quay) and Grouse Mountain (10 minutes further along). Grouse is the end of the line, so don't worry about getting off at the right stop. You can do both these attractions in one day: start with Capilano (before it gets too crowded) then continue on to Grouse (which you'll want to take more time for). Alternatively, both Grouse and Capilano can be accessed by free summer shuttle buses from downtown Vancouver.

For exploring West Vancouver, your best bet is catching bus 250 from downtown. It'll take you along Marine Dr, which is right in the heart of the area.

Skiers can take the good-value Cypress and Seymour shuttle buses from Lonsdale Quay during the season.

Local Life

- **Alternative suspension bridge** Capilano is great but the locals prefer the less-crowded Lynn Canyon Park (p179) as a gratis alternative.
- **Cut-price Grouse** If you're fit, hike the Grouse Grind (p179) and you'll be able to enjoy all the attractions up top as if you paid the regular Skyride fee. You'll have to pay $10 to get back down, though.
- **Farmers market** Few North Vancouverites do their regular shopping at Lonsdale Quay Public Market (p184), but many drop by for its May to October farmers market.

Getting There & Away

- **SeaBus** From downtown's Waterfront Station, it takes just 12 minutes to reach Lonsdale Quay on the transit network's ferry service.
- **Bus** Lonsdale Quay has a bus terminal where services depart for North and West Vancouver. Bus 236 is key: it runs to both Capilano and Grouse Mountain.

SIGHTS

North Vancouver

CAPILANO SUSPENSION BRIDGE PARK

Map p284 (www.capbridge.com; 3735 Capilano Rd; adult/youth/child $34.95/21.05/12; ⌚9am-7pm Apr & May, 8:30am-8pm Jun-Aug, reduced off-season; 👪; 🚌236 from Lonsdale Quay) As you walk gingerly onto one of the world's longest (140m) and highest (70m) suspension bridges, swaying gently over the roiling Capilano Canyon, remember that its thick steel cables are embedded in concrete. That should steady your feet – unless there are teenagers stamping across. Added park attractions include a glass-bottomed cliffside walkway and an elevated canopy trail through the trees.

This is a hugely popular attraction (hence the summer tour buses); try to arrive early during peak months so you can check out the historic exhibits, totem poles and tree-shaded nature trails on the other side of the bridge in relative calm. On your way out, peruse what must be the city's largest souvenir shop for First Nations artworks, 'moose dropping' choccies and a full-range of T-shirts and ball caps. From May to September, Capilano makes it very easy for you to get here from downtown by running a free shuttle from Canada Place and area hotels. Check the website for details.

GROUSE MOUNTAIN OUTDOORS

Map p284 (www.grousemountain.com; 6400 Nancy Greene Way; Skyride adult/youth/child $39.95/23.95/13.95; ⌚9am-10pm; 👪; 🚌236 from Lonsdale Quay) Calling itself the 'Peak of Vancouver,' this mountaintop playground offers smashing views of downtown, shimmering in the water below. In summer, **Skyride** gondola tickets include access to lumberjack shows, alpine hiking, movie presentations and a grizzly-bear refuge. Pay extra for ziplining and **Eye of the Wind**, a 20-story, elevator-accessed turbine tower with a panoramic viewing pod that will have your camera itching for action.

There are also restaurants up here if you fancy dining: it's an ideal sunset-viewing spot. You can reduce the gondola fee by hiking the ultrasteep Grouse Grind (p180) up the side of the mountain – it costs $10 to get back down on the Skyride. Like Capilano, Grouse lures visitors from downtown in summer by offering a free shuttle from Canada Place. And in winter, it's all about skiing and snowboarding as Grouse becomes the locals' fave powder-bound playground.

MT SEYMOUR PROVINCIAL PARK OUTDOORS

Map p284 (www.bcparks.ca; 1700 Mt Seymour Rd; ⌚dawn-dusk) A popular, rustic retreat from the downtown clamor, this giant, tree-lined park is suffused with more than a dozen summertime hiking trails that suit walkers of most abilities (the easiest path is the 2km Goldie Lake Trail). Many trails wind past lakes and centuries-old Douglas firs. This is also one of the city's three main winter playgrounds.

The park is a great spot for mountain biking and has many dedicated trails. It's around 30 minutes from downtown Vancouver by car; drivers can take Hwy 1 to the Mt Seymour Parkway (near the Second Narrows Bridge) and follow it east to Mt Seymour Rd.

LYNN CANYON PARK PARK

Map p284 (www.lynncanyon.ca; Park Rd; ⌚7am-9pm summer, reduced hours off-season; 👪; 🚌229 from Lonsdale Quay) Amid a dense bristling of ancient trees, the main feature of this provincial park is its suspension bridge, a free alternative to Capilano. Not quite as big as its tourist-magnet rival, it nevertheless provokes the same jelly-legged reaction as you sway over the river that runs 50m below – and it's always far less crowded. Hiking trails, swimming areas and picnic spots will keep you busy here as well.

The **Ecology Centre** (Map p284; www.dnv.org/ecology; 3663 Park Rd; by donation $2; ⌚10am-5pm Jun-Sep, reduced off-season) houses interesting displays, including dioramas and video presentations, on the area's rich biodiversity. It stages regular talks and events for kids, especially in summer.

MAPLEWOOD FARM FARM

Map p284 (www.maplewoodfarm.bc.ca; 405 Seymour River Place; adult/child $7.50/4.50; ⌚10am-4pm Apr-Dec, closed Mon Jan-Mar; 👪; 🚌239 from Lonsdale Quay, then C15) A popular family-friendly site, this farmyard attraction includes plenty of hands-on displays plus a collection of more than 200 domestic animals. Your wide-eyed kids can pet some critters, watch the milking demonstration and feed some squawking, ever-hungry ducks and chickens. The highlight

MOTHER NATURE'S STAIRMASTER

If you're finding your vacation a little too relaxing, head over to North Vancouver and join the perspiring throng snaking – almost vertically – up the **Grouse Grind** trail. The entrance is near the parking lot, across the street from where slightly more sane Grouse Mountain visitors pile into the Skyride gondola and trundle up to the summit without breaking a sweat.

Around 3km in total, this steep, rock-studded forest trek will likely have your joints screaming for mercy within 15 minutes as you focus on the feet of the person in front of you. Most people take around an hour to reach the top, where they collapse like fish gasping on the rocks. If you're feeling energetic, you might want to try and beat the record of Vancouverite Sebastian Albrecht, who nailed the trail 14 times in one day in 2010.

Things to keep in mind if you're planning to join the 110,000 who hike the Grind every year: take a bottle of water, dress in thin layers so you can strip down, and bring $10 with you: the trail is one way, so when you reach the summit you have to take the Skyride back down – your consolation is that you get to enjoy the summit's many attractions for free in exchange for your exploding calf muscles.

is the daily (around 3:30pm) 'running of the goats,' when starving hairballs streak from the paddock to their barn for dinner.

The top 'extra,' though, is the behind-the-scenes tour where your sprogs can learn what it's like to be a farmer, from grooming (the animals, not the kids) to egg collecting and getting the feed ready. Book ahead: these hour-long tours are popular.

FERRY BUILDING ART GALLERY GALLERY

Map p284 (www.ferrybuildinggallery.com; 1414 Argyle Ave; ⏲11am-5pm Tue-Sun; 🚌255) FREE Housed in a cute wooden heritage building, which was once a ferry terminal when transit boats plied the waters between West Van and Vancouver, this popular waterfront community gallery is well worth a look if you're in the Ambleside Park vicinity. Shows change once or twice a month and there's a strong commitment to showcasing local artists.

Time your visit well and you can drop in for an opening reception and meet the artists themselves.

CAPILANO RIVER HATCHERY FARM

Map p284 (4500 Capilano Park Rd; ⏲8am-8pm Jun-Aug, to 7pm May & Sep, reduced off-season) FREE Just 2km north of Capilano Suspension Bridge, this government-run fish farm works to protect coho, chinook and steelhead salmon stocks. Visit from July to November and you'll likely catch adult salmon swimming through fish ladders past the rapids in a heroic effort to reach their spawning grounds upstream, after which they promptly die in a scripted lifecycle possibly penned by Samuel Beckett.

Eye-level tanks display the creatures while enlightening exhibits help explain the entire mysterious process. If you're driving here (rather than swimming with the salmon) head north along Capilano Rd, then turn left onto Capilano Park Rd and continue for 1km.

West Vancouver

CYPRESS PROVINCIAL PARK OUTDOORS

Map p284 (www.bcparks.ca; Cypress Bowl Rd; ⏲dawn-dusk) Around 8km north of West Van via Hwy 99, Cypress offers great summertime hikes, including the Baden-Powell, Yew Lake and Howe Sound Crest trails, which plunge through forests of cedar, yellow cypress and Douglas fir, and wind past little lakes and alpine meadows. It's also a popular area for mountain bikers, and Cypress becomes a snowy playground in winter.

If you're driving from downtown Vancouver, cross the Lions Gate Bridge to the Upper Levels Hwy via Taylor Way in West Vancouver. Then, follow the signs to the park entrance.

LIGHTHOUSE PARK PARK

Map p284 (www.lighthousepark.ca; cnr Beacon Lane & Marine Dr; ⏲dawn-dusk; 🚌250) Some of the region's oldest trees live within this accessible 75-hectare park, including a rare stand of original coastal forest and plenty of those gnarly, copper-trunked arbutus trees. About 13km of hiking trails criss-cross the area, including a recommended trek that leads to the rocky perch of Point Atkinson Lighthouse, ideal for capturing shimmering, camera-worthy views over Burrard Inlet.

If you're driving from downtown, turn left on Marine Dr after crossing the Lions Gate Bridge to reach the park.

WEST VANCOUVER SEAWALL — WATERFRONT

Map p284 (🚌250) Take bus 250 from downtown Vancouver and hop off on Marine Dr at the intersection with 24th St. Peruse the stores and coffee shops in Dundarave Village, then stroll downhill to the waterfront. Take in the panoramic coastline from Dundarave Pier, then weave eastwards along the shore-hugging Centennial Seawalk route. On West Van's favorite promenade, you'll pass joggers, herons and public artworks.

After 2km, the trail comes to a halt. From here, head back up to the Marine Dr shops or weave over to Ambleside Park, where you'll find a dramatic First Nations carved welcome figure facing the water.

HORSESHOE BAY — VILLAGE

Map p284 (www.horseshoebay.bc.ca; 🚌257) This small coastal community marks the end of West Vancouver and the starting point for trips to Whistler, via the Sea to Sky Hwy (Hwy 99). It's a pretty village with views across the bay and up glassy-watered Howe Sound. Cute places to eat and shop line waterfront Bay St, from where you can also take a whale-watching boat trek with Sewell's Sea Safari (p248).

The BC Ferries terminal for aquatic hops to Bowen Island, Vancouver Island and beyond is also located here.

WHYTECLIFF PARK — PARK

Map p284 (Marine Dr, 7100-block; ⌚dawn-dusk; 🚌250) Just west of Horseshoe Bay, this is an exceptional little waterfront green space. Trails lead to vistas and a gazebo, from where you can watch the Burrard Inlet boat traffic. The rocky beach is a great place to scamper over the large rocks protruding from the beach. It's also one of region's favorite dive spots for scuba fans.

But humans are not the only divers who like this place: the park is a popular area for lounging seals.

EATING

The North Shore has plenty of dine-out options. You'll find a concentrated cluster of eateries radiating up Lonsdale Ave from the waterfront, with many more dotted around both North and West Van.

ARTISAN BAKE SHOPPE — BAKERY $

Map p284 (www.artisanbakeshoppe.ca; 127 Lonsdale Ave, North Vancouver; mains $4-9; ⌚7am-5:30pm Mon-Sat; 🚌230) One of a string of German-heritage businesses on this Lonsdale stretch, the Artisan Bake Shoppe has hearty, house-baked European-style breads that are about as far from factory-made products as possible. Be sure to pick up some pumpkin-seed bread (it'll keep you going all week) then indulge in some instant treats: banana pecan cookies and the region's best pretzels are recommended. Soups and sandwiches are available.

If you still have room (or even if you don't) consider some eye-rollingly-good apple strudel for the road.

★TOMAHAWK RESTAURANT — DINER $$

Map p284 (www.tomahawkrestaurant.com; 1550 Philip Ave, North Vancouver; mains $8-16; ⌚8am-9pm Sun-Thu, to 10pm Fri & Sat; 🚌240) A colorful blast from North Van's pioneering past, the family-run Tomahawk has been heaping its plates with comfort food since 1926. A bustling weekend brunch spot – if the massive Yukon bacon and eggs grease-fest

NORTH SHORE'S BEST FEST

Late July is the time when everyone on the North Shore finds their party groove in one of metro Vancouver's best community events. The weekend-long **Caribbean Days Festival** (www.caribbeandays.ca) in the city's Waterfront Park – not far from the SeaBus dock – includes a street parade; live music and dance; a food fair of epic, spicy proportions; and a popular art and clothing market. Luring thousands to area, it never fails to put smiles on faces.

or the frightening Skookum Chief burger don't kill your hangover, nothing will – it's also fun for lunch or dinner, when bulging burgers and chicken potpies hit the menu.

Grab a spot at the counter on one of the swivel stools, and check out the surfeit of First Nations artifacts lining the walls: it's like stuffing your face in a museum.

BURGOO BISTRO WEST COAST **$$**

Map p284 (www.burgoo.ca; 3 Lonsdale Ave, North Vancouver; mains $10-18; ⌚11am-10pm Sun-Wed, to 11pm Thu-Sat; ⛴SeaBus from Waterfront Station) With the feel of a cozy, rustic cabin – complete with large stone fireplace – Burgoo's menu of comfort food with a twist aims to warm up North Van's winter nights: the spicy apricot lamb tagine or smile-triggering butter chicken would thaw a glacier from 50 paces. There's also a wide array of house-made soups and salads. Drinks-wise, try the tasty craft beers. There's live jazz on Sunday nights (from 7pm) to keep your toes tapping.

SAVARY ISLAND PIE COMPANY BAKERY, CAFE **$$**

Map p284 (www.savaryislandpiecompany.com; 1533 Marine Dr, West Vancouver; mains $8-14; ⌚6am-7pm, to 9pm in summer; 🚌250) Ask North Shore locals where to get a great slice of pie and they'll point you to this popular bakery cafe. The bulging, fresh-baked pies remain the mainstay of the business (do not miss the raspberry rhubarb) but since opening in 1989 they've extended to a menu – think breakfasts or soup and sandwiches – that suggests dessert is not the only meal. It's also a great place to pop-in for coffee: see if you can resist the fresh-baked muffins (hint: don't even try).

RAGLAN'S BURGERS, BREAKFAST **$$**

Map p284 (www.raglans.ca; 15 Londsale Ave, North Vancouver; $10-18; ⌚10am-midnight Sun-Thu, to 1am Fri & Sat; ⛴SeaBus from Waterfront Station) Friendly and funky (hence the eye-popping fusion of surfer and tiki decor), this is the most laid-back of the small, side-by-side, patio-fronted restaurants and bars calling your name at the bottom of Lonsdale. Expect jaw-disclocatingly huge burgers and nacho plates that would satisfy a biblical plague of locusts, but go for the excellent garden pesto quesadilla if you can't decide.

Arguably the best time to come is at the end of the day, when you can slide onto the patio and work your way down a cocktail menu that feels like it's from a beach bar in Maui. Return in the morning, so your inevi-

SURFING THE SEABUS

Sashaying between downtown Vancouver's Waterfront Station and the North Shore's Lonsdale Quay, the 400-seat SeaBus vessels easily divide the locals from the tourists. Vancouverites barely raise a glance when the boats arrive in their little docks to pick up passengers for the 12-minute voyage across Burrard Inlet. In contrast, wide-eyed visitors excitedly crowd the automatic doors as if they're about to climb onto a theme park ride.

Once on board, it's a similar story: locals shuffle to the back and open their newspapers, while out-of-towners glue themselves to the front seats for a panoramic view of the glittering crossing, with the looming North Shore mountains growing in stature ahead of them as the voyage gets underway.

The pair of boxy, low-slung catamarans – joined by a third sibling in 2012 – first hit the waves in 1977. But they weren't the first boats to take passengers over the briny. The first regular private ferry covering this route launched in 1900. It was taken over and run as a public service by the City of North Vancouver a few years later, when the route's two vessels were imaginatively renamed *North Vancouver Ferry 1* and *North Vancouver Ferry 2*. No prizes for guessing what the third ferry was named when it was added in 1936. The opening of the Lions Gate Bridge, linking the two shores by road, a couple of years later slowly pulled the rug from under the ferry service, and the last sailing took place in 1958. It would be almost 20 years before a new public service was restored to the route, when *MV Burrard Beaver* and *MV Burrard Otter* (and, later, the new *MV Pacific Breeze*) took to the waves.

A fourth SeaBus vessel is expected to enter service in 2014, at which time the older two vessels will be retired or kept on standby.

DRINKING & NIGHTLIFE

The North Shore isn't a great place for a destination night out, but there are some standouts worth pulling over for (with a designated driver, of course).

RAVEN — PUB

Map p284 (www.theravenpub.com; 1052 Deep Cove Rd, North Vancouver; 11am-midnight; 212) This instantly welcoming Deep Cove joint effortlessly mixes blokey barflies and twenty-something lads within an inviting interior illuminated by red-glass candleholders. But it's not just about looks. The Raven serves great pizzas – the pesto chicken is recommended – and has a beer list with top BC quaffs by Storm, Phillips, Driftwood and Howe Sound Brewing. To be honest, the beer selection is good enough to make this your local wherever you might live.

CAFE FOR CONTEMPORARY ART — COFFEE

Map p284 (www.cafeforcontemporaryart.com; 104 East Esplanade, North Vancouver; 8am-6pm; SeaBus from Waterfront Station) A sign that North Van is developing its own hipster scene, every plaid shirt in the area gravitates toward this grandly named hangout to sup 49th Parallel coffee – the best java you'll likely find on this side of Burrard Inlet. With its polished concrete floors and industrial ducts, it's a bit spartan, but lively chat from the MacBookers warms things up.

Save time to peruse the artwork in the adjoining gallery. Typically of the challenging, thought-provoking kind, the shows change every month.

BUDDHA-FULL — JUICE BAR

Map p284 (www.buddha-full.ca; 106 W 1st St, North Vancouver; 10am-6pm Mon-Fri, to 5pm Sat & Sun; ; SeaBus from Waterfront Station) Tucked just off Lower Lonsdale, this eclectic little cafe – just look for the yellow bike suspended in the window – is a bright and cheery smoothie bar. Pull up a telegraph cable table (actually don't: they're quite heavy) and slurp a Peaceful Warrior or Vibrant C, then stick around for a vegetarian sandwich lunch. Cakes and cookies also available.

The cafe has a funky interior with lots of found-art (and created-art) flourishes. This is also a good place to meet the local bike community, who fuel up for their next assault on the mountain trails.

QUEEN'S CROSS PUB

Map p284 (www.queenscross.com; 2989 Lonsdale Ave, North Vancouver; ⏲11am-midnight Sun-Thu, to 1am Fri & Sat; 📶; 🚌230 from Lonsdale Quay) It's a hike from the SeaBus up Lonsdale Ave for this trad-style, gable-roofed neighborhood pub, but just think how easy it will be to roll back downhill at the end of the night (stop when you hit the water). Formerly the kind of place where you had choice of Bud or Molson, it now has a tasty commitment to craft brews with around a dozen BC faves to choose from.

Food-wise, you'll find all the usual pub-grub classics (half-price wings from 3pm to 5pm weekdays). It's a good place to catch a hockey game with the locals: you'll find out just how angry those so-called mild-mannered Canadians can get.

SHOPPING

Outdoor stores are a specialty here, particularly those that can help you hit the bike trails or gear-up for an assault on area ski slopes. But it's not all about action.

LONSDALE QUAY PUBLIC MARKET MARKET

Map p284 (www.lonsdalequay.com; 123 Carrie Cates Ct, North Vancouver; ⏲9am-7pm; ⛴SeaBus from Waterfront Station) As well as being a transportation hub – the SeaBus from downtown docks here and you can pick up transit buses to Capilano, Grouse and beyond – this waterfront facility houses a colorful public market. Look for fresh fruit and glassy-eyed whole fish on the main floor, and trinkets and clothing on the 2nd floor. There's also a lively food court (Montgomery's Fish & Chips recommended).

It's an easy afternoon jaunt from downtown, with many visitors scooping up an ice cream and lingering over the boardwalk views of Vancouver. If you're eating at the food court (in summer), snag one of the alfresco tables.

MOUNTAIN EQUIPMENT CO-OP OUTDOOR EQUIPMENT

Map p284 (www.mec.ca; 212 Brooksbank Ave, North Vancouver; ⏲10am-9pm Mon-Fri, 9am-6pm Sat, 11am-5pm Sun) Smaller than its Vancouver parent, this M a friendlier, more neighbo everyone here – staff an seems to know each other a of the North Shore outdc It's a great place to stock your nature-loving adventu everything from perfect sof waterproofs.

You'll need to be a memb from this nonprofit co-op: range and costs just $5 (for l

SHIPYARDS NIGHT MARKET

Map p284 (www.northshoregr Shipbuilders Sq, North Vancouve & Fri May-Sep; ⛴SeaBus from Wa Muscling in on the region's night-market scene, North is a few steps east of Lonsd a fun way to spend a balmy the ocean lapping nearby. Sc a dozen or so food trucks, ta live bands on the little stag unusual souvenir or two fro of vendors.

It's an easy spot to end your day; the SeaBus back to the c away.

COVE BIKE SHOP OUT

Map p284 (www.covebike.com; 1 North Vancouver; ⏲9:30am-5pm; North Shore's favorite store f mountain bikers, the Cove bikes but it sells and services f serious biker dudes. An excellen clists to rub shoulders with the ing community; it's worth dro a chat and some expert tips on a

PARK ROYAL

Map p284 (www.shopparkroyal.com West Vancouver ; ⏲10am-7pm Mon & Wed-Fri, 9:30am-6pm Sat, to 6pm Sun the region's oldest mall but Park a good job of keeping up with t tition. With 280 stores (includi usual suspects), its ever-expandi area emulates an outdoor UK high street with strollable big s restaurants. The indoor area is a tion when the the region's 'Wet C name is in full force.

Park Royal is easy to access from downtown Vancouver; buse over the picturesque Lions Gate B stop just outside.

table hangover ca receive some brunch plate salvation (go for pulled pork hash).

FRAICHE WEST COAST $$$

Map p284 (☎604-925-7595; www.fraicherestaurant.ca; 2240 Chippendale Rd, West Vancouver; mains $18-42; ⏰11am-3pm & 5-10pm Tue-Sun; 🚌256) It's worth tearing your gaze from the mesmerizing shoreline vistas here to focus on your plate. Perfect Canadian gourmet is the approach, with typical highlights on the seasonal menu including charred octopus or juicy roast duck. If you fancy a taste of the high life without the price, drop in for lunch or weekend brunch when many dishes hover around $20.

OBSERVATORY WEST COAST $$$

Map p284 (☎604-980-9311; www.grousemountain.com; Grouse Mountain, North Vancouver; mains $39; ⏰5-10pm; 🚌236 from Lonsdale Quay) Crowning Grouse Mountain, the fine-dining Observatory serves its chorizo scallops and lamb medleys alongside breathtaking views over Stanley Park and Vancouver's twinkling towers far below. A perfect romantic dinner venue – you wouldn't be the first to propose here – there's an excellent wine list if you suddenly need to console yourself. Reserve in advance and you'll also get free Skyride passes.

The atmosphere is more laid-back at the adjacent, pub-like **Altitudes Bistro**, which offers comfort grub of the burgers and fish and chips variety in a casual ski-lodge ambience.

SALMON HOUSE ON THE HILL SEAFOOD $$$

Map p284 (☎604-926-3212; www.salmonhouse.com; 2229 Folkestone Way, West Vancouver; mains $30-40; ⏰5-9:30pm Sun-Thu, 6-10pm Fri & Sat, brunch Sat & Sun 10:30am-2:30pm) West Vancouver's old-school destination restaurant, this landmark has been luring locals for special occasion dinners for years. But Salmon House doesn't rest on its laurels – if laurels can be defined as a gable-roofed wooden interior and floor-to-ceiling windows with sunset clifftop city views. Instead, you'll find a menu of delectable seasonal British Columbia (BC) seafood with serious gourmet credentials. There are also top-notch duck and lamb dishes for those nonaquatic scoffers. And if you just want to check it out without the top-end dinner price, drop by for weekend brunch (crab eggs Benedict recommended).

DRINKING & NIGHTLIFE

The North Shore isn't a great place for a destination night out, but there are some standouts worth pulling over for (with a designated driver, of course).

RAVEN PUB

Map p284 (www.theravenpub.com; 1052 Deep Cove Rd, North Vancouver; ⏰11am-midnight; 🚌212) This instantly welcoming Deep Cove joint effortlessly mixes blokey barflies and twenty-something lads within an inviting interior illuminated by red-glass candleholders. But it's not just about looks. The Raven serves great pizzas – the pesto chicken is recommended – and has a beer list with top BC quaffs by Storm, Phillips, Driftwood and Howe Sound Brewing. To be honest, the beer selection is good enough to make this your local wherever you might live.

CAFE FOR CONTEMPORARY ART COFFEE

Map p284 (www.cafeforcontemporaryart.com; 104 East Esplanade, North Vancouver; ⏰8am-6pm; ⛴SeaBus from Waterfront Station) A sign that North Van is developing its own hipster scene, every plaid shirt in the area gravitates toward this grandly named hangout to sup 49th Parallel coffee – the best java you'll likely find on this side of Burrard Inlet. With its polished concrete floors and industrial ducts, it's a bit spartan, but lively chat from the MacBookers warms things up.

Save time to peruse the artwork in the adjoining gallery. Typically of the challenging, thought-provoking kind, the shows change every month.

BUDDHA-FULL JUICE BAR

Map p284 (www.buddha-full.ca; 106 W 1st St, North Vancouver; ⏰10am-6pm Mon-Fri, to 5pm Sat & Sun; 📶; ⛴SeaBus from Waterfront Station) Tucked just off Lower Lonsdale, this eclectic little cafe – just look for the yellow bike suspended in the window – is a bright and cheery smoothie bar. Pull up a telegraph cable table (actually don't: they're quite heavy) and slurp a Peaceful Warrior or Vibrant C, then stick around for a vegetarian sandwich lunch. Cakes and cookies also available.

The cafe has a funky interior with lots of found-art (and created-art) flourishes. This is also a good place to meet the local bike community, who fuel up for their next assault on the mountain trails.

QUEEN'S CROSS PUB

Map p284 (www.queenscross.com; 2989 Lonsdale Ave, North Vancouver; ⏲11am-midnight Sun-Thu, to 1am Fri & Sat; 📶; 🚌230 from Lonsdale Quay) It's a hike from the SeaBus up Lonsdale Ave for this trad-style, gable-roofed neighborhood pub, but just think how easy it will be to roll back downhill at the end of the night (stop when you hit the water). Formerly the kind of place where you had choice of Bud or Molson, it now has a tasty commitment to craft brews with around a dozen BC faves to choose from.

Food-wise, you'll find all the usual pub-grub classics (half-price wings from 3pm to 5pm weekdays). It's a good place to catch a hockey game with the locals: you'll find out just how angry those so-called mild-mannered Canadians can get.

SHOPPING

Outdoor stores are a specialty here, particularly those that can help you hit the bike trails or gear-up for an assault on area ski slopes. But it's not all about action.

LONSDALE QUAY PUBLIC MARKET MARKET

Map p284 (www.lonsdalequay.com; 123 Carrie Cates Ct, North Vancouver; ⏲9am-7pm; ⛴SeaBus from Waterfront Station) As well as being a transportation hub – the SeaBus from downtown docks here and you can pick up transit buses to Capilano, Grouse and beyond – this waterfront facility houses a colorful public market. Look for fresh fruit and glassy-eyed whole fish on the main floor, and trinkets and clothing on the 2nd floor. There's also a lively food court (Montgomery's Fish & Chips recommended).

It's an easy afternoon jaunt from downtown, with many visitors scooping up an ice cream and lingering over the boardwalk views of Vancouver. If you're eating at the food court (in summer), snag one of the alfresco tables.

MOUNTAIN EQUIPMENT CO-OP OUTDOOR EQUIPMENT

Map p284 (www.mec.ca; 212 Brooksbank Ave, North Vancouver; ⏲10am-9pm Mon-Fri, 9am-6pm Sat, 11am-5pm Sun) Smaller than its Vancouver parent, this MEC branch has a friendlier, more neighborly feel. Almost everyone here – staff and customers – seems to know each other and is a member of the North Shore outdoor community. It's a great place to stock up on gear for your nature-loving adventures; you'll find everything from perfect soft hikers to great waterproofs.

You'll need to be a member to purchase from this nonprofit co-op: it's easy to arrange and costs just $5 (for life).

SHIPYARDS NIGHT MARKET MARKET

Map p284 (www.northshoregreenmarket.com; Shipbuilders Sq, North Vancouver; ⏲5-10pm Thu & Fri May-Sep; ⛴SeaBus from Waterfront Station) Muscling in on the region's summertime night-market scene, North Van's version is a few steps east of Lonsdale Quay. It's a fun way to spend a balmy evening, with the ocean lapping nearby. Scoff grub from a dozen or so food trucks, tap your toes to live bands on the little stage and buy an unusual souvenir or two from the dozens of vendors.

It's an easy spot to end your North Shore day; the SeaBus back to the city is a stroll away.

COVE BIKE SHOP OUTDOOR EQUIPMENT

Map p284 (www.covebike.com; 1389 Main St, North Vancouver; ⏲9:30am-5pm; 🚌250) The North Shore's favorite store for hardcore mountain bikers, the Cove doesn't rent bikes but it sells and services for the area's serious biker dudes. An excellent spot for cyclists to rub shoulders with the region's biking community; it's worth dropping in for a chat and some expert tips on area trails.

PARK ROYAL MALL

Map p284 (www.shopparkroyal.com; Marine Dr, West Vancouver ; ⏲10am-7pm Mon & Tue, to 9pm Wed-Fri, 9:30am-6pm Sat, to 6pm Sun; 🚌250) It's the region's oldest mall but Park Royal does a good job of keeping up with the competition. With 280 stores (including all the usual suspects), its ever-expanding Village area emulates an outdoor UK shopping high street with strollable big stores and restaurants. The indoor area is a good option when the the region's 'Wet Coast' nickname is in full force.

Park Royal is easy to access on transit from downtown Vancouver; buses trundle over the picturesque Lions Gate Bridge and stop just outside.

SNOWSHOE SHENANIGANS

If you lack the pose-worthy skills for the ski and snowboard slopes around Vancouver but you'd still like to gambol through the powder, snowshoeing is an ideal alternative – especially since the only requirement is the ability to walk. If you can manage that, head to Grouse Mountain, where you can rent shoes and hit the 10km of winding trails in Munday Alpine Snowshoe Park.

Within minutes you'll feel like you're the only person on the mountain; the sound of voices fades and is replaced by the crunch of ice-caked snow, along with the ever-present cawing of scavenging ravens. You might also glimpse an eagle or two. Passing through the forest of mountain hemlocks and Pacific silver fir trees – many with straggles of moss hanging from them like Marxian beards – you'll sometimes break into open ground and catch some stunning panoramic views. Burnaby Mountain, topped by Simon Fraser University, is usually visible, while the ghostly face of Mt Baker can often be glimpsed shimmering 130km away.

Continuing upward, you'll eventually hit the park's broad Evian Express Trail. The route overlooks the silver surface of Capilano Reservoir far below and the distant crags of Vancouver Island on the watery horizon. Once you've had enough of the view, head downhill (at a rate of knots) to the lodge for a well-deserved Granville Island brew or two.

SPORTS & ACTIVITIES

In winter, Grouse Mountain, Cypress Mountain and Mt Seymour are the three favorite winter destinations for Vancouverites. You can be on the slopes within 30 minutes of downtown. In summer, hiking and mountain biking lures locals to the North Shore, with the latter especially taking off in the past decade. Check in with the North Shore Mountain Bike Association (www.nsmba.ca) for a handle on the local scene.

GROUSE MOUNTAIN SKIING

Map p284 (www.grousemountain.com; 6400 Nancy Greene Way, North Vancouver; adult/youth/child $58/45/25, reduced in summer; ⌚9am-10pm mid-Nov–mid-Apr; 🚌236 from Lonsdale Quay) Vancouver's favorite winter hangout, family-friendly Grouse offers 26 ski and snowboard runs (including 14 night runs). There are classes and lessons available for beginners and beyond, and the area's forested snowshoe trails are magical. There are also a couple of dining options if you just want to relax and watch the snow with hot chocolate in hand.

If you're here in December, this is a great place to soak up some Christmas spirit; if you're looking for Santa in Vancouver, this is where you'll find him, along with a reindeer or two.

CYPRESS MOUNTAIN SKIING

Map p284 (www.cypressmountain.com; Cypress Bowl Rd, West Vancouver; adult/youth/child $60/46/26; ⌚9am-4pm Dec, to 10pm Jan-Mar, 10am-5pm Apr–season end) Around 8km north of West Van via Hwy 99, Cypress Provincial Park transforms into Cypress Mountain resort in winter, attracting well-insulated locals with its 53 runs, snowshoe trails and snowtubing course. Upgraded for the 2010 Winter Olympics, the resort's new facilities include an expanded lodge and improvements to several runs, including Lower Panorama, where Canada won its first Olympic gold on home soil.

If you don't want to drive, consider taking the seasonal Cypress Coach Lines bus ($23 return), which can pick you up from the city or Lonsdale Quay.

MT SEYMOUR SKIING, MOUNTAIN BIKING

Map p284 (www.mountseymour.com; 1700 Mt Seymour Rd, North Vancouver; adult/youth/child $51/44/24; ⌚9:30am-10pm Mon-Fri, 8:30am-10pm Sat & Sun Dec-Apr) A year-round outdoor hangout for Vancouverites, this branch of the region's winter playgrounds offers ski and snowboarding areas, plus toboggan and tubing courses. The snowshoe trails and tours are also popular – check out the nighttime snowshoeing and chocolate fondue tour ($57). You'll also find excellent mountain-biking trails through forested terrain.

This is usually the least crowded snowy destination in the region, so you're likely to meet locals here. Seymour runs a winter-season shuttle bus from Lonsdale Quay ($6 each way).

ENDLESS BIKING MOUNTAIN BIKING

Map p284 (www.endlessbiking.com; 1401 Hunter St, North Vancouver; ⏲10am-6pm Mon-Fri, 9am-5pm Sat, 10am-4pm Sun) The first stop for anyone looking to access the local bike scene. The friendly folks here can take you on a guided tour or just rent you a bike and point you in the right direction. Lessons are also available if you're a newbie and you want to learn how to negotiate those gnarly tree roots without wiping out.

Beginners should consider the scenic tour (from $129), which includes bike, helmet and a trundle into the wilderness for mountain-and-waterfront views.

DEEP COVE CANOE & KAYAK CENTRE KAYAKING

Map p284 (☎604-929-2268; www.deepcovekayak.com; 2156 Banbury Rd, North Vancouver; kayak rental per 2hr/day $39/84; ⏲9am-dusk May-Aug, reduced off-season; 🚌212) Enjoying Deep Cove's sheltered waters, this is an ideal – and idyllic – spot for first-timers to try their hand at paddling. Lessons and tours are available (the Full Moon Evening Explorer is recommended), and stand-up paddleboarding (SUP) has also been added to the mix – try it out with a two-hour introductory class ($60).

For those with a little more experience, the center also sponsors Tuesday evening race nights (www.tuesdaynightracing.com), where fun contests for all abilities are staged. These evenings are a great way to hang out with North Shore boaty types.

EDGE CLIMBING CENTRE ROCK CLIMBING

Map p284 (www.edgeclimbing.com; Suite 2, 1485 Welch St, North Vancouver; ⏲1-11pm Mon-Fri, noon-9pm Sat & Sun; 🚌240) This high-tech North Van facility has a large climbing gym with more than 15,000 sq ft of climbing surfaces for those who like hanging around for fun. There are plenty of courses, from introductory level to advanced classes where you can learn all about diagonalling and heel-and-toe hooking. If you enjoy this, you can drive straight from here to the Stawamus Chief in Squamish. A giant granite rock face looming over the town and studded with climbers in summer, it's an hour's drive north via Hwy 99.

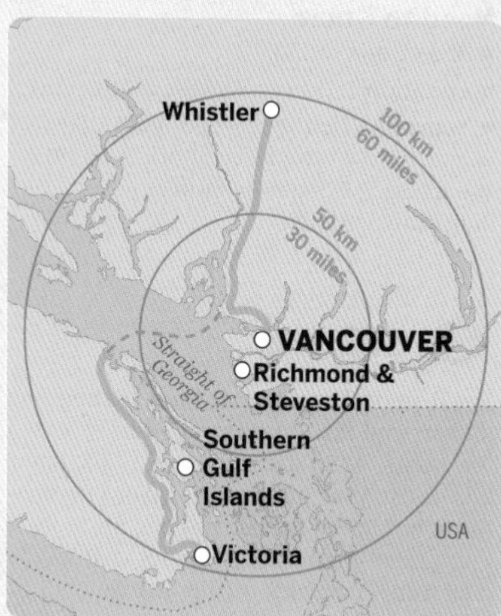

Day Trips from Vancouver

Victoria p188

A fast floatplane hop or languid ferry trip away, British Columbia's historic waterfront capital combines colonial charm, a brilliant museum and a pub-tastic craft-beer scene.

Whistler p194

In the shadow of the mountains, this idyllic gable-roofed ski resort also becomes Canada's favorite outdoor activity destination in summer.

Richmond & Steveston p200

Richmond's modern-day Chinatown is home to North America's best Asian shopping and dining scenes, from authentic stores and restaurants to cool summertime night markets. Steveston is a historic waterfront fishing village with great museums.

Southern Gulf Islands p204

A scenic floatplane trip (or leisurely ferry voyage, if time allows) from Vancouver, Salt Spring is the main escape here, while the other islands – each with their own distinctive feel – are not far away.

Victoria

Explore

Centered on the twin Inner Harbour landmarks of the Parliament Buildings and the Empress Hotel, downtown Victoria is compact and strollable. Stretching north from here, Government St is the main shopping promenade (especially for souvenirs) and leads to historic Bastion Sq, which is colonized by restaurants and a summer market. At downtown's northern edge, Victoria's small Chinatown is the oldest in Canada. Nearby is Market Sq, adjoined by the funky Lower Johnson (LoJo) shopping area. A few minutes southeast of the Inner Harbour lies Beacon Hill Park, Victoria's clifftop waterfront gem. In summer, you can expect the city's streets to be awash with visitors: hop a miniferry around the harbor or rent a bike (Victoria has more cycle routes than any other Canadian city) to escape the crowds.

The Best...

- **Sight** Royal BC Museum (p188)
- **Place to Eat** Red Fish Blue Fish (p192)
- **Place to Drink** Spinnakers Gastro Brewpub (p193)

Top Tip

For a meal with a difference, show your ID at security and nip into the old-school, white-tableclothed politicians' dining room in the Parliament Buildings; it's open to everyone.

Getting There & Away

- **Air** The scenic downtown-to-downtown floatplane services operated from Vancouver by Harbour Air Seaplanes (www.harbour-air.com) take around 30 minutes.
- **Bus** Downtown-to-downtown Pacific Coach Lines (www.pacificcoach.com) services arrive, via ferry, several times daily. Hop transit bus 70 to downtown Victoria from the island's Swartz Bay ferry terminal.
- **Car** Drive to the mainland Tsawwassen BC Ferries terminal, board the Victoria-bound ferry, then hit the island's Hwy 17 into Victoria (32km).

Need to Know

- **Area Code** ☎250
- **Location** 112km southwest of Vancouver
- **Tourist Office** ☎800-663-3883, 250-953-2033; www.tourismvictoria.com; 812 Wharf St; ⊙8:30am-8:30pm Jun-Aug, 9am-5pm Sep-May

SIGHTS

You'll find plenty to keep you occupied in and around the Inner Harbour for at least a few hours. But if it's time to move on, hop a bus or use your hire car to explore further-flung hot spots, or just wander up to little Chinatown for a camera-loving visit. If you have time, consider hitting a bike trail or taking a whale-watching tour.

ROYAL BC MUSEUM — MUSEUM

(www.royalbcmuseum.bc.ca; 675 Belleville St; adult/child from $16/10; ⊙10am-5pm Sun-Wed, to 10pm Thu-Sat, reduced hours off-season) At the province's best museum, start at the 2nd-floor natural-history gallery with its beady-eyed woolly mammoth and realistic dioramas (the shady forest of elk and grizzlies peeking from behind trees is highly evocative). Then peruse the First Peoples culture showcase, which includes a fascinating mask gallery. Don't miss the walk-through colonial street, complete with detailed storefronts and a chatty Chinatown.

The museum also has an IMAX theater and, especially in summer, there's usually a blockbuster visiting exhibition to add to the city's appeal.

PARLIAMENT BUILDINGS — HISTORICAL BUILDING

(www.leg.bc.ca; 501 Belleville St; ⊙tours 9am-5pm daily mid-May–Aug, to 5pm Mon-Fri Sep–mid-May) FREE Across from the Royal BC Museum, this handsome confection of turrets, domes and stained glass is the province's working legislature, but it's also open to history-loving visitors. Peek behind the facade on a colorful 30-minute tour led by costumed Victorians, then stop for lunch at the 'secret' politicians' restaurant (photo ID required). Check out the building's attractive nighttime exterior; it's lit like a Christmas tree. This is one of Victoria's most-photographed landmarks, so keep your camera handy.

WORTH A DETOUR

TOFINO

Lovely Tofino, hugging itself against the crashing surf on the west coast of Vancouver Island, has boomed in recent years to become the de facto capital of the rainforested **Pacific Rim National Park**. It's a great place to head if you're planning to extend your Vancouver Island stay beyond Victoria, and the drive there will take you through the heart of the region.

You'll find plenty of seaside hotels and resorts and a smattering of good seafood restaurants in and around the town, but really it's all about the outdoors. The area's tumultuous waves attract surfers and storm watchers in equal measure, while **Clayoquot Sound** is famed for its idyllic kayaking. There are also plenty of hiking trails and wilderness treks, and popular whale-watching excursions on offer.

Drive here via Hwy 1 and Hwy 4 from Victoria (314km). The way becomes increasingly windy as you thread through the mountains before reaching the country's real West Coast. From here, you could swim all the way to Japan if you desired – but that might be extending your vacation a little too far.

CRAIGDARROCH CASTLE MUSEUM

(www.thecastle.ca; 1050 Joan Cres; adult/youth/child $13.75/8.75/5; ⌚9am-7pm mid-Jun–Aug, 10am-4:30pm Sep–mid-Jun) A grand Victorian folly, this elegant turreted mansion a short bus hop from downtown is not to be missed. The handsome 39-room landmark was built by a 19th-century coal baron who had money to burn; unfortunately he died before it was completed. It's dripping with period features and antique-packed rooms. Climb the tower's 87 steps (perusing the stained-glass windows en route) for snow-capped mountain views.

If you're here in December, you'll find many of the rooms beautifully decorated for Christmas.

ART GALLERY OF GREATER VICTORIA GALLERY

(www.aggv.bc.ca; 1040 Moss St; adult/child $13/2.50; ⌚10am-5pm Mon-Wed, Fri & Sat, to 9pm Thu, noon-5pm Sun, closed Mon off-season) Hop a bus downtown via Fort St and follow the gallery signs to find one of Canada's best collections of works by Emily Carr, one of the leading historic art figures in British Columbia (BC). Aside from Carr's swirling nature canvases, you'll find an ever-changing array of temporary exhibitions. Check online for a lively roster of events, including tours, lectures, presentations and film screenings.

The gallery is close to Craigdarroch Castle, handy if you want to combine your visits. And if you're on a budget, entry on the first Tuesday of the month is by donation.

ROBERT BATEMAN CENTRE GALLERY

(www.batemancentre.org; Steamship Terminal Bldg, 470 Belleville St; adult/child $12.50/6; ⌚10am-6pm Sun-Wed, to 9pm Thu-Sat Jun-Sep, reduced hours off-season) Worried locals wondered what would become of the grand Inner Harbour building that had housed a creaky old waxworks museum for many years. But most were delighted when a new art center celebrating the work of arguably Canada's foremost nature painter moved in. Expect plenty of beady-eyed artworks on display, plus the chance to buy your own on the way out.

Check the events calender online before you visit: if you're really lucky, Bateman himself will be here to give a talk.

BEACON HILL PARK PARK

Fringed by crashing ocean, this dramatic park is perfect for weathering a wild storm – check out those windswept trees along the cliff top. You'll also find one of the world's tallest totem poles, a Victorian cricket pitch and a marker for Mile 0 of Hwy 1, alongside a statue of Terry Fox, the one-legged runner whose cross-Canada trek gripped the nation (p102).

If you're here with kids, head for the children's farm to hang out with its baby pigs and wandering peacocks. There are also goat races twice daily.

BUTCHART GARDENS GARDENS

(www.butchartgardens.com; 800 Benvenuto Ave; adult/youth/child $30/15/10.30, reduced prices off-season; ⌚9am-10pm mid-Jun–Aug, reduced

Victoria

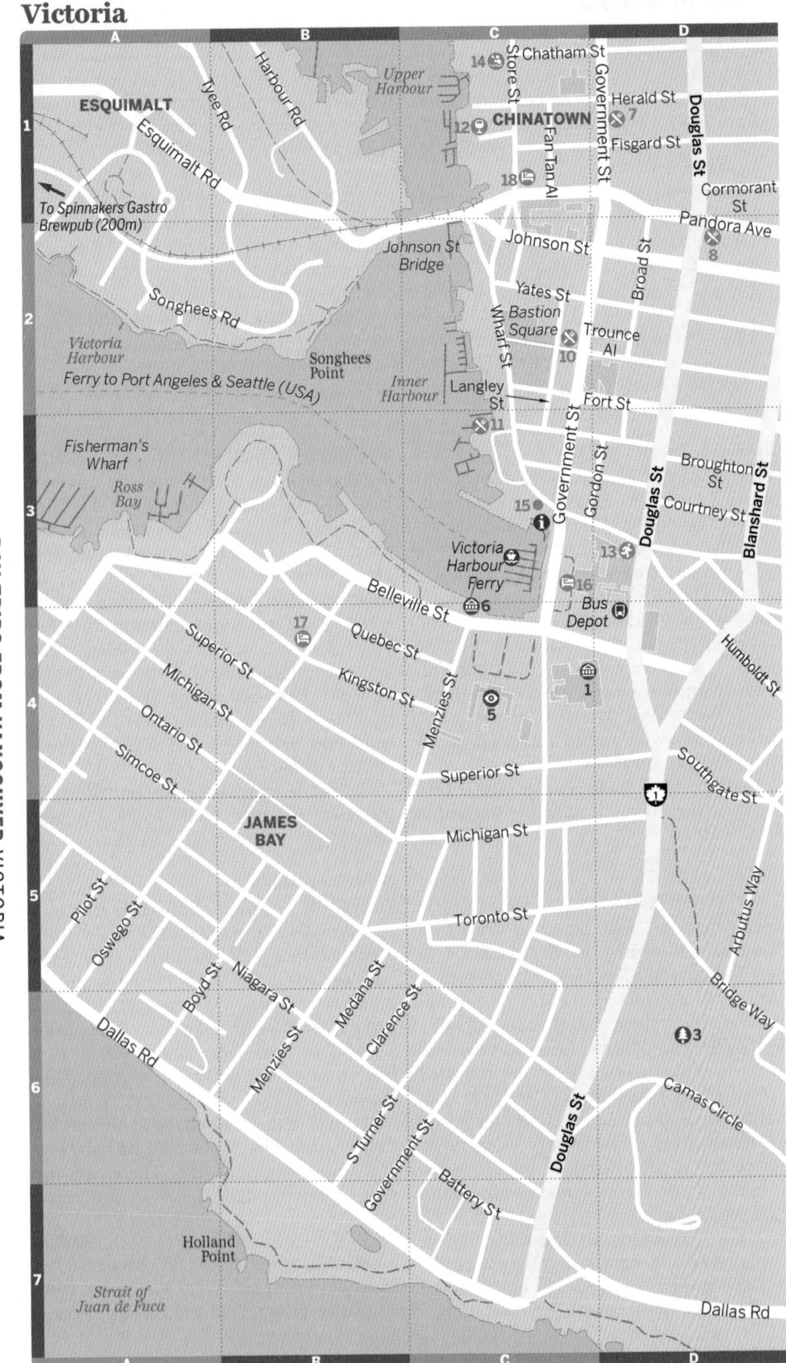

A
B
C
D
1
2
3
4
5
6
7
ESQUIMALT
Esquimalt Rd
Tyee Rd
Harbour Rd
Upper Harbour
Store St
Chatham St
14
Government St
Herald St
Douglas St
CHINATOWN
7
12
Fan Tan Al
Fisgard St
18
Cormorant St
To Spinnakers Gastro Brewpub (200m)
Pandora Ave
8
Johnson St Bridge
Johnson St
Broad St
Songhees Rd
Yates St
Bastion Square
Wharf St
Trounce Al
10
Victoria Harbour
Songhees Point
Ferry to Port Angeles & Seattle (USA)
Inner Harbour
Langley St
Fort St
11
Fisherman's Wharf
Ross Bay
Gordon St
Broughton St
Blanshard St
Courtney St
15
Victoria Harbour Ferry
13
16
Belleville St
6
Bus Depot
17
Superior St
Quebec St
Humboldt St
Michigan St
Kingston St
Menzies St
1
5
Ontario St
Simcoe St
Superior St
Southgate St
JAMES BAY
Michigan St
Pilot St
Oswego St
Toronto St
Arbutus Way
Niagara St
Boyd St
Medana St
Clarence St
Bridge Way
Dallas Rd
Menzies St
3
Camas Circle
S Turner St
Government St
Battery St
Holland Point
Strait of Juan de Fuca
Dallas Rd

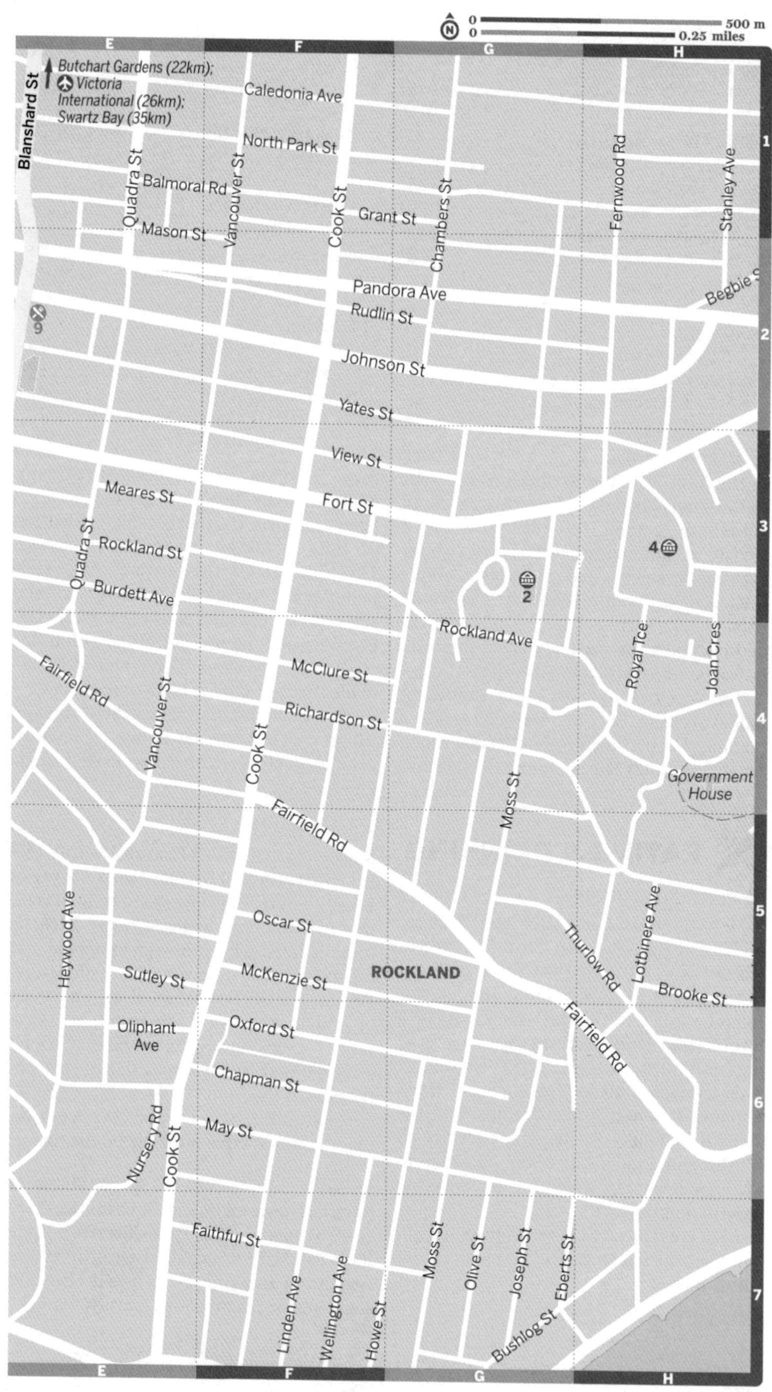

500 m
0.25 miles
Butchart Gardens (22km); Victoria International (26km); Swartz Bay (35km)
Blanshard St
Quadra St
Vancouver St
Cook St
Chambers St
Fernwood Rd
Stanley Ave
Caledonia Ave
North Park St
Balmoral Rd
Mason St
Grant St
Pandora Ave
Begbie St
Rudlin St
Johnson St
Yates St
View St
Fort St
Meares St
Rockland St
Burdett Ave
Rockland Ave
Royal Tce
Joan Cres
McClure St
Richardson St
Fairfield Rd
Government House
Moss St
Oscar St
Thurlow Rd
Lotbinere Ave
Brooke St
Heywood Ave
Sutley St
McKenzie St
ROCKLAND
Oliphant Ave
Oxford St
Chapman St
May St
Nursery Rd
Faithful St
Linden Ave
Wellington Ave
Howe St
Olive St
Joseph St
Eberts St
Bushlog St

Victoria

Top Sights
1 Royal BC Museum C4

Sights
2 Art Gallery of Greater Victoria G3
3 Beacon Hill Park D6
4 Craigdarroch Castle H3
5 Parliament Buildings C4
6 Robert Bateman Centre C4

Eating
7 Brasserie L'Ecole D1
8 John's Place D2
9 Pig BBQ Joint E2
10 ReBar C2
11 Red Fish Blue Fish C3

Drinking & Nightlife
12 Canoe Brewpub C1

Sports & Activities
13 Cycle BC Rentals D3
14 Ocean River Adventures C1
15 Prince of Whales C3

Sleeping
16 Fairmont Empress Hotel C3
17 Oswego Hotel B4
18 Swans Suite Hotel C1

hours off-season; 75) If you're driving back to the ferry en route to Vancouver, detour to this hugely popular, perfectly manicured garden attraction. It's especially worth a visit in summer when it hosts regular evening concerts and fireworks events (included with admission). A year-round kaleidoscope of colors, the grounds are divided into separate garden areas – the tranquil Japanese Garden is a favorite.

A great spot to spend a balmy Vancouver Island evening, Butchart Gardens is also a popular destination for a spot of afternoon tea in its chintzy Dining Room Restaurant.

EATING & DRINKING

★RED FISH BLUE FISH SEAFOOD $

(www.redfish-bluefish.com; 1006 Wharf St; mains $6-20; 11:30am-7pm Mon-Thu, to 8pm Fri-Sun, reduced hours off-season) On the waterfront boardwalk at the foot of Broughton St, this freight-container takeout shack serves a loyal clientele who just can't get enough of its fresh, sustainable seafood. Highlights such as scallop tacone (cone-shaped taco), tempura battered fish and chips, and the signature chunky Pacific Rim chowder all hit the spot. Find a waterfront perch to enjoy your nosh, but watch out for hovering seagull mobsters.

It's a good idea to arrive off-peak here in summer: the lineup can be very long on hot sunny days.

PIG BBQ JOINT BARBECUE $

(www.pigbbqjoint.com; 1325 Blanshard St; mains $7.50-15; 11am-10pm) A larger new location hasn't dimmed the meat-loving credentials of this good-value vegetarian-free zone. The signature is the bulging, Texas-style pulled-pork sandwiches (beef brisket and smoked-chicken variations are also offered). Consider perking up your order with a side of succulent cornbread or a pail of house-made iced tea. Expect lunchtime queues.

This is the kind of place where you can fill up for an entire day at one meal. Wash your grub down with some locally made Phillips beer.

JOHN'S PLACE DINER $$

(www.johnsplace.ca; 723 Pandora Ave; mains $7-16; 7am-9pm Mon-Fri, 8am-4pm & 5-9pm Sat & Sun) Victoria's best weekend brunch spot, this wood-floored, high-ceilinged heritage room is lined with funky memorabilia and the menu is a cut above standard diner fare. For dinner, you'll get started with a basket of addictive house-made bread, but save room for heaping pasta or pierogy. Don't leave without trying a thick slab of pie from the case at the front.

Good value and friendly service have made John's Place a local legend for years.

REBAR WEST COAST $$

(www.rebarmodernfood.com; 50 Bastian Sq; mains $8-16; 11am-9pm Mon-Thu, to 10pm Fri, 8:30am-10pm Sat, to 8pm Sun;) There's a strong vegetarian focus here, but you'll also find some options for visiting carnivores. The funky laid-back interior has a diner-esque feel, and if you snag a sun-dappled table you'll likely bask in the cozy ambience way longer than you intended. Also a good spot to drop into for a midafternoon pie and java break if you're exploring downtown on foot.

ReBar has also produced its own cookbook so, if you like what you eat, you can pretend you're still here when you get back home (especially if you've also mastered that subtle Canadian accent).

BRASSERIE L'ECOLE FRENCH **$$$**

(☎250-475-6260; www.lecole.ca; 1715 Government St; mains $18-26; ⏲5:30pm-11pm Tue-Sat) This country-style French bistro has a warm, casual atmosphere and a delectable menu. Locally sourced produce is de rigueur, so the dishes constantly change to reflect seasonal highlights such as figs, salmonberries and heirloom tomatoes. We recommend the beef paleron in a bacon and mushroom sauce. There's also an excellent French-focused wine menu, plus some tasty (mostly Belgian) beers.

★**SPINNAKERS GASTRO BREWPUB** PUB

(www.spinnakers.com; 308 Catherine St; ⏲11am-10:30pm) This wood-floored brewpub is a short miniferry hop from the Inner Harbour but it's worth it for the copper-colored Nut Brown Ale and the smashing Hoptoria American-style IPA. Save room to eat: the gourmet-yet-comfort grub menu includes hearty pizzas and locally made sausages, and an ale-braised beef dish that'll fill you up for the week.

Beer fans should ask about the daily special cask – a different one is tapped every night.

CANOE BREWPUB PUB

(www.canoebrewpub.com; 450 Swift St; ⏲11:30am-11pm Sun-Wed, to midnight Thu, to 1pm Fri & Sat) A pioneer of the Victoria brewpub scene, this cavernous brick-lined bar is popular on rainy days but it also has the best patio in the city, with handsome views over the waterfront. Indulge in treats that are brewed on-site: the tasting sample is recommended, but make sure it includes crisp Red Canoe Lager and the lovely, copper-colored Siren's Song Pale Ale.

Food is hearty pub grub here, so you'll find plenty of ways to soak up all the booze. Be sure to ask about the seasonal beers.

SPORTS & ACTIVITIES

PRINCE OF WHALES BOAT TOUR

(☎888-383-4884, 250-383-4884; www.princeofwhales.com; 812 Wharf St; adult/child from $110/85) This long-established downtown Victoria operator specializes in whale-watching tours. You'll be whisked out on the comfortable cruiser or alternatively the more spray-in-your-face zodiacs for possible viewing of migrating orcas. If the aquatic faves are nowhere to be seen on your trip, the team will almost always be able to find some lolling seals (and maybe a sea otter or two) for you to gawp at.

OCEAN RIVER ADVENTURES KAYAKING

(☎800-909-4233, 250-381-4233; www.oceanriver.com; 1824 Store St; rental per 2hr $40, tours from $75; ⏲9:30am-6pm Mon-Wed & Sat, to 8pm Thu & Fri, 10am-5pm Sun) One of the best ways to see Victoria's antique skyline is from the glassy-calm water. You can do it yourself with a kayak rental via these friendly folks, but an even better option is to go on a guided tour (May to September). The Urban Kayak Tour introduces the busy harbor's balance of history, development and wildlife, but the twice-weekly sunset tours are especially recommended.

VICTORIA'S BEST FESTS

Time your visit well and you can hang with the locals at one of these popular Victoria festivals:

Victoria Day Parade Marking Queen Victoria's birthday on the Monday before 25 May, this colorful street fiesta shimmies with dancers, musical floats and a full complement of marching bands.

Victoria International JazzFest (www.jazzvictoria.ca) The city's biggest music festival takes place in late June over 10 days. Jazz performances pop up in venues in and around the city, including some free alfresco shows.

Victoria Fringe Theater Festival (www.victoriafringe.com) Hundreds of quirky short plays, reviews and wacky stand-up acts are staged at venues throughout the city over 11 days in late August.

You'll have a great time catching the city and shoreline illuminated under a gently fading golden light and you'll likely catch a surprising amount of birdlife looking for supper before turning in for the night.

CYCLE BC RENTALS CYCLING
(☎866-380-2453, 250-380-2453; www.cyclebc.ca; 685 Humboldt St; ⏰9am-5pm; 🚌1) Victoria is one of Canada's most cycle-friendly cities, so it's a great place to explore on two wheels. Since you probably didn't bring your own, the folks at Cycle BC can you rent a bike and also point out some attractive area routes. You don't have to let your legs do all the work, either: electric bikes, scooters and motorcycle rentals are also available.

Bike rentals include helmets (which are mandatory in BC).

SLEEPING

Prices indicated are for the May to September peak season (sans taxes), when it is difficult to find anything central for less than $100 a night; rooms are reduced by up to 50% off-peak, when the weather is often pleasantly mild. Tourism Victoria's **room reservation service** (☎800-663-3883, 250-953-2033; www.tourismvictoria.com/hotels) books B&Bs, hotels and everything else.

SWANS SUITE HOTEL HOTEL $$
(☎800-668-7926, 250-361-3310; www.swanshotel.com; 506 Pandora Ave; d incl breakfast $185;) This former brick warehouse has been transformed into art-lined boutique accommodation. Most rooms are spacious loft suites where you climb upstairs to sleep in a gabled nook, and each is decorated with a comfy combination of wood beams, rustic yet chic furniture and deep leather sofas. The full kitchens are handy. There's also a brewpub downstairs.

OSWEGO HOTEL HOTEL $$
(☎250-294-7500, 877-767-9346; www.oswegovictoria.com; 500 Oswego St; d $205;) Well hidden on a residential side street but only a short stroll from the Inner Harbour, this contemporary boutique sleepover is an in-the-know favorite. Rooms come with granite floors, cedar beams and (in most units) small balconies. All have kitchens (think stainless steel) and deep baths, making them more like apartments than hotel rooms. Cleverly, the smaller studio rooms have space-saving high-end Murphy (pull down) beds.

FAIRMONT EMPRESS HOTEL HOTEL $$$
(☎866-540-4429, 250-384-8111; www.fairmont.com/empress; 721 Government St; d $250;) Rooms at this ivy-covered, century-old Inner Harbour landmark are elegant but conservative, and some are quite small, yet the overall effect is grand and classy – from the Raj-style curry and cocktail restaurant to the sumptuous high tea sipped while overlooking the waterfront. Even if you don't stay, make sure you stroll through and soak up the old-world charm.

Whistler

Explore

Nestled in the shade of the formidable Whistler and Blackcomb Mountains, wintertime Whistler has a frosted, Christmas-card appeal, perfect for skiing. Summer draws even greater numbers though, with Vancouverites and international travelers lured to the lakes and crags by a wide array of activities, from mountain biking to hair-raising zipline runs. Whistler centers on four main neighborhoods. Approaching via Hwy 99 from the south, you'll hit Creekside first. Whistler Village is the key hub for shops, restaurants and activity operators. You'll find quieter walks around and beyond the Village North area, while the Upper Village is home to swanky hotels and a summertime farmers market. Don't be surprised if you get lost when wandering around the labyrinthine village, but there are always lots of people around to help with directions.

The Best...

- **Sight** Peak 2 Peak Gondola
- **Place to Eat** Rimrock Café
- **Place to Drink** Longhorn Saloon (p196)

Top Tip

Skiers can bypass the crowded slopes with Fresh Tracks tickets, available in advance at Whistler Village Gondola Guest Relations. Be at the gondola by 7:30am the next day.

Getting There & Away

* **Bus** Services from Vancouver take 2½ hours. Catch Greyhound (www.greyhound.ca, from $15) or the Whistler Express, operated by Pacific Coach Lines (www.pacificcoach.com, from $49).
* **Car** Take W Georgia St through Stanley Park and over the Lions Gate Bridge then follow the signs to Hwy 99 north, which takes you straight to Whistler.
* **Train** Trundle in from North Vancouver over three hours on the Rocky Mountaineer Whistler Sea to Sky Climb (www.rockymountaineer.com; tickets from $129; May to mid-Oct).

Need to Know

* **Area Code** 250
* **Location** 122km north of Vancouver
* **Tourist Office** 604-935-3357, 800-944-7853; www.whistler.com; 4230 Gateway Dr; 8am-8pm

SIGHTS

PEAK 2 PEAK GONDOLA GONDOLA
(4545 Blackcomb Way; adult/youth/child $49/42/25; 10am-4:45pm) Linking the Whistler-Blackcomb sister mountains for the first time when it opened in 2009, the resort's mammoth 4.4km Peak 2 Peak Gondola takes 11 breathtaking minutes to shuttle wide-eyed powder hogs between the two high alpine areas, so you can hit the slopes on both mountains in the same day. In summer, it's one of the region's most popular sightseeing attractions.

SQUAMISH LIL'WAT CULTURAL CENTRE MUSEUM
(www.slcc.ca; 4584 Blackcomb Way; adult/child $18/8; 9:30am-5pm, closed Mon off-season) This handsome wood-beamed facility showcases two quite different First Nations groups – one coastal and one interior. Take a tour for the vital context behind the exhibits, which include four newly carved totem poles and a new upstairs gallery that features a 1200-year-old ceremonial bowl. Ask about the summer barbecue dinners ($58) or nip into the downstairs cafe for delicious venison chili with traditional bannock.

EATING & DRINKING

GONE VILLAGE EATERY CAFE $
(www.gonevillageeatery.com; 4205 Village Sq; mains $6-12; 6:30am-9pm; @) Hidden behind Armchair Books, this chatty, wood-floored haunt is a local fave. It serves up hearty breakfast grub (try the omelet burrito), lunch specials (sandwiches, falafel or the $10 burger-and-beer deal should do the trick) and baked treats (snag a chewy toffee cookie). A good spot to fire up your laptop and update your travel blog.

★**RIMROCK CAFÉ** WEST COAST $$
(604-932-5565; www.rimrockwhistler.com; 2117 Whistler Rd; mains $16-28; 5:45pm-9:30pm) On the edge of Creekside, accessible just off Hwy 99, this locals' favorite includes highlights such as seared scallops, venison tenderloin and a recommended Seafood Trio of grilled prawns, ahi (yellowfin) tuna and nut-crusted sablefish. All are served in an intimate room with two fireplaces and on a large, flower-lined patio, where you can watch the harried highway drivers zipping past.

Fancy restaurants have come and gone in Whistler over the years, but the Rimrock continues to deliver, which is why you'll see more Whistlerites enjoying a fine-dining night out here than anywhere else.

CREPE MONTAGNE FRENCH $$
(www.crepemontagne.com; 4368 Main St; mains $8-24; 8am-10:30pm) This small, authentic creperie – hence the French accents percolating among the staff – offers an incredible array of sweet and savory buckwheat crepes with fillings including ham, brie, asparagus, banana, strawberries and more. It's a good breakfast spot: go for eggs Benedict or waffles and you'll be perfectly set up for a day of working it off on the slopes.

It's also a cozy little nook for dinner, when raclette as well as fondues (meat or cheese) are added to the mix. All of which means any benefit you derived from working off your breakfast will soon be forgotten.

SACHI SUSHI JAPANESE $$
(www.sachisushi.com; 106-4359 Main St; mains $8-22; 5:30pm-10pm) Popular with Vancouverites missing their daily raw fish fix, this ever-busy sushi spot doesn't stop at California rolls but serves everything from crispy popcorn shrimp to seafood salads and stomach-warming udon noodles (the

Whistler

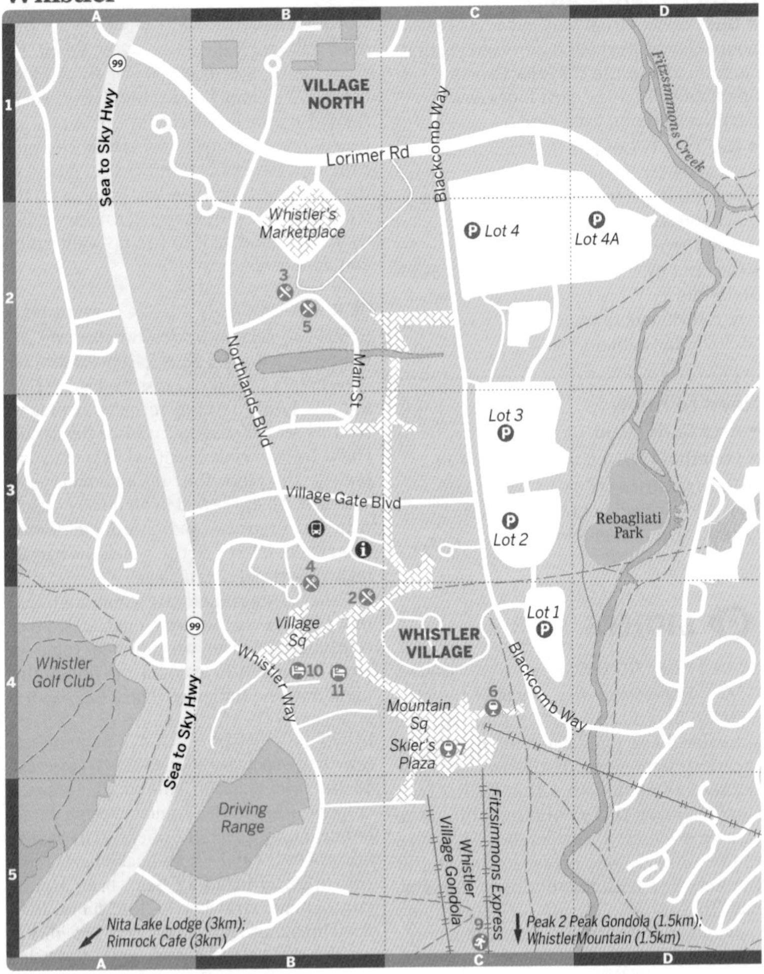

tempura noodle bowl is best). Expect attentive service. Consider a glass of hot sake on a cold winter's day.

Arrive early: Sachi Sushi doesn't take reservations and the lineups you'll encounter at peak times can be lengthy.

ARAXI RESTAURANT & BAR WEST COAST **$$$**
(☎604-932-4540; www.araxi.com; 4222 Village Sq; mains $24-41; ⏲5-11pm daily, brunch 10am-2pm Sat & Sun) If you're in the village center and it's time for a splurge, get your smart togs on and head over to Araxi. An inventive and exquisite menu is served up with charming and courteous service. Try dishes such as perfectly prepared Haida Gwaii halibut and east coast lobster. Then make a bold attempt to drain the 15,000-bottle wine selection. Save room for a selection of piquant regional cheeses.

Araxi is at the top end of pricing in Whistler, so you might also consider the weekend brunch, which offers a taste of the high life for less than $20 a dish.

LONGHORN SALOON & GRILL PUB
(www.longhornsaloon.ca; 4284 Mountain Sq; ⏲9am-1am) Drinking here is all about the

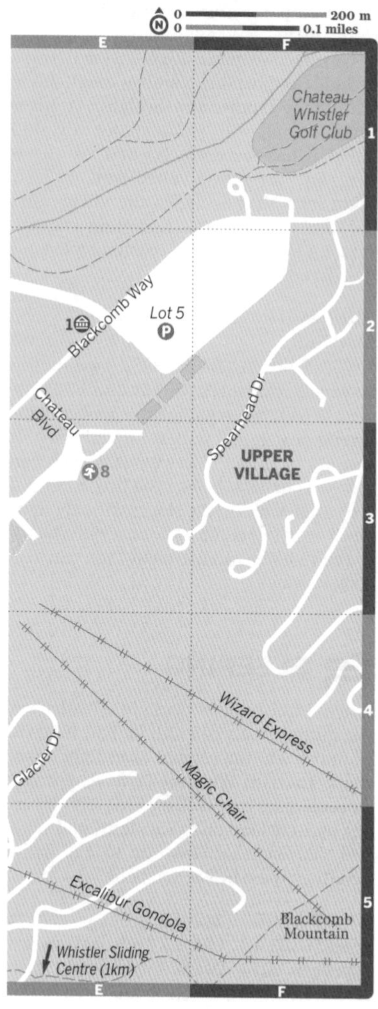

Whistler

Sights

1 Squamish Lil'wat Cultural Centre........E2

Eating

2 Araxi Restaurant & Bar........B4
3 Crepe Montagne........B2
4 Gone Village Eatery........B3
5 Sachi Sushi........B2

Drinking & Nightlife

6 Black's Restaurant & Pub........C4
7 Longhorn Saloon & Grill........C4

Sports & Activities

8 Mountain Adventure Centres........E3
9 Whistler Mountain Bike Park........C5

Sleeping

10 Adara Hotel........B4
11 Crystal Lodge & Suites........B4

scene: spread out on the sprawling patio at the base of Whistler Mountain and you'll be in the heart of the ski action. The pub food is nothing special (eat before you arrive) but it's hard to beat the atmosphere on a hopping winter evening as the jugs of fizzy booze come out and the electric party vibe kicks off.

It's all about the patio here at Longhorn; drinking outside in winter has rarely been more fun.

BLACK'S RESTAURANT & PUB PUB

(www.blackspub.com; 4270 Mountain Sq; ⏲7am-11pm) This trad retro-pub leans toward pasta and pizza but also has a good draft- and bottled-beer selection. Among its BC drafts, the Russell Cream Ale is recommended. And if you indulge too much, come back for a hearty, hangover-busting breakfast next morning. Black's is located across from the Village Gondola; the heated patio is perfect for sitting and watching skiers slide downhill.

SPORTS & ACTIVITIES

WHISTLER-BLACKCOMB OUTDOORS

(www.whistlerblackcomb.com; 1-day winter lift ticket adult/child $98/52) Comprising almost 82 sq km of skiable terrain and more than 200 runs (over half for intermediate-level skiers), the sister mountains of Whistler and Blackcomb were physically linked in 2009 when the mammoth 4.4km Peak 2 Peak Gondola opened. It takes 11 minutes to shuttle between the two high-alpine areas, so you can hit both mountains in one day.

The resort's winter season usually starts in late November and runs to April on Whistler and May/June on Blackcomb – December to February is the peak. Snowboard fans should also check out the freestyle terrain parks mostly located on Blackcomb, including the Snow Cross and the Big Easy Terrain Garden. In summer, the whole area becomes an outdoor adventure playground with hiking, climbing and biking particularly popular.

WHISTLER SLIDING CENTRE ADVENTURE SPORTS

(www.whistlerslidingcentre.com; 4910 Glacier Lane; ⏲10am-5pm Dec-Mar) Perched just above the village on Blackcomb, Whistler Sliding Centre hosted the 2010 Winter Olympic bobsled, luge and skeleton events and is now open to the public. You can grit your teeth and try them for yourself, full training included (from $159). Or if you're not quite such a daredevil, take a free self-guided Olympic facilities tour.

Fans of the five rings should also ask about the Whistler Olympic Park, which nestles south of town in the Callaghan Valley and can be visited.

WHISTLER MOUNTAIN BIKE PARK MOUNTAIN BIKING

(http://bike.whistlerblackcomb.com; base of Whistler Mountain; 1-day pass adult/child $53/31; ⏲mid-May–mid-Oct) Colonizing the melted ski slopes, this lift-accessed summer park offers an orgy of jumps and beams on 200km of forested trails. You don't have to be a bike courier to stand the pace: easier routes are marked in green, while blue intermediate trails and black diamond advanced paths are for those who want to Crank It Up – a popular route.

Outside the park area, regional trails include Comfortably Numb (a tough 26km with steep climbs and bridges); A River Runs Through It (suitable for all skill levels, it has teeter-totters and log obstacles); and the gentle Valley Trail, an easy 14km loop that encircles the village and its lake, meadow and mountain chateau surroundings – this is recommended for first-timers.

WHISTLER FESTIVALS

Whistler hosts some great annual events worth timing your visit for.

Winterpride (www.gaywhistler.com) A week of gay-friendly snow action and late-night partying in early February, this event has grown exponentially in recent years.

World Ski & Snowboard Festival (www.wssf.com) A nine-day showcase in mid-April of pro ski and snowboard competitions, with a full menu of live music and events.

Crankworx (www.crankworx.com) Mid-August sees an adrenalin-filled celebration of bike stunts, speed and shenanigans; BC's biggest mountain bike fest.

MOUNTAIN ADVENTURE CENTRES OUTDOORS

(☎800-766-0449, 604-967-8950; www.whistlerblackcomb.com/rentals; 4599 Chateau Blvd) The resort's official equipment supplier runs several gear rental outlets around town. It also offers online reservations, so you can choose your look before you arrive. And if you're a newbie on the slopes with about as much experience on skis or a snowboard as you've had as an astronaut, you can also book lessons.

SLEEPING

Winter is the peak for prices in Whistler, but last-minute deals can still be had if you're planning an impromptu overnight visit; check **Tourism Whistler** (www.whistler.com) for room sales and packages. Most hotels extort parking fees (up to $20 daily) and some also slap on resort fees (up to $25 daily) – confirm these before you book.

CRYSTAL LODGE & SUITES HOTEL $$

(☎800-667-3363, 604-932-2221; www.crystal-lodge.com; 4154 Village Green; d/ste from $130/175; ❄ 🏊 🐾) With both chic, loungey rooms and motel-style options, there's something to suit most budgets here. You're also in the heart of the action, less than 100m from the Village Gondola lift.

ADARA HOTEL HOTEL $$

(☎866-502-3272, 604-905-4009; www.adarahotel.com; 4122 Village Green; r from $149; ❄ 📶 🐾) Sophisticated and quirky, this joint offers art-lined interiors and dramatic mod rooms where the fireplaces look like TVs and faux-fur throws abound. Despite the ultracool aesthetics, service is warm and relaxed.

WORTH A DETOUR

SQUAMISH

Midway between Vancouver and Whistler on Hwy 99, Squamish enjoys an incredible natural setting at the fingertips of Howe Sound. Once little more than a rough-and-ready logging town, it's undergone an Olympics-triggered boom and is now a popular base for outdoor activities, especially in summer.

For mountain bikers, the 100 or so forested trails around Squamish are ideal – especially if you've had enough of the crowds at the ever-popular Whistler Mountain Bike Park. Check out the **Cheekeye Fan trail** near Brackendale, or join the downhill thrill seekers in the **Diamond Head/Power Smart** area, where the routes have inviting names like Dope Slope and Icy Hole of Death.

If you're looking for some sights that are a little less strenuous, there are plenty other must-sees in the area.

Just before Squamish on Hwy 99, the **Britannia Mine Museum** (www.britanniaminemuseum.ca; adult/child $21.50/13.50; ⏲9am-5pm) is a popular stop. Once the British Empire's largest copper mine, it's been preserved with an impressive restoration. Its underground train tour into the pitch-black mine tunnels is a highlight and there are plenty of additional kid-friendly exhibits – including gold panning – plus a large artsy gift shop.

Historic-train nuts should continue just past Squamish to the popular **West Coast Railway Heritage Park** (www.wcra.org; 39645 Government Rd; adult/child $15/10; ⏲10am-5pm, reduced hours off-season). This large, mostly alfresco museum is the final resting place of BC's legendary *Royal Hudson* steam engine and has around 90 other historic rail cars, including 10 working engines and the original prototype SkyTrain car. Check out the new Roundhouse building, housing the park's most precious artifacts.

Attracting hardy climbers, the highlight of **Stawamus Chief Provincial Park** (www.bcparks.ca) is 'The Chief'. You don't have to be geared up to experience the summit's breathtaking vistas: there are hiking routes up the back for anyone who wants to have a go. Consider **Squamish Rock Guides** (☎604-892-7816; www.squamishrockguides.com; guided rock climbs half-/full day from $75/115) for climbing assistance or lessons.

If you prefer to travel under your own steam, the **Squamish Spit** is a popular kiteboarding (and windsurfing) hot spot; the kiteboarding season runs from May to October. The **Squamish Windsports Society** (www.squamishwindsports.com) should be your first point of contact for information on weather, water conditions and access to the spit.

For an overnighter, try the quality rustic approach of the comfortable **Howe Sound Inn & Brewing Company** (☎604-892-2603; www.howesound.com; 37801 Cleveland Ave; d from $99;). Rooms are warm and inviting with plenty of woodsy touches. There's an outdoor climbing wall where you can train for your attempt on the nearby Stawamus Chief, and a sauna where you can recover afterwards. The downstairs brewpub is worth a visit even if you're not staying – yam fries and Oatmeal Stout recommended.

NITA LAKE LODGE HOTEL **$$$**
(☎888-755-6482, 604-966-5700; www.nitalakelodge.com; 2135 Lake Placid Rd; d from $199;) Adjoining Creekside train station – handy if you're coming up on the Rocky Mountaineer Whistler Sea to Sky Climb – this swanky timber-framed lodge has lakefront views and pampering rooms with rock fireplaces and small kitchenettes. Creekside lifts are just a few minutes away.

Richmond & Steveston

Explore

The handy Canada Line SkyTrain link has made the region's modern-day Chinatown much easier to reach from downtown Vancouver, which means Vancouverites have been visiting their southern neighbor more often in recent years. Hop aboard and head down the line for a culturally immersive half-day of bustling Asian shopping malls – centered on the Golden Village area – followed by a taste-trip through authentic Chinese, Japanese and Vietnamese restaurants. And don't miss the city's historic waterfront Steveston village. This is a charming, museum-full area that's popular with sunset-viewing locals...especially those with a penchant for great fish and chips.

The Best...

- **Sight** Gulf of Georgia Cannery
- **Place to Eat** Pajo's (p203)
- **Place to Drink** Leisure Tea & Coffee (p203)

Top Tip

Coming from Vancouver on the Canada Line, alight at Aberdeen Station, then explore the streets to the next stop, Lansdowne. This is the heart of the Golden Village.

Getting There & Away

- **Train** Canada Line trains trundle into Richmond from Vancouver every few minutes. It's a two-zone fair from the city and the journey from downtown Vancouver to central Richmond takes 15 to 20 minutes, depending on where you're stopping. Make sure you board a Richmond–Brighouse train in Vancouver or otherwise you'll be heading to the airport; you can change to the correct train anywhere up to Bridgeport Station.
- **Bus** For Steveston, first take the Canada Line train to Bridgeport Station, then transfer to the 401, 402, 407 or 410 bus. Your transit ticket covers you for both parts of this journey.

Need to Know

- **Area Code** 604
- **Location** 16km south of Vancouver
- **Tourist Office** www.tourismrichmond.com; 3811 Moncton St, Steveston; 9:30am-6pm daily Jul-Aug, 9:30am-5pm Mon-Sat & noon-4pm Sun Sep-Jun; 402

SIGHTS

GULF OF GEORGIA CANNERY MUSEUM

(www.gulfofgeorgiacannery.com; 12138 4th Ave, Steveston; adult/child/senior $7.80/3.90/6.55; 10am-5pm Feb-Oct; M Richmond-Brighouse, then 401) After perusing the boats hawking the day's fresh catch, check out this excellent museum that illuminates the sights and sounds (and smells) of a bygone era of labor-intensive fish processing. Most of the machinery remains – polished and cleaned of its film of blood and oil – and there's an evocative focus on the people who worked here before the plant's 1979 closure.

You'll hear recorded testimonies from former workers present in the air like ghosts and see large black-and-white blow-ups of some of the staff who spent their days immersed in entrails in order to roll thousands of cans down the production line. Take one of the free hourly tours, sometimes run by former cannery workers.

SUMMER NIGHT MARKET MARKET

(www.summernightmarket.com; 12631 Vulcan Way, Richmond; 7pm-1am Fri & Sat, to midnight Sun mid-May–early Oct; 407) Much larger than downtown Vancouver's Chinatown version, this market lures thousands of hungry locals on summer weekends. Check out the tacky vendor stands and, more importantly, the dozens of hawker food stalls. Make sure you come hungry so you can taste-trip through steaming Malaysian, Korean, Japanese and Chinese treats. Be sure to compare it with the Richmond Night Market, the region's other summer-season night market.

The adventurous grub to look out for here includes stinky tofu (the blue cheese of the Asian dining world), and dragon's-beard candy – a sweet, whispy treat that's unlike anything else we've tried.

Richmond & Steveston

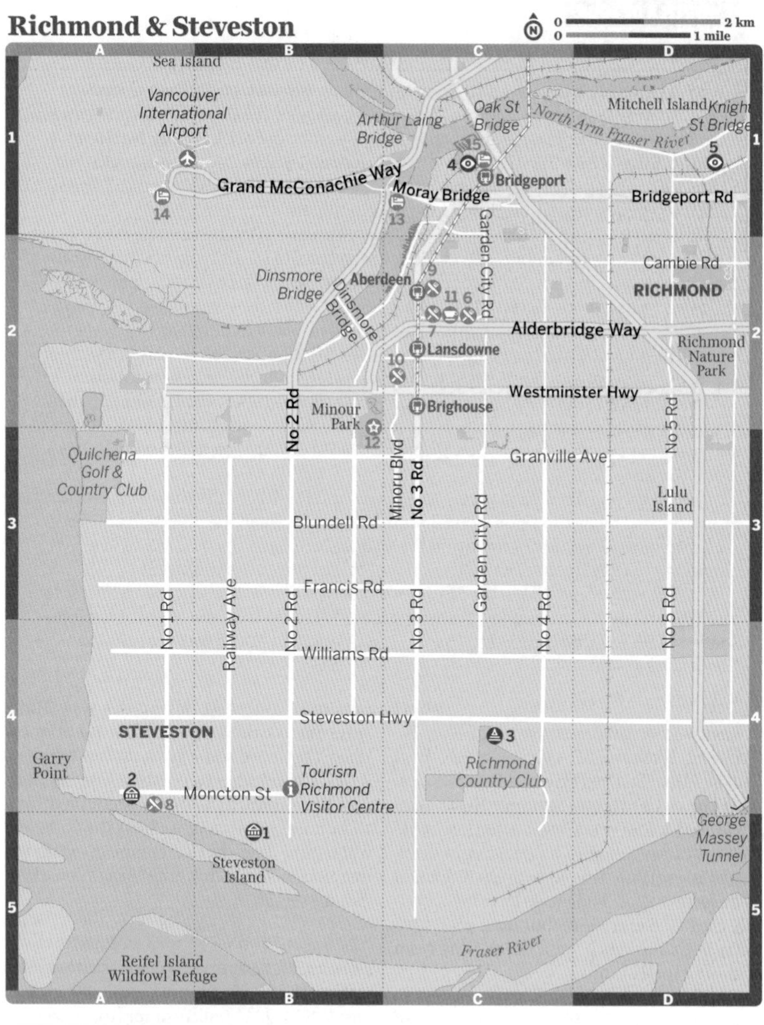

Richmond & Steveston

Sights

1 Britannia Shipyard B5
2 Gulf of Georgia Cannery A4
3 Kuan Yin Temple C4
4 Richmond Night Market C1
5 Summer Night Market D1

Eating

6 Cattle Cafe C2
7 Jang Mo Jib C2
8 Pajo's A4
9 Parker Place C2
10 Shanghai River Restaurant C2

Drinking & Nightlife

11 Leisure Tea & Coffee C2

Entertainment

12 Terminal City Rollergirls B2

Sleeping

13 Delta Vancouver Airport C1
14 Fairmont Vancouver Airport A1
15 River Rock Casino Resort C1

WORTH A DETOUR

FORT LANGLEY

Little Fort Langley's tree-lined streets and 19th-century storefronts make it one of the Lower Mainland's most picturesque historic villages, ideal for an afternoon away from Vancouver. Its main historic highlight is the colorful **Fort Langley National Historic Site** (☎604-513-4777; www.pc.gc.ca/fortlangley; 23433 Mavis Ave; adult/child $7.80/3.90; ⊙10am-4pm mid-Jun–Aug, reduced hours off-season; 🚌501, then C62), perhaps the region's most important old-school landmark.

A fortified trading post since 1827, this is where James Douglas announced the creation of British Columbia (BC) in 1858, giving the site a legitimate claim to being the province's birthplace. With costumed re-enactments, re-created artisan workshops and a gold-panning area that's very popular with kids – who also enjoy charging around the wooden battlements – this is an ideal place for families who want to add a little education to their trip. If you need an introduction before you start exploring, there's a surprisingly entertaining time-travel-themed movie presentation.

Make sure you check the website before you arrive, so you can plan ahead: there are a wide array of events that bring the past evocatively back to life, including a summertime evening campfire program that will take you back to the pioneer days of the 1800s.

If you're driving from Vancouver, take Hwy 1 east for 40km, then take the 232nd St exit north. Follow the signs along 232nd St until you reach the stop sign at Glover Rd. Turn right here, and continue into the village. Turn right again on Mavis Ave, just before the railway tracks. The fort's parking lot is at the end of the street.

If traveling by transit, take the SkyTrain to Surrey Central Station, then transfer to bus 501, 502 or 320 to Langley. Transfer in Langley to the C62 and alight at the intersection of 96 Ave and Glover Rd. The fort is a signposted 400m walk from here.

RICHMOND NIGHT MARKET MARKET

(www.richmondnightmarket.com; 8351 River Rd, Richmond; admission $2; ⊙7pm-midnight Fri & Sat, 6pm-11pm Sun mid-May–mid-Oct; Ⓜ Bridgeport) The city's original Summer Night Market closed a few years back after losing its venue, but reopened in a new spot in 2012. In the meantime, this new market opened in its former spot. The locals have been happily confused ever since, but it's a good idea to try both markets if you love scoffing from steaming food stands.

Of the two markets, this one is easiest to reach on transit. It offers the usual mix of cheap, blingy trinkets, live entertainment and – the main lure – many chances to stuff your face.

BRITANNIA SHIPYARD MUSEUM

(www.britannia-hss.ca; 5180 Westwater Dr, Steveston; ⊙10am-6pm Tue-Sun May-Sep, to 4pm Sat, noon-4pm Sun Oct-Apr; Ⓜ Richmond-Brighouse, then 🚌410) FREE Though not as slick as the Gulf of Georgia Cannery museum, this is a fascinating complex of creaky old sheds that house dusty tools, boats and reminders of the region's maritime past. Check out the preserved Murakami House, where a large Japanese family lived before being unceremoniously interned during the war. Make sure you ask the volunteers plenty of questions: they have some great stories to tell.

It's a good idea to combine the cannery and the shipyard. The two are joined by a 15-minute stroll along Steveston's lovely waterfront boardwalk, complete with art installations evoking the area's bustling fishing sector.

KUAN YIN TEMPLE BUDDHIST TEMPLE

(www.buddhisttemple.ca; 9160 Steveston Hwy, Steveston; ⊙9:30am-5:30pm; Ⓜ Richmond-Brighouse, then 🚌403) FREE Called simply the 'Buddhist Temple' by most, this attractive classical Chinese complex is an intriguing stop. The highlight is the sumptuous Gracious Hall, complete with deep-red exterior walls and a gently flaring orange porcelain roof. Check out the colorful 100m-long Buddha mural and the golden, multiarmed Bodhisattva figure here. The surrounding landscaped garden, with sculptures and bonsai trees, is also not to be missed.

Allow yourself time to enjoy a lip-smacking veggie lunch in the ground-floor cafeteria. You don't have to be Buddhist to visit and the monks are highly welcoming if you just want to have a respectful look around.

EATING & DRINKING

★PAJO'S
SEAFOOD $

(www.pajos.com; The Wharf, Steveston; mains $6-9; 11am-dusk Feb-Nov; Richmond-Brighouse, then 402) After perusing the fresh catches on the nearby fishing boats, follow your nose and descend the ramp to Pajo's little ordering hatch. You'll be greeted by a friendly face and a menu more extensive than your average chippy. Go the traditional fresh-fried cod, salmon or halibut route (with secret-recipe tartar sauce) or mix things up with a yellowfin tuna burger and zucchini sticks.

It's hard to think of a better spot to enjoy fish and chips than the boat-bobbing wharf at Steveston.

CATTLE CAFE
ASIAN $

(www.cattlecafe.ca; 8580 Alexandra Rd, Richmond; mains $6-14; 11am-1am; Lansdowne) Richmond's lip-smacking Asian dining scene is its main lure; if you want to get to heart of the matter, head straight to Alexandra Rd, aka 'Eat Street', where dozens of restaurants await. This Hong Kong–style joint is among the funkiest eateries and great for trying barbecued eel sandwiches, washed down with some delectable bubble tea.

You'll be hanging out with a young crowd here, including many local ESL students missing their comfort grub back home.

PARKER PLACE
FOOD COURT $

(www.parkerplace.com; 4380 No 3 Rd, Richmond; mains $5-10; 11am-7pm Sun-Thu, to 9pm Fri & Sat; Aberdeen) There are several popular Asian shopping malls in Richmond; Aberdeen Centre and Lansdowne Centre are the bigger, but Parker Place has a highly authentic food court that feels like a Singaporean hawker market. It's beloved of Asian-Canadian locals, and you too can dive in for good-value noodle, fish-ball and dragon's-beard-candy dishes: buy a few plates and share 'em at your table.

Once you're full, peruse the labyrinth of surrounding retailers (you'll feel like you're in another country) or nip outside to the food court's adjoining parking lot for a surprise: a shimmering shrine.

JANG MO JIB
ASIAN $$

(www.jangmojib.com; 8230 Alexandra Rd, Richmond; mains $12-24; 10am-1am Mon-Thu, to 2am Fri & Sat; Lansdowne) If you're in the mood for a spot of Korean hotpot and barbecue, this friendly restaurant is for you. Just look for the wacky carved poles outside, then nip into the gable-roofed resto for a host of immersive, mostly meaty dishes. The must-have specialty here? The pork-blood sausage. It divides the table between real and pretend carnivores.

And if you're wondering: Jang Mo Jib translates as 'mother-in-law's house.'

SHANGHAI RIVER RESTAURANT
CHINESE $$

(7381 Westminster Hwy, Richmond; mains $6-18; 11am-2:30pm & 5:30-11pm; Richmond-Brighouse) Grab a seat overlooking the kitchen window at this contemporary northern Chinese eatery and you'll be mesmerized by the intricate handiwork that goes into folding some of the best dim-sum dumplings around. Order plates to share – one dish per person is the usual ratio – and be careful not to squirt everyone with the delicate but juicy pork or shrimp dumplings.

The braised duck and ham soup is a great winter warmer, too. This place fills up at peak times, when it becomes animated with Chinese chatter. Note: the servers are often not fluent in English.

LEISURE TEA & COFFEE
TEAHOUSE

(8391 Alexandra Rd, Richmond; 10am-6pm Mon-Thu, to midnight Fri & Sat, noon-8pm Sun; Lansdowne) This delightfully eclectic tea (including bubble tea) and coffee spot has an Asian-influenced love for European ski-lodge interiors fused with a clientele of young locals missing home (especially late at night). Go for a Taiwan-style shaved ice treat or warm up in winter with a fruit-packed peach warmer tea. This cozy joint is one of Metro Vancouver's most authentic Asian hangouts.

ENTERTAINMENT

TERMINAL CITY ROLLERGIRLS
SPECTATOR SPORT

(www.terminalcityrollergirls.com; Minoru Arena 7551 Minoru Gate, Richmond; adult/child $20/10) Head to Richmond to cheer on the all-female flat-track roller derby teams as they whistle around at breakneck speeds. Teams such as Riot Girls and Bad Reputations are often part of the action here and they've lured a loyal local following in recent years. This is Metro Vancouver's most popular alternative sports league, and possibly the most fun you'll have on your Richmond day out.

WORTH A DETOUR

BURNABY

Immediately east of Vancouver via Hastings St, Burnaby – the birthplace of Michael J Fox, no less – is a no-frills residential suburb with an elongated strip-mall feel. Luckily, there are a handful of attractions to keep you away from the shops. Check in with **Tourism Burnaby** (☎604-419-0377; www.tourismburnaby.com) for tips and information.

Nestled among Burnaby's labyrinth of residential side streets, tranquil **Deer Lake Park** (⊙dawn-dusk) is crisscrossed with verdant meadow and waterfront walks, and also offers boat rentals. Nearby, the popular **Burnaby Village Museum** (www.burnabyvillagemuseum.ca; 6501 Deer Lake Ave; ⊙11am-4:30pm May-Aug) FREE recreates the atmosphere of a British Columbia (BC) pioneer town, with replica homes and businesses of the time and a wonderfully restored 1912 carousel. Entry to the museum is half-price on Tuesdays and it's also open off-season for special Christmas and Halloween displays.

Topping Burnaby Mountain, **Simon Fraser University** (www.sfu.com; 8888 University Dr) is the Lower Mainland's second main campus community. Visitor attractions here include the **Museum of Archaeology & Ethnology** (⊙10am-4pm Mon-Fri) FREE and the **SFU Gallery** (⊙10am-4pm Tue-Fri, noon-5pm Sat) FREE.

Burnaby is a 20-minute SkyTrain hop from downtown Vancouver – alight at Metrotown Station for bus connections throughout Burnaby.

Southern Gulf Islands

Explore

When Canadians refer to BC as 'lotusland,' the Gulf Islands are really what they're thinking about. Languidly strung between the mainland and Vancouver Island, Salt Spring, Galiano, Mayne, Saturna and the North and South Penders are the natural retreat of choice for Vancouverites and in-the-know visitors looking for some extra tranquillity during their stay. Combining a mild climate, gentle natural beauty and an infectious, laid-back ambience, these small communities seem remote but are generally easy to access from the mainland by ferry. The most popular destination for day-trippers is Salt Spring (best accessed by floatplane), while Galiano (best accessed by boat) is also ideal if you crave a quieter, more rustic retreat. Wherever you go, turn off your electronic communications devices and sink into zen-like calm.

The Best...

- **Sight** Saturday Market
- **Place to Eat** Tree House Café
- **Place to Drink** Hummingbird Pub (p206)

Top Tip

Day-trippers can floatplane onto Salt Spring (especially for the Saturday Market). But these islands are best experienced without rushing, so consider a long, languid weekend stay.

Getting There & Away

- **Air** Services from Salt Spring Air (www.saltspringair.com) arrive throughout the Southern Gulf Islands from downtown Vancouver and Vancouver International Airport. Check its website for the myriad schedules.
- **Ferry** Services from BC Ferries (www.bcferries.com) depart from Tsawwassen Ferry Terminal and arrive at Galiano, with connections from there to North Pender. There are also direct weekend services to Mayne (Sunday only) and Salt Spring (Friday to Sunday). For more frequent services to these and other islands, you

will need to travel from Tsawwassen to Vancouver Island's Swartz Bay terminal, then board connecting ferries. Fares from Tsawwassen to the Gulf Islands are $17.85/8.95/57.05 per adult/child/vehicle.

Need to Know

- **Area Code** ☎250
- **Location** Southwest from Vancouver (one to three hours by ferry; 20 minutes by plane)
- **Salt Spring Island Tourist Office** ☎250-537-5252; www.saltspringtourism.com; 121 Lower Ganges Rd; ⊙9am-5pm Jul & Aug, reduced hours off-season
- **Galiano Island Tourist Office** ☎250-539-2507; www.galianoisland.com; 2590 Sturdies Bay Rd; ⊙Jul & Aug

SIGHTS

Salt Spring Island

SATURDAY MARKET MARKET

(www.saltspringmarket.com; Centennial Park; ⊙8am-4pm Sat Apr-Oct) If you arrive on a summer weekend, the best way to dive into the community is at this thriving market where you can tuck into luscious island-grown fruit and piquant cheeses made right on the market's doorstep and then peruse a wide range of locally created arts and crafts: this is a very arty island, so there's often lots of tempting goodies.

You can also visit artisans around the island. Among the best place is the rustic Blue Horse Folk Art Gallery, complete with some funky carvings of horses. The friendly owners also run an on-site B&B, if you're looking for an excuse to stay a little longer.

SALT SPRING ISLAND CHEESE FARM

(www.saltspringcheese.com; 285 Reynolds Rd; ⊙10am-5pm May-Sep, to 4pm Oct-Apr) Among a tasty host of island farm and dairy producers, this lovely spot is a standout. You can take a self-guided tour of the facilities – be sure to check out the miniature ponies – then sample up to 10 curdy treats in the winery-style tasting room. You're almost certain to fall in love with a cheese here: consider a picnic for the road.

Ruckle Provincial Park is a short drive away and perfect for a spot of relaxing alfresco picnic dining.

RUCKLE PROVINCIAL PARK PARK

(www.bcparks.ca) Pack up your picnic and head over to Ruckle Provincial Park, a southeast Salt Spring Island gem that's ever-popular for its ragged shorelines, arbutus forests and sun-kissed farmlands. There are hiking trails here for all skill levels, with Yeo Point making an ideal pit stop: feel free to eat your picnic en route.

The island is crisscrossed with other trails. Consult the locals: they usually have suggestions for favored rambles.

Galiano Island

Once you've got your bearings – ie driven off the ferry – head for Montague Harbour Marine Provincial Park for trails to beaches, meadows and a cliff carved by glaciers. In contrast, Bodega Ridge Provincial Park is renowned for its eagle, loon and cormorant birdlife and has some spectacular drop-off viewpoints. The protected waters of Trincomali Channel and the more chaotic waters of Active Pass satisfy paddlers of all skill levels. **Gulf Island Kayaking** (☎250-539-2442; www.seakayak.ca; 3451 Montague Rd; 2hr/day rental from $32/58, tours from $55) can help with rentals and guided tours.

EATING

★**TREE HOUSE CAFÉ** CAFE $$

(www.treehousecafe.ca; 106 Purvis Lane, Salt Spring Island; mains $10-16) At this magical outdoor cafe in the heart of Ganges you'll be sitting in the shade of a large plum tree as you choose from a menu of comfort pastas, Mexican specialties and gourmet burgers – the Teriyaki salmon burger is recommended, washed down with a hoppy bottle of Salt Spring Pale Ale. There's live music every night in summer; on balmy nights, it feels like everyone on the island is hanging out here.

This is also a good spot for breakfast (the hearty Tree House Breakfast is excellent).

Southern Gulf Islands

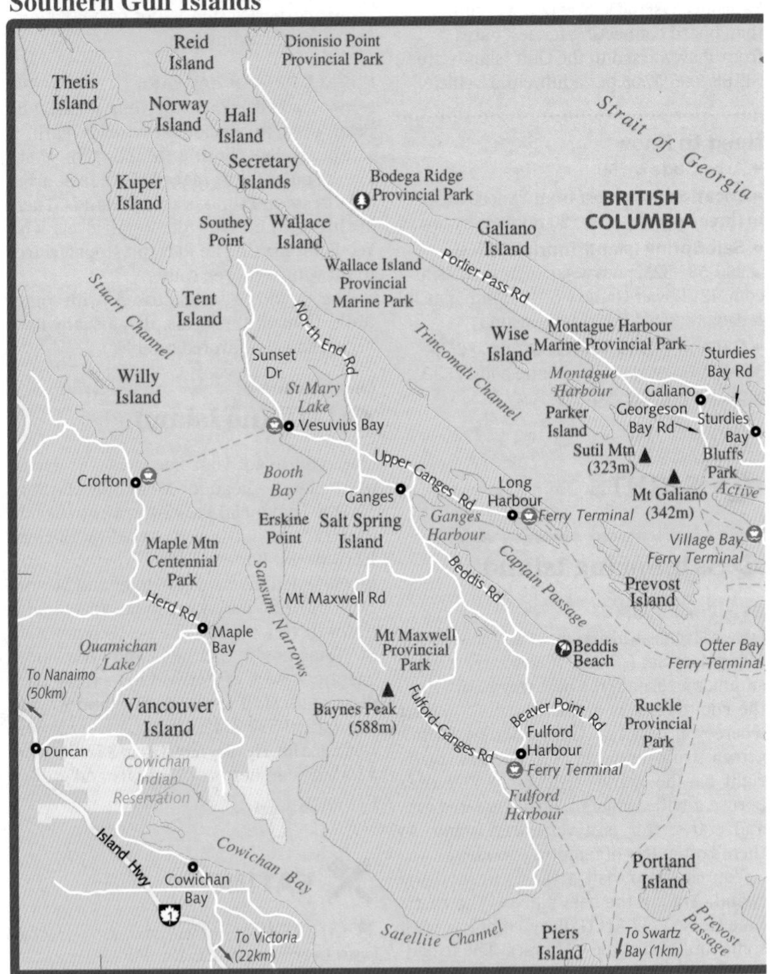

RESTAURANT

HOUSE PICCOLO WEST COAST $$

(www.housepiccolo.com; 108 Hereford Ave, Salt Spring Island; mains $14-24; ⏲5-10pm Wed-Sun) White-tableclothed dining, along with Salt Spring's best wine list, makes this a popular spot among islanders looking for a special night out. Expect lots of local and regional ingredients of the seasonal variety, and there's usually some sumptuous seafood available: go for the perfect crab cakes and some pan-seared local scallops. Then, if you're really feeling greedy, consider the lamb shank.

★**HUMMINGBIRD PUB** PUB

(www.hummingbirdpub.com; 47 Sturdies Bay Rd, Galiano Island; mains $8-12) Sup ale with the locals on the patio here and you'll hear all the latest island gossip. Make sure you save room for a fruity Galiano Island Rum Punch chaser. There's plenty of pub grub to keep you glued to your perch for the evening, too, and the pub runs its own bus around the island if you've somehow forgotten how to find your bed.

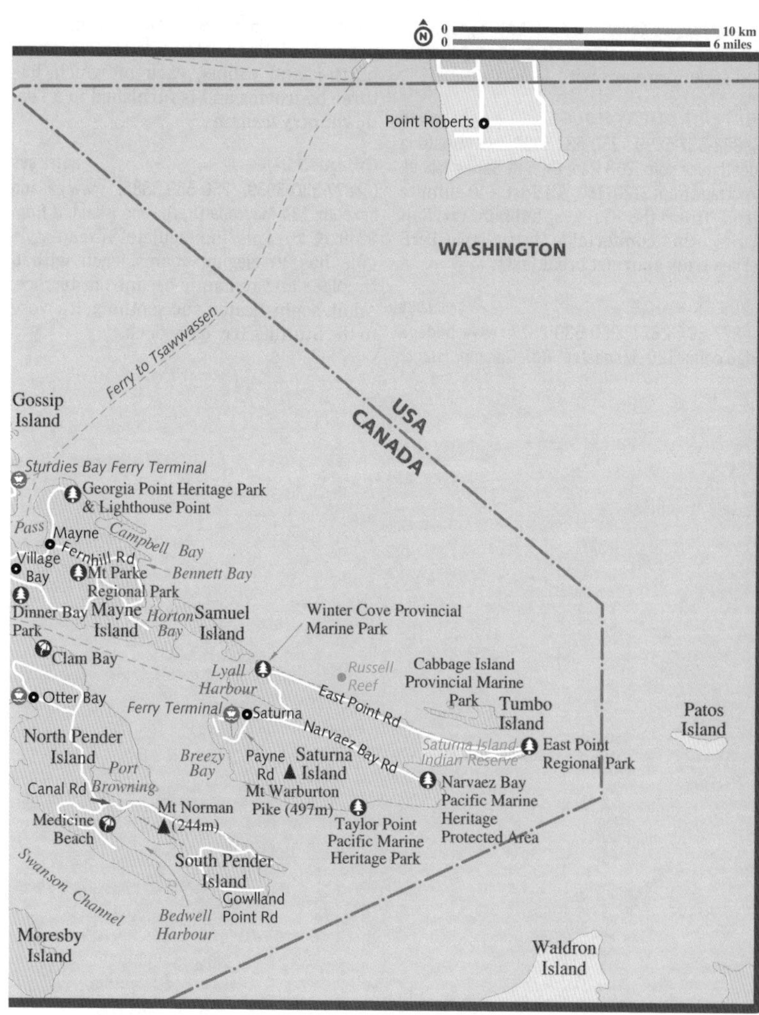

SPORTS & ACTIVITIES

SALT SPRING ADVENTURE CO KAYAKING

(☎250-537-2764, 877-537-2764; www.saltspringadventures.com; 124 Upper Ganges Rd, Salt Spring Island; tours from $50) It's not all about culinary-related hedonism on Salt Spring. If you crave some activity (especially if you've overindulged in samples at the Saturday Market), touch base with Salt Spring Adventure Co. The friendly folks here can kit you out for a kayak tour around Ganges Harbour that will make it seem like you're a million miles from bustling downtown Vancouver.

This operator also rents bikes if you feel like exploring the island on two wheels.

SLEEPING

HARBOUR HOUSE HOTEL HOTEL $$

(☎888-799-5571, 250-537-5571; www.saltspringharbourhouse.com; 121 Upper Ganges Rd, Salt Spring Island; d from $149; 📶) Situated in a great Ganges location, this Salt Spring Island hotel has a combination of motel-style and superior rooms with Jacuzzis.

WISTERIA GUEST HOUSE B&B **$$**

(☎888-537-5899, 250-537-5899; www.wisteriaguesthouse.com; 268 Park Dr, Salt Spring Island; d/cottage from $120/180; 📶) Just a 10-minute stroll from the Ganges hubbub on Salt Spring, this comfortable, home-style B&B serves truly gourmet breakfasts.

BODEGA RIDGE CABIN **$$$**

(☎877-604-2677, 250-539-2677; www.bodegaridge.com; 120 Manastee Rd, Galiano Island; cabins from $250; 📶🐾) Bodega Ridge is a peaceful Galiano Island retreat of seven north-island cabins, each of which has three bedrooms and is furnished in a rustic country fashion.

GALIANO INN HOTEL **$$$**

(☎877-530-3939, 250-539-3388; www.galianoinn.com; 134 Madrona Dr, Galiano Island; d from $249; 📶🐾) This immaculate Tuscan-style villa has 10 elegant rooms, each with a fireplace and romantic oceanfront terrace. Adult, sophisticated and soothing, it's close to the Sturdies Bay ferry dock.

Sleeping

Metro Vancouver is home to more than 25,000 hotel rooms – many in or around the downtown core. The city is packed with visitors in summer, so book ahead...unless you fancy sleeping against a damp log in Stanley Park. Rates peak in July and August, but there are good spring and fall deals, at which time of year you can also expect some accompanying 'Wet Coast' rainfall.

Hotels

Vancouver's 2010 Winter Olympics triggered a rash of hotel building, mostly in the high-end range. The Shangri-La, the Fairmont Pacific Rim and the Rosewood Hotel Georgia have all opened their doors recently, becoming the 'it' sleepovers for visitors with healthy travel budgets. Older 'it' properties such as the Opus Hotel and the St Regis Hotel have polished their appeal anew to draw attention away from the newbies, creating some healthy competition: off-season you'll find there are often seriously good rates available at these signature Vancouver properties. There are also plenty of attractive midrange options, many of which include great-value kitchen facilities that can save you a considerable amount on your dining-out costs. Consider staying downtown: there are lots of options in the area and much of the neighborhood is easily accessed on foot. Wi-fi (typically free) is common, and most properties are nonsmoking, although some still cater to visiting puffers.

B&Bs

The closest B&Bs to downtown are in the West End, and are typically sumptuous heritage homes of the romantic, high-end variety. Prices vary more in neighborhoods a little further out – especially Kitsilano and Fairview – where you usually won't be far from a bus or SkyTrain route that can have you downtown in a few minutes. Keep in mind that some B&Bs require a two-night minimum stay – especially on summer weekends – and cancellation policies can cost you an arm and a leg if you decide not to turn up.

Budget Sleepovers

There are many low-cost options in the city, but keep in mind that hostels, in particular, are not all created equal. While some offer great value, others can be smelly fleapits that you'll be itching (quite literally) to get out of. Consider the popular YWCA, Samesun or HI Hostel options as well as accommodation at the University of British Columbia (UBC). There are also a couple of respectable but low-cost guesthouse-style options in the city. When traveling off-season, your budget will likely stretch to a bargain rate at a midrange property.

Taxes & Fees

Be aware that there will be some significant additions to most quoted room rates. You'll pay an extra 7% Provincial Sales Tax (PST) plus 5% Goods and Services Tax (GST) above the advertised rate. Also, in common with other large cities in BC, Vancouver charges an additional 2% Hotel Room Tax. On top of all this, some hotels also charge a Destination Marketing Fee of around 1.5%. Parking fees don't help either: overnight parking, especially at higher-end downtown hotels, can be expensive. You'll be charged $43 at the Fairmont Pacific Rim and $39 at the Pan Pacific, for example. Keep in mind that B&Bs usually include parking free of charge.

NEED TO KNOW

Price Ranges

Our listings use the following price guide based on a double room with private bathroom.

$	less than $100
$$	$100 to $250
$$$	over $250

Online Booking Services

Lonely Planet (www.lonelyplanet.com/hotels)

Tourism Vancouver (www.tourismvancouver.com)

Hello BC (www.hellobc.com)

BC Bed & Breakfast Innkeepers Guild (www.bcsbestbnbs.com)

Tipping

Bellhops typically get tipped $2 to $5 for hailing you a cab at the front of the hotel, and up to $5 for carrying your bags to your room. Housekeepers can be tipped $2 to $5 per night of your stay, although this is entirely optional.

Lonely Planet's Top Choices

Rosewood Hotel Georgia (p213) Swanky, art-lined, landmark city hotel that's recently been reinvented.

Fairmont Pacific Rim (p214) Chic new downtown sleepover with some winning waterfront views.

St Regis Hotel (p212) Amenity-packed boutique property with a great central location.

Times Square Suites Hotel (p215) Comfortable and popular home-away-from-home near Stanley Park.

Sylvia Hotel (p215) Ivy-covered heritage charmer with some lovely beachfront views.

Opus Hotel (p218) Stylish boutique option in Yaletown; perfect for see-and-be-seen coolsters.

Best by Budget

$

YWCA Hotel (p217) Centrally located tower with comfortable rooms that offer great value (especially for families).

Urban Hideaway Guesthouse (p213) Homely little house with an excellent location.

$$

Victorian Hotel (p212) Wood-floored, bay-windowed heritage inn; good location in the heart of downtown.

Sylvia Hotel (p215) Charming beachfront sleepover in the West End, overlooking English Bay.

$$$

Rosewood Hotel Georgia (p213) Vancouver's top 'it' hotel for stylish overnighting.

Fairmont Pacific Rim (p214) Chic and luxurious waterfront hotel with a swanky air.

Best Boutique Hotels

Loden Hotel (p217) A slick and alluring Coal Harbour property just steps from the downtown core.

Opus Hotel (p218) Sexy and chic hotel in the heart of Yaletown; close to many restaurants.

St Regis Hotel (p212) City-center accommodations with some excellent value-added amenities.

Le Soleil (p213) Versace-esque interiors with a perfect, central location.

Wedgewood Hotel & Spa (p214) Classic and classy European-feel decor, plus a popular spa.

Best Historic Hotels

Fairmont Hotel Vancouver (p214) The city's lovely, gargoyle-topped grand hotel has had several royal guests over the years.

Rosewood Hotel Georgia (p213) Recently restored to its 1920s golden-age glory; glam former guests include Sinatra, Dietrich and Presley (not on the same night).

Sylvia Hotel (p215) Ivy-covered West End landmark where Errol Flynn is said to have had more than a drink or two.

Pan Pacific Vancouver (p214) Glam waterfront hotel where Princess Diana and Prince Charles stayed when they were together.

Where to Stay

Neighborhood	For	Against
Downtown	Walking distance to stores, restaurants, nightlife and some attractions; great transit links to wider region; good range of hotels	Can be pricey; streets can be clamorous; some accommodations overlook noisy traffic areas
West End	Walking distance to Stanley Park; many midrange restaurants nearby; heart of the gay district; quiet residential streets	Mostly high-end B&Bs with a couple of additional chain hotels; can be a bit of a hike to the city center and attractions other than Stanley Park
Yaletown & Granville Island	Close to shops and many restaurants; good transport links to other areas	Few accommodation options to choose from
Fairview & South Granville	Quiet residential streets; well-priced heritage B&B sleepovers; good bus and SkyTrain access to downtown	Most options are B&Bs; few local nightlife options
Kitsilano & UBC	Comfy heritage houses and good UBC budget options; direct transit to downtown; on the doorstep of several beaches	Not the center of the action; scant nightlife options; can feel a bit too quiet and laid-back
North Shore	Better hotel rates than city center; handy access to downtown via SeaBus; close to popular attractions such as Grouse Mountain and the Capilano Suspension Bridge	Away from the heart of the action; takes time to get to other major attractions

AIRPORT ACCOMMODATIONS

Staying near the airport in Richmond is not required since downtown Vancouver is only a 25-minute SkyTrain ride away on the Canada Line. But if you're a dogged plane spotter or have an early-morning flight to catch (or a late-night one to recover from), there are some choice options to consider.

The slick **River Rock Casino Resort** (Map p201; ☎866-748-3718, 604-247-8900; www.riverrock.com; 8811 River Rd; d from $190; ❄︎ 📶; Ⓜ Bridgeport Station) hotel is a 10-minute Canada Line train hop from the airport. And if you don't lose your shirt on the slots, there are some good deals on rooms here, each finished with a comfortable contemporary look.

Situated on 9 acres fronting the Fraser River and just a five-minute drive from the airport, the **Delta Vancouver Airport** (Map p201; ☎888-890-2322, 604-278-1241; www.deltavancouverairport.ca; 3500 Cessna Dr, Richmond; d from $159; 📶 🏊 🐾) has standard, comfortable, business-class rooms. It provides a 24-hour airport shuttle (or free taxi during the wee hours). There's also a 24-hour health club and an outdoor pool.

You can wave from the overhead walkway to the harried economy-class plebs below as you stroll toward the lobby of the **Fairmont Vancouver Airport** (Map p201; ☎866-540-4441, 604-207-5200; www.fairmont.com/vancouverairport; Vancouver International Airport, Richmond; d from $250; ❄︎ @ 📶 🏊; Ⓜ YVR Airport), a luxe airport hotel in the US departure hall. Rooms are elegantly furnished with high-end flourishes including remote-controlled curtains and marble-lined bathrooms. It's ideal for boarding long-haul flights in a Zen-like state of calm.

Downtown

HI VANCOUVER CENTRAL HOSTEL $

Map p266 (866-762-4122, 604-685-5335; www.hihostels.ca/vancouver; 1025 Granville St; dm with shared bathroom incl breakfast $40, r incl breakfast $113; 10) Located across from the Samesun, this warren-like hostel is more of a party joint than its HI Downtown sibling. Some of the benefits of its past hotel incarnation remain, such as air-conditioning and small dorms. There are dozens of two-bed dorms (some with ensuite) for privacy fans. Snag a back room to avoid Granville St noise issues.

Kitchen facilities are limited to microwaves and toasters but a continental breakfast is included. There's a brimming roster of social activities, including regular sightseeing tours. Locationwise, this hostel is within staggering distance of the Granville Strip's bars and clubs.

SAMESUN BACKPACKERS LODGE HOSTEL $

Map p266 (877-972-6378, 604-682-8226; www.samesun.com; 1018 Granville St; dm with shared bathroom incl breakfast $35, r incl breakfast $95; 10) Vancouver's party hostel, the brightly painted Samesun is on the city's nightlife strip. Ask for a back room if you fancy a few hours of kip or just head down to the on-site bar (provocatively called the Beaver) to join the beery throng. Dorms are comfortably small, and there's a large kitchen for your mystery-meat pasta dishes. Continental breakfast is included.

This sociable hostel has daily events (including free tours), a large guest lounge with pool table and a large-screen TV room. Staff can sell you tickets to local hockey, soccer and football games. The downstairs bar is also a good spot to catch a game, along with a few beer specials.

★**ST REGIS HOTEL** BOUTIQUE HOTEL $$

Map p266 (800-770-7929, 604-681-1135; www.stregishotel.com; 602 Dunsmuir St; d incl breakfast $220; Granville) Transformed in recent years, the St Regis is now an art-lined boutique sleepover in a 1913 heritage shell. Befitting its age, almost all the rooms seem to be a different size, and they exhibit a loungey élan with leather-look wallpaper, earth-toned bedspreads, flatscreen TVs and multimedia hubs. Rates include cooked breakfast, access to the nearby gym and free international phone calls.

The St Regis is well located in the heart of the action, offers top-notch service and has a business center if you have left your laptop at home.

VICTORIAN HOTEL HOTEL $$

Map p266 (877-681-6369, 604-681-6369; www.victorianhotel.ca; 514 Homer St; r incl breakfast $159, with shared bathroom incl breakfast $99; Granville) The high-ceilinged rooms at this popular Euro-style, heritage-building hotel combine glossy hardwood floors, a sprinkling of antiques, an occasional bay window and plenty of historical charm. The best rooms are in the renovated extension, where raindrop showers, marble bathroom floors and flatscreen TVs add a slice of luxe. Rates include continental breakfast, and rooms are provided with fans in summer.

Go for room 203: a spacious corner room with views and a cool mod chair. The Victorian has friendly staff and an excellent location just steps from the downtown action.

BURRARD HOTEL HOTEL $$

Map p266 (800-663-0366, 604-681-2331; www.theburrard.com; 1100 Burrard St; d $150; 22) A long-overdue makeover is finally capitalizing on the Burrard's kitsch-cool 1950s motel credentials, which for years had relied solely on its retro neon sign and nothing else. Now the rooms have been spruced up with mod flourishes and contemporary amenities such as Nespresso coffee machines and flatscreens. Not everything has changed, though: the hidden interior courtyard of Florida-style palm trees is *tres* cool.

When the new owners took over, they also added some enticing freebies: loaner bikes, North American phone calls and access to a nearby gym. There's also a handy late-opening cafe in the building.

L'HERMITAGE HOTEL BOUTIQUE HOTEL $$

Map p266 (888-855-1050, 778-327-4100; www.lhermitagevancouver.com; 788 Richards St; r $220; Vancouver City Centre) This classy, well-located property is divided between longer-stay suites that attract visiting movie-industry types and guests just dropping in for the night. Whichever you are, you'll find a contemporary, designer feel combined with artsy flourishes in the rooms – some of which offer full kitchens. A library-style common lounge has a secret garden terrace, and there's an adjoining Jacuzzi and lap pool.

Free loaner bikes are available on request if you fancy exploring the city's ever-expanding network of urban bicycle lanes.

METROPOLITAN HOTEL BOUTIQUE HOTEL **$$**

Map p266 (800-667-2300, 604-687-1122; www.metropolitan.com/vanc; 645 Howe St; r $225; ; Burrard) This swish boutique property has a contemporary take on style that will appeal to urban sophisticates. It's also handily located in the heart of downtown. Bold modern artworks add a splash of color to the atmospheric, subtly decorated rooms, and there's a good on-site restaurant, an indoor pool and a squash court to keep you busy.

Unusually for Vancouver, there are also some smoking rooms available. And if you really want to show your class, hop in the hotel's Jaguar: it'll take you anywhere you want as part of the hotel's morning downtown limo service. When you finally get back to the hotel, you can play a little pitch-and-put on the outdoor minigolf course. Excellent service.

URBAN HIDEAWAY GUESTHOUSE GUESTHOUSE **$$**

Map p266 (604-694-0600; www.urban-hideaway.com; 581 Richards St; d with shared bathroom $109, suite $159; @; Granville) This cozy but fiendishly well-hidden guesthouse is a word-of-mouth favorite in the heart of the city. Tuck yourself into one of the comfy rooms (the loft is recommended) or spend your time in the lounge areas downstairs. There are laundry facilities, a computer that's free to use and loaner bikes that are also gratis. Bathrooms are mostly shared; the loft's bathroom is private.

The hosts are highly welcoming and full of suggestions for what to do in the area if you need some ideas.

MODA HOTEL HOTEL **$$**

Map p266 (877-683-5522, 604-683-4251; www.modahotel.ca; 900 Seymour St; d $159; ; 10) Moda will never be in the big league of fancy local boutiques, but that's fine because it has two key things going for it: an excellent heart-of-the-city location and better rates than its posher siblings.The mostly small rooms combine mod, 'cheap chic' flourishes with quirky heritage holdovers (the building opened in 1908). Light sleepers should avoid lower floors.

If you're traveling with your pooch, there are also some dog-friendly rooms here ($15 extra per night). Alternatively, if you're missing your pet back home, pad down to the excellent on-site wine bar for a consoling nightcap.

CENTURY PLAZA HOTEL & SPA HOTEL **$$**

Map p266 (800-663-1818, 604-687-0575; www.century-plaza.com; 1015 Burrard St; r $169; ; 22) This centrally located tower sleepover combines standard business hotel-style rooms (all with handy kitchenettes) plus a raft of on-site amenities: there can't be many North American hotels that have both their own spa and comedy club. There's also an indoor pool and steam room, and you're just a couple of downhill blocks from the tumult of Robson St shops.

There are many restaurants within strolling distance, but the hotel also has its own loungey, modern eatery if you're feeling too lazy to leave the building.

ROSEWOOD HOTEL GEORGIA HOTEL **$$$**

Map p266 (604-682-5566; www.rosewoodhotels.com; 801 W Georgia St; d $410; @; Vancouver City Centre) Vancouver's current 'it' hotel underwent a recent spectacular renovation that brought the 1927-built landmark back to its golden-age glory. Despite the abstract modern art lining its public areas, the hotel's rooms take a classic, elegant approach with warming earth and coffee tones, pampering treats such as deep soaker tubs and (in some rooms) sparkling downtown cityscape views.

Save time for the the lobby-level restaurant. Alongside the hotel's successful resurrection, Hawksworth (p63) has become the place to be seen for the city's movers and shakers – and you, if you look the part.

HOTEL LE SOLEIL BOUTIQUE HOTEL **$$$**

Map p266 (604-632-3000; www.hotellesoleil.com; 567 Hornby St; d $289; ; Burrard) One of Vancouver's most stylish boutique hotel towers, Le Soleil is lined with classical European furnishings and bold flourishes that have a chic, Versace-esque appeal. Most rooms are compact but elegantly designed (corner roome have balconies), and you'll be steps from the center of all the downtown nightlife action – although those on the higher floors will feel loftily far from the bustling streets.

If you don't fancy straying too far from your room, the hotel's lobby-level bistro serves great cocktails as well as some unexpectedly excellent Indian tapas dishes. And if you catch the eye of someone at the next table, rest assured: your in-room honor bar contains an 'intimacy kit' with two condoms. It costs $8, though, so make sure you've chosen well. Rates include access to a nearby gym.

FAIRMONT PACIFIC RIM HOTEL $$$

Map p266 (☎877-900-5350, 604-695-5300; www.fairmont.com/pacificrim; 1038 Canada Place; d $249; ; MWaterfront) Near the convention center, this chic 377-room property is Vancouver's newest Fairmont. While many rooms have city views, the ones with waterfront vistas will blow you away, especially as you sit in your jetted tub or cube-shaped Japanese bath with a glass of bubbly. In-room flourishes include iPod docks and Nespresso machines, but the rooftop swimming pool should monopolize most of your time.

Check out the wrap-around text art installation on the hotel's glass exterior. And stick around for a drink: the lobby bar is popular with local cocktail-quaffing movers and shakers. Soothe your hangover away the next day at the Willow Stream Spa, one of the area's most popular pampering options.

FAIRMONT HOTEL VANCOUVER HOTEL $$$

Map p266 (☎866-540-4452, 604-684-3131; www.fairmont.com/hotelvancouver; 900 W Georgia St; r $369; @; MVancouver City Centre) Opened in 1939 by visiting UK royals, this sparkling grand dame is a Vancouver landmark. Despite the provenance, the hotel carefully balances comfort with elegance: the lobby is bedecked with crystal chandeliers but the rooms have an understated business-hotel feel. If you have the budget, check in to the Gold Floor for a raft of pampering services.

And if you'd rather not pay for internet access, join the President's Club loyalty program for free and it won't cost you a penny (this applies to all Fairmont properties). If you're staying in the city at Christmas, this place is a good option: the lobby is always beautifully decorated for the season.

WEDGEWOOD HOTEL & SPA BOUTIQUE HOTEL $$$

Map p266 (☎800-663-0666, 604-689-7777; www.wedgewoodhotel.com; 845 Hornby St; r $310; @; 5) The last word in personalized luxury, the elegant Wedgewood is dripping with top-hatted charm. The friendly staff are second to none, rooms are stuffed with reproduction antiques and the balconies enable you to smirk at the seemingly grubby plebs shuffling past below. Steam up your monocle with a trip to the spa, then sip a signature cocktail in the fireplace-warmed lobby bar.

The fitness center has had a recent upgrade and is now lined with slick, state-of-the-art equipment.

PAN PACIFIC VANCOUVER HOTEL $$$

Map p266 (☎800-663-1515, 604-662-8111; www.vancouver.panpacific.com; 999 Canada Place; d $319; @; MWaterfront) This luxe Canada Place hotel starts with a cavernous lobby, complete with its own clutch of totem poles. The large rooms, many with

VANCOUVER'S TALLEST HOTEL TOWER

Standing at the corner of Thurlow and W Georgia Sts and craning your neck skywards to the building dominating the intersection is a somewhat futile gesture: however hard you try, you won't see much of the rooftop garden sitting up top. The city's loftiest artificial green space, it resides at the apex of what became Vancouver's tallest building when it opened its doors in 2009. Housing the ultraluxurious Shangri-La Hotel (p217) on its first 15 floors, the Shangri-La is a sheer 201m glass box that beats the city's previous record holder – the dark-glassed One Wall Centre at 1088 Burrard St – by more than 50m. Slick condominiums occupy the rest of the building above the hotel, including one 'penthouse estate' that was reputedly sold for $15 million. Check out the raised box blip that sticks out a little from the rest of the building's mirror-like fascia: its location marks the previous height limit for buildings in the city.

panoramic Burrard Inlet vistas, are no less impressive; they come with decadent maple-wood furnishings and the kind of beds where the linen thread-count is off the scale. More pampering required? Hit the luxurious on-site spa, a city fave.

The downtown core is minutes away by foot, and Gastown (great for nightlife) is just around the corner.

West End

BUCHAN HOTEL HOTEL $

Map p270 (☎800-668-6654, 604-685-5354; www.buchanhotel.com; 1906 Haro St; d $139, with shared bathroom $99; ; 5) The cheap and cheerful 1926-built Buchan has bags of charm and is located just steps from Stanley Park. Along corridors lined with old prints of yesteryear Vancouver, its budget rooms – most with shared bathrooms – are clean, cozy and well maintained, although some furnishings have seen better days. The pricier rooms are correspondingly prettier, while the eastside rooms are brighter. The front desk is friendly.

There's also a comfy guest lounge, and other extras include storage facilities for bikes and skis as well as handy laundry machines. Wi-fi costs $2 per day. If you're driving, there's some free parking around the neighborhood, or you can pay $10 to park overnight at the hotel. There are many midrange dining options nearby, including a charming Italian restaurant at the base of the building.

HI VANCOUVER DOWNTOWN HOSTEL $

Map p270 (☎866-762-4122, 604-684-4565; www.hihostels.ca/vancouver; 1114 Burnaby St; dm/r incl breakfast $42/108; ; 6) It says 'downtown' but this purpose-built hostel is on a quiet residential West End side street. Popular with older hostelers and families, the dorms are all mercifully small and rates include continental breakfast. Private rooms are available. There's also bike storage, a full kitchen, and TV and games rooms, plus twice-weekly tours from April to November with legendary local guide Erik.

The most 'institutional' of Vancouver's three HI hostels, the front-deskers are especially friendly here. Book well ahead for private rooms.

TIMES SQUARE SUITES HOTEL APARTMENT $$

Map p270 (☎877-684-2223, 604-684-2223; www.timessquaresuites.com; 1821 Robson St; ste $225; ; 5) Superbly located a short walk from Stanley Park, this excellent West End hidden gem (even the entrance can be hard to spot) is the perfect apartment-style Vancouver sleepover. Rooms are mostly one-bedroom suites and are spacious, with tubs, laundry facilities, full kitchens and superbly well-maintained (if slightly 1980s) decor. Rates include access to a neaby gym. There's a supermarket just across the street.

Choose a back suite if you want to be away from the busy road. Up to three adults can be accommodated in each suite (all are equipped with sofa beds). Make sure you visit the shared rooftop patio: the ideal place to while away an evening with a glass of wine, it has a communal barbecue if you fancy grilling a few burgers. There's often a two-night minimum stay in July and August.

SUNSET INN & SUITES HOTEL $$

Map p270 (☎800-786-1997, 604-688-2474; www.sunsetinn.com; 1111 Burnaby St; ste incl breakfast $175; ; 6) A generous cut above most of the West End's self-catering suite hotels, the popular Sunset Inn offers larger-then-average rooms with full kitchenettes. Each has a balcony, and some – particularly those on south-facing higher floors – have partial views of English Bay. Rates include continental breakfast and, rare for Vancouver, free parking. The attentive staff are among the best in the city.

Sunset Inn is sitting pretty near the Robson St shopping action, popular Sunset Beach and the bustling gay village around Davie St. If you're planning to stay longer, it also offers good monthly rates.

SYLVIA HOTEL HOTEL $$

Map p270 (☎604-681-9321; www.sylviahotel.com; 1154 Gilford St; r $189; ; 5) Built in 1912, the ivy-covered Sylvia enjoys a prime location overlooking English Bay. Generations of guests keep coming back – many requesting the same room every year – for a dollop of old-world charm, plus a side order of first-name service. The rooms have a wide array of comfortable configurations, but best are the bedsit suites, which have kitchens and waterfront views.

If you don't have a room with a view, decamp to the lobby-level lounge to nurse a beer and watch the sun set over the beach.

ENGLISH BAY INN B&B **$$**

Map p270 (☎866-683-8002, 604-683-8002; www.englishbayinn.com; 1968 Comox St; r incl breakfast $175; 🚭📶; 🚌6) Each of the six antique-lined rooms in this Tudoresque B&B near Stanley Park has a private bathroom, and two have sumptuous four-poster beds. You'll think you've arrived in Victoria, BC's determinedly Olde English capital, by mistake. There's complimentary port in the parlor, a secluded garden for hanging out and a three-course breakfast – arrive in the dining room early for the alcove table.

This property has been a charmer for years with many loyal guests coming back. It's the warm welcome from host Greg, who's the star of the show, that makes all the difference. Ask him for a few tips about what to see in the area on your visit and he'll have plenty of perfect suggestions for you.

LISTEL HOTEL BOUTIQUE HOTEL **$$**

Map p270 (☎800-663-5491, 604-684-8461; www.thelistelhotel.com; 1300 Robson St; d $180; 🚭❄@📶; 🚌5) A sophisticated, self-described 'art hotel,' the Listel attracts grown-ups through its on-site installations and package deals with local art galleries. Many rooms display original artwork, including contemporary installations and First Nations works, and all have a relaxing, mood-lit West Coast feel. Artsy types should also check out the adjoining private gallery, as well as Forage (p64), the hotel's new farm-to-table on-site restaurant.

Check the hotel's website for an ever-changing roster of good-value, art-themed package deals. And don't worry about finding the shops on your visit: you're steps away from Robson St's retailing center.

BARCLAY HOUSE B&B B&B **$$**

Map p270 (☎800-971-1351, 604-605-1351; www.barclayhouse.com; 1351 Barclay St; d $120; @📶; 🚌5) This magnificent bright-yellow Victorian property (built in 1904) takes a sophisticated boutique twist on the usual heritage B&B. Rather than a mothballed museum look with delicate and overly chintzy antiques, the six rooms have a sophisticated, designer feel and are lined with modern artsy flourishes. But home comforts haven't been lost to aesthetics, and several rooms have gratifyingly deep soaker tubs.

Our favorite room? The lovely Haidaway, which has original First Nations artworks and a huge jetted bathtub.

BLUE HORIZON HOTEL HOTEL **$$**

Map p270 (☎800-663-1333, 604-688-1411; www.bluehorizonhotel.com; 1225 Robson St; r $169; 🚭❄@📶🏊; 🚌5) Despite being located in a 1960s tower, the recently refurbished Blue Horizon feels modern. The good-value suites have the kind of quality, business-hotel furnishings common in pricier joints and all have corner balconies. Those on the top floors look across

VANCOUVER'S HISTORIC SLEEPOVERS

While shiny new towers are de rigueur among Vancouver hotels these days, the city has a colorful heritage of older accommodations with bags of character. Leading the pack is the ivy-shrouded Sylvia Hotel (p215), which was named after the owner's daughter when it opened in 1912. By the late 1940s, the Sylvia had become a glam city hangout and, in 1954, it became the home of Vancouver's first cocktail bar. Errol Flynn propped up the bar here once or twice during a prolonged bender just before dying of a heart attack in the city in October 1959. You can visit the bar today, although it's moved on from its cocktail-exclusive heyday.

The Sylvia was designated as a local heritage building in 1975, but it's not the only historic hotel in town. The Canadian Pacific Railway company built a string of castle-like sleepovers across Canada around the turn of the 19th century for first-class train passengers planning countrywide jaunts. The company's first hotel in Vancouver was knocked down and replaced by a larger second version, which was also superseded and eventually demolished in favour of the current gargoyle-topped Hotel Vancouver (p214). This was opened in 1939 by King George VI and Queen Elizabeth, who were on their own cross-Canada tour at the time. Nip into the hotel's lobby and you'll see a copy of the lunch menu that greeted the royals on their first day in the city.

to English Bay or the mountain-framed North Shore. The revamped on-site restaurant has also moved up a notch with a focus on fresh comfort food.

The hotel is right on the city's main shopping strip, so you won't have far to transport your purchases. In addition, Stanley Park is a 15-minute walk away.

RIVIERA HOTEL HOTEL **$$**

Map p270 (888-699-5222, 604-685-1301; www.rivieravancouver.com; 1431 Robson St; d $149; ; 5) One of several well-located apartment-style hotels crowding the Robson St and Broughton St intersection, the Riviera has undergone a recent and long-overdue makeover, adding new interiors to its generally spacious rooms. Complete with kitchens, many rooms can easily fit a small family. Parking is free and there are often excellent off-season deals. There are restaurants nearby if you don't want to cook.

The Riviera is a good choice for those who want to be near Stanley Park and downtown shopping options.

COAST COAL HARBOUR HOTEL HOTEL **$$**

Map p270 (604-697-0202; www.coasthotels.com; 1180 W Hastings St; d $239; ; M Burrard) A modern and popular business hotel that also lures leisure travelers with its proximity to both Stanley Park and the downtown core, the bright and breezy Coast Coal Harbour often has some screamingly good deals on last-minute hotel-booking sites. For your money, you'll get a comfortable if generic-looking room with the possibility of waterfront views through those floor-to-ceiling windows.

If you need to cool off after hiking the seawall, there's also an outdoor heated pool.

LODEN HOTEL BOUTIQUE HOTEL **$$$**

Map p270 (877-225-6336, 604-669-5060; www.theloden.com; 1177 Melville St; r $300; ; M Burrard) The stylish Loden is the real designer deal, and one of the first boutique properties in years to give Yaletown's Opus a run for its money. The chic, chocolate-hued rooms have a contemporary feel, with luxe accoutrements such as marble-lined bathrooms and those oh-so-civilized heated floors. Service is top-notch – make sure you try the complimentary London taxicab limo service.

Free loaner bikes are also available; they're perfect for hitting the nearby Stanley Park seawall.

SHANGRI-LA HOTEL HOTEL **$$$**

Map p270 (604-689-1120; www.shangri-la.com/vancouver; 1128 W Georgia St; r/ste $340/425; ; M Burrard) Occupying the lower floors of the city's tallest tower, the Shangri-La redefined opulent Vancouver sleepovers when it opened in 2010. Its sleek, mood-lit rooms (some compact and others palatially large) are lined with artwork and dark-wood paneling, while pampering flourishes include L'Occitane products, bathroom mirrors embedded with TVs and automatic blinds so you can shower behind the floor-to-ceiling windows without being seen from outside.

Service is of the highly attentive, first-name variety and is second to none. The hotel's celebrated on-site restaurant, Market, is a winner even among those not staying here. Drop by in summer and you'll even find an indoor farmers market of gourmet goodies. There's also an excellent full-service spa.

Yaletown & Granville Island

★YWCA HOTEL HOSTEL **$**

Map p274 (800-663-1424, 604-895-5830; www.ywcahotel.com; 733 Beatty St; s/d/tr with shared bathroom $73/90/117; ; M Stadium-Chinatown) A good-value, well-located option offering nicely maintained (if spartan) rooms of the student accommodation variety. There are a wide range of configurations here, from singles to five-bed rooms that are ideal for groups, and shared, semiprivate or private bathrooms. Each room has a minifridge and guests can use the communal kitchens. Rates include access to the YWCA Health & Fitness Centre, a 10-minute walk away.

This is a great option for budget-conscious families; kids get a toy upon check-in. Despite the slightly institutionalized feel, the staff are friendly and helpful.

GEORGIAN COURT HOTEL HOTEL **$$**

Map p274 (800-663-1155, 604-682-5555; www.georgiancourt.com; 773 Beatty St; r $190; ; M Stadium-Chinatown) This under-the-radar, European-style property has never changed its old-school approach to good service and solid, dependable amenities. Rooms have an elegant, business-hotel feel but the spacious, apartment-style corner suites – with their quiet, recessed bedrooms – are best. There's a small on-site fitness room and the hotel runs a shuttle bus around the city throughout the day.

A good location near the city center adds to the appeal here, and if you're planning to catch a hockey, football or soccer game, the city's two main stadiums are just steps away.

GRANVILLE ISLAND HOTEL

BOUTIQUE HOTEL **$$**

Map p275 (800-663-1840, 604-683-7373; www.granvilleislandhotel.com; 1253 Johnston St; r $220; 50) This gracious boutique property hugs Granville Island's quiet northeastern tip, enjoying tranquil views across False Creek to Yaletown's mirrored towers. You'll be a five-minute walk from the Public Market, with shopping and theater options on your doorstep. Rooms have an elegant, West Coast feel with some exposed wood flourishes. There's also a cool rooftop Jacuzzi, and the on-site brewpub-restaurant has a great patio.

You're close to the seawall bike trail here (the hotel can rent you a bike) if you fancy pedaling to UBC or, in the opposite direction, Stanley Park.

OPUS HOTEL

BOUTIQUE HOTEL **$$$**

Map p274 (866-642-6780, 604-642-6787; www.opushotel.com; 322 Davie St; r $299; Yaletown-Roundhouse) The Opus kick-started Vancouver's boutique hotel scene and, with its recent full-on revamp, it's still high up on the city's most stylish sleepovers list. The spruced-up rooms have contemporary-chic interiors with bold colors, mod furnishings and feng-shui bed placements, while the luxe bathrooms have clear windows overlooking the streets (visiting exhibitionists take note).

A model of excellent service, the Opus has a slick on-site bar and a quality Italian restaurant, while all rooms come with iPads or Samsung Galaxy tablet loaners. And if you need to get around town, you can borrow a bike or hop in the hotel's freebie limo service.

ARTSY HOTELS

While visiting art lovers might find it difficult to roll out a sleeping bag and kip among the exhibits at the Vancouver Art Gallery, there are some places in town that positively encourage it (*sans* sleeping bag). The newly revamped Rosewood Hotel Georgia (p213) has arguably the city's best hotel art collection. Dominated by modern Canadian art, the hotel's public spaces have a gallery feel with abstract works by the likes of Alan Wood, Marcel Baebeau and Guido Molinari studding the walls. The highlight, though, is in the lobby and it's the only piece by a non-Canadian artist. Entitled *Internity*, the 3D work by Brit artist Patrick Hughes shifts perspective as you move in front of it and is a real eye-popper.

But the Hotel Georgia isn't the only Vancouver hotel with an artistic bent. Calling itself the city's 'art hotel', the Listel Hotel (p216) has a curatorial arrangement with several local galleries and museums that means its corridors are lined with display cases of intriguing art; First Nations carvings and contemporary abstract works dominate. Many of its rooms eschew generic landscapes in favor of limited-edition prints. Attached to the hotel is the Stewart Stephenson Modern Art Gallery, where you can watch artwork being created and maybe pick up a top-notch piece to hang on your wall back home. Adding to its creative credentials, the Listel has even produced its own book: an anthology of Vancouver-themed short stories, with contributions from Douglas Coupland and William Gibson, among others.

Guests who stay at the Shangri-La Hotel (p217) should be a bit bookish, since on their pillow they'll find a copy of the 1930s novel *Lost Horizons*, which details the discovery of a hidden utopia in the Himalayas. Alongside its own impressive wall-mounted art collection, the hotel has also made a fantastic artistic contribution to the city in creating the Vancouver Art Gallery Offsite, just outside the hotel's entrance. This new free-access public art area includes a couple of eye-catching alfresco art shows every year. These have so far included a series of giant photos of Chinese children and a clutch of highly detailed scale models of cannery sheds that recall the area's fishing industry past.

Fairview & South Granville

SHAUGHNESSY VILLAGE HOTEL $

Map p280 (☎604-736-5511; www.shaughnessyvillage.com; 1125 W 12th Ave; s/d incl breakfast $79/89; ; 9) This entertainingly kitsch tower block sleepover – think pink carpets, flowery sofas and maritime memorabilia – offers well-maintained, perfectly shipshape, basic budget rooms. Like boat cabins, they are lined with wooden cupboards and include microwaves, refrigerators and tiny private bathrooms. Rates include use of an outdoor pool, laundry facilities and, of course, a large display of petrified wood.

Aimed primarily at longer-stay residents, there are good deals here if you're sticking around for a while.

WINDSOR GUEST HOUSE B&B $$

Map p280 (☎888-872-3060, 604-872-3060; www.dougwin.com; 325 W 11th Ave; r incl breakfast $105, with shared bathroom incl breakfast $85; ; MBroadway-City Hall) This 1895 wood-built mansion has a lived-in, homey feel, complete with a charming veranda and stained-glass windows. The good-value rooms vary greatly in size and some have shared bathrooms. The recommended top floor 'Charles Room' is quaint and quiet with a patio overlooking downtown that's shared with the neighbouring room. Cooked breakfast is included, along with free off-street parking.

The Windsor is on a quiet residential street with plenty of restaurants in the vicinity. The Canada Line's Broadway-City Hall station is a short walk away, so you can be in the heart of downtown in less than 10 minutes.

Kitsilano & University of British Columbia (UBC)

HI VANCOUVER JERICHO BEACH HOSTEL $

(☎866-762-4122, 604-224-3208; www.hihostels.ca/vancouver; 1515 Discovery St, Kitsilano; dm/r with shared bathroom $36/88; May-Sep; @; 4) One of Canada's largest hostels looks like a Victorian hospital from the outside but has a great location if you're here for the sun-kissed Jericho Beach vibe; downtown is a 40-minute bus ride away. Basic rooms make this the least palatial Vancouver HI, but it has a large kitchen, bike rentals and a recently revamped cafe. Dorms are also larger here. Book ahead for private rooms.

For many, this hostel delivers more of a vacation than its downtown siblings due to its beach proximity. Unlike other HI's, rates do not include continental breakfast. Take bus 4 west along 4th Ave and disembark at the intersection with NW Marine Dr. The hostel is a short stroll downhill from there.

UNIVERSITY OF BRITISH COLUMBIA ACCOMMODATION ACCOMMODATION SERVICES $$

Map p286 (☎888-822-1030, 604-822-1000; www.ubcconferences.com; 5961 Student Union Blvd, UBC; r $35-199; May-Aug; @; 99B-Line) Pretend you're still a student at this UBC campus sleepover. Well-maintained accommodation options include good-value college-dorm units at Pacific Spirit Hostel; private rooms in shared apartments at Gage Towers (most with great views); and impressive, hotel-style suites at West Coast Suites, including flatscreen TVs and slick interiors. Of the three, only the latter is available year-round and also includes breakfast and wi-fi.

Ideal for groups or budget travelers who want to be close to UBC's array of museum, garden and gallery attractions. Downtown is 45 minutes away by bus.

CORKSCREW INN B&B $$

Map p282 (☎877-737-7276, 604-733-7276; www.corkscrewinn.com; 2735 W 2nd Ave, Kitsilano; d incl breakfast $180; ; 84) This immaculate, gable-roofed property appears to have a drinking problem: it houses a little museum, available only to guests, that's lined with quirky corkskrews and antique vineyard tools. Aside from the boozy paraphernalia, this lovely century-old Craftsman home has five artsy rooms (we like the art deco room) and is just a short walk from the beach. Sumptuous breakfast included.

A three-night minimum stay typically applies, but the owners can be flexible about this if there's availability (especially outside summer). Parking is on the street and it's free.

KITSILANO SUITES APARTMENT $$

Map p282 (☎604-732-4038; www.kitsilanosuites.com; 2465 W 6th Ave, Kitsilano; ste $159; ; 9) This shingle-sided Arts and Crafts heritage house is divided into three self-catering, home-away-from-home suites. Each has been immaculately renovated and lined with modern appliances without spoiling the historic feel: think hardwood floors, claw-foot bathtubs and stained-glass windows. All have full kitchens and a welcome pack is included for your first breakfast if you're staying four nights or more. Shops and restaurants abound nearby.

A three-night minimum rule often applies (this may be relaxed off-season); weekly rates are also available.

North Shore

PINNACLE HOTEL AT THE PIER HOTEL **$$**

Map p284 (877-986-7437, 604-986-7437; www.pinnaclehotelatthepier.com; 138 Victory Ship Way, North Vancouver; d $169; ; SeaBus to Lonsdale Quay) North Van's new Pinnacle is an excellent option if you want to stay on this side of the water and hop to the city center on the nearby SeaBus. Rooms are furnished with contemporary elegance, calming hues favored over bold colors. The hotel balances itself between business and leisure travelers. Harbor view rooms are recommended (typically $10 to $20 extra per night).

Fitness buffs will enjoy the property's large gym and pool. The Lonsdale Quay Public Market is just steps away.

THISTLEDOWN HOUSE B&B B&B **$$**

Map p284 (888-633-7173, 604-986-7173; www.thistle-down.com; 3910 Capilano Rd, North Vancouver; d incl breakfast $165; ; 236) Located on the road to Grouse Mountain, this adult-oriented 1920s Craftsman-style house is a notch above standard B&Bs: just check out its gourmet breakfast menu. Among its elegantly decorated rooms, the most palatial suite (called Under the Apple Tree) is surprisingly secluded and includes a beautiful fireplace, sunken sitting room, Jacuzzi and large windows opening onto a private patio.

The owners (plus Tosh, the house terrier) are friendly and helpful – join them for afternoon tea during your stay.

LONSDALE QUAY HOTEL BOUTIQUE HOTEL **$$**

Map p284 (800-836-6111, 604-986-6111; www.lonsdalequayhotel.com; 123 Carrie Cates Ct, North Vancouver; d $195; ; SeaBus to Lonsdale Quay) This well-located North Van waterfront sleepover has upgraded its rooms to include granite bathroom counters and (in the higher-end executive suites) flatscreen TVs, new artworks and dark-wood furnishings. It's attached to the market building a short walk from the SeaBus terminal. There are numerous restaurants nearby, and you can work off any naughty vacation excesses in the gym.

If you really want to indulge, the executive suites have curved window views of the downtown towers twinkling across Burrard Inlet.

Understand Vancouver

Vancouver Today

Despite the prevalence of Lycra, Vancouverites are not just a bunch of bike-riding hippies. It likely won't be long before you've told the locals how much you love their beautiful city and they've replied that it's not all perfect. House prices have been shooting skywards here since the 1990s – those 'best places in the world to live' surveys that routinely place Vancouver near the top come with a hefty cost-of-living price tag. It's a very real issue on everyone's mind.

Best in Print

City of Glass (Douglas Coupland; 2000) Affectionate homage to the city by one of its leading authors.

Vancouver Special (Charles Demers; 2009) Black-and-white images and warts-and-all reflections on the city.

Runaway: Diary of a Street Kid (Evelyn Lau; 2001) Deeply personal memoir about life on the streets in Vancouver.

The Jade Peony (Wayson Choy; 1995) Immersive memoir of growing up in a Chinese immigrant family in Vancouver in the 1930s.

Vancouver Stories (2005) Collection of evocative short stories on the city from authors including Coupland and Timothy Taylor.

Best on Film

On the Corner (2003) Fictional account of life on the Downtown Eastside.

Carts of Darkness (2008) Documentary exploring the 'extreme sport' of shopping-cart racing among local bottle pickers.

Double Happiness (1994) Generational differences in a colorful Chinese-Canadian family in Vancouver.

The Delicate Art of Parking (2003) Documentary-style comedy about Vancouver parking enforcers.

Income Issues

Get any two Vancouverites in a room and you can take bets on how long it will be before they start talking about house prices. Many locals will tell you they've been priced out of the market and expect to be renting forever (or else moving to suburban Abbotsford). Those who do buy property appear to have healthy joint incomes but still only just squeak by.

It's sometimes said that Vancouver has become the victim of its own success. It's reputedly one of the best places in the world to live – according to various global surveys – and was thrust into the international spotlight as the host of a highly regarded 2010 Olympic and Paralympic Winter Games. All of which means that even traditionally grungy or cheap neighborhoods such as Gastown, Strathcona, Main St and Commercial Dr – areas that have a long track record of housing the city's artists, bohemians and low-income locals – have become trendy, sought-after spots that command prices unheard of in the city just a few years ago.

Gentrification

The city's sprawling Downtown Eastside district – which includes Gastown and Chinatown – has been rapidly gentrifying in recent years, with historic old buildings now repaired and repainted into live-work spaces and hip coffee shops. Heritage spaces are being restored, but transforming grungy old neighborhoods into cool new hipster havens has a flip side. The locals who have called this area home for decades – many of whom have long-standing drug, poverty or mental-health issues – don't necessarily want to leave and are in no mood to be priced out of the neighborhood. There are dozens of social-housing developments in this area and there likely always will be. While the mayor has stated publicly that the city will end homelessness in Vancouver by 2015, the Downtown Eastside continues on a tense path of development, balancing the needs of those who want to improve the area and those who have always lived here and don't want their home to change.

No Fun City?

In the years leading up to the 2010 Olympics, Vancouver gained a reputation for bureaucratic stickling that made it difficult for new events and festivals to take off, and for existing businesses – especially those related to booze – to expand their offerings. The phrase 'no fun city' emerged to cover what many saw as a small-minded, parochial approach, despite Vancouver's claim to being a world-class city. But the 2010 Games were a turning point. Locals showed that they could party without causing trouble and city officials responded by trying to recapture the positive street vibe after the event was over. It wasn't long before a food-truck program was launched – emulating Portland – while several new grassroots summer events were also introduced.

British Columbia has also been at the forefront of Canada's recent microbrewery surge. It's taken years, however, for Vancouver to begin catching up to Victoria and its surfeit of tasty beer makers. The 'no fun' label hasn't been far from the lips of some locals; Vancouver ale fans blame the slow pace on city bureacrats. An associated issue has been liquor licensing, primarily controlled by the province rather than the city, which has seen local movie houses and theaters struggle to gain the ability to sell alcohol to their patrons. Whatever the reasons behind this, Vancouver – according to many locals – simply has far too many rules. Which partly explains why the city's mooted public bike-share program is taking a while to get moving: helmets are mandatory here, which makes success a greater challenge.

if Vancouver were 100 people

48 would be Caucasian
28 would be Chinese
9 would be Southeast Asian
6 would be South Asian
9 would be other

languages spoken at home (% of population)

population per sq km

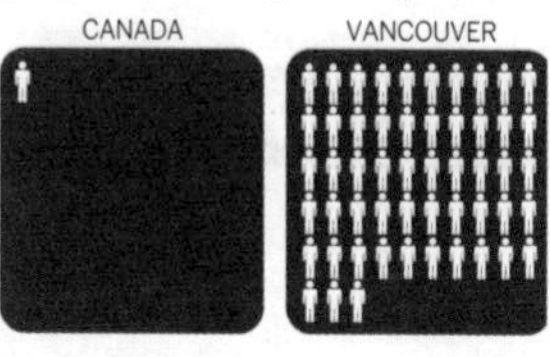

History

Vancouverites often say there's no history here, usually in jealous reference to 'all those old buildings in Europe.' But the fact is Vancouver has a rich and tumultuous past stretching back thousands of years. Stand by for tales of First Nations communities from more than 10,000 years ago; Spanish and English explorers who poked around the region for the first time; and an Englishman who kick-started the modern-day city with a barrel of whiskey and a pub-building project.

Living off the Land

The ancestors of Vancouver's First Nations people were in British Columbia (BC) at least 10,000 years ago, with many setting up camp along the coastline in areas still regarded as important First Nations lands to this day.

These first people lived in villages comprising wood-plank houses arranged in rows, often surrounded by a stockade. Totem poles were set up as an emblem of family or clan. It's not surprising these groups settled this area: the local beaches and rivers teemed with seafood; the forests bristled with tasty wildlife, including deer and elk; and fat silvery salmon were abundantly available to anyone who fancied outsmarting the odd bear for the privilege.

Several distinct communities formed. The Musqueam populated Burrard Inlet, English Bay and the mouth of the Fraser River, although they shared some of this area with the Squamish, who were largely based at the head of Howe Sound, but also had villages in North and West Vancouver, Kitsilano Point, Stanley Park and Jericho Beach. The Kwantlen controlled the area around New Westminster, while Delta and Richmond were home to the Tsawwassen. The Tsleil-Waututh occupied much of North Vancouver, while Coast Salish tribes, such as the Cowichan, Nanaimo and Saanich, set up seasonal camps along the Fraser River when the salmon were running.

Scant evidence exists about this intriguing period in Vancouver's history: most settlements have crumbled to dust and few have been rediscovered by archaeologists. In addition, these early settlers gener-

History Books

Chuck Davis' History of Metropolitan Vancouver (Chuck Davis)

Vanishing Vancouver (Michael Kluckner)

Vancouver Noir (Diane Purvey, John Belshaw)

TIMELINE

8000 BC

Evidence of the region's first inhabitants date from this time; whether they arrived from Asia across the Bering Strait or were here already is contentious among historians.

1774

The Spanish arrive in the area in search of the fabled Northwest Passage. They don't venture any further than Vancouver Island's Nootka Sound.

1791

A little more adventurous than his colleagues, Spanish explorer José María Narváez edges into the Strait of Georgia.

ally maintained oral records – they told each other (often in song) the stories of their ancestors, rather than writing things down for posterity. This method would have been highly successful until the arrival of the Europeans.

Captain Van Hits Town

After centuries of unhindered First Nations occupation, Europeans began arriving in the late 18th century. The Spanish sent three expeditions between 1774 and 1779 in search of the fabled Northwest Passage. British explorer Captain James Cook elbowed into the area from the South Pacific in 1779. He had a similar Northwest Passage motive but when he hit the west coast of Vancouver Island, he believed it to be the mainland. It wasn't until 1791 that the Strait of Georgia near what we call Vancouver was properly explored. Spanish navigator José María Narváez did the honors, sailing all the way into Burrard Inlet.

Next up was Captain George Vancouver, a British navigator. In 1792 he glided into the inner harbor and spent one day here – an auspicious day, as it turned out. When he arrived, he discovered that the Spanish, in ships under the command of captains Valdez and Galiano, had already claimed the area. Meeting at what is today known as Spanish Banks, the men shared area navigational information. Vancouver made a note of the deep natural port, which he named Burrard after one of his crew. Then he sailed away, not thinking twice about a place that would eventually be named after him.

As Spanish influence in the area waned over the next few years in favor of the more persistent British, explorers such as Simon Fraser and Alexander Mackenzie began mapping the region's interior, opening it up for overland travelers, the arrival of the legendary Hudson's Bay Company, and the eventual full entry of the region into the British Empire.

The Spanish landed here before the Brits. Captain José María Narváez named the shoreline stretch where he set foot Islas de Langara, now Spanish Banks. This early influence is reflected around the BC coastline, where islands are called Saturna, Galiano and Texada.

Gold Rush

In 1858 gold was discovered on the banks of the Fraser River, and more than 25,000 shiny-eyed prospectors rapidly swept in. To maintain order and control, the mainland officially became part of the British Empire at this time. James Douglas was sworn in as the governor of the region, which included Vancouver Island. In a proclamation at Fort Langley on November 19, 1858, British Columbia officially came into being.

The first lumber mills were set up along the Fraser River in 1860, and their logging operations cleared the land for farms across the region. It wasn't long before operators began chewing northward through the trees toward Burrard Inlet. In 1867 Edward Stamp's British-financed

1792
The Brits join the party when Royal Navy Captain George Vancouver sails into Burrard Inlet. He stays just 24 hours before setting sail again.

1827
The Hudson's Bay Company builds Fort Langley, the first European settlement to grace the region.

1858
Gold is discovered on the banks of the Fraser River, prompting more than 25,000 prospectors to arrive with picks and pans. Most leave empty-handed.

1867
'Gassy' Jack Deighton rows in with a barrel of whiskey and some big ideas. He opens a saloon, and a small, thirsty settlement, called Gastown, springs up near the entrance.

Hastings Mill, on the south shore of the inlet, established the starting point of a town that would eventually become Vancouver.

With the promise of access to a new national railway network, BC joined the Canadian Confederation in 1871. It would be another 16 years before the railway actually rolled into the region.

Among the reminders of early Vancouver are Kitsilano's Old Hastings Mill Store Museum and Gassy Jack's statue in Maple Tree Sq. The Byrnes Block, the oldest Vancouver building still in its original location, recalls the city's swift reconstruction after the 1886 Great Fire.

The City's Boozy Start

In 1867 Englishman 'Gassy' Jack Deighton rowed into Burrard Inlet with his First Nations wife, a small dog and a barrel of whiskey. He knew the nearest drink for thirsty mill workers was 20km away so he asked them to help him build a tavern. Within 24 hours the Globe Saloon was in business. And when a village sprang up around the establishment it was quickly dubbed 'Gastown.' In 1870, in an attempt to formalize the ramshackle township, the colonial administration renamed it 'Granville,' although almost everyone still called it Gastown.

Selected over Port Moody, a rival mill town, as the new western railway terminus for the Canadian Pacific Railway (CPR), the town of Granville was incorporated as the City of Vancouver in April 1886. According to legend, this name was chosen by CPR manager William Van Horne, who reasoned the new city needed a grand moniker to live up to its future as a great metropolis. He is said to have selected the name 'Vancouver' to recall the historic seafarer who literally put the area on the map.

The first piece of business for Vancouver's new council was to establish the city's first park – and so Stanley Park was born. But the city faced a less enjoyable task at the tender age of two months: on June 13, 1886, a fire lit by CPR workers to clear brush rapidly spread out of control. The 'Great Fire,' as it came to be known, took 45 minutes to destroy Vancouver's 1000 wooden structures, killing as many as 28 people (the number remains disputed) and leaving 3000 homeless.

Within hours, reconstruction was underway. But this time the buildings were fashioned from stone and brick. A few months later, on May 23, 1887, Locomotive 374 pulled the first transcontinental passenger train into the city and Vancouver was back in business. Within four years it grew to a population of 13,000, and between 1891 and 1901 the population skyrocketed to more than double that.

Locomotive 374 pulled the first transcontinental passenger train into Vancouver, but was left to rot on a local beach for decades after its retirement. A long-overdue campaign to restore it culminated in its unveiling in a purpose-built Yaletown home in time for Expo '86.

Growing Pains

The railway was responsible for shaping much of the city as it exists today, with the CPR developing several key neighborhoods for new residential developments. During the first 30 years of the 20th century, the suburbs around the city also grew substantially. When Point Grey

1871

With the promise of access to a new national railway network, BC joins the Canadian Confederation. Sixteen years later, the railway rolls into the region.

1886

The fledgling town is incorporated as the City of Vancouver. Within weeks, the new city burns to the ground in just 45 minutes. No one is pleased.

1887

Locomotive 374 pulls the first transcontinental passenger train into a rebuilt Vancouver, and the town is back in business.

1901

First Nations communities, who have lived here for thousands of years, are displaced from their settlements in the Vanier Park area, as colonials fell forests.

and South Vancouver amalgamated with the city in 1929, Vancouver became Canada's third-largest city – a ranking it retains today.

While the 1930s Great Depression saw the construction of several public works – the Marine Building, Vancouver City Hall, the third and present Hotel Vancouver and the Lions Gate Bridge, to name a few – many people were unemployed, as was the case throughout Canada. This marked a time of large demonstrations, violent riots and public discontent.

WWII helped to pull Vancouver out of the Depression by creating instant jobs at shipyards, aircraft-parts factories and canneries, and in construction with the building of rental units for the increased workforce. Japanese Canadians didn't fare so well. In 1942, following the bombing of Pearl Harbor, they were shipped to internment camps and had to endure the confiscation of their land and property, much of which was never returned.

Chinese, Japanese and First Nations people were finally given the provincial vote in 1949.

Expo-Sing the City

By the start of the 1950s, Vancouver's population was 345,000 and the area was thriving. The high-rise craze hit in the middle of the decade, mostly in the West End. During the next 13 years, 220 apartment buildings went up – and up – in this area alone.

In the 1960s and '70s, Vancouver was known for its counterculture community, centered on Kitsilano. Canada's gay-rights movement began here in 1964 when a group of feminists and academics started the Association for Social Knowledge, the country's first gay and lesbian discussion group. In 1969 the Don't Make a Wave Committee formed to stop US nuclear testing in Alaska, sending a protest vessel to the region in 1971. A few years later, the group morphed into the environmental organization Greenpeace.

As the years passed, the city's revolutionary fervor dissipated and economic development became the region's main pastime. Nothing was more important to Vancouver in the 1980s than Expo '86, the world fair that many regard as the city's coming of age. The six-month event, coinciding with Vancouver's 100th birthday, brought millions of visitors to the city and kick-started a rash of regeneration in several tired neighborhoods. New facilities built for Expo included the 60,000-seat BC Place Stadium, which has since played a starring role in the opening and closing ceremonies of the 2010 Olympic and Paralympic Winter Games.

Marking its 75th birthday in 2013, the Lions Gate Bridge was officially opened, a year after its 1938 completion, by King George VI and Queen Elizabeth, who were on a cross-Canada tour.

1949

The region's Chinese, Japanese and First Nations peoples eventually gain the right to vote in provincial elections.

1956

The West End is rezoned for greater population density. Hundreds of wooden homes are bulldozed for apartment blocks.

1964

Canada's gay-rights movement begins when feminists and academics create the Association for Social Knowledge, the country's first gay and lesbian discussion group.

1979

Granville Island is developed from an industrial wasteland into one of Vancouver's most popular hangouts. A cement factory remains to keep the faith.

Multicultural Milestones

The brewing issue of First Nations land rights spilled over in the late 1980s, with a growing number of rallies, road blockades and court actions in the region. Aside from a few treaties covering a tiny portion of the province, land-claim agreements had not been signed and no clear definition of the scope and nature of First Nations rights existed. Until 1990 the provincial government refused to participate in treaty negotiations. That changed in December of that year when the BC Claims Task Force was formed among the Canadian and BC governments and the First Nations Summit with a mission to figure out how the three parties could solve land-rights matters. It has been a slow-moving, ongoing process that in Vancouver's case involves the Tsawwassen, Tsleil-Waututh, Katzie, Squamish and Musqueam nations.

The 1990s saw the region become even more multicultural. Prior to the British handover of Hong Kong to China in 1997, tens of thousands of wealthy Hong Kong Chinese migrated to BC's Lower Mainland area, boosting the area's permanent Asian population by about 85% and creating the largest Asian population in any North American city. Real-estate prices rose, with Vancouver's cost-of-living figures suddenly rivaling those of London, Paris and Tokyo. Many of the new arrivals shunned the city proper in favor of the suburbs, especially Richmond. By 1998 immigration had tapered off but the city's transformation into a modern, multicultural mecca was already complete. By then, about 40% of Vancouver residents were foreign-born, and an ethnic smorgasbord of restaurants, stores and cultural activities had emerged, solidifying the worldly reputation the city earned by hosting Expo '86.

A few steps from Chinatown's Millennium Gate, Shanghai Alley was once home to hundreds of immigrant Chinese men, domiciled in cheap lodgings. With its own shops, eateries and 500-seat theater, it was designed as a one-way street that could be defended in the event of attack from locals.

Going for Gold

In the opening decade of the new millennium, Vancouver became a regular on those global surveys that designate the best places in the world to live. Seizing the initiative and recalling the success of Expo '86, the region again looked to the future, winning the bid to host the 2010 Olympic and Paralympic Winter Games.

With events staged in and around the city, and also at Whistler, a global TV audience of more than two billion gazed admiringly at picture-perfect snow-and-blue-sky vistas, while athletes from 80 countries competed for gold. And while many locals had grumbled about the cost of the Games, the entire city exploded in a 17-day mardi gras of support that surprised even the organizers.

Upwards of 200,000 Maple Leaf–waving partiers hit the streets around Robson and Granville Sts every night to hang out with overseas visitors, catch LiveSite music shows and break into impromptu rendi-

The 2010 Olympics saw a record haul of Canadian medals, but it wasn't just athletes who were popular with the crowds. Among several merchandise-friendly mascots introduced by organizers, Quatchi the gigantic but ever-cuddly sasquatch, was far and away the biggest hit.

1983

BC Place Stadium polishes its roof and opens for business, and the old courthouse building is transformed into the Vancouver Art Gallery.

1985

The first SkyTrain line opens, creating a link between the communities of New Westminster and Vancouver.

1986

The international spotlight shines on Vancouver as the Expo '86 world fair dominates the summer, bringing Sheena Easton and Depeche Mode to local stages.

1996

With the Hong Kong handover to China imminent, Vancouver sees a massive influx of Asian immigrants into the city. Richmond transforms into the region's new Chinatown.

tions of the national anthem. This all-enveloping Canadian pride hit fever pitch during the men's gold medal hockey game, when the host nation beat the US with a dream-like last-gasp goal. For many Vancouverites, this moment was the best thing that's ever happened in the city's short modern history.

Gentrification

After the Olympics, a new wave of development took hold in the city, especially in those areas that had traditionally seen little change in decades past. One such controversial neighborhood in particular was suddenly part of these new plans.

Long-blighted by drugs, prostitution and a concentration of mentally ill residents, the Downtown Eastside – centered on Main and Hastings Sts – had been a no-go skid row for many years. While nearby Gastown was the historic genesis of the city, the key streets of the Downtown Eastside were also once lined with the banks, shops and bustling commercial enterprises of the region's main business district. When new development shifted the city center across to the Robson and Granville Sts area of downtown in the 1940s, though, this old 'hood began a graceless decline. City and provincial policies that concentrated services for the poor and homeless in the area didn't help, with squalid rooming houses and dodgy pubs soon becoming standard fixtures.

Politicians have made regular pronouncements about solving the area's problems since the 1990s. Current mayor Gregor Robinson has claimed he will end homelessness across the city by 2015, and a new wave of gentrification is finally changing the neighborhood. The opening of a large, new housing, shops and university-campus complex on the old Woodward's department-store site in 2009 was the catalyst for change, with new businesses recolonizing the area's paint-peeled storefronts for the first time in decades.

The gentrification drive is not without controversy, though. While city hipsters move into pricey loft apartments and populate exposed-brick coffee shops, the residents who have called this area home for the last few decades are feeling threatened and increasingly marginalized. In 2013 antigentrification protesters began picketing new restaurants in the area and appealing for more social housing to be part of all future plans. Finding the right balance between rampant development and support for the people who already live in the city's Eastside will be one of Vancouver's biggest challenges over the coming years.

For decades a neon-lit 'W' stood atop the old Woodward's department store. But when the building was redeveloped it was found to be severely corroded. A new one was created in its place, while the old one was preserved in a glass case at ground level.

2003

BC and Ontario lead North America by making same-sex marriage legal. Vancouver becomes a hotspot for elopements.

2010

Locals party as Vancouver hosts the Olympic and Paralympic Winter Games. Flags are waved, national anthems sung and Canada wins gold in hockey.

2011

Vancouver celebrates its 125th birthday, but the party doesn't quite match that of the Olympics.

2013

Decades after Vancouver's Brewery Creek lost its last independent brewery, new craft-beer makers begin popping up in the neighborhood.

Food & Drink

The height of fine dining in Vancouver used to be an overdone steak with exotic prawn cocktail starter. But the past decade has seen a culinary sea change. It began when international influences imported by immigrants from around the world swept across the restaurant scene. The next development was closer to home: Vancouver and the rest of British Columbia (BC) is currently undergoing a golden age of farm-to-table cuisine, transforming local restaurant menus with a taste-bud-popping cornucopia of unique regional flavors.

What Is West Coast Dining?

Eating local used to be about cheapskates growing produce in their own backyards, but now you'll find restaurants at the highest levels eager to boast that their ingredients come from just down the road. The movement has even transformed the 'West Coast dining' label itself. Once lazily applied to humdrum salmon dinners available at innumerable restaurants, it's been revitalized as a dining category and now signifies amazing dishes showcasing the rich variety of ingredients grown, foraged, fished and raised around the province. Finally, West Coast dining is something worth drooling over. But what does the label actually mean?

Vancouver Cookbooks

Gorilla Food: Living and Eating Organic, Vegan and Raw (Aaron Ash)

Fresh (John Bishop)

Flavours of the West Coast (Steve Walker-Duncan)

West Coast dining is the Canadian arm of the Pacific Northwest dining scene, which covers Oregon, Washington and BC. Vancouverites generally don't call what they eat 'Pacific Northwest dining' because they consider themselves West Coast Canadians rather than citizens of the Pacific Northwest, which is more often regarded as a US region. The key point, though, is that Pacific Northwest and West Coast Canadian cuisine take the same approach: local dishes that celebrate the region's natural bounty.

In Vancouver this bounty typically includes seafood and shellfish, as well as duck, chicken, lamb and pork raised at farms around the Lower Mainland and beyond. In the way of vegetables, West Coast dishes often include seasonal local favorites such as foraged mushrooms and locally farmed potatoes, squash and heirloom tomatoes. Many of Vancouver's West Coast restaurants include international influences in their dishes – salmon with a miso-flavored sauce, for example – while typical West Coast ingredients on tables around the city include juicy halibut from Haida Gwaii, velvet-soft lamb shank from Salt Spring Island and free-range duck or chicken from the Fraser Valley. Desserts often feature seasonal local fruit including cherries, peaches, blueberries and apples, and cheese plates are rich in piquant treats from farm producers across the region, including favorites such as Agassiz's Farmhouse Natural Cheese and Salt Spring Island's Moonstruck Organic Cheese.

Seafood

Don't tell Atlantic Canada, but BC is the nation's seafood capital and Vancouver arguably has the country's best marine-loving restaurants. A trip here that doesn't include face-planting into Canada's brimming aquatic larder is like visiting New York without having a slice of pizza: you can do it but why would you want to? The abundance of fresh fish here is the main reason Vancouver has the best sushi scene outside Japan, as well as being home to a full menu of Chinese restaurants that are simply falling over themselves to feature everything from fresh crab to local-caught geoduck (pronounced 'gooey duck'), a giant saltwater clam that's a delicacy in Chinese dining and is even shipped from here to chefs across the world.

But the region's seafood surfeit isn't only a feature of the city's ethnic dining scene. Vancouver's West Coast eateries almost always feature seasonal catches. Buttery wild salmon is a signature dish that dominates autumn menus – this is something not to be missed. Almost as popular is the early spring spot prawn; in season these sweet, crunchy critters turn up on tables across the city. And keep your appetite primed for delicious scallops and crab. If you fancy meeting the fishers and choosing some grub straight off the back of their boats, head to Granville Island and the nearby Fisherman's Wharf. Alternatively, take a trip to Richmond's Steveston village: the boats bobbling alongside the boardwalk there sell fresh catch, while local museums recall the area's days as the home of the once-mighty regional fishing fleet. Not surprisingly, Steveston is also a good spot for excellent fish and chips. Back in Vancouver, head to Yaletown for some of the city's best and most sophisticated West Coast seafood dining.

Food Magazines

Eat Magazine (www.eatmagazine.ca)

City Food (www.cityfood.com)

Edible Vancouver (www.ediblecommunities.com/vancouver)

Carnivores to Herbivores

From Gelderman Farms' pork from Abbotsford to free-range eggs laid at Rabbit River Farm in Richmond, you'll find restaurants across the city making strong farm-to-table claims by directly naming local producers on their menus. But while Vancouverites are increasingly keen to know where their food is coming from, dining off local producers isn't just about food security. The quality and flavor of BC-sourced ingredients is also top-notch and is alone reason enough for eating local. Sinking your teeth into a burger made from Pemberton Valley beef is an eye-rollingly tasty meal, while a rich dish of slow-cooked pork belly from the Fraser Valley is silkily addictive. Look for great meat-loving West Coast dining options in Gastown, downtown and on Granville Island.

An interesting offshoot of the local West Coast noshing scene is also benefiting vegetarians. Local veggies and vegans used to be limited to gloomily tucking into heaping bowls of mung beans here, but the farm-to-table renaissance has not only delivered great sides for meat and fish

MEET YOUR MAKER

Ask Vancouverites where the food on their tables comes from and some will confidently tell you about the Fraser Valley. This lush interior region starts about 50km from the city and has been studded with busy farms for decades. In recent years, farmers and the people they feed have started to get to know one another on a series of five **Circle Farm Tours**. These self-guided driving tours take you around the communities of Langley, Abbotsford, Chilliwack, Agassiz & Harrison Mills and Maple Ridge & Pitt Meadows, pointing out recommended pit stops – farms, markets, wineries and dining suggestions – along the way.

One of the most popular excursions – especially for wine lovers – is the Langley tour, which starts at **Vista D'oro Farms and Winery**, a welcoming family-run operation specializing in seasonal preserves that are sold in Vancouver and beyond. Go for their blackberry jam plus a bottle of fortified walnut wine, made from nuts grown right here on the farm. Vista D'Oro is only one of several wineries in the Langley region. On this Circle Farms Tour, also check out the bucolic vineyards and warming tasting room at **Domaine de Chaberton Winery** or compare locally made fruit wines at **Krause Berry Farms & Estate Winery** with the cranberry-focused tipples at **Fort Wine Company**.

Maps for all City Farm Tours routes can be downloaded free at www.circlefarmtour.ca.

eaters but has inspired a mini-wave of tasty new vegetarian restaurants around the city, many of them successfully luring and satisfying carnivorous diners as well. Look for some of these new veggie hot spots on Main St, in South Granville and on Kitsilano's West 4th Ave. And don't forget the city's food-truck scene: some of Vancouver's surfeit of 100-plus mobile food vendors have a strong focus on West Coast seasonal produce.

Drink & Be Merry

BC's locavore movement doesn't begin and end with what's on your plate. The drive for area-made treats also extends to drink. Wine kick-started the local trend around 20 years ago when vineyards started popping up in the Okanagan region in the BC interior. Now rivaling Ontario's Niagara as Canada's leading wine area, the Okanagan's success has sparked smaller winery regions across the province, from the Fraser Valley to Vancouver Island. You'll find some BC wine on the majority of restaurant menus – look out for tipples by Burrowing Owl, Quail's Gate and Nk'Mip Cellars, a celebrated First Nations–owned winery.

This thriving wine industry has paved the way for another local scene to develop. From just a handful of producers 10 years ago, BC now has more than 40 microbreweries and is arguably the craft-beer capital of Canada. Pent-up demand from Vancouver drinkers, fed up with years of generic beer, has been such that almost everywhere in the city now has at least a few BC brews to sample. Ask for anything local and you'll likely be pleasantly surprised. Province-based brewers to look out for include Driftwood and Phillips from Victoria, Crannog from Sorrento, Howe Sound Brewing from Squamish and Central City Brewing from Surrey.

Vancouver itself is on the cusp of a new age of hyperlocal beer making. Alongside city-made faves such as Storm Brewing and R&B Brewing, a new wave of local microbreweries and nanobreweries are opening, many with tasting rooms. Look out for Powell Street Craft Brewing, Parallel 49, 33 Acres and Brassneck Brewery. And if you can't make it to the maker, just head to the bars of Gastown, Main St or Commercial Dr, where you'll find a full round of craft brews at many neighborhood bars.

And don't forget the hard stuff. The success of wine and beer makers has also sparked a small but growing craft distilling sector. The sign of a maturing own-made-booze region, the top-notch products from Victoria Spirits (go for their excellent dry gin) to Pemberton Distillery (ultra-smooth potato vodka) are available at discerning bars around the city. And, like the beer scene, Vancouver's own-made distillers are just starting to emerge as well.

SIDEWALK DINING

Vancouver's sidewalk dining revolution started mid-2010 with the introduction of 17 diverse food trucks across the city. Suddenly, barbecued pulled pork, fresh fish tacos and Korean-fusion takeout were available to hungry locals. There are now more than 100 trucks on streets around the city.

Festivals & Events

In summer Vancouver is teeming with farmers markets, highly recommended for their great local produce. They also offer a chance to get out and meet food-loving Vancouverites. Additional events happen throughout the year for those who time their visit well. January's Dine Out Vancouver delivers discount restaurant meals at restaurants around the city, meaning you can sample some top fare for a good-value price; May's Spot Prawn Festival is a chance to hang out at Fisherman's Wharf and stuff your face with the first of the season's catch; June's Vancouver Craft Beer Week is a multiday extravaganza of burp-triggering tastings and parties; February's Vancouver International Wine Festival does the same for wine; September's Feast of Fields showcases local produce and top chefs at an alfresco one-day party; and October's UBC Apple Festival brings a bounty of varieties to the city for a weekend-long family-friendly event – don't miss the apple tastings or the stand hawking huge, fresh-baked slices of pie.

Green Vancouver

It's hard to see Vancouver as anything but a green city: its dense forests and verdant, rain-fed plant life make nature an ever-present fact of life here. But beyond the breathtaking visuals, how does the city measure up to its environmental responsibilities? And – just as importantly – what can a Vancouver-bound visitor do to reduce their own eco-footprint in the region without turning their vacation into a monastic, fun-free zone?

Painting the Town Green

Vancouver has an international reputation for being a green city, but that doesn't mean everyone here wears biodegradable socks and eats only elderly vegetables that have died of natural causes. In fact, if you stroll the Robson St boutiques or dip into a takeout coffee shop, it's easy to think that 'green Vancouver' doesn't exist at all. As with many of the city's best features, you have to do a little digging.

Vancouver has an active plan to be the world's greenest city by 2020. Among its raft of goals, the city aims to drastically cut waste and carbon emissions as well as improve regional ecosystems.

Given the city's breathtaking natural surroundings, it was just a matter of time before Vancouver's residents were inspired to protect the planet, which explains why a few of them began gathering in a Kitsilano basement in 1969 to plan the fledgling Don't Make a Wave Committee's first protest against nuclear testing in Alaska. By the time their campaign boat entered the Gulf of Alaska in 1971, they had renamed themselves Greenpeace and sailed into environmental history. Greenpeace set the tone, and the city has since become a headquarters for environmental groups from the Wilderness Committee to Farm Folk City Folk and the David Suzuki Foundation.

Actions speak louder than words, however, and Vancouver's green scene is not just about protest and discussion. The city is home to dozens of large and small eco-initiatives, enabling many locals to color their lives as green as they choose. Vancouver has one of the largest hybrid-vehicle taxi fleets in North America and has a commitment to mass public transportation, including electric trolley buses and a light-rail train system. Carpooling is also big, with the Jack Bell Foundation's ride-share scheme (www.rideshare.com) matching travelers with shared vehicle trips throughout the region. In construction, the green potential of any design project is always part of the plan here. And while developers tout their green credentials as if they're saving the planet single-handed, few of the new towers are built without key environmental considerations.

Vancouver is also a leader in 'green roofs' – planted rooftops that curb wasted energy through natural evaporation in summer and natural insulation in winter. The Shangri-La Hotel tower and Vancouver's landmark, Colosseum-shaped central library building have these, as does the giant convention center West Building next to Canada Place: it's a shaggy grass covering that looks like it could use a hungry goat or two to keep it in shape. In addition, many city restaurants and food stores are now bringing British Columbia (BC) seafood, meat, vegetables and even beer to the tables and kitchens of city diners from just a few kilometers away, vastly reducing the 'food miles' attached to them.

On the Ground

Several Vancouver accommodation options have some kind of environmental program. Opus Hotel, for example, has a water and energy conservation scheme; the Fairmont Hotel Vancouver deploys energy-efficient lighting and purchases green power for its property; and the Listel Hotel has installed its own power-generating solar panels.

Dining is also firmly on the green agenda. Spearheaded by the Vancouver Aquarium and a growing menu of city restaurants, Ocean Wise (www.oceanwise.ca) encourages sustainable fish and shellfish supplies that minimize environmental impact. The website lists participating restaurants; check local menus for symbols indicating Ocean Wise dishes. A similar, smaller movement called the Green Table Network (www.greentable.net) can help you identify considerate area restaurants that try to source all their supplies – not just seafood – from sustainable, mostly local sources.

Sustainability also has a social side in Vancouver with Green Drinks (www.greendrinks.org), a monthly drop-in gathering for anyone interested in environmental issues. The meetings take place at Gastown's Steamworks Brewing Company bar and usually attract more than 100 regulars for beer-fueled discussions on alternative energy, global warming and the sky-high price of organic groceries. Speaking of groceries, there are lots of sustainable-food shopping options around the city, but the area's farmers markets are the ideal way to eat well and do your bit for the world. See www.eatlocal.org for listings of several area markets.

Consider hopping on two wheels to get around the city. Vancouver has more than 300km of designated bike lanes, so you can see the sights without burning up the planet. Bike rentals are easy to come by and many operators can get you out for a citywide pedal. The city is also working to introduce a public bike-share scheme similar to those in London and Montreal, due to launch early 2014.

Great Green Attractions

- *Stanley Park (p52)*
- *Lost Lagoon Nature House (p53)*
- *UBC Botanical Garden (p166)*
- *Lynn Canyon Park & Ecology Centre (p179)*
- *Vancouver Compost Demonstration Garden (p166)*

Tree Hugging

It's hard not to be impressed by the towering Douglas firs in Stanley Park or the cherry blossom trees that bloom around the city in spring. But for many, fall is the best time to hang out with the trees. Burnished copper, pumpkin-orange, deep candy-apple red: the seemingly infinite colors of autumn under cloudless blue skies make this the fave time of year for many Vancouverites, and it's one of the rare times you'll see locals reaching for their cameras. If you're here in October, charge up your camera, slip into comfortable walking shoes and hunt down the following pigment-popping locations.

NEWEST GREEN ATTRACTION

North Vancouver's Grouse Mountain offers great views over the city, shimmering by the water far below, and recently this became even better (or at least higher). The outdoor attraction has added a 20-story wind turbine tower. Visitors can take an elevator to a glass-encased viewing pod at the top of the turbine, halting just 3m away from the giant, moving blades. The view, to say the least, is spectacular and it's a rare opportunity to see wind turbines in action. The power generated by the turbines is fed into the system at Grouse and helps to power the mountain-top complex. Once you've snapped your photos, stick around: in summer you can walk Grouse's alpine trails and visit the grizzly bear sanctuary, while in winter you can hit the snowy slopes. It's a perfect way to touch base with the outdoors without having to travel far from the city.

ECO SAVINGS

Green-minded travelers who want to save the planet and save a few bucks should consider picking up a Greenster book (www.greenster.com). The bulging coupon book – available online or via the businesses listed on their website – costs $29 and offers deals and discounts at eco-minded shops, spas, restaurants and attractions around the region.

Make a beeline for Stanley Park. Hit the seawall – by bike or on foot – to find rusty amber hues and Japanese maple reds studding the evergreen Douglas firs. If you don't have time for a full-on Stanley Park jaunt, weave towards nearby English Bay. The beach at the end of Denman St will require your camera's panorama setting. You'll find a glittering, gently rippling waterfront, backed by a stand of achingly beautiful mature trees, each seemingly a different color. Not surprisingly, this is also a great location for sunset shots. If it's raining, nip into the lounge bar of the nearby ivy-shrouded Sylvia Hotel: it faces the water, so you'll still have a great view.

Across town at Queen Elizabeth Park, weave uphill among the trees from the Cambie St entrance. Aim towards the Bloedel Conservatory dome at the summit for a spectacular squirrel's-eye view across the foliage. On a fine day, you'll also have one of the best wide-angled vistas over the glass-towered city, framed by ice-frosted mountains. And if it's time to warm up? Nip inside the Conservatory where the tropical plants and neon-bright birds are guaranteed to give your day a splash of extra color.

It's not all parks, of course. Many of Vancouver's older residential neighborhoods resemble spilled paintboxes of color every fall. The West End neighborhood is striped with residential streets where fall-flavored trees mix with bright-painted heritage houses: on a honey-lit, sunshine-steeped day, you can hear the photographers clicking madly here. One of the best spots is Mt Pleasant's 10th Ave, especially in the section running east from City Hall. Like a walk-through kaleidoscope, the dozens of century-old chestnut trees here create a tunnel of rich orange and yellow – above a dense carpet of fallen chestnuts that's like walking on shiny cobbles.

Every year, typically in June, Vancouver hosts Epic (www.epicfest.ca), a weekend-long sustainable-living fair. The popular event includes food, workshops, live music and features some engaging speakers. There's also a marketplace of lifestyle products for greenies looking for everything from hemp shoes to eco make-up.

At the Grassroots

Many Vancouver green initiatives are at the grassroots community level and one of our favorites is the city's Pop-Up Library phenomenon. Several neighborhoods across Vancouver have built their own pop-up minilibraries for all to use. These free-to-use book exchanges sit outside on residential streets, covered of course to stop the dog-eared tomes suffering on Vancouver's frequent rainy days. There are at least five dotted around local communities. One of the largest is the St George Sharing Library, a double-shelved covered table a few steps from the intersection of East 10th Ave and St George St. It's always bulging with well-used paperbacks from pulp fiction to self-published screeds on communism and the occasional Lonely Planet guidebook.

Vancouver's City Farm Boy (www.cityfarmboy.com) uses tiny, often forgotten green spaces to grow fruit and vegetables right on people's doorsteps, turning urban residents' unloved and unused garden plots into mini produce-growing areas for everything from carrots, lettuce and beans to chard, rhubarb and garlic.

Vancouver recently introduced a pilot scheme to support the use of plug-in electric vehicles. The initiative, the first of its kind in BC, has seen the introduction of car-charging ports at parking lots around the city. Charging costs $1 per hour.

CHRISTOPHER HERWIG / GETTY IMAGES ©

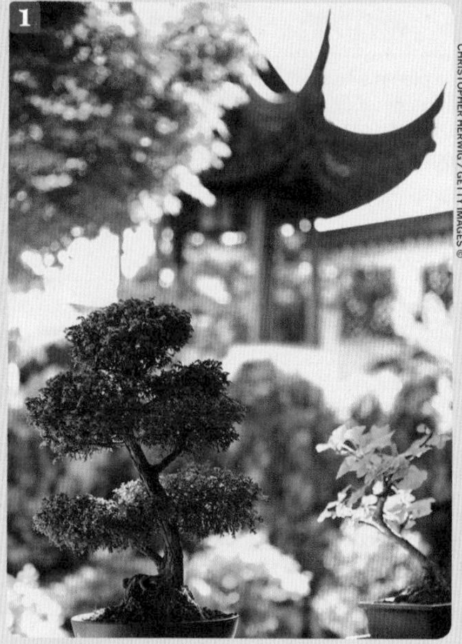

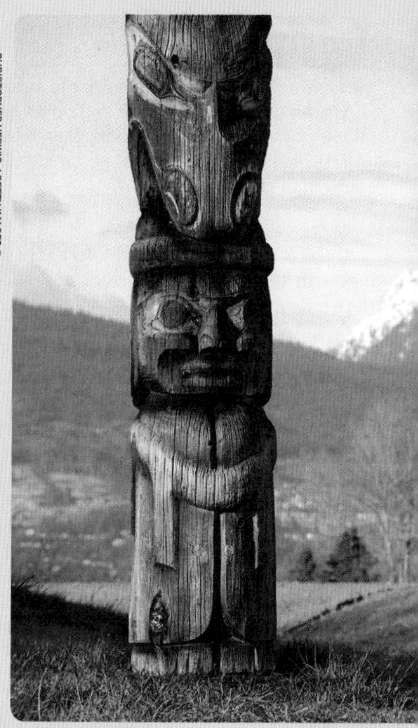

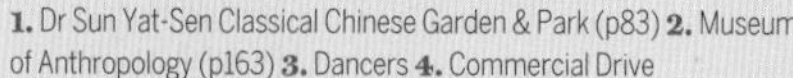

1. Dr Sun Yat-Sen Classical Chinese Garden & Park (p83) **2.** Museum of Anthropology (p163) **3.** Dancers **4.** Commercial Drive

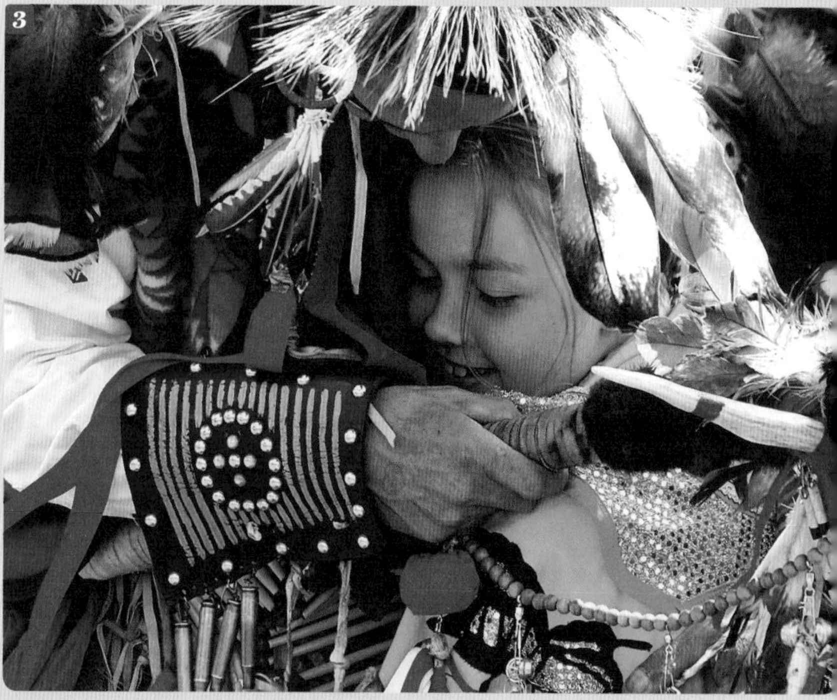

2

CHRISTIAN KOBER / GETTY IMAGES ©

Multicultural Vancouver

Long-regarded as Canada's most multicultural metropolis, Vancouver offers uncountable ways to dive into the food, traditions and artistic side of nations near and far. For many visitors, this rich international accessibility is a highlight of their trip.

Festivals

From giant Chinese New Year parades to grass-roots events such as Greek Day, Italian Day, Caribbean Days Festival and the Japanese-themed Powell Street Festival, it's hard not get swept up in Vancouver's heady mix of great cultural events. Dive right in, and be sure to eat as much as you can.

Chinatown

Canada's largest historic Chinatown is as vibrant as ever. But it's not just about the visuals of dragon-topped street lamps and terracotta-tiled heritage buildings. The bustling grocery stores show that this neighborhood is grounded in tradition, while its newly reinvented summertime night market indicates it's still evolving.

4

Aboriginal Art

The region's first inhabitants have a rich heritage of creativity, which visitors have many opportunities to discover. From thrilling carvings at UBC's Museum of Anthropology to a stunning collection at the Bill Reid Gallery of Northwest Coast Art, you'll also find aboriginal public art studding the streets and buildings around the city.

Commercial Drive

Coffee is a way of life on the Drive, where generations of Italian families have been serving the city's best java since arriving in the 1950s. Here you'll find elderly Italian grandparents rubbing shoulders with hipsters; they're all after the same thing – that perfect cup to see them through the day.

1

J. A. KRAULIS / GETTY IMAGES ©

2

4

MICHAEL WHEATLEY / GETTY IMAGES ©

1. Stanley Park (p52)
This 400-hectare woodland is studded with nature trails, beaches and a plethora of picnic spots – look out for scavenging raccoons.

2. Mt Seymour Provincial Park (p179)
One of Vancouver's three main winter playgrounds, this giant tree-lined park is also suffused with more than a dozen summertime hiking trails.

3. Salt Tasting Room, Gastown (p91)
Atmospheric Gastown is home to many of the best bars in the city, making it an ideal spot for an evening aperitif.

4. Coal Harbour Seawall (p59)
The seawall makes an idyllic waterfront stroll from Canada Place to Stanley Park; the perfect way to spend a sunny afternoon.

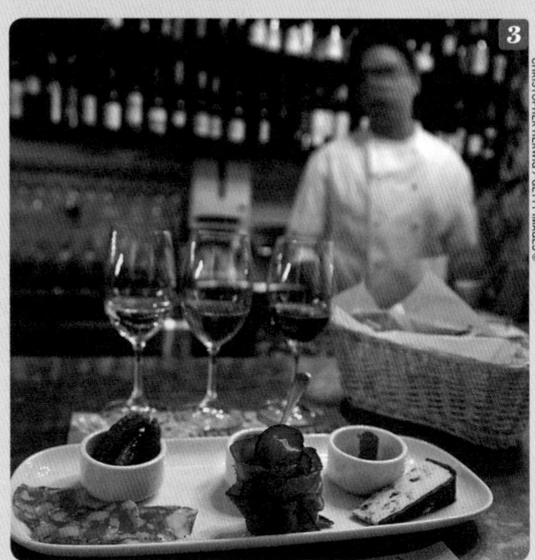

CHRISTOPHER HERWIG / GETTY IMAGES ©

Arts & Culture

It's easy to think Vancouver's outdoorsy locals must be philistines when it comes to arty pursuits – how can mountain bikers be interested in galleries, dance and literature, you might ask? But in reality, this city by the sea is a major Canadian cultural capital. With a little digging, visitors will be able to tap into the primarily grassroots scene. Ask the locals for tips and pick up a copy of the free, weekly *Georgia Straight*. You'll be fully rewarded for your efforts.

Look out for paintings by Emily Carr (1871–1945). Regarded as Canada's first major female artist, she painted swirling, nature-themed canvases depicting the West Coast landscape. The Vancouver Art Gallery has a large collection. Other local art legends include painters Jack Shadbolt and EJ Hughes, and photographer Fred Herzog.

Visual Arts

British Columbia (BC) is strongly identified with three main forms of visual arts, and each is well represented in galleries and public spaces throughout Vancouver. Historic and contemporary aboriginal works are displayed at unique institutions such as the UBC Museum of Anthropology and downtown's Bill Reid Gallery of Northwest Coast Art; contemporary painting and photoconceptualism (often called the 'Vancouver School' of photography) are exhibited at the Vancouver Art Gallery and the many spaces located in the Flats, an emerging new gallery district just off Main St; finally, the city's neighborhoods are studded with intriguing public art installations – see www.vancouver.ca/publicart for locations and look out for the next Vancouver Biennale, a showcase of outdoor public art staged every two years. For further information on the local art scene, visit www.art-bc.com.

It's the outdoor public-art scene that captures the attention (and the cameras) of many Vancouverites. The city has a fascination for dressing its streets with artworks, look out for the series of smiling, oversized bronze figures near the shoreline of English Bay, which form one of Canada's most-photographed public artworks; the towering neon cross near East Vancouver's Commercial Dr; and let's not forget the poodle sculpture on Main St, which even has its own Twitter account. *Public Art in Vancouver: Angels Among Lions* (by John Steil and Aileen Stalker) is a handy guide to the hundreds of works around the city, so you can plot your own chin-rubbing walking tour. Even Vancouver International Airport is worthy of a photographic snap or two for its visual art: between the international and US check-in desks, the hulking, magnificent bronze *Spirit of Haida Gwaii* by Bill Reid is the terminal's focal point and also its main meeting spot.

Vancouver provides plenty of opportunity to meet some of the region's creative types face to face. November's excellent weekend-long Eastside Culture Crawl (p93) is when hundreds of East Vancouver artists open their studios large and small for locals to wander around. It's arguably the best art event in the city, and it's a firm local favorite.

Performance Arts

Vancouver has a strong reputation for stage performance and is especially well represented in dance and live theater.

Second only to Montréal as a hotbed of contemporary Canadian dance, Vancouver is home to dozens of professional companies. The Dance Centre

RIOTOUS ARTWORK

Look for the large London Drugs shop in the Woodward's (p82) building on W Hastings St and enter the building's courtyard, carved from what was originally the interior of one of the city's largest department stores. The space is now dominated by one of Vancouver's most evocative public artworks. Measuring 15m by 9m and created by Stan Douglas, *Abbott & Cordova, 7 August 1971* is a mammoth black-and-white photo montage depicting a key moment in the history of local social protest: the night when police in full riot gear broke up a pro-marijuana smoke-in being staged in the Downtown Eastside. The action – the image shows mounted police pushing against unarmed locals and miscreants being stuffed into police wagons – soon spiraled out of control, with pitched battles and general chaos triggering a siege-like atmosphere on the area's streets. Later, the event became known as the 'Gastown Riot' and 'The Battle of Maple Tree Square.'

(p71) is the main twinkle-toes resource in the province. Its range of activities is unparalleled in Canada, including support for professional artists, operation of western Canada's flagship dance facility, and presentation of a huge number of programs and events for the public. Dance events are scheduled throughout the city, including the three-week-long Vancouver International Dance Festival in spring and the 10-day Dancing on the Edge event in July.

Despite losing its long-established Playhouse Theatre Company to a funding crisis in 2012, Vancouver is also home to a vibrant theater scene. But rather than one or two major theaters, you'll find dozens of smaller stages dotted around the city. The Arts Club Theatre Company (www.artsclub.com) is the city's largest theatrical troupe, and the host of fringe-like smaller venues and companies, include the Cultch (p126) and the Firehall Arts Centre (p95). Events-wise, plan your visit for the Bard on the Beach (p173) Shakespeare festival, the Vancouver International Fringe Festival (p112) or the PuSh International Performing Arts Festival (p20). And if you're a fan of alfresco shows, the outdoor Malkin Bowl in Stanley Park is home to the summer season Theatre Under the Stars (p71) troupe.

Pauline Johnson (1861–1913) is Vancouver's most famous poet. The daughter of a Mohawk chief and a middle-class Englishwoman, she recited her works dressed in traditional First Nations buckskin. Hugely popular, her funeral was the largest ever held in Vancouver at the time of her death, and there is a memorial to her in Stanley Park.

Literature

Vancouver is a highly bookish city, home to a healthy round of bookstores and a large volume of literary events to keep local and visiting bookworms fully enthralled. Among the city's favorite bookshop hangouts are Macleod's Books (p72) and Pulpfiction (p143), where stacks of used tomes invite cozy browsing on rainy days. If you really want to see how serious the city is about books, visit the landmark Vancouver Public Library, shaped like the Colosseum. There are plenty of ways to rub bookish shoulders with the locals at events that include poetry slams, the Word on the Street book and magazine festival and the Vancouver International Writers Festival (p24), where you're likely to run into every book lover in town.

Local authors past and present who have garnered international reputations include Douglas Coupland, William Gibson and Malcolm Lowry. Coupland is the city's most famous living author, with celebrated works including *Generation X*, *J-Pod* and his latest title: *Worst. Person. Ever.*

A strong nonfiction bent also exists within the local literary scene. Two local authors have produced back-to-back wins in Canada's prestigious Charles Taylor Prize for Literary Nonfiction in recent years. Charles Montgomery's *The Last Heathen: Encounters with Ghosts and*

Ancestors in Melanesia (later published around the world as *The Shark God*) led the way, followed by his colleague James Mackinnon who won for *Dead Man in Paradise*. Mackinnon also partnered with Alisa Smith to produce the best-selling *100-Mile Diet: A Year of Local Eating*, which charted their attempts to only consume food made from ultralocal ingredients.

The website of the BC Film Commission (www.bcfilmcommission.com) should be the first stop for anyone interested in working in the film industry in Vancouver. It gives the weekly lowdown on what's filming and who's in the cast and crew, and provides contact information for productions seeking extras.

Film

The movie industry has a starring role in Vancouver's 'Hollywood North' economy. True, not many stories are set here – and few know that *X-Men 2* and the *Twilight* series were filmed in metro Vancouver – but the industry is home to a couple of hundred productions every year. Vancouver's influential Vancouver Film School counts director/actor/screenwriter Kevin Smith (of *Clerks* fame) as its most famed alumnus, and actors who have moved on to global acclaim from the city include Seth Rogen, Ryan Reynolds and Michael J Fox. The city also has a growing reputation for postproduction special effects, with *Avatar*, *District 9* and *Life of Pi* using area studios for their whizz-bang enhancements.

Alongside a full range of local movie theaters, Vancouver is home to many niche film festivals staged in the city throughout the year, and the giant Vancouver International Film Festival (p24) is one of the city's most popular annual cultural events. Second only to Toronto's film festival in size, it's a 17-day showcase of great flicks from Canada and around the world. The city also nurtures budding filmmakers through the likes of the Celluloid Social Club; held monthly at the Anza Club near Main St, it's a hangout for aspiring movie creatives and is open to all comers.

Music

Vancouver has a strong and diverse musical tradition founded on decades of homegrown talent. Sarah McLachlan, Nickelback, the New Pornographers and Michael Bublé are based here, along with jazz diva Diana Krall and her husband Elvis Costello, who reside in West Vancouver. The city's music scene is at its liveliest at the grassroots level, where local indie acts hit stages small and slightly larger every night of the week. There are a number of top venues worth catching shows in, including the Commodore (p69), Biltmore Cabaret (p139), Rickshaw Theatre (p94) and the Railway Club (p66), and local stores such as Zulu Records (p174) and Main St's Red Cat Records (p143) are great for recommendations, as is the free local-music magazine *Discorder,* produced by the University of British Columbia's Student Radio Society.

Blog It

Before you hit town, jump into the indie scene via these eclectic local-music blogs:

Van Music (www.vanmusic.ca)

Backstage Rider (www.backstagerider.com)

Winnie Cooper (www.winniecooper.net)

Vancouver also has one of North America's most vital classical-music scenes, with chamber and choral groups particularly well represented. Favorites include the Vancouver Bach Choir, whose Messiah sing-along is a Christmastime legend; the internationally renowned Vancouver Chamber Choir, which covers everything from jazz to avant-garde; and the Vancouver Symphony Orchestra, which effortlessly draws serious music fans and first timers with a stirring mix of classics and 'pops'. Jazz is also well represented at the Cellar Jazz Club, an ever-popular spot for intimate muso nights.

Vancouver hots live music events throughout the year with summer the best time for some outdoor tunes. Among the most popular events are the Vancouver International Jazz Festival (p23) and the Vancouver Folk Music Festival (p23).

Survival Guide

Transportation

ARRIVING IN VANCOUVER

Most visitors will arrive by air at Vancouver International Airport (YVR), south of the city on Sea Island in Richmond. Alternatively, US trains trundle in from Seattle to Pacific Central Station, located on the southern edge of Vancouver's Chinatown district. Cross-border bus services also arrive at this terminal. Vancouver is only an hour or so from several US border crossings, so driving is a popular way to access the city from the US, while cruise ships plying the Alaska route dock on the city's waterfront. Cross-Canada rail, bus and flight operations also service the city, which is the main gateway for accessing destinations throughout British Columbia (BC).

Flights, cars and tours can be booked online at www.lonelyplanet.com.

Vancouver International Airport

Canada's second-busiest airport, **Vancouver International Airport** (YVR; Map p201; www.yvr.ca) lies 13km south of downtown in the city of Richmond. There are two main terminals – international (including flights to the US) and domestic – just a short stroll apart. The smaller South Terminal is located a quick drive away: free shuttle-bus links are provided. This tiny terminal services floatplanes, helicopters and smaller aircraft traveling on lower capacity routes to small communities in BC and beyond. In addition, short-hop floatplane and helicopter services to and from Vancouver Island and beyond also have a terminal on the city's downtown waterfront near Canada Place.

The main airport has shops, food courts, currency exchange booths and a tourist information desk. It's also dotted with First Nations artworks. Baggage carts are free (no deposit required) and there is also free wi-fi.

Train

SkyTrain's 16-station **Canada Line** (www.translink.bc.ca; adult one-way fare $2.75-5.50, plus extra $5 from airport) operates a rapid-transit train service from the airport to downtown. Trains run every few minutes from early morning until after midnight and take around 25 minutes to reach downtown's Waterfront Station. The airport station is located outside between the domestic and international terminals. Follow the signs from inside either terminal and buy your ticket from the platform vending machines. These accept cash, credit and debit cards – look for green-jacketed Canada Line staff if you're bleary-eyed and need assistance after your long-haul flight. Fares from the airport cost between $7.75 and $10.50, depending on your destination and the time of day.

Taxi

Follow the signs from inside the main airport terminal to the cab stand just outside. The fare to downtown will usually cost between $30 and $40, plus tip (15% is the norm). Alternatively, limo car services are also available close to the main taxi stand. Expect to pay around $20 more for your ride to the city if you want to arrive in style.

Car

Most major car-rental agencies have desks at the airport, as well as multiple offices around the city. Once you're strapped in – seat belts are compulsory here – proceed east after leaving the airport on Grant McConachie Way, and follow the Vancouver signs over the Arthur Laing Bridge. Take the Granville St exit and travel north along Granville St with the mountains ahead of you, and you'll soon be in the downtown core.

Pacific Central Station

On the edge of Chinatown, the grand-looking white-stucco **Pacific Central Station** (1150 Station St, Chinatown) is the city's main terminus for long-distance train services – from across Canada on VIA Rail, and from Seattle (just south of the

CLIMATE CHANGE & TRAVEL

Every form of transport that relies on carbon-based fuel generates CO_2, the main cause of human-induced climate change. Modern travel is dependent on airplanes, which might use less fuel per kilometer per person than most cars but travel much greater distances. The altitude at which aircraft emit gases (including CO_2) and particles also contributes to their climate change impact. Many websites offer 'carbon calculators' that allow people to estimate the carbon emissions generated by their journey and, for those who wish to do so, to offset the impact of the greenhouse gases emitted with contributions to portfolios of climate-friendly initiatives throughout the world. Lonely Planet offsets the carbon footprint of all staff and author travel.

border) and beyond on Amtrak. It's also the main arrival point for major intercity bus services: Canada and cross-border buses on Greyhound; cross-border budget bus services on Bolt Bus; Victoria and Whistler services on Pacific Coach Lines; Sunshine Coast services on Malaspina Coach Lines.

While the station building itself has seen better days, Pacific Central has places to pick up coffee, snacks and sandwiches, and it also has free wi-fi. Keep in mind that although this part of Vancouver is not far from the city center on maps, it can be confusing to navigate from here to downtown on foot: best to hop on the nearby SkyTrain or take a cab.

Train

Main Street-Science World SkyTrain Station (on the Expo and Millennium Lines) is just across the street from Pacific Central. If you're heading downtown (which is a five-minute trundle away), jump on any train bound for Waterfront Station. The fare will be $2.50.

Taxi

There are usually a few cabs just outside Pacific Central Station. The ride to most downtown hotels from Pacific Central will take around 10 minutes, depending on traffic. It should cost around $10, or more if you're staying deep in the wilds of the West End.

Car

Hertz offers car-rental services in the train station. From the station, turn right along Main St and, within a minute or two, turn left onto the signposted 'City Centre' ramp that leads straight into the heart of downtown. You'll be there (traffic depending) in less than 10 minutes.

GETTING AROUND VANCOUVER

Downtown Vancouver is easily navigated on foot, with lots of transit services (bus and SkyTrain) for those hopping to other neighborhoods.

TransLink

TransLink (www.translink.bc.ca) oversees public bus, SkyTrain light rail and SeaBus commuter boat services. Its website has handy route maps and a trip-planning tool.

Tickets bought on any of these services are valid for up to 90 minutes of travel on the entire network. One-zone tickets cost adult/child $2.75/1.75, two-zone tickets $4/2.75 and three-zone tickets $5.505/3.75. An all-day, all-zone DayPass costs $9.75/7.50. After 6:30pm or on weekends or holidays, all trips are classed as one-zone fares and cost $2.75/1.75.

Books of 10 FareSaver tickets (adult one/two/three zones $21/31.50/42, child all zones $17.50) are a good way to save if you're planning multiple trips. They are sold at many convenience stores and drugstores throughout the city.

Children under five travel for free on all transit services.

At the time of research, fare gates were being installed in SkyTrain stations for the introduction of a new card ticketing system called Compass, currently scheduled to start between late 2013 and early 2014; check the Translink website before you arrive for the latest information.

Bus

Vancouver's bus network is extensive in central areas. All vehicles are equipped with bike racks and all are wheelchair accessible. Exact change (or more) is required; buses use fare machines and change is not given. Day passes, FareSaver tickets and the new Compass card can be used on buses.

There is a handy night-bus system that runs every 30 minutes between 1:30am and 4am. The last bus leaves downtown Vancouver at 3:09am. Look for night-bus signs at designated stops.

SeaBus

This iconic aquatic shuttle service operates throughout the day, taking 12 minutes to cross Burrard Inlet between Waterfront Station and Lonsdale Quay in North Vancouver. At Lonsdale you can then connect to buses servicing North Vancouver and West Vancouver; this is where you pick up bus 236 to both Capilano Suspension Bridge and Grouse Mountain.

SeaBus services leave from Waterfront Station between 6:16am and 1:22am Monday to Saturday (8:16am to 11:16pm Sunday). Vessels are wheelchair accessible and bike-friendly.

Tickets must be purchased from vending machines on either side of the route before boarding. The machines take cards and also give change for cash transactions up to $20.

Train

The SkyTrain rapid-transit network currently consists of three routes and is a great way to move around the region. A fourth route, the Evergreen Line, is scheduled for completion in 2016 and will link the suburban communities of Burnaby, Coquitlam and Port Moody.

Tickets for all services must be purchased from station vending machines (change is given; machines also accept debit and credit cards) prior to boarding. Checks by fare inspectors are frequent; they can issue on-the-spot fines. Fare gates were being introduced at the time of writing, requiring tickets to be scanned before you enter platform areas.

Expo Line

The original 35-minute Expo Line takes passengers to and from downtown Vancouver and Surrey, via stops in Burnaby and New Westminster. Trains run every two to eight minutes, with services departing Waterfront Station between 5:35am and 1:15am Monday to Friday (6:50am and 1:15am Saturday; 7:15am and 12:15am Sunday).

Millennium Line

Alights near shopping malls and suburban districts in Coquitlam and Burnaby. Trains run every five to eight minutes, with services departing Waterfront Station between 5:54am and 12:31am Monday to Friday (6:54am and 12:31am Saturday; 7:54am and 11:31pm Sunday).

Canada Line

Added in 2009, links the city to the airport and Richmond. Trains run every six to 20 minutes. Services run from the airport to downtown between 5:07am and 12:56am and from Waterfront Station to the airport between 4:48am and 1:05am. If you're heading for the airport from the city, make sure you board a YVR-bound train – some head to Richmond but not to the airport.

Miniferries

Operators offer day passes (from $10 to $15) as well as discounted books of tickets for those making multiple watery hops.

Aquabus Ferries (www.theaquabus.com; adult/child from $3/1.50) Runs frequent minivessels (some big enough to carry bikes) between the foot of Hornby St and Granville Island. It also services several additional spots along the False Creek waterfront as far as Science World.

ARRIVING BY FERRY

BC Ferries (www.bcferries.com) services arrive at Tsawwassen, an hour south of Vancouver, and at Horseshoe Bay, 30 minutes from downtown in West Vancouver. The company operates one of the world's largest ferry networks, including some spectacular routes throughout the province.

Main services to Tsawwassen arrive from Vancouver Island's Swartz Bay, near Victoria (adult/child/vehicle $14.85/7.45/49.25, 90 minutes), and Duke Point, near Nanaimo (adult/child/vehicle $14/7/47, two hours). Services also arrive from the Southern Gulf Islands. Services to Horseshoe Bay arrive from Nanaimo's Departure Bay (adult/child/vehicle $14.85/6.40/49.25, 90 minutes). Services also arrive here from Bowen Island (adult/child/vehicle $8.80/3.75/35.35, 20 minutes) and from Langdale (adult/child/vehicle $10.90/2.75/32.25, 40 minutes) on the Sunshine Coast.

You can buy walk-on tickets at the ferry terminals (no reservations required). You can also make vehicle reservations for a $15 fee – recommended for travel on weekends or during July and August.

To depart Tsawwassen by transit, take bus 620 (adult/child $5.50/3.50) to Bridgeport Station and transfer to the Canada Line. It takes about 40 minutes to reach downtown.

From Horseshoe Bay to downtown, take bus 257 (adult/child $4/2.75, 45 minutes), which is faster than bus 250. It takes about 35 minutes.

False Creek Ferries (Map p270; www.granvilleisland ferries.bc.ca; adult/child from $3/1.50) Operates a similar Granville Island service from Sunset Beach, and has additional ports of call around False Creek.

Bicycle

Vancouver is a relatively good cycling city. More than 300km of designated routes crisscross the region. Cyclists can take their bikes for free on SkyTrains, SeaBuses and bike-rack-fitted transit buses, as well as on some larger miniferries. Cyclists are required by law to wear helmets. In recent years, dedicated bike lanes have been created downtown and a public bike-share scheme is scheduled to be introduced in early 2014.

Pick up a *Metro Vancouver Cycling Map* ($3.95) from a convenience store for details on area routes and bike-friendly contacts and resources – or download it for free via the TransLink website.

If you're traveling sans bike, you can also rent wheels (often including in-line skates) from businesses around the city, especially on Denman St near Stanley Park – home of Vancouver's most popular scenic cycling route.

Handy resources:

City of Vancouver (www.vancouver.ca/cycling) Route maps and bike-friendly info.

University of British Columbia (www.cyclevancouver.ubc.ca) Handy route planner.

HUB (www.bikhub.ca) The locals' main bike-based resource.

Car & Motorcycle

For sightseeing in the city, you'll be fine without a car (the city center is especially easy to explore on foot and transit routes are extensive). For visits that incorporate the wider region's mountains and communities, however, a vehicle makes life much simpler: the further you travel from downtown, the more limited your transit options become.

Driving

With few exceptions, you can legally drive in Canada with a valid driver's license issued by your home country. You may be required to show an international driving permit if your license isn't written in English (or French). If you've rented a car in the US and you are driving it into Canada, bring a copy of the rental agreement to save any possible hassles by border officials. Seat belts are mandatory here, and there is also a ban on using handheld electronic devices while driving.

Vancouver doesn't have any expressways going through its core, which can lead to some major congestion issues. Evening rush-hour traffic can be a nightmare, with enormous lines of cars snaking along W Georgia St waiting to cross the Lions Gate Bridge. Try the Second Narrows Ironworkers Memorial Bridge (known simply as the Second Narrows Bridge to most locals) if you need to access the North Shore in a hurry. Other peak-time hot spots to avoid are the George Massey Tunnel and Hwy 1 to Surrey.

For suggested driving routes around the region, visit www.hellobc.com/drive. For route planning and driving conditions throughout the province, try www.drivebc.ca.

Parking

Parking is at a premium in downtown Vancouver: there are some free spots on residential side streets but many require permits, and traffic wardens are predictably predatory. Many streets also have metered parking (from $1 to $5 per hour). Pay-parking lots (typically from $4 per hour) are a better proposition – arrive before 9am at some for early-bird, day-rate discounts. For an interactive map of parking-lot locations, check **EasyPark** (www.easypark.ca).

Rental

Major car-rental agencies with offices around the city and at Vancouver International Airport:

Avis (☎800-230-4898, 604-606-2847; www.avis.ca)

Budget (☎800-219-3199, 604-668-7000; www.budgetbc.com)

Enterprise (☎800-261-7331, 604-688-5500; www.enterprisecar.ca)

Hertz (☎800-654-3131, 604-606-4711; www.hertz.ca)

Thrifty (☎800-847-4389, 604-606-1655; www.thrifty.com)

Taxi

Try the following taxi companies:

Black Top & Checker Cabs (☎604-731-1111)

Vancouver Taxi (☎604-871-1111)

Yellow Cab (☎604-681-1111)

TOURS

Most tour operators offer several different options – check their websites for the full selection.

Boat Tours

Accent Cruises (Map p275; ☎604-688-6625; www.accentcruises.ca; 1698 Duranleau St, Granville Island; dinner cruise $89; ⏰May–mid-Oct; 🚌50) Popular salmon-buffet cruise along the coastlines of English Bay, Stanley Park and Ambleside Beach in West Vancouver. Departures are from Granville

Island and it's a relaxing way to spend your evening after a long day trawling the sights on foot.

Harbour Cruises (Map p270; 604-688-7246, 800-663-1500; www.boatcruises.com; north foot of Denman St, West End; adult/child/concession $30/10/25; May-Oct) View the city – and some unexpected wildlife – from the water on a 75-minute narrated harbor tour, weaving past Stanley Park, Lions Gate Bridge and the North Shore mountains. There's also a 2½-hour sunset dinner cruise (adult/child $79/69) plus a long, languid lunch trek to lovely Indian Arm ($69).

Bus Tours

Big Bus (877-299-0701, 604-299-0700; www.bigbus.ca; adult/child/concession $40/37/22; year-round) Stay for the full 90-minute narrated loop or use your ticket as a hop-on hop-off pass for up to 21 stops around the city. Departures are every 15 to 20 minutes during peak season, and the $90 family tickets are good value. There's also a two-day option for a few dollars more.

Landsea Tours (877-669-2277, 604-255-7272; www.vancouvertours.com; adult/child $69/45; year-round) Landsea's comfortable tours in 24-passenger minibuses attract an older crowd. Treks include a four-hour city-highlights tour (adult/child $69/45) and a six-hour Vancouver and the North Shore excursion (adult/child $165/109).

Vancouver Trolley Company (888-451-5581, 604-801-5515; www.vancouvertrolley.com; adult/child/concession from $40/22/37; year-round) Red replica San Francisco trolley cars (without the tracks) provide a hop-on hop-off tour around the main city sites. One or two-day options are available. Look out for Halloween and Christmas-themed tours as well.

Walking & Cycling Tours

Architectural Institute of British Columbia (604-683-8588; www.aibc.ca; tours $10; Tue-Sun Jul & Aug) Local architecture students conduct these excellent one- to two-hour wanders, focusing on the buildings, history and heritage of several key Vancouver neighborhoods. There are six tours in all, and areas covered include Gastown, Strathcona, Yaletown, Chinatown, downtown and the West End.

Forbidden Vancouver (www.forbiddenvancouver.ca; adult/concession $22/19; Apr-Nov) This quirky company offers highly entertaining tours: delve into prohibition-era Vancouver and poke around the seedy underbelly of historic Gastown. Not recommended for kids. Book ahead: they fill-up quickly. At the time of research, a third tour was planned to cover Granville St's colorful nightlife history.

Vancouver Foodie Tours (877-804-9220; www.foodietours.ca; $49-69; year-round) The perfect way to dive into the city's food scene, these belt-busting guided tours include a street food crawl and a gourmet drink-and-dine tour.

Vancouver Tour Guys (866-251-1888; www.tourguys.ca; free-$45; year-round) Free neighborhood tours (gratuities of $5 to $10 encouraged) plus a couple of walks you'll pay for (consider the $45 craft-beer option if you're thirsty). Booking ahead is recommended on busy summer days.

Specialty Tours

Harbour Air Seaplanes (800-665-0212, 604-274-1277; www.harbour-air.com; tours from $69; year-round) A thrilling way to explore Vancouver's breathtaking natural setting, these panoramic floatplane flights will have you soaring over mountains, forests and coastlines – before a dramatic water landing brings you back down to earth.

Sewell's Sea Safari (Map p284; 604-921-3474; www.sewellsmarina.com; 6409 Bay St, Horseshoe Bay; adult/youth/child $83/74/53; Apr-Oct; 250) West Vancouver's Horseshoe Bay is the departure point for this two-hour marine-wildlife-watching boat tour. Orcas are always a highlight but even if they're not around, you'll almost certainly spot harbor seals lolling on the rocks and pretending to ignore you. Seabirds and bald eagles are also a frequent part of the show.

Stanley Park Horse-Drawn Carriages (888-681-5110, 604-681-5115; www.stanleypark.com; Stanley Park; adult/child/concession $32/17/30; Mar-Oct; 19) These narrated, one-hour tours offer a leisurely but informative way to see the park without having to walk. Tours depart from near the information booth, not far from the park's W Georgia St entrance.

Directory A–Z

Customs Regulations

Adults aged 19 or older can bring in 1.5L of wine or 1.14L of liquor or 8.5L of beer. You can also bring in 200 cigarettes, 50 cigars and 200g of tobacco (combined). In addition, you can bring in gifts valued up to $60 plus a 'reasonable amount' of personal effects, including cars, computers and outdoor equipment. Dispose of any perishable items, such as fruit, vegetables or plants, before crossing the border. Mace, pepper spray and many firearms are also prohibited. For the latest regulations, contact the **Canada Border Services Agency** (☎800-461-9999, 204-983-3500; www.cbsa.gc.ca).

Discount Cards

Aside from the city's free attractions, there are other ways to stretch your visitor dollars here. If you're planning to take in lots of sights in a few days, the **Vancouver City Passport** (www.citypassports.com; $24.95) can be a good idea. It offers discounts at attractions, restaurants and activities across the city for one adult and two children.

You can save on entry to a triumvirate of Kitsilano attractions with a combined **Vanier Park Explore Pass** (www.

PRACTICALITIES

Maps

The Tourism Vancouver Visitor Centre (p253) provides free downtown maps. Alternatively, the comprehensive *Greater Vancouver Streetwise Map Book* ($5.95) is sold at convenience stores. For free online maps, check out the **VanMap** (www.vancouver.ca/vanmap) system.

Newspapers

- **Georgia Straight** (www.straight.com) Alternative weekly providing Vancouver's best entertainment listings. Free every Thursday.
- **Province** (www.theprovince.com) Vancouver's 'tabloid' daily newspaper.
- **Tyee** (www.thetyee.ca) Award-winning online local news source.
- **Vancouver Sun** (www.vancouversun.com) Main city daily, with Thursday arts and entertainment listings pull-out.
- **Xtra!** (www.xtra.ca) Free, gay-oriented, alternative paper, distributed biweekly.

Radio

Around Vancouver, flip the dial to these stations or listen in online before you arrive:

- **CBC Radio One** (690AM, 88.1FM; www.cbc.ca/bc) Canadian Broadcasting Corporation's commercial-free news, talk and music station.
- **CKNW** (980AM; www.cknw.com) News, traffic, sports and talk.
- **Fox** (99.3FM; www.cfox.com) New rock and chatter.
- **JACK-FM** (96.9FM; www.jackfm.com) Pop mix station.
- **News 1130** (1130AM; www.news1130.com) News 24/7.
- **Peak** (102.7FM; www.thepeak.fm) Popular mainstream new-rock station.

spacecentre.ca/explore-pass; adult/child $30/24) which covers the Museum of Vancouver, Vancouver Maritime Museum and HR MacMillan Space Centre. The pass includes one entry to each attraction, has no time restrictions and is available at any of the three attractions. It saves you around $10 on separate admissions.

The University of British Columbia (UBC) also offers a combined-entry discount passport for some of its campus-based attractions, available at participating attractions. This card also includes discounts for campus parking and dining.

It's also a good idea to drop by the Tourism Vancouver Visitor Centre for a free visitor guide, which has pages of coupons in the back. And don't forget **Greenster** (www.greenster.com/guide), a coupon book covering the region's eco-supporting stores, eateries and activities.

Electricity

Canada, like the USA, operates on 120V, 60Hz AC.

Emergency

Police, Fire & Ambulance (☎911)

Police (☎604-717-3321) Nonemergency number.

Internet Access

Most Vancouver hotels provide in-room wi-fi or high-speed cable internet services for guests, but not always for free: check with your hotel when booking.

If you're toting your hardware around town and it's time to update your travel blog, drop into one of the many branches of **Blenz** (www.blenz.com), **Take 5** (www.take5cafe.com) and **Waves** (www.wavescoffee.com) coffee shops for free wi-fi. The **Vancouver Public Library** (☎604-331-3603; 350 W Georgia St; ⏲10am-9pm Mon-Thu, to 6pm Fri & Sat, noon-5pm Sun; Ⓜ Stadium-Chinatown) also has free wi-fi and free-access internet-enabled computers: ask at the information desk for wi-fi guest cards. Check www.wififreespot.com/can.html for other free hot spots across the region.

If you don't have your computer with you, check your email for free in the Apple Store in downtown's Pacific Centre mall.

Medical Services

There are no reciprocal healthcare arrangements between Canada and other countries. Non-Canadians usually pay cash up front for treatment, so taking out travel insurance with a medical-cover component is strongly advised. Medical treatment in Canada is expensive: hospital beds can cost up to $2500 a day for nonresidents.

Clinics

The following walk-in clinics cater to visitors:

Care Point Medical Centre (⏲daily, hours vary) Branches at Commercial Dr (☎604-254-5554; 1623 Commercial Dr; 🚌20); Downtown (☎604-687-4858; 711 W Pender St; Ⓜ Granville) and West End (☎604-681-5338; 1175 Denman St; 🚌5). For additional locations, see www.carepoint.ca. Appointments not necessary.

Stein Medical Clinic (☎604-688-5924; www.steinmedical.com; Bentall 5, Suite 188, 550 Burrard St; ⏲8am-5:30pm Mon-Fri; Ⓜ Burrard) Appointments not necessary.

Travel Medicine & Vaccination Centre (☎604-681-5656; www.tmvc.com; Suite 314, 1030 W Georgia St; Ⓜ Burrard) Specializing in travel shots; appointments necessary.

Ultima Medicentre (☎604-683-8138; www.

ultimamedicentre.ca; Bentall Centre Plaza Level, 1055 Dunsmuir St; ⌚8am-5pm Mon-Fri; MBurrard) Appointments not necessary.

Emergency Rooms

Vancouver's emergency rooms include the following:

BC Children's Hospital (☎604-875-2345; www.bcchildrens.ca; 4480 Oak St; 🚌17)

St Paul's Hospital (☎604-682-2344; 1081 Burrard St; 🚌22) Downtown accident-and-emergency hospital.

Vancouver General Hospital (☎604-875-4111; 855 W 12th Ave; MBroadway-City Hall)

Pharmacies

Vancouver is well stocked with pharmacies.

Pharmasave (☎604-801-6991; 499 Granville St; ⌚7am-8pm Mon-Fri, 9am-5:30pm Sat, to 5pm Sun; MGranville)

Shoppers Drug Mart (☎604-669-2424; 1125 Davie St; ⌚24hr; 🚌6) Pharmacy chain.

Money

Canadian dollars come in $5 (blue), $10 (purple), $20 (green), $50 (red) and $100 (brown) denominations. New bills are currently being introduced: colors will remain the same but the paper has a plastic feel. It will be several years before all the older bills are replaced, though. The penny (1¢) was recently phased out, but nickel (5¢), dime (10¢), quarter (25¢), 'loonie' ($1) and 'toonie' ($2) coins persist.

Most Canadians do not carry large amounts of cash for everyday use, relying instead on electronic transactions: credit cards, ATMs and direct-debit cards.

ATMs

Interbank ATM exchange rates usually beat the rates offered for traveler's checks or foreign currency. Canadian ATM fees are generally low, but your home bank may charge another fee on top of that. Some ATM machines also dispense US currency; ideal if you're planning a trip across the border. ATMs abound in Vancouver, with bank branches congregating around the business district bordered by Burrard, Georgia, Pender and Granville Sts. Drugstores also frequently have ATMs.

Changing Money

You can exchange currency at most main bank branches, which often charge less than the *bureaux de change* dotted around the city. In addition to the banks, try **Vancouver Bullion & Currency Exchange** (☎604-685-1008; www.vbce.ca; 800 W Pender St; ⌚9am-5pm Mon-Fri; MGranville), which often offers a wider range of currencies and competitive rates.

Credit Cards

Visa, MasterCard and American Express are widely accepted in Canada. Credit cards can get you cash advances at bank ATMs, usually for an additional surcharge. Be aware that many US-based credit cards now convert foreign charges using unfavorable exchange rates and fees.

Opening Hours

Standard business hours are 9am to 5pm weekdays. Some postal outlets may stay open later and on weekends. Most banks adhere to standard hours but some branches keep shorter hours and others also open on Saturday mornings. Usual retail shopping hours are from 10am to 6pm Monday to Saturday, and noon to 5pm on Sunday in the city center, although in neighborhoods such as Main St and Commercial Dr stores typically open from 11am. Twenty-four-hour supermarkets, pharmacies and convenience stores are dotted around the city, particularly in the West End.

Shopping malls often stay open later than regular stores. Many supermarkets stay open until 9pm or beyond. Restaurants are usually open for lunch on weekdays from 11:30am until 2:30pm and serve dinner from 5pm until 9pm or 10pm daily, later on weekends. Many are open all day; some close between lunch and dinner; some open only for dinner. Those serving breakfast often open at 7am, and many that don't serve breakfast do serve weekend brunch. If restaurants take a day off, it is usually Monday.

Pubs and bars that serve lunch open before midday; others wait it out until 5pm before opening their doors. Clubs may open in the evening around 9pm, but most don't get busy before 11pm. Bars and clubs, especially those downtown, may serve liquor until 3am.

Tourist attractions often keep longer hours in summer and reduce their opening hours during winter.

Post

Canada Post (www.canadapost.ca) may not be remarkably quick, but it is reliable. The standard (up to 30g) letter and postcard rate to destinations within Canada is 63¢. Postcards and standard letters to the US cost $1.10. International airmail postcards cost $1.85.

Postal outlets are dotted around the city, many

of them at the back of drugstores – look for the blue-and-red window signs. Handy branches:

- **Canada Post Main Outlet** (Map p266; ☎604-662-5723; 349 W Georgia St; ⌚8:30am-5:30pm Mon-Fri; Ⓜ Stadium-Chinatown)
- **Howe St Postal Outlet** (Map p266; ☎604-688-2068; 732 Davie St; ⌚9am-7pm Mon-Fri, 10am-5pm Sat; 🚌6)

Public Holidays

During national public holidays, all banks, schools and government offices (including post offices) are closed, and transportation, museums and other services often operate on Sunday schedules. Holidays falling on weekends are usually observed the following Monday.

Major public holidays in Vancouver:

- **New Year's Day** 1 January
- **Family Day** Second Monday in February
- **Good Friday & Easter Monday** Late March to mid-April
- **Victoria Day** Third Monday in May
- **Canada Day** 1 July
- **BC Day** First Monday in August
- **Labour Day** First Monday in September
- **Thanksgiving** Second Monday in October
- **Remembrance Day** 11 November
- **Christmas Day** 25 December
- **Boxing Day** 26 December

Safe Travel

Vancouver is relatively safe for visitors. Purse-snatching and pickpocketing do occur, however, so be vigilant with your personal possessions. Theft from unattended cars is not uncommon, so never leave valuables in vehicles where they can be seen.

Persistent street begging is a big issue for many visitors; just say 'Sorry' and pass on if you're not interested and want to be polite. A small group of hardcore scam artists also works the downtown core, singling out tourists and asking for 'help to get back home.' They never seem to make it home and locals roll their eyes when they see them approaching unsuspecting visitors. Do not engage in conversation.

The city's Downtown Eastside area has a depressing history of lives blighted by drugs, prostitution and mental illness. Crime against visitors is rare in this area but you are advised to be vigilant and stick to the main streets, especially at night. You will likely be discreetly offered drugs here by a small-fry pusher or two at some point – just walk on and they won't bother you again.

Taxes & Refunds

After British Columbia (BC) backtracked in its attempt to unite its Goods and Services Tax (GST) and Provincial Sales Tax (PST) into a single levy, the two separate taxes were reintroduced in 2013. You will now pay 5% GST on almost almost all purchases as well as an additional 7% PST on some purchases. For example, you will be charged 5% for restaurant meals and attraction entries but a combined 12% – GST and PST – for accommodation (plus any additional hotel taxes).

Tax rebates for visitors have mostly been discontinued in recent years. If you booked your trip as part of a package, however, you may be able to claw back some of the tax paid for your accommodation. Don't hold your breath but check in with the **Canada Revenue Agency** (☎800-668-4748, 902-432-5608; www.ccra.gc.ca/visitors) for the latest information.

Telephone

Local calls cost 50¢ from public pay phones, but it's increasingly difficult to find such phones in the city. Gas stations are usually a good bet if you need to make a call in a hurry. If calling from a private phone, local calls are free – a gratis approach that often doesn't apply to calls made from hotel rooms.

Most Vancouver-area phone numbers have the area code ☎604, although you can also expect to see ☎778, ☎250 and the new ☎236 codes across the region. Dial all 10 digits of a given phone number, including the three-digit area code and seven-digit number, even for local calls. In some instances (eg between Vancouver and Whistler), numbers will have the same area code but will be long-distance; at such times you need to dial ☎1 before the area code.

Always dial ☎1 before other domestic long-distance and toll-free (☎800, ☎888, ☎877 etc) numbers. Some toll-free numbers are good anywhere in North America, others within Canada only. International rates apply for calls to the US, even though the dialing code (☎1) is the same as for Canadian long-distance calls. Dial ☎011 followed by the country code for all other overseas direct-dial calls.

Cell Phones

Cell phones use the GSM and CDMA systems, depending on your carrier. Check with your cellular service provider before you leave about using your phone in Canada. Calls may be routed internationally, and US travelers should beware roaming surcharges (it can become very expensive for a 'local' call).

Phonecards

Prepaid phonecards for long-distance and international calls can be purchased at convenience stores, gas stations and some post offices. Beware some phonecards that advertise the cheapest per-minute rates, as they may also charge hefty connection fees for each call. Leading local phone company **Telus** (www.telus.com) offers a range of reliable phonecards available in retail outlets around the city.

Time

Vancouver is in the Pacific time zone (PST/PDT), the same as the US West Coast. At noon in Vancouver it's the following:

- 11am in Anchorage
- 3pm in Toronto
- 2pm in Chicago
- 8pm in London
- 9pm in Paris
- 6am (the next day) in Sydney
- 8am (the next day) in Auckland

During Daylight Saving Time (from the second Sunday in March to the first Sunday in November), the clock moves ahead one hour.

Tourist Information

The **Tourism Vancouver Visitor Centre** (Map p266; ☎604-683-2000, 877-826-1717; www.tourismvancouver.com; 200 Burrard St; ⏰8:30am-6pm ; Ⓜ Waterfront) is a large repository of resources for visitors, with a staff of helpful advisers ready to assist in planning your trip. Services and info available here include free maps, visitor guides, half-priced theater tickets, accommodation and tour bookings, plus a host of glossy brochures on the city and the wider BC region. At time of writing, the main downtown Visitor Centre was being refurbished; a temporary counter was running across the street at the Convention Centre. There is also a small satellite information kiosk near the Vancouver Art Gallery.

Travelers with Disabilities

Vancouver is an accessible city. On arrival at the airport, vehicle-rental agencies can provide prearranged cars with hand controls. Accessible cabs are also widely available at the airport and throughout the city, on request.

All TransLink SkyTrain, SeaBus and transit bus services are wheelchair accessible. Check the TransLink website (www.translink.bc.ca) for a wide range of information on accessible transport around the region. Head to www.accesstotravel.gc.ca for information and resources on accessible travel across Canada.

Guide dogs may legally be brought into restaurants, hotels and other businesses in Vancouver. Many public-service phone numbers and some pay phones are adapted for the hearing impaired. Almost all downtown sidewalks have sloping ramps, and most public buildings and attractions are wheelchair accessible. Check the City of Vancouver's dedicated website (www.vancouver.ca/accessibility) for additional information and resources.

Other helpful resources:

BC Coalition of People with Disabilities (☎800-663-1278, 604-875-0188; www.bccpd.bc.ca) Programs and support for people with disabilities.

Canadian National Institute for the Blind (☎604-431-2121; www.cnib.ca) Support and services for the visually impaired.

Western Institute for the Deaf & Hard of Hearing (☎604-736-7391; www.widhh.com) Interpreter services and resources for the hearing impaired.

Visas

Citizens or permanent residents of all countries – including the US – need a passport to enter Canada. Visitors from the US, Scandinavia, European Union and most Commonwealth nations do not need a visa for tourist visits, but citizens of more than 100 other nations do. For further information as well as the latest updated passport and visa rules, see the website of **Citizenship & Immigration Canada** (www.cic.gc.ca).

A passport and/or visa does not guarantee entry. Proof of sufficient funds or return ticket out of the country may be required. Visitors with medical conditions may only be refused if they 'might reasonably be expected to cause excessive demands on health and social services' (ie they admit to needing treatment during their stay in Canada).

If you are refused entry but have a visa, you have the right of appeal at the port of entry. If you're arriving by land, the best course is simply to try again later (after a shift change) or at a different border crossing.

Women Travelers

Vancouver is generally quite safe for women traveling solo, although jogging alone after dark in parks and hanging out late at night in the Downtown Eastside without company is best avoided. Note it is illegal to carry pepper spray or mace in Canada. The **Vancouver Women's Health Collective** (☎604-736-5262; www.womenshealthcollective.ca; 29 W Hastings St, Chinatown; Ⓜ Stadium-Chinatown) provides advice and referrals for health issues as well as free yoga classes.

Behind the Scenes

SEND US YOUR FEEDBACK

Things change – prices go up, schedules change, good places go bad and bad places go bankrupt. So if you find things better or worse, recently opened or long since closed, or you just want to tell us what you loved or loathed about this book, please get in touch and help make the next edition even more accurate and useful. We love to hear from travelers – your comments keep us on our toes and our well-traveled team reads every word. Although we can't reply individually to postal submissions, we always guarantee that your feedback goes straight to the appropriate authors, in time for the next edition. Each person who sends us information is thanked in the next edition – the most useful submissions are rewarded with a selection of digital PDF chapters.

Visit **lonelyplanet.com/contact** to submit your updates and suggestions or to ask for help. Our award-winning website also features inspirational travel stories, news and discussions.

Note: We may edit, reproduce and incorporate your comments in Lonely Planet products such as guidebooks, websites and digital products, so let us know if you don't want your comments reproduced or your name acknowledged. For a copy of our privacy policy visit lonelyplanet.com/privacy.

AUTHOR THANKS

John Lee

Heartfelt thanks go to my dad for first bringing me to Vancouver from the UK for a visit back in 1986 – see you soon, Dad! I'd also like to thank my friends and family for not totally abandoning me during the write-up period – and, especially, for still being able to recognize me despite the giant 'book beard' I grew in the process. It's now time for a shave...

ACKNOWLEDGMENTS

Cover photograph: Totem poles in Stanley Park, Vancouver; Totem Pole Artist © Ellen Neel; Photographer Bert Klassen/Alamy. Illustration pp50-1 by Michael Weldon.

THIS BOOK

This 6th edition of Lonely Planet's *Vancouver* guidebook was researched and written by John Lee. The previous two editions were also written by John Lee. This guidebook was commissioned in Lonely Planet's Oakland office, and produced by the following:

Commissioning Editor Korina Miller
Coordinating Editors Samantha Forge, Susan Paterson
Senior Cartographers Mark Griffiths, Alison Lyall
Coordinating Layout Designer Jessica Rose
Managing Editors Sasha Baskett, Martine Power
Senior Editor Catherine Naghten
Managing Layout Designer Chris Girdler
Assisting Editors Judith Bamber, Rosie Nicholson, Gabrielle Stefanos, Fionnula Twomey
Assisting Cartographer Jennifer Johnston
Cover Research Naomi Parker
Internal Image Research Aude Vauconsant
Thanks to Nicholas Colicchia, Brendan Dempsey, Ryan Evans, Larissa Frost, Jennye Garibaldi, Scott Hymen, Genesys India, Jouve India, Asha Ioculari, Andi Jones, Katherine Marsh, Darren O'Connell, Trent Paton, Emily Pietropaolo, Kerrianne Southway, Gerard Walker, Daniëlle Wolbers, Emily K Wolman

Index

See also separate subindexes for:

EATING P259
DRINKING & NIGHTLIFE P260
ENTERTAINMENT P261
SHOPPING P261
SPORTS & ACTIVITIES P262
SLEEPING P262

Sights 000
Map Pages **000**
Photo Pages **000**

Sights 000
Map Pages **000**
Photo Pages **000**

L

M

N

O

P

Sights 000
Map Pages **000**
Photo Pages **000**

EATING

DRINKING & NIGHTLIFE

Sights 000
Map Pages **000**
Photo Pages **000**

ENTERTAINMENT

SHOPPING

SPORTS & ACTIVITIES

SLEEPING

Sights 000
Map Pages **000**
Photo Pages **000**

Vancouver Maps

Map Legend

Sights
- Beach
- Buddhist
- Castle
- Christian
- Hindu
- Islamic
- Jewish
- Monument
- Museum/Gallery
- Ruin
- Winery/Vineyard
- Zoo
- Other Sight

Eating
- Eating

Drinking & Nightlife
- Drinking & Nightlife
- Cafe

Entertainment
- Entertainment

Shopping
- Shopping

Sleeping
- Sleeping
- Camping

Sports & Activities
- Diving/Snorkelling
- Canoeing/Kayaking
- Skiing
- Surfing
- Swimming/Pool
- Walking
- Windsurfing
- Other Sports & Activities

Information
- Post Office
- Tourist Information

Transport
- Airport
- Border Crossing
- Bus
- Cable Car/Funicular
- Cycling
- Ferry
- Monorail
- Parking
- S-Bahn
- Taxi
- Train/Railway
- Tram
- Tube Station
- U-Bahn
- Underground Train Station
- Other Transport

Routes
- Tollway
- Freeway
- Primary
- Secondary
- Tertiary
- Lane
- Unsealed Road
- Plaza/Mall
- Steps
- Tunnel
- Pedestrian Overpass
- Walking Tour
- Walking Tour Detour
- Path

Boundaries
- International
- State/Province
- Disputed
- Regional/Suburb
- Marine Park
- Cliff
- Wall

Geographic
- Hut/Shelter
- Lighthouse
- Lookout
- Mountain/Volcano
- Oasis
- Park
- Pass
- Picnic Area
- Waterfall

Hydrography
- River/Creek
- Intermittent River
- Swamp/Mangrove
- Reef
- Canal
- Water
- Dry/Salt/ Intermittent Lake
- Glacier

Areas
- Beach/Desert
- Cemetery (Christian)
- Cemetery (Other)
- Park/Forest
- Sportsground
- Sight (Building)
- Top Sight (Building)

MAP INDEX

0 5 km
0 2.5 miles
Capilano Lake
Capilano River Regional Park
Capilano River
WEST VANCOUVER
Queen Charlotte Channel
Passage Island
HORSESHOE BAY
Lighthouse Park
Sandy Cove
West Bay
DUNDARAVE
Lynn Canyon Park
Lynn Creek
NORTH VANCOUVER
QUEENSDALE
Burrard Inlet
First Narrows
Stanley Park
Vancouver Harbour
11
2
1
3
English Bay
WEST END
DOWNTOWN
HASTINGS
CHINATOWN
5
YALETOWN
4
8
7
RENFREW
GRANDVIEW
12
10
6
Marine Drive Foreshore Park
Pacific Spirit Regional Park
KITSILANO
FAIRVIEW
UNIVERSITY OF BRITISH COLUMBIA (UBC)
POINT GREY
SOUTH GRANVILLE
SOUTH MAIN
RENFREW HEIGHTS
ARBUTUS
Pacific Spirit Regional Park
CAMBIE
QUILCHENA
DUNBAR
WEST SIDE
9
Queen Elizabeth Park
KNIGHT ROAD
COLLINGWOOD
Strait of Georgia
Central Park

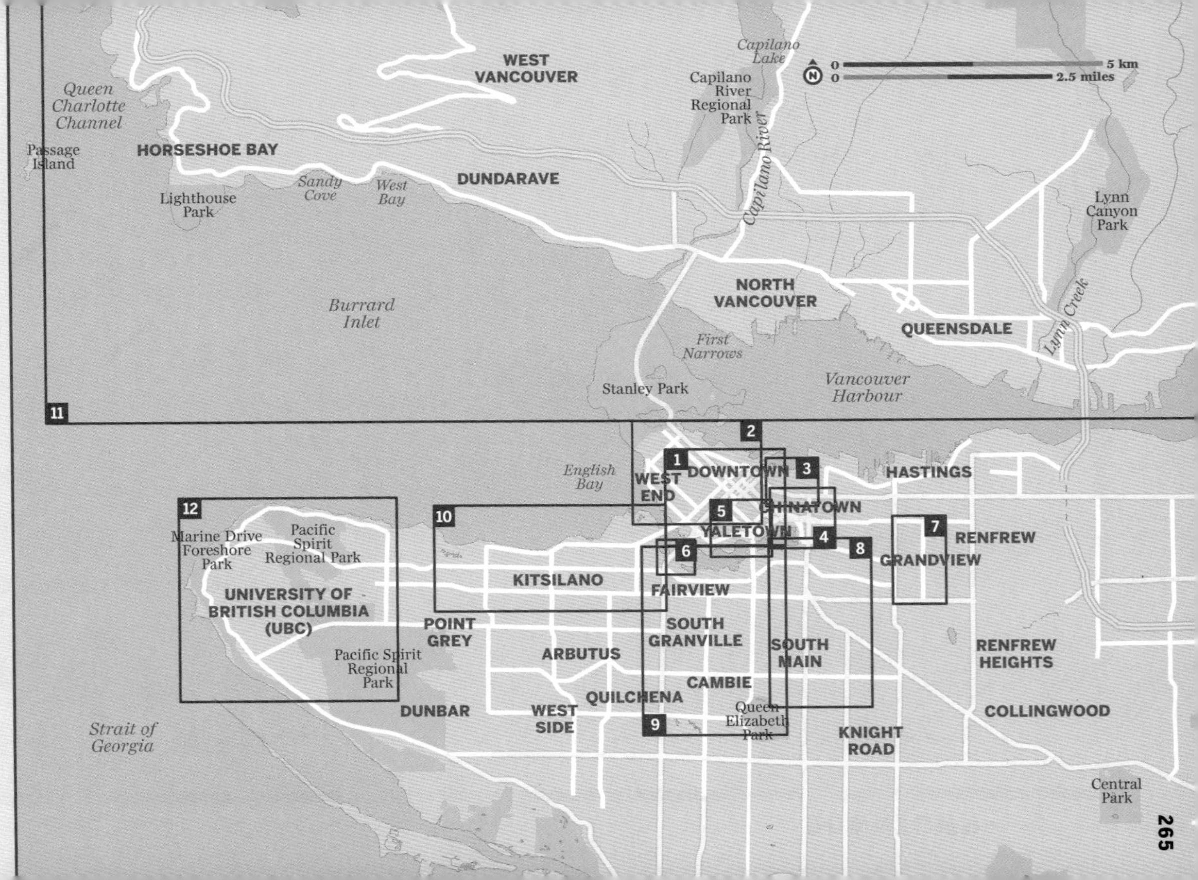

Key on p268

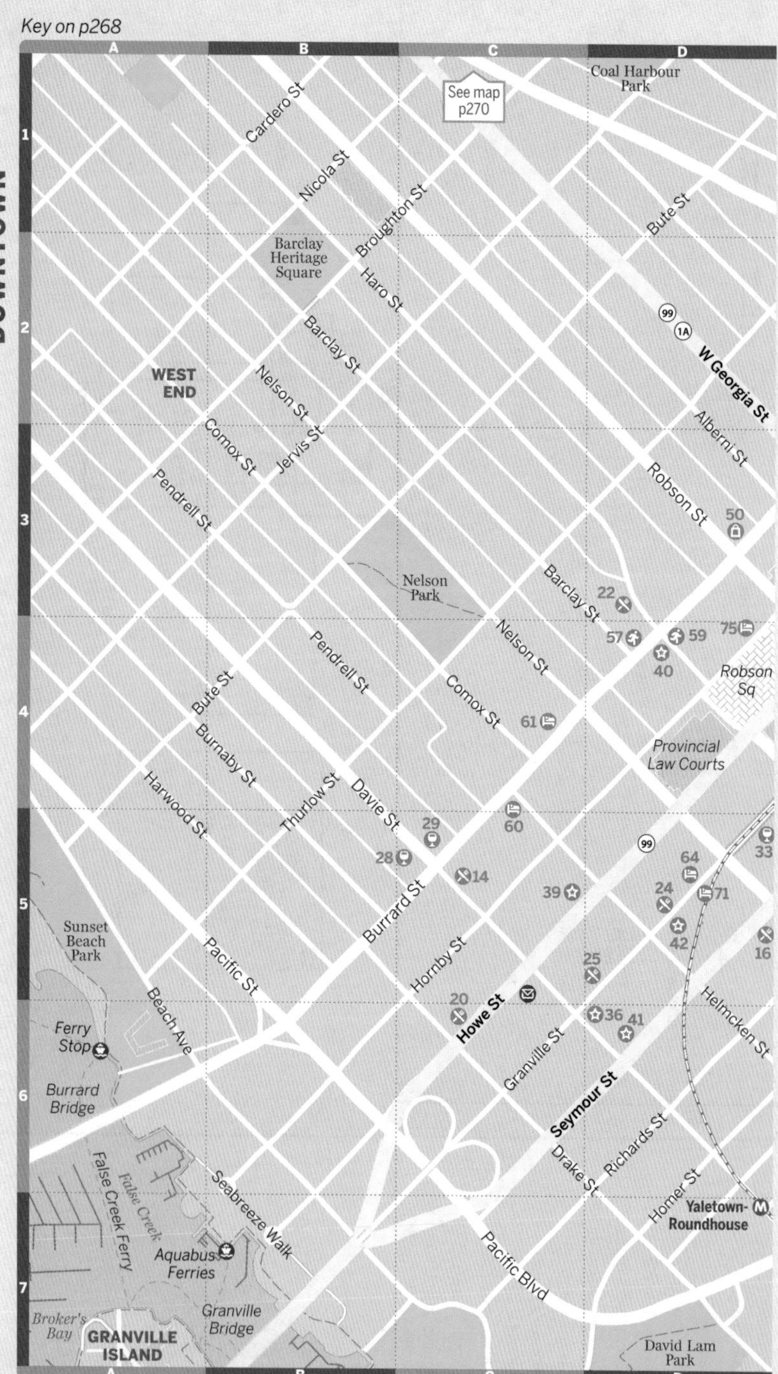
DOWNTOWN
See map p270
Coal Harbour Park
Cardero St
Nicola St
Broughton St
Bute St
Barclay Heritage Square
Haro St
Barclay St
W Georgia St
Alberni St
WEST END
Nelson St
Comox St
Jervis St
Pendrell St
Robson St
50
Nelson Park
Barclay St
22
57
59
75
40
Robson Sq
Pendrell St
Nelson St
Comox St
Bute St
61
Burnaby St
Provincial Law Courts
Harwood St
Thurlow St
Davie St
29
60
28
14
99
64
33
39
24
71
Burrard St
42
16
Sunset Beach Park
Pacific St
Hornby St
25
Helmcken St
Beach Ave
20
Howe St
36
41
Ferry Stop
Granville St
Burrard Bridge
Seymour St
False Creek Ferry
False Creek
Seabreeze Walk
Drake St
Richards St
Homer St
Yaletown-Roundhouse
Aquabus Ferries
Pacific Blvd
Granville Bridge
Broker's Bay
GRANVILLE ISLAND
David Lam Park

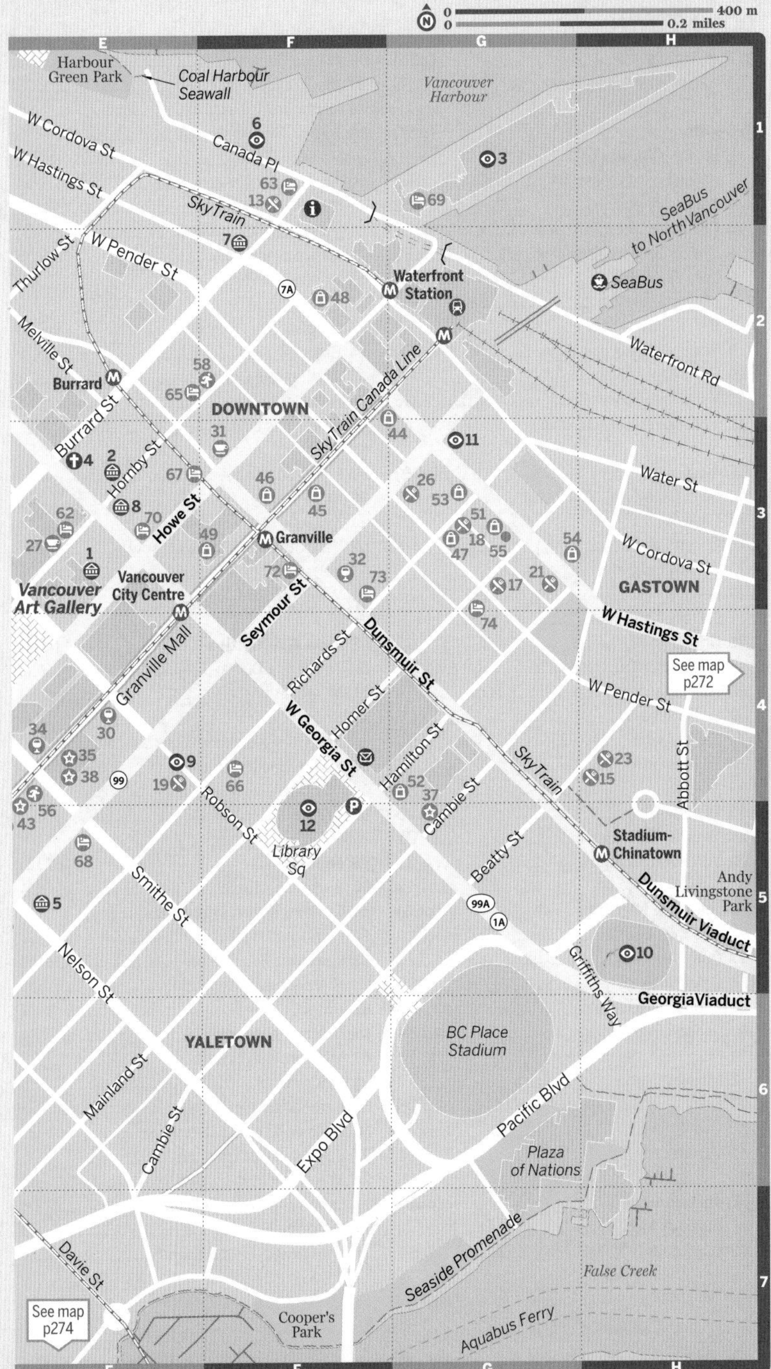

0 400 m
0 0.2 miles
E
F
G
H
1
2
3
4
5
6
7
Harbour Green Park
Coal Harbour Seawall
Vancouver Harbour
W Cordova St
Canada Pl
W Hastings St
SkyTrain
SeaBus to North Vancouver
SeaBus
Thurlow St
W Pender St
Waterfront Station
Waterfront Rd
Melville St
Burrard
Burrard St
SkyTrain Canada Line
DOWNTOWN
Hornby St
Water St
Howe St
Granville
W Cordova St
GASTOWN
Vancouver Art Gallery
Vancouver City Centre
Seymour St
Dunsmuir St
W Hastings St
Richards St
See map p272
Granville Mall
W Pender St
W Georgia St
Homer St
Hamilton St
SkyTrain
Abbott St
Robson St
Cambie St
Library Sq
Beatty St
Stadium-Chinatown
Smithe St
Andy Livingstone Park
Dunsmuir Viaduct
Nelson St
Griffiths Way
Georgia Viaduct
BC Place Stadium
YALETOWN
Mainland St
Pacific Blvd
Cambie St
Expo Blvd
Plaza of Nations
Seaside Promenade
Davie St
False Creek
See map p274
Cooper's Park
Aquabus Ferry

DOWNTOWN *Map on p266*

WEST END *Map on p270*

Key on p269

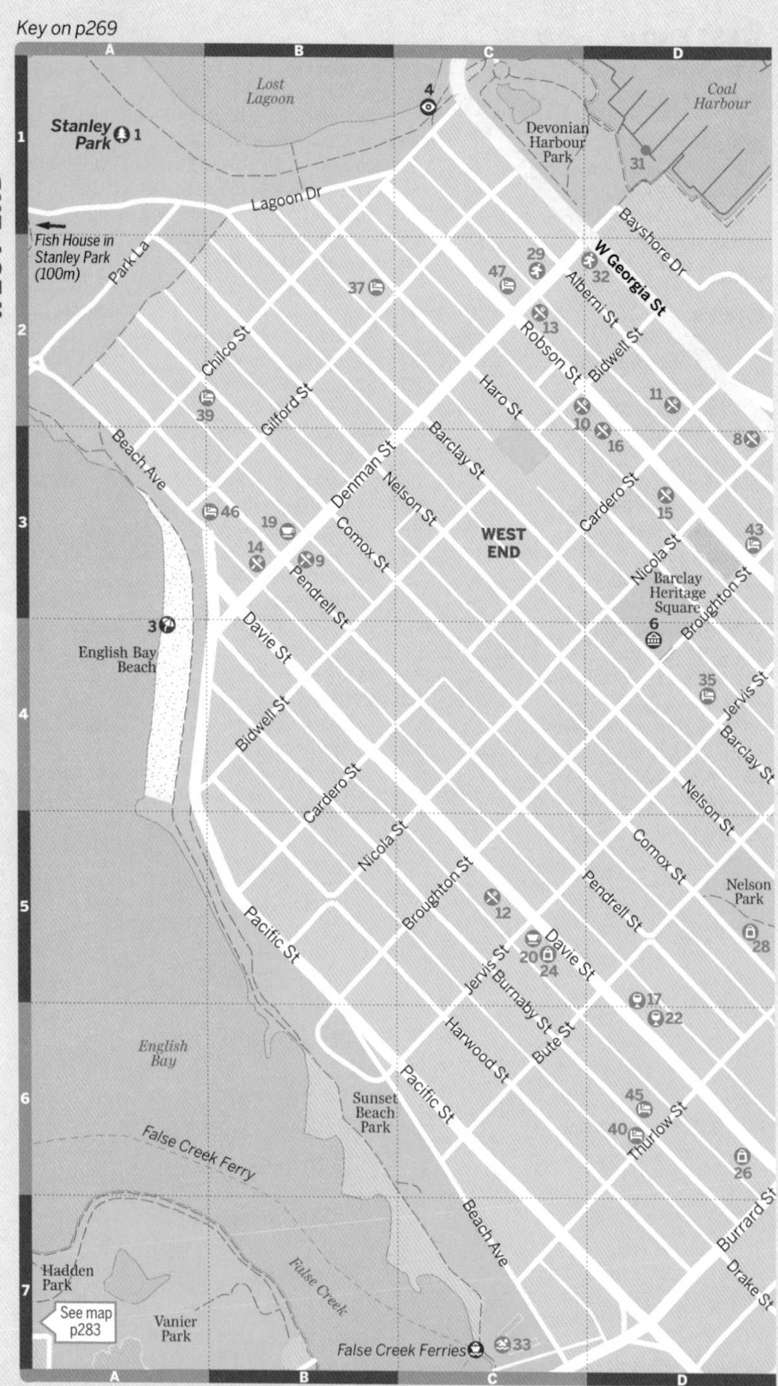
WEST END
Lost Lagoon
Coal Harbour
Stanley Park 1
4
Devonian Harbour Park
31
Lagoon Dr
Fish House in Stanley Park (100m)
Park La
Bayshore Dr
W Georgia St
Alberni St
Robson St
Bidwell St
Haro St
Barclay St
Chilco St
Gilford St
Denman St
Nelson St
Beach Ave
Comox St
Pendrell St
Cardero St
Nicola St
Broughton St
Jervis St
WEST END
Barclay Heritage Square
English Bay Beach
Davie St
Pacific St
Burnaby St
Harwood St
Bute St
Thurlow St
Burrard St
Drake St
Nelson Park
English Bay
Sunset Beach Park
False Creek Ferry
False Creek
Hadden Park
Vanier Park
See map p283
False Creek Ferries
33

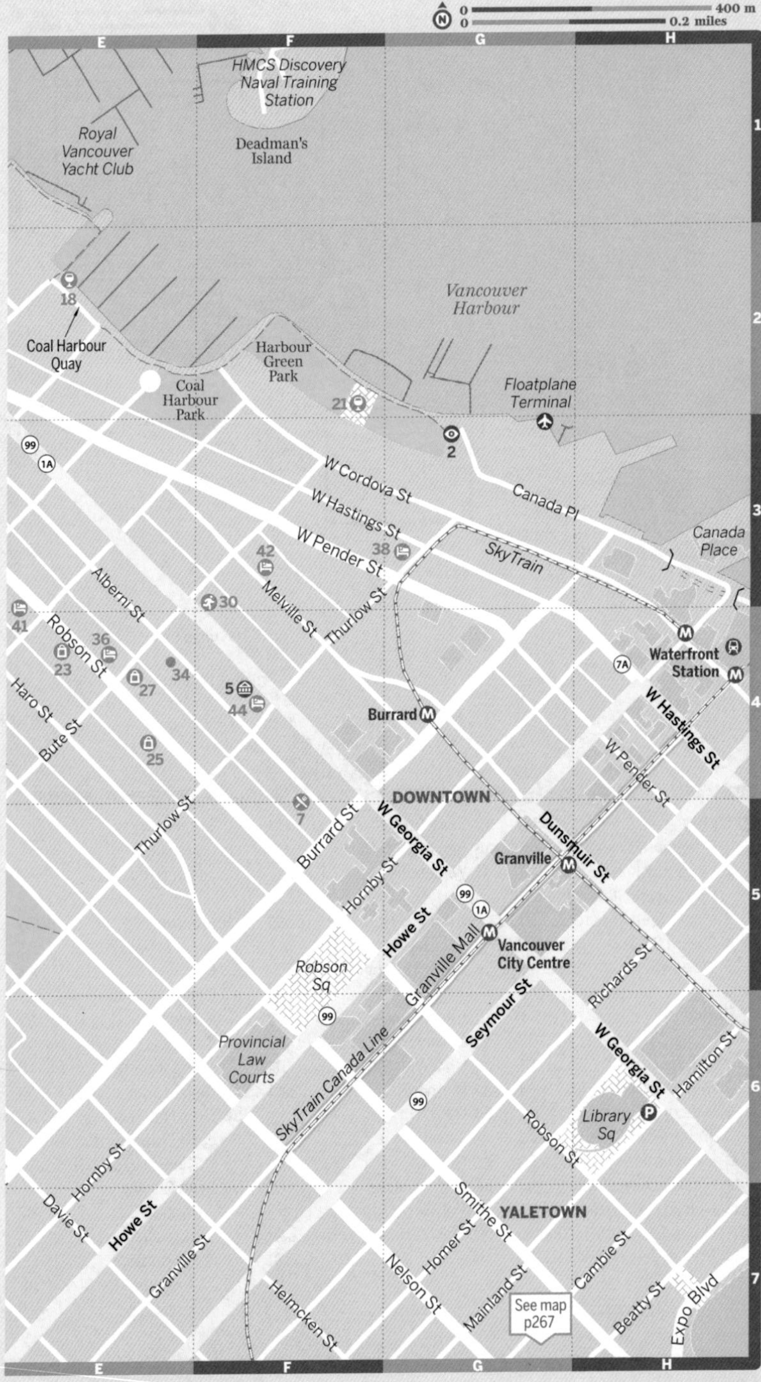

HMCS Discovery Naval Training Station
Deadman's Island
Royal Vancouver Yacht Club
Vancouver Harbour
Coal Harbour Quay
Harbour Green Park
Coal Harbour Park
Floatplane Terminal
W Cordova St
Canada Pl
W Hastings St
W Pender St
SkyTrain
Canada Place
Alberni St
Melville St
Thurlow St
Robson St
Haro St
Bute St
Waterfront Station
Burrard
DOWNTOWN
Burrard St
W Georgia St
Dunsmuir St
Granville
Hornby St
Howe St
Granville Mall
Vancouver City Centre
Robson Sq
Provincial Law Courts
SkyTrain Canada Line
Seymour St
Richards St
Hamilton St
Library Sq
Davie St
Smithe St
YALETOWN
Homer St
Cambie St
Granville St
Nelson St
Mainland St
Beatty St
Expo Blvd
Helmcken St
See map p267
400 m
0.2 miles

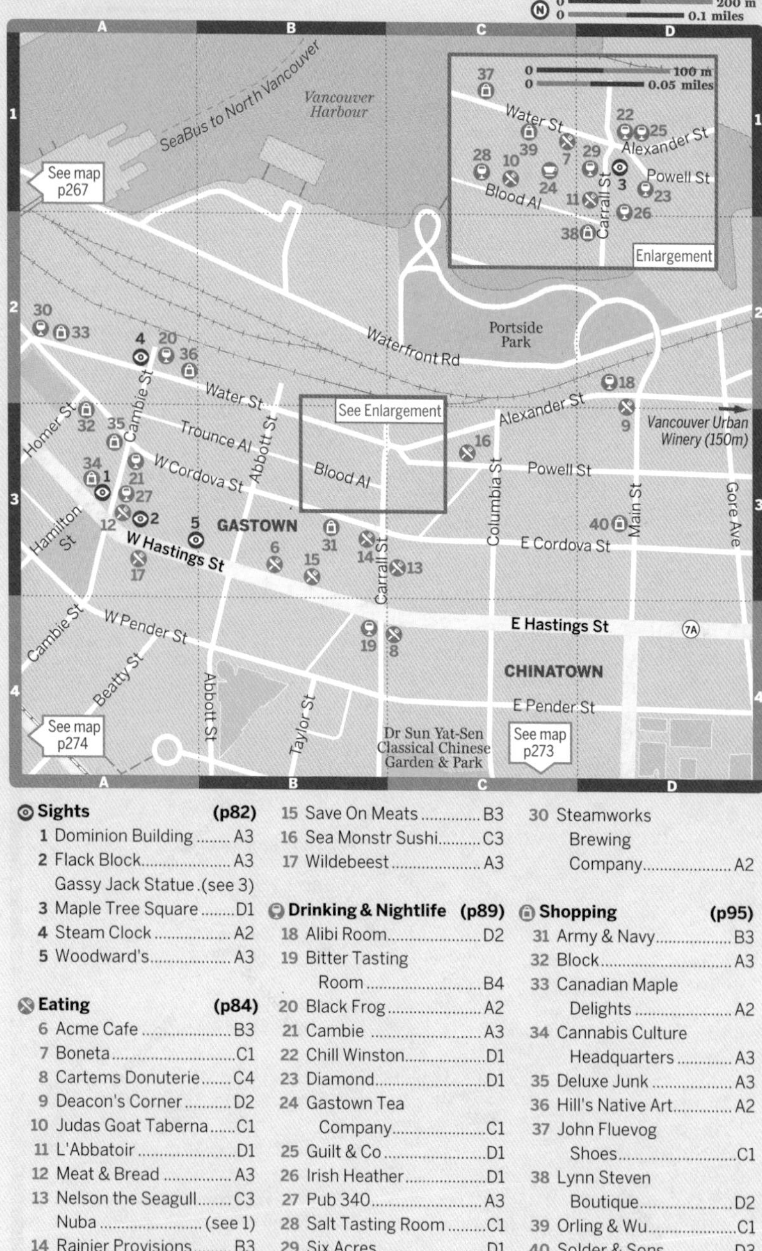

Sights (p82)

1 Dominion Building........A3
2 Flack Block........A3
Gassy Jack Statue.(see 3)
3 Maple Tree Square........D1
4 Steam Clock........A2
5 Woodward's........A3

Eating (p84)

6 Acme Cafe........B3
7 Boneta........C1
8 Cartems Donuterie........C4
9 Deacon's Corner........D2
10 Judas Goat Taberna........C1
11 L'Abbatoir........D1
12 Meat & Bread........A3
13 Nelson the Seagull........C3
Nuba........(see 1)
14 Rainier Provisions........B3
15 Save On Meats........B3
16 Sea Monstr Sushi........C3
17 Wildebeest........A3

Drinking & Nightlife (p89)

18 Alibi Room........D2
19 Bitter Tasting Room........B4
20 Black Frog........A2
21 Cambie........A3
22 Chill Winston........D1
23 Diamond........D1
24 Gastown Tea Company........C1
25 Guilt & Co........D1
26 Irish Heather........D1
27 Pub 340........A3
28 Salt Tasting Room........C1
29 Six Acres........D1
30 Steamworks Brewing Company........A2

Shopping (p95)

31 Army & Navy........B3
32 Block........A3
33 Canadian Maple Delights........A2
34 Cannabis Culture Headquarters........A3
35 Deluxe Junk........A3
36 Hill's Native Art........A2
37 John Fluevog Shoes........C1
38 Lynn Steven Boutique........D2
39 Orling & Wu........C1
40 Solder & Sons........D3

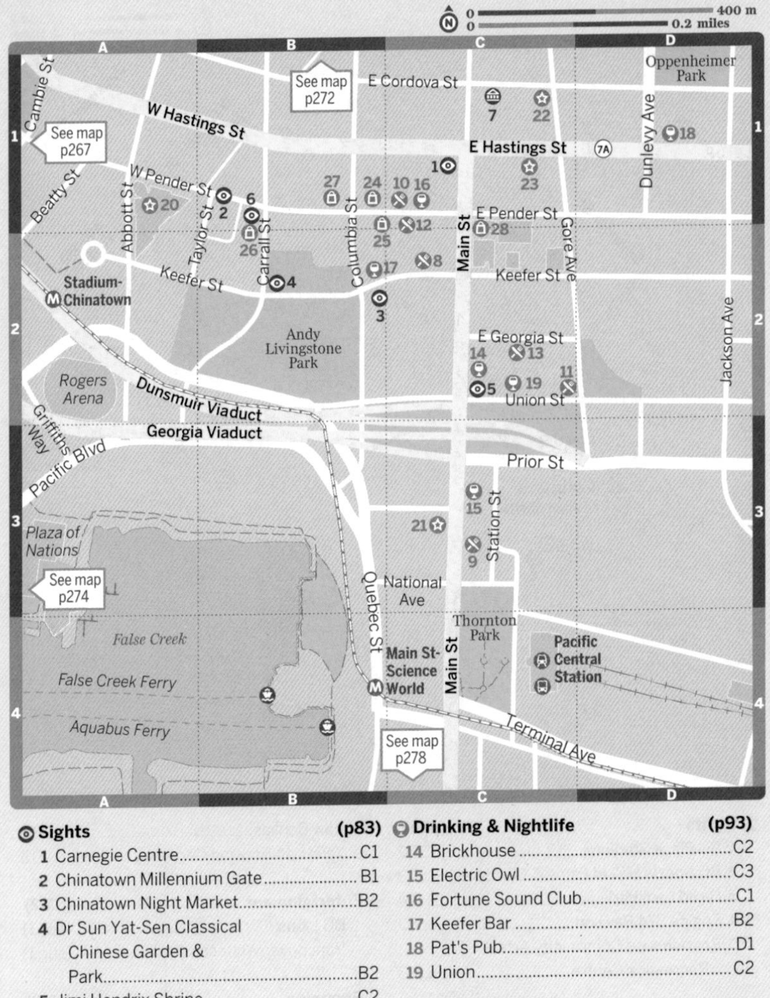

Sights **(p83)**

1 Carnegie Centre ... C1
2 Chinatown Millennium Gate ... B1
3 Chinatown Night Market ... B2
4 Dr Sun Yat-Sen Classical Chinese Garden & Park ... B2
5 Jimi Hendrix Shrine ... C2
6 Sam Kee Building ... B1
7 Vancouver Police Museum ... C1

Eating **(p88)**

8 Bao Bei ... C2
9 Campagnolo ... C3
10 Gam Gok Yuen ... C1
11 Hogan's Alley Cafe ... C2
12 New Town Bakery & Restaurant ... C1
13 Phnom Penh ... C2

Drinking & Nightlife **(p93)**

14 Brickhouse ... C2
15 Electric Owl ... C3
16 Fortune Sound Club ... C1
17 Keefer Bar ... B2
18 Pat's Pub ... D1
19 Union ... C2

Entertainment **(p94)**

20 Cineplex Odean International Village ... A1
21 Cobalt ... C3
22 Firehall Arts Centre ... C1
23 Rickshaw Theatre ... C1

Shopping **(p95)**

24 Blim ... B1
25 Eastern Gifts ... B1
26 Erin Templeton ... B2
27 Peking Lounge ... B1
28 Ten Lee Hong Enterprises ... C2

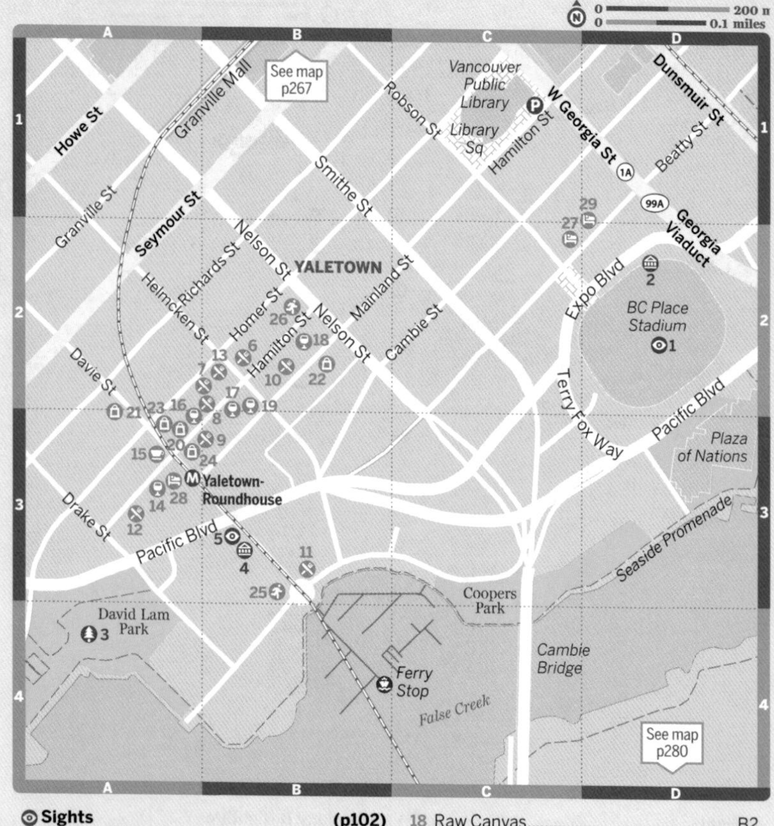

Sights (p102)

1 BC Place Stadium D2
2 BC Sports Hall of Fame & Museum D2
3 David Lam Park A4
4 Engine 374 Pavilion B3
5 Roundhouse Community Arts & Recreation Centre B3

Eating (p103)

6 Blue Water Café + Raw Bar B2
7 Brix B2
8 Cioppino's Mediterranean Grill B2
9 Flying Pig B3
10 Glowbal Grill Steak & Satay B2
11 Provence Marinaside B3
12 Rodney's Oyster House A3
13 Yopo Cafe B2

Drinking & Nightlife (p108)

14 Bar None A3
15 Caffe Artigiano A3
16 George Lounge A3
17 Killjoy Cocktail Tavern B2
18 Raw Canvas B2
19 Yaletown Brewing Company B2

Entertainment (p112)

BC Lions .... (see 1)
Vancouver Whitecaps .... (see 1)

Shopping (p113)

20 Basquiat A3
21 Brooklyn Clothing A3
22 Coastal Peoples Fine Arts Gallery B2
23 Cross A3
24 Goorin Bros Hat Shop A3

Sports & Activities (p116)

25 Reckless Bike Stores B3
26 Skoah B2

Sleeping (p217)

27 Georgian Court Hotel C2
28 Opus Hotel A3
29 YWCA Hotel D1

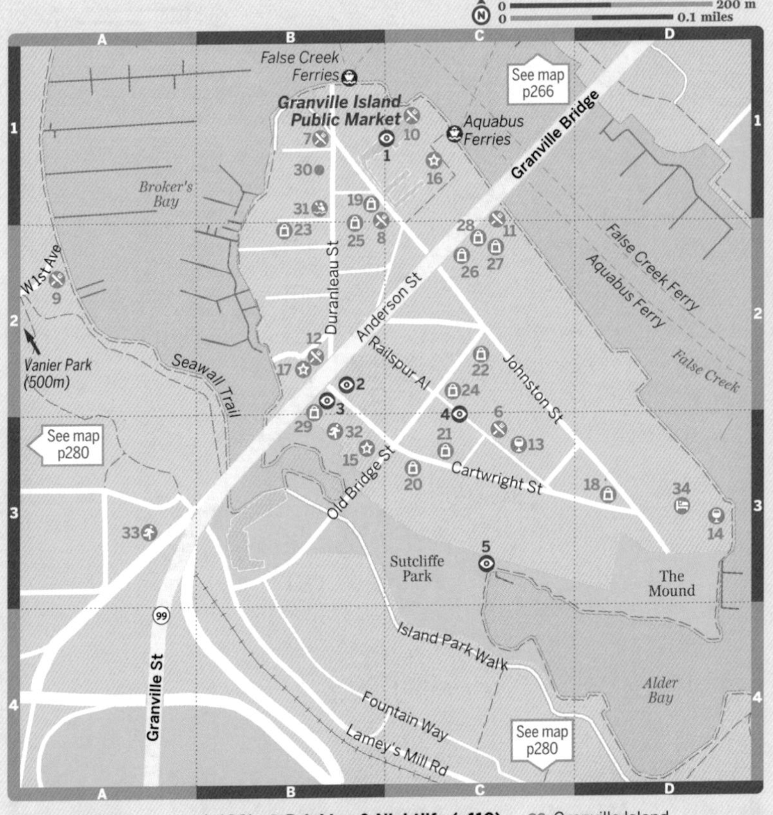

False Creek Ferries
Granville Island Public Market
Aquabus Ferries
See map p266
Granville Bridge
Broker's Bay
W 1st Ave
Duranleau St
Anderson St
Railspur Al
Johnston St
False Creek Ferry
Aquabus Ferry
False Creek
Vanier Park (500m)
Seawall Trail
See map p280
Old Bridge St
Cartwright St
Sutcliffe Park
The Mound
Granville St
Island Park Walk
Alder Bay
Fountain Way
Lamey's Mill Rd
See map p280
200 m
0.1 miles

COMMERCIAL DRIVE

0 — 200 m
0 — 0.1 miles

A B C D
1 2 3 4 5 6 7

La Casa Gelato (250m)

EAST VANCOUVER
GRANDVIEW

Adanac St
Venables St
Parker St
Napier St
William St
Charles St
Kitchener St
Grant St
Graveley St
E 1st Ave
E 2nd Ave
E 3rd Ave
E 4th Ave
McSpadden Ave
E 5th Ave
E 6th Ave
E 7th Ave
E 8th Ave
E Broadway
Grandview Hwy N

McLean Dr
Woodland Dr
Commercial Dr
Salsbury Dr
Semlin Dr
Odlum Dr
Cotton Dr
Clark Dr
Victoria Dr
McLean Cr

Grandview Park
Victoria Park
McSpadden Park

Commercial-Broadway
Commercial-Broadway

1 2 3 4 5 6 7 8 9 10 11 12 13 14 15 16 17 18 19 20 21 22 23 24 25 26 27 28 29 30 31 32 33 34 35 36 37 38 39 40 41 42 43 44 45 46 47 48 49 50

COMMERCIAL DRIVE

Sights **(p119)**
1 Grandview Park........C2

Eating **(p119)**
2 Belgian Fries........C5
3 Cannibal Café........C5
4 Carthage Cafe........C5
5 Falconetti's East Side Grill........C4
6 Fratelli Baking........C4
7 Havana........C2
Kishimoto Japanese Kitchen + Sushi Bar........(see 20)
8 La Mezcaleria........C4
9 Merchant's Oyster Bar........C4
10 Palki Restaurant........C2
11 Prophouse Cafe........C1
12 Reef........C2
13 Sweet Cherubim........C2
14 Timbre........C5
15 Uprising Breads Bakery Cafe........C1
16 Via Tevere........D2

Drinking & Nightlife **(p122)**
17 Biercraft Tap & Tapas Bar........C2
18 Bump N Grind........C1
19 Café Calabria........C4
20 Cafe Deux Soleils........C6
21 Caffe Roma........C3
22 Charlatan........C3
23 JJ Bean........C6
24 Prado Café........C5
25 Renzo's........C3
26 Royal Canadian Legion........C6
27 St Augustine's........C6
28 Storm Crow Tavern........C3

Entertainment **(p126)**
29 Cultch (Vancouver East Cultural Centre)........D1
30 Grandview Lanes Bowling Centre........C6
31 Libra Room........C4
32 Rio Theatre........C7
Vancouver Poetry Slam........(see 20)
33 Wise Hall........D1

Shopping **(p128)**
34 Attic Treasures........C1
35 Audiopile........C6
36 Barefoot Contessa........C5
37 Canterbury Tales........C5
38 Dream Designs........C1
39 Kalena's Shoes........C3
40 La Grotta Del Formaggio........C4
41 Licorice Parlour........C2
42 Mintage........C4
43 Mis'cel'la'ny Finds........C2
44 People's Co-Op Bookstore........C3
45 Pulpfiction Books East........C5
46 Riot Clothing........C3
47 Urban Empire........C2
48 Womyns' Ware........C1
49 Wonderbucks Wonderful Living........C4

Sports & Activities **(p130)**
50 Britannia Community Centre........C2

MAIN ST

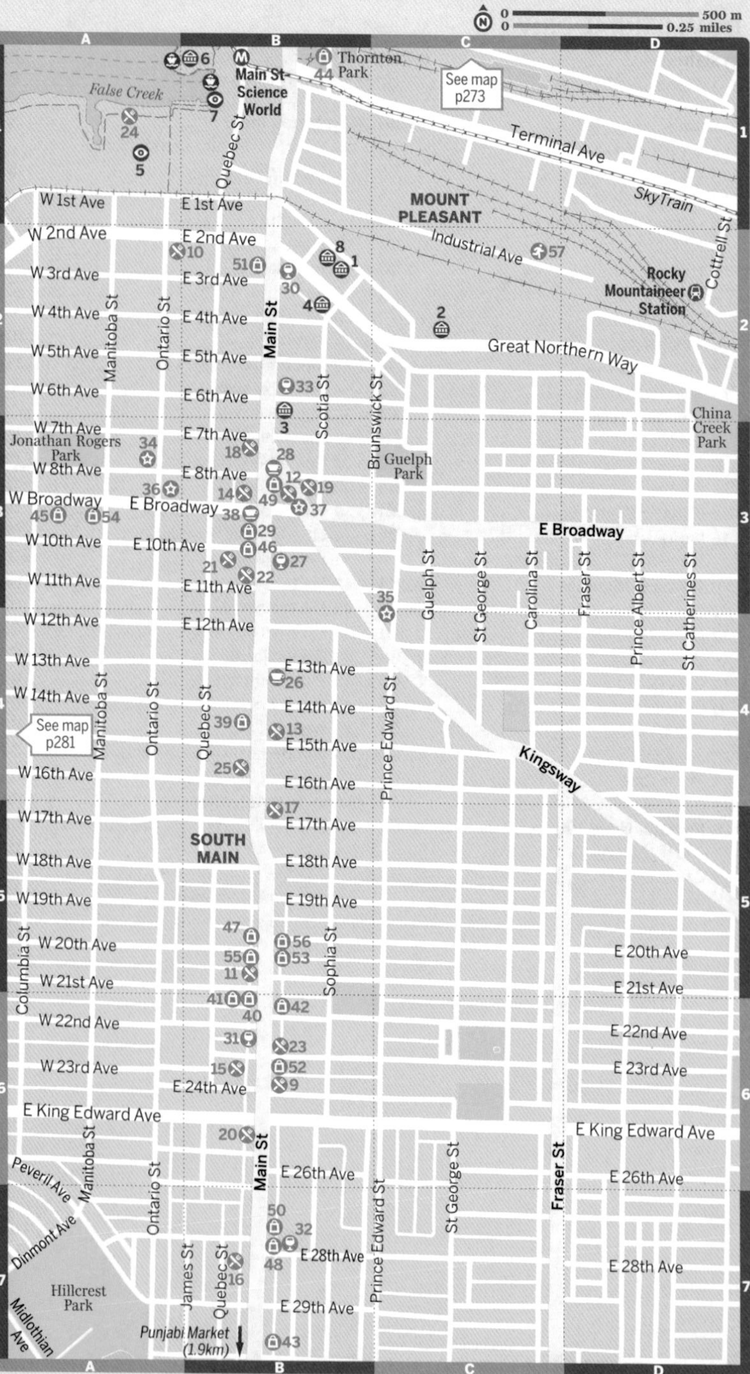

500 m
0.25 miles
False Creek
Main St-Science World
Thornton Park
See map p273
Terminal Ave
SkyTrain
MOUNT PLEASANT
Industrial Ave
Rocky Mountaineer Station
Cottrell St
Great Northern Way
China Creek Park
W 1st Ave
E 1st Ave
W 2nd Ave
E 2nd Ave
W 3rd Ave
E 3rd Ave
W 4th Ave
E 4th Ave
W 5th Ave
E 5th Ave
W 6th Ave
E 6th Ave
W 7th Ave
E 7th Ave
Jonathan Rogers Park
W 8th Ave
E 8th Ave
W Broadway
E Broadway
W 10th Ave
E 10th Ave
W 11th Ave
E 11th Ave
W 12th Ave
E 12th Ave
W 13th Ave
E 13th Ave
W 14th Ave
E 14th Ave
See map p281
E 15th Ave
W 16th Ave
E 16th Ave
W 17th Ave
E 17th Ave
SOUTH MAIN
W 18th Ave
E 18th Ave
W 19th Ave
E 19th Ave
W 20th Ave
E 20th Ave
W 21st Ave
E 21st Ave
W 22nd Ave
E 22nd Ave
W 23rd Ave
E 23rd Ave
E 24th Ave
E King Edward Ave
E 26th Ave
E 28th Ave
E 29th Ave
Quebec St
Main St
Manitoba St
Ontario St
Scotia St
Brunswick St
Guelph Park
Guelph St
St George St
Carolina St
Fraser St
Prince Albert St
St Catherines St
Kingsway
Prince Edward St
Sophia St
Columbia St
Peveril Ave
Dinmont Ave
Hillcrest Park
Midlothian Ave
James St
Punjabi Market (1.9km)

MAIN STREET

Sights (p133)

1 Catriona Jeffries B2
2 Equinox Gallery C2
3 Hot Art Wet City B2
4 Macaulay & Co Fine Art B2
Monte Clark Gallery .... (see 2)
5 Olympic Village A1
Portobello West .... (see 5)
6 Science World B1
7 South False Creek Seawall B1
8 Winsor Gallery B2

Eating (p135)

9 Acorn B6
10 Argo Cafe A2
11 Bob Likes Thai Food B5
12 Budgie's Burritos B3
13 Burgoo Bistro B4
14 Chutney Villa B3
15 Crave B6
16 East is East B7
17 El Camino's B5
18 Foundation B3
19 French Made Baking B3
20 Hawkers Delight B6
21 Holy Trinity Ukrainian Orthodox Church B3
22 Rumpus Room B3
23 Sun Sui Wah Seafood Restaurant B6
24 Tap & Barrel A1
25 Toshi Sushi B4

Drinking & Nightlife (p137)

26 49th Parallel Coffee B4
27 Cascade Room B3
28 Gene Cafe B3
29 Kafka's B3
30 Narrow Lounge B2
31 Portland Craft B6
32 Shameful Tiki Room B7
33 Whip B2

Entertainment (p139)

34 Anza Club A3
35 Biltmore Cabaret C4
36 Celluloid Social Club A3
Pacific Bluegrass Jam Night .... (see 34)
37 Vancouver Ukulele Circle B3

Shopping (p140)

38 Bird on a Wire Creations B3
39 Brewery Creek Liquor Store B4
40 Choclolatene de la Nouvelle France B6
41 Eugene Choo B6
42 Front & Company B6
43 Giving Gifts & Company B7
44 Main Street Station Farmers Market B1
45 Mountain Equipment Co-Op A3
46 Much & Little B3
47 Neptoon Records B5
48 Nineteen Ten B7
49 Pulpfiction Books B3
50 Red Cat Records B7
51 Refind B2
52 Regional Assembly of Text B6
53 Smoking Lily B5
54 Sports Junkies A3
55 Twigg & Hottie B5
56 Vancouver Special B5

Sports & Activities (p145)

57 Cliffhanger Climbing C2

FAIRVIEW & SOUTH GRANVILLE

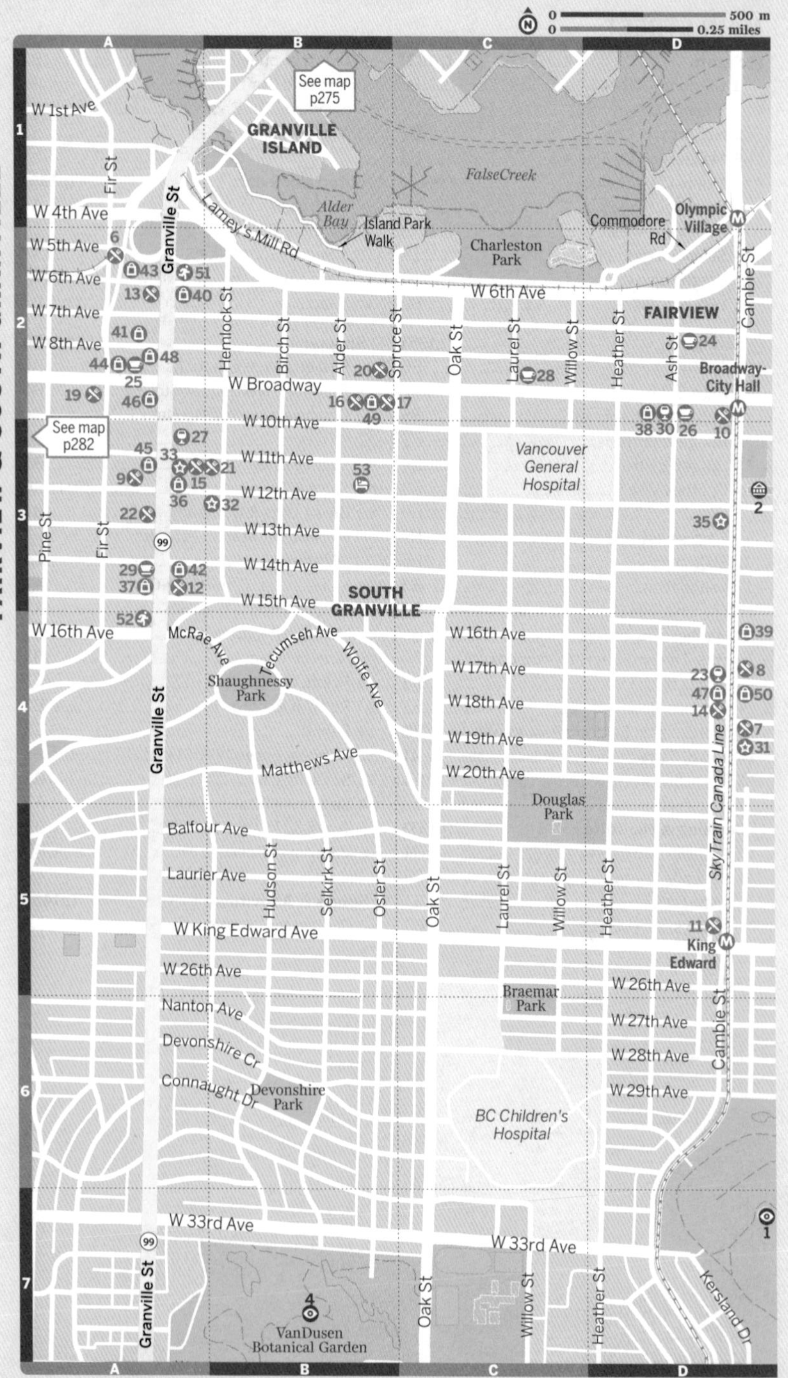

See map p275
See map p282
GRANVILLE ISLAND
False Creek
Alder Bay
Island Park Walk
Charleston Park
Commodore Rd
Olympic Village
FAIRVIEW
Broadway-City Hall
Vancouver General Hospital
SOUTH GRANVILLE
Shaughnessy Park
Douglas Park
King Edward
Braemar Park
Devonshire Park
BC Children's Hospital
VanDusen Botanical Garden
SkyTrain Canada Line
W 1st Ave
W 4th Ave
W 5th Ave
W 6th Ave
W 7th Ave
W 8th Ave
W Broadway
W 10th Ave
W 11th Ave
W 12th Ave
W 13th Ave
W 14th Ave
W 15th Ave
W 16th Ave
W 17th Ave
W 18th Ave
W 19th Ave
W 20th Ave
Balfour Ave
Laurier Ave
W King Edward Ave
W 26th Ave
W 27th Ave
W 28th Ave
W 29th Ave
Nanton Ave
Devonshire Cr
Connaught Dr
W 33rd Ave
Lamey's Mill Rd
McRae Ave
Tecumseh Ave
Wolfe Ave
Matthews Ave
Kersland Dr
Pine St
Fir St
Granville St
Hemlock St
Birch St
Alder St
Spruce St
Oak St
Laurel St
Willow St
Heather St
Ash St
Cambie St
Hudson St
Selkirk St
Osler St

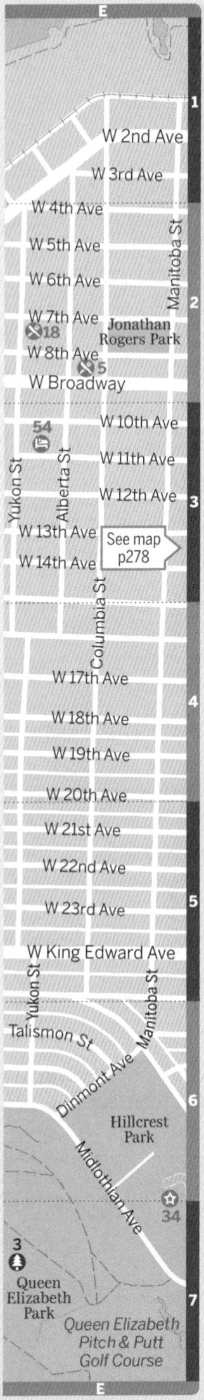

Sights (p148)

1 Bloedel Conservatory D7
2 City Hall D3
3 Queen Elizabeth Park E7
4 VanDusen Botanical Garden B7

Eating (p149)

5 Aperture Coffee Bar E2
6 Beaucoup Bakery & Cafe A2
7 Benton Brothers Fine Cheese D4
8 Dutch Wooden Shoe Cafe D4
9 Heirloom Vegetarian A3
10 La Taqueria Pinche Taco Shop D2
11 Landmark Hotpot House D5
12 Ouisi Bistro A3
13 Paul's Omelettery A2
14 Pied-a-Terre D4
15 Rangoli A3
16 Salmon n' Bannock B2
17 Shizen Ya B2
18 Solly's Bagelry E2
19 Suika A2
20 Tojo's B2
21 Vij's B3
22 West A3

Drinking & Nightlife (p153)

23 Biercraft Bistro D4
24 Caffe Cittadella D2
25 Dose Espresso Bar A2
26 Elysian Coffee D2
27 Marquis A3
28 Pekoe Tea Lounge C2
29 Phoscao Cafe A3
30 Rogue Kitchen & Wet Bar D2

Entertainment (p155)

31 Cineplex Park Theatre D4
Kino Cafe .... (see 31)
32 Pacific Theatre B3
33 Stanley Theatre A3
34 Vancouver Canadians E6
35 Yuk Yuk's Comedy Club D3

Shopping (p156)

36 Bacci's A3
37 Bau-Xi Gallery A3
38 Book Warehouse D2
39 Fabtabulous Thrift D4
40 Ian Tan Gallery A2
41 Lusso Verde A2
42 Meinhardt Fine Foods A3
43 Oliver + Lilly's A2
44 Oscar's Art Books A2
45 Purdy's Chocolates A3
46 Restoration Hardware A2
47 Shop Cocoon D4
48 Tilley Endurables A2
49 Umbrella Shop B2
50 Walrus D4

Sports & Activities (p160)

51 Miraj Hammam Spa A2
52 Suki's Salon & Spa A4

Sleeping (p219)

53 Shaughnessy Village B3
54 Windsor Guest House E3

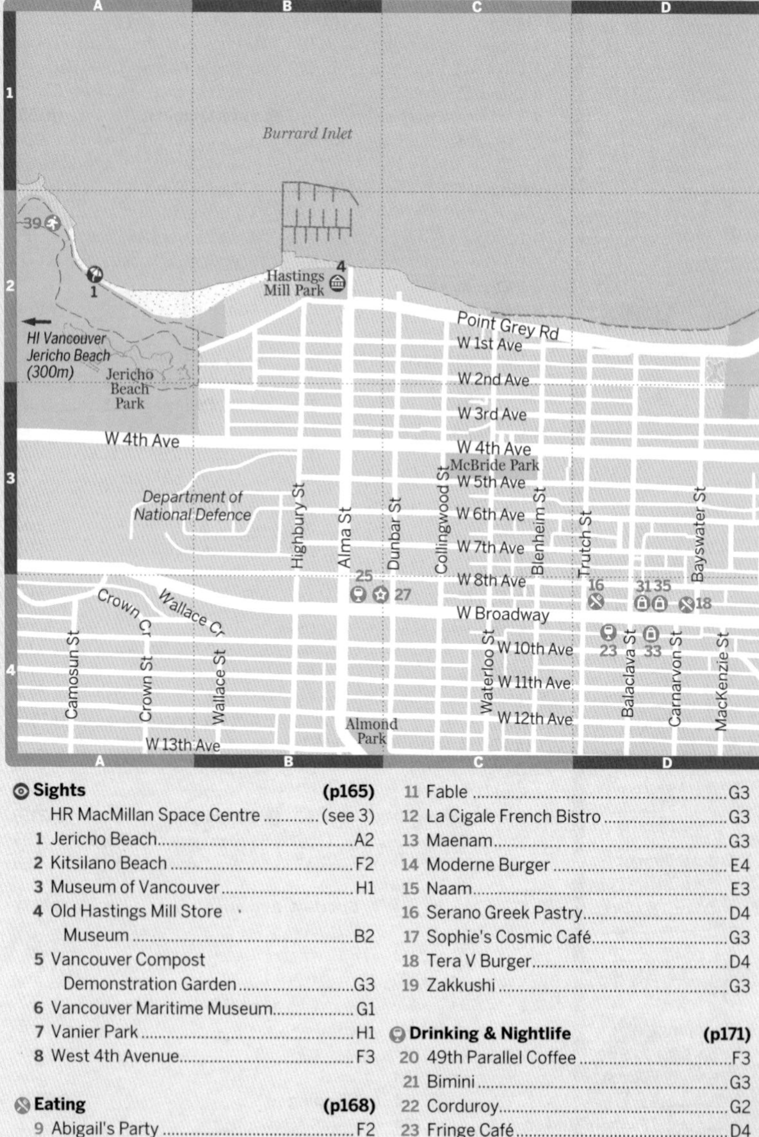

Sights (p165)

HR MacMillan Space Centre .... (see 3)
1 Jericho Beach A2
2 Kitsilano Beach F2
3 Museum of Vancouver H1
4 Old Hastings Mill Store Museum B2
5 Vancouver Compost Demonstration Garden G3
6 Vancouver Maritime Museum G1
7 Vanier Park H1
8 West 4th Avenue F3

Eating (p168)

9 Abigail's Party F2
10 Bishop's F3
11 Fable G3
12 La Cigale French Bistro G3
13 Maenam G3
14 Moderne Burger E4
15 Naam E3
16 Serano Greek Pastry D4
17 Sophie's Cosmic Café G3
18 Tera V Burger D4
19 Zakkushi G3

Drinking & Nightlife (p171)

20 49th Parallel Coffee F3
21 Bimini G3
22 Corduroy G2
23 Fringe Café D4
Galley Patio & Grill .... (see 39)

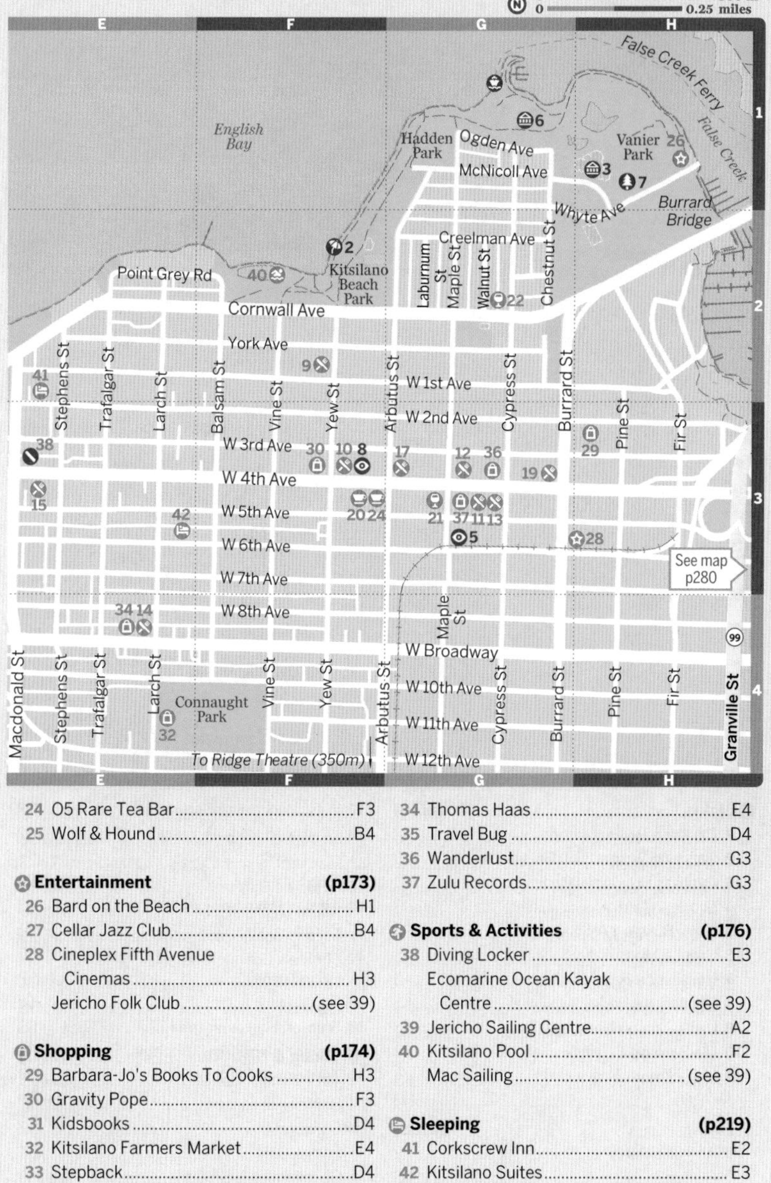

24 O5 Rare Tea Bar....F3
25 Wolf & Hound....B4

Entertainment (p173)
26 Bard on the Beach....H1
27 Cellar Jazz Club....B4
28 Cineplex Fifth Avenue Cinemas....H3
Jericho Folk Club....(see 39)

Shopping (p174)
29 Barbara-Jo's Books To Cooks....H3
30 Gravity Pope....F3
31 Kidsbooks....D4
32 Kitsilano Farmers Market....E4
33 Stepback....D4
34 Thomas Haas....E4
35 Travel Bug....D4
36 Wanderlust....G3
37 Zulu Records....G3

Sports & Activities (p176)
38 Diving Locker....E3
Ecomarine Ocean Kayak Centre....(see 39)
39 Jericho Sailing Centre....A2
40 Kitsilano Pool....F2
Mac Sailing....(see 39)

Sleeping (p219)
41 Corkscrew Inn....E2
42 Kitsilano Suites....E3

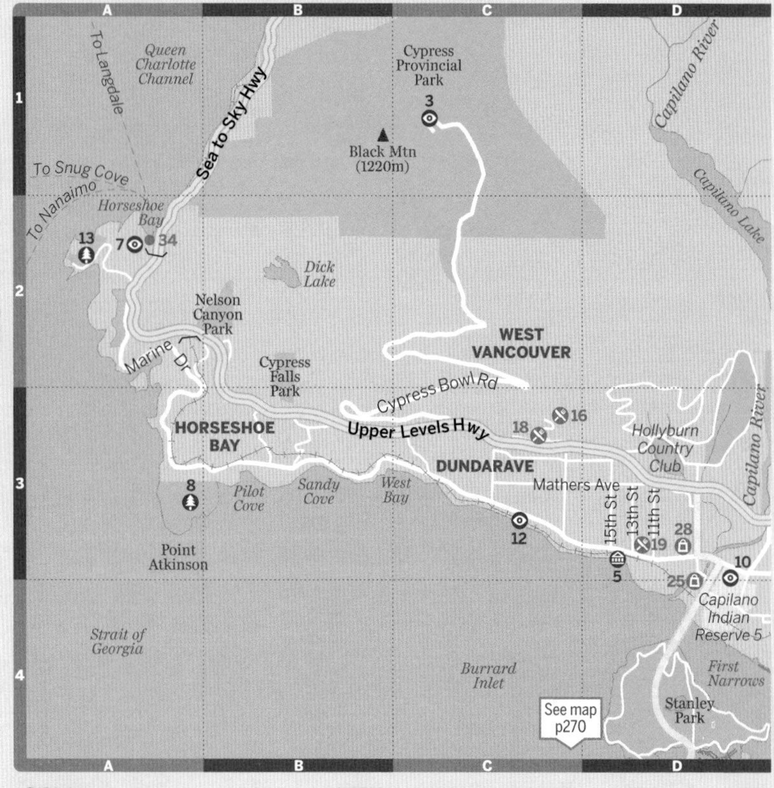

Sights **(p179)**

1 Capilano River Hatchery E2
2 Capilano Suspension Bridge E3
3 Cypress Provincial Park C1
4 Ecology Centre G3
5 Ferry Building Art Gallery D3
6 Grouse Mountain E1
7 Horseshoe Bay A2
8 Lighthouse Park A3
9 Lynn Canyon Park G3
10 Maplewood Farm D3
11 Mt Seymour Provincial Park H3
12 West Vancouver Seawall C3
13 Whytecliff Park A2

Eating **(p181)**

14 Artisan Bake Shoppe G1
15 Burgoo Bistro G1
16 Fraiche C3
Observatory .... (see 6)
17 Raglan's G1
18 Salmon House on the Hill C3
19 Savary Island Pie Company D3
20 Tomahawk Restaurant E4

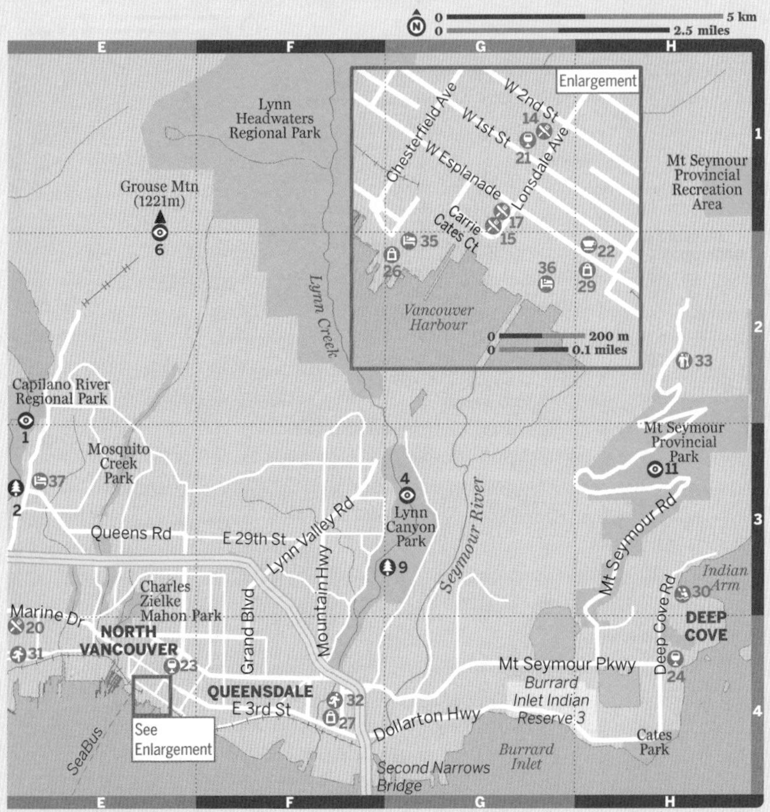

NORTH SHORE

Drinking & Nightlife (p183)

21 Buddha-Full G1
22 Cafe for Contemporary Art H2
23 Queen's Cross E4
24 Raven H4

Shopping (p184)

25 Cove Bike Shop D4
26 Lonsdale Quay Public Market G2
27 Mountain Equipment Co-op F4
28 Park Royal D3
29 Shipyards Night Market H2

Sports & Activities (p185)

Cypress Mountain .... (see 3)
30 Deep Cove Canoe & Kayak Centre H3
31 Edge Climbing Centre E4
32 Endless Biking F4
Grouse Mountain .... (see 6)
33 Mt Seymour H2
34 Sewell's Sea Safari A2

Sleeping (p220)

35 Lonsdale Quay Hotel G2
36 Pinnacle Hotel at the Pier G2
37 Thistledown House B&B E3

UNIVERSITY OF BRITISH COLUMBIA (UBC)

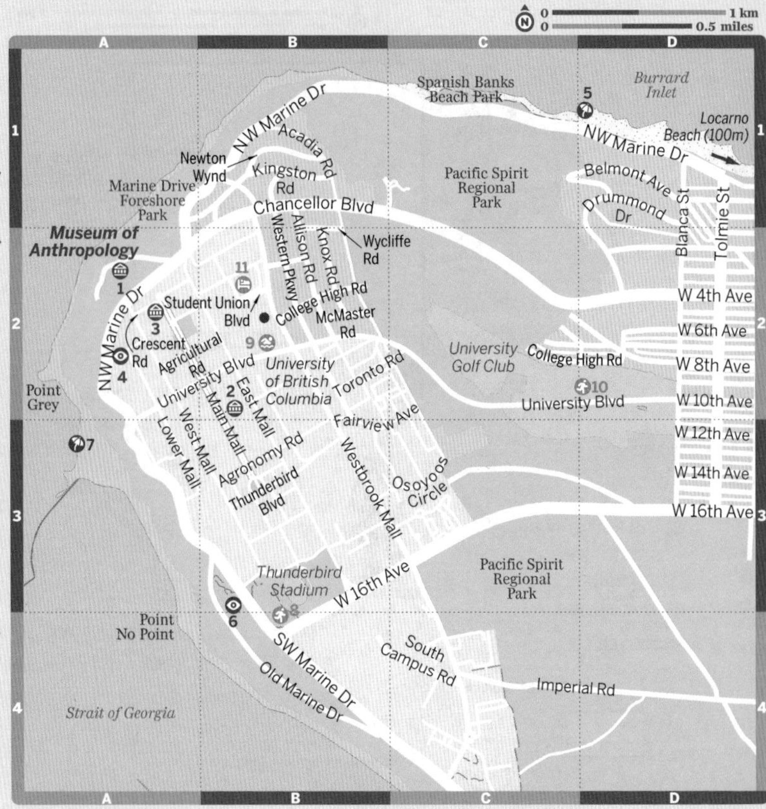

Top Sights (p163)

1 Museum of Anthropology A2

Sights (p165)

2 Beaty Biodiversity Museum B2
3 Morris and Helen Belkin Gallery A2
4 Nitobe Memorial Garden A2
5 Spanish Banks D1
6 UBC Botanical Garden B3
7 Wreck Beach A3

Sports & Activities (p176)

8 Greenheart Canopy Walkway B4
9 UBC Aquatic Centre B2
10 University Golf Club D2

Sleeping (p219)

11 University of British Columbia Accommodation B2